A joint publication of
Music Sales Corporation and **Hal Leonard Publishing Corporation**

Exclusive Distributor in the United States and Canada:
Music Sales Corporation

Amsco Publications
New York/London/Paris/Sydney

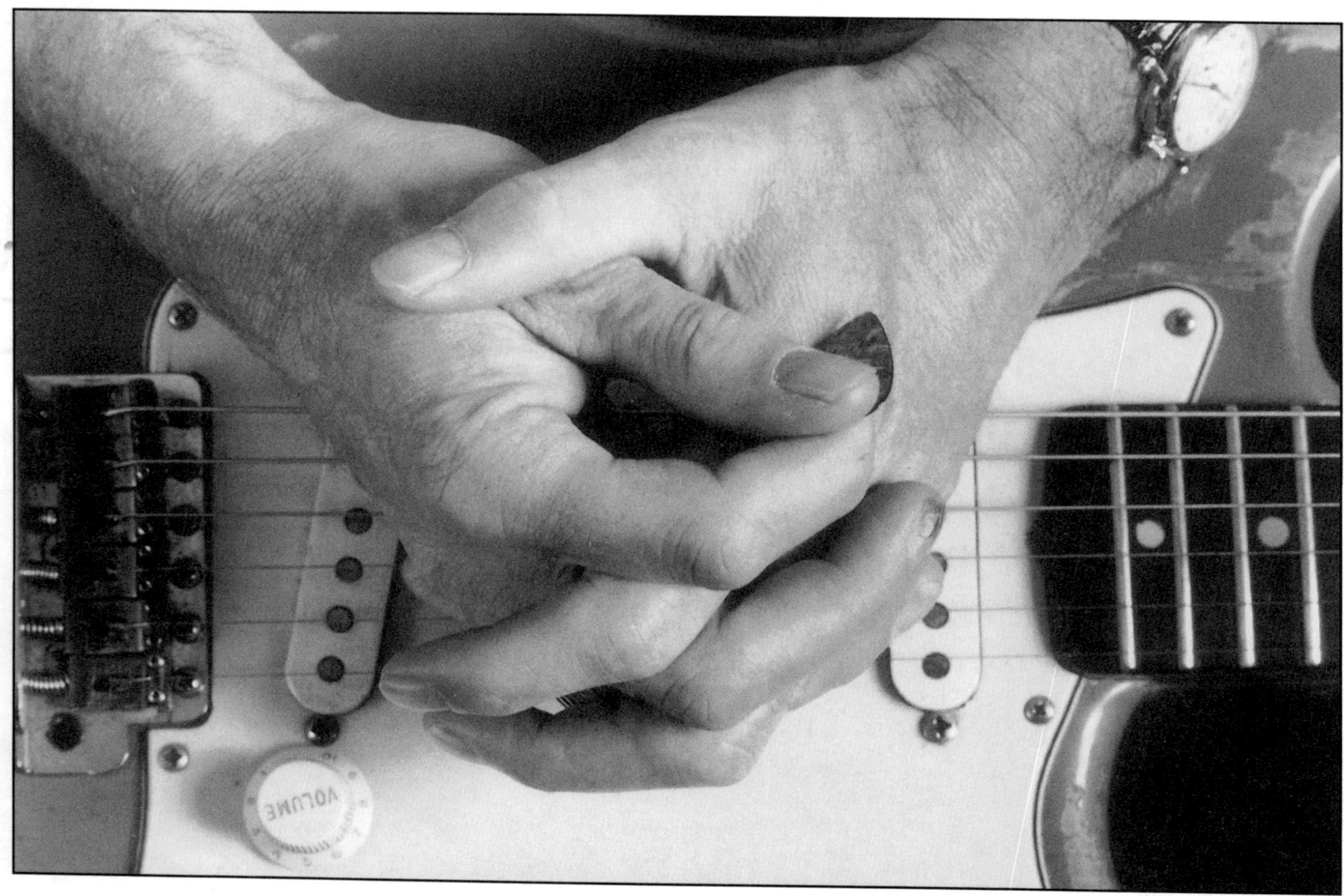

Photography:
Front cover, Page 18 (top left): Mick Hutson/Redfern/Retna Ltd.
Back cover, Page 5, 15 (bottom), 16 (bottom left), 17 (top right), 18 (bottom left): Larry Busacca/Retna Ltd.
Page 2, 17 (top left): Luiciano Viti/Retna Ltd.
Page 5, 7, 8 (top and bottom): David Redfern/Redfern/Retna Ltd.
Page 9, 13: David Gahr
Page 10: London Features International
Page 11, 12, 14 (top and bottom): Michael Putland/Retna Ltd.
Page 15 (top left), 17 (bottom right): Gary Gershoff/Retna Ltd.
Page 15 (top right): Chris Walter/Retna Ltd.
Page 16 (bottom right): David Corio/Retna Ltd.
Page 16 (top): Paul Slattery/Retna Ltd.
Page 17 (bottom left): Paul Studna/Retna Ltd.
Page 18 (top right): Ed Sykes/Retna Ltd.
Page 18 (bottom right), 19: Letto/Stills/Retna Ltd.

Text by Kalen Rogers
Project editor: Edward J. Lozano

Order No. AM 931216
International Standard Book Number: 0.8256.1484.8

Exclusive Distributor for the United States and Canada:
Music Sales Corporation
257 Park Avenue South, New York, New York 10010

Printed in the United States of America by
Vicks Lithograph and Printing Corporation

Legend of Music Symbols

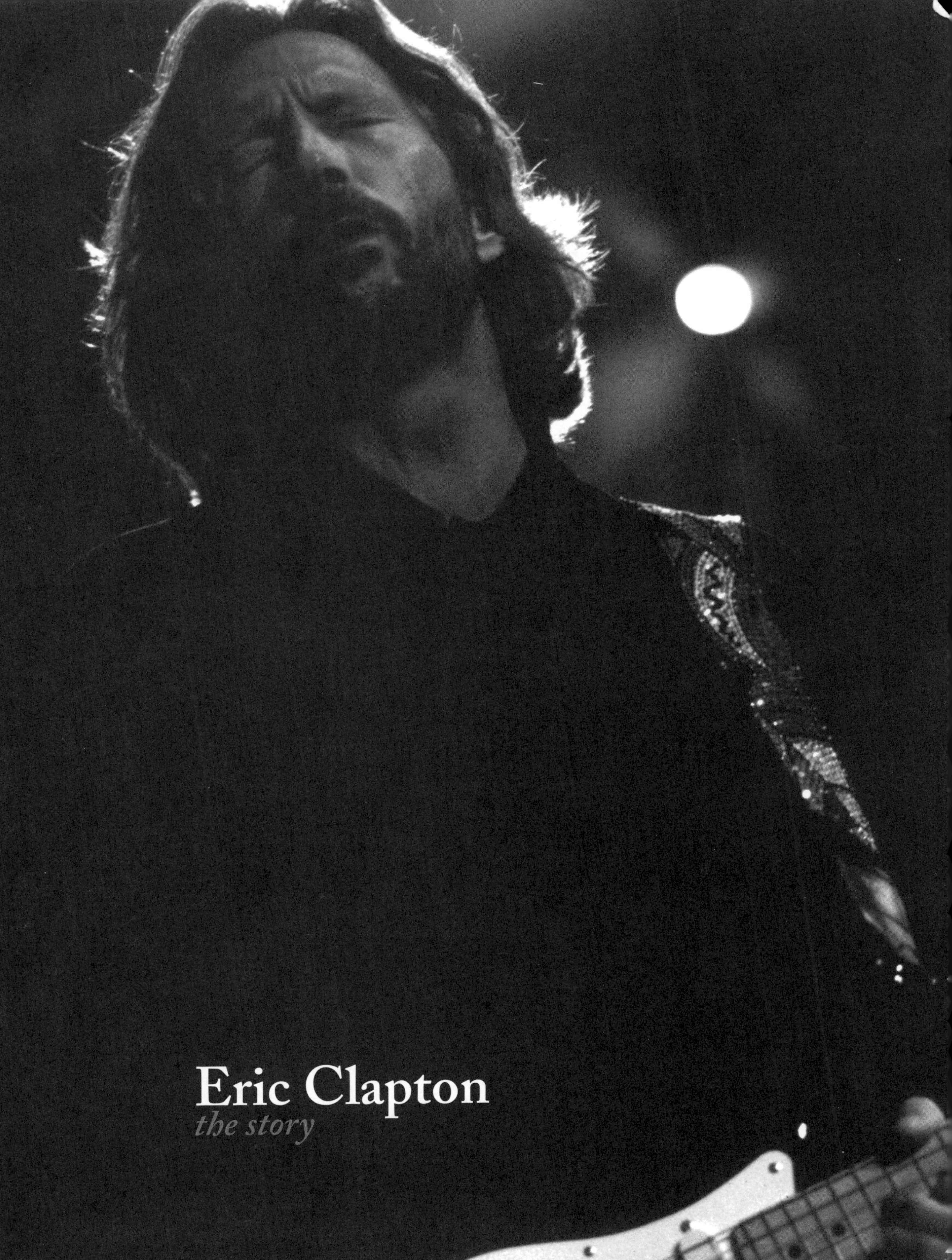
Eric Clapton
the story

Eric Clapton was born in Ripley, Surrey on March 30, 1945, the illegitimate son of Patricia Molly Clapton and a Canadian soldier named Edward Fryer who was stationed in England. Brought up by his grandparents in a small village, his first exposure to the instrument which would later shape his life and career was via the television. Eric recalls watching Jerry Lee Lewis perform "Great Balls of Fire" and that "it was like seeing someone from outer space." Clapton now says he saw the bass player and thought, "That's a guitar. That's the future. And that's what I want."

Setting out to get what he wanted with admirable, if not successful, resolve, young Eric attempted to carve himself a wooden Stratocaster. His grandparents intervened and bought him a "plastic Elvis Presley guitar" which, needless to say, didn't quite suit his burgeoning ambitions and was soon replaced with an inexpensive acoustic. Eric's penchant for bringing the guitar with him to Kingston Art College, where he was studying graphic design, reportedly proved to be the reason for his being asked to leave the school at age sixteen.

Meanwhile, Clapton was becoming increasingly entranced with American blues, and began fraternizing with fellow "blues fanatics" who recognized and emulated the tortured and intense music of Blind Willie Johnson, B.B. King, Muddy Waters, and Robert Johnson. According to Clapton, the first time he heard Robert Johnson's *King of the Delta Blues Singers* album, he "couldn't take it... it was just too much anguish to take on." Clapton took the blues seriously, and began what was to become a life-long exploration into the history and structure of its music. He joined his first band, The Roosters, in 1963, and the rhythm and blues group secured a few opening gigs at the Marquee in London before breaking up later that year.

The second band Eric joined was destined to be much more high-profile; they were called The Yardbirds. The band spent all of 1964 playing clubs in and around London, topping the year off by supporting The Beatles' Christmas Show in December. Eric at this point was firmly entrenched in his purist blues mode, and the pop success of The Yardbirds was not the path he wanted to follow. "My attitude within the group got really sour," he recalls, "and it was kind of hinted that it would be better for me to leave." Weeks later he joined John Mayall's Bluesbreakers in which he found a more musically and creatively sympathetic atmosphere and through which he met up with bassist Jack Bruce.

After a successful stint with The Bluesbreakers during which Clapton became better-known in his own right—his name appearing on the cover of the 1966 *Bluesbreakers with Eric Clapton* album—Clapton, Jack Bruce, and drummer Ginger Baker started rehearsing together secretly. The trio, officially named Cream, began performing in the summer of '66, launching a not-quite three year period of intense and fruitful musical endeavor. In December they released their first album *Fresh Cream.*

The very individual personalities within the group made for a dynamic, if volatile team; as Clapton put it, "there was a constant battle between Ginger and Jack. They loved one anothers' playing but they couldn't stand the sight of each other." Extensive touring and the release of two more albums, November 1967's *Disraeli Gears* (recorded at Atlantic's New York studios) and August 1968's double LP *Wheels Of Fire* established Cream as one of the foremost musical influences of the time. The trio's inventive style, featuring lengthy solos and virtuoso improvisation, was to influence many bands in the years to come. The group "broke" America and established a wide-spread following. After farewell tours of both America and the UK, Cream released their last album, aptly entitled *Goodbye*, in March of 1969.

It was during his time with Cream that Clapton embarked on what was to become a vital part of his career in playing as a guest session artist on a variety of musician's records, including George Harrison and The Beatles. Clapton also became a staple in the musical scene of the day whose other major guitarists comprised the likes of Pete Townshend and Jimi Hendrix. Of Hendrix, Clapton said, "He became a soul mate for me." After Jimi joined Cream on-stage for a jam session, Eric remembers, "I knew it was all over in terms of guitar heroes. Jimi had everything." Cream embraced the era of psychedelia through both its music and its style, and Clapton, ever fashion-conscious, took on the flamboyant trends of the sixties with often fantastic result, sporting an afro and a wonderful variety of colorful costumes. Even his guitar took on a new persona as he began playing a Gibson SG covered in a near-hallucinogenic pattern that the Beatles' Fool design team had devised for him.

During his lengthy stint in America with Cream, Clapton had become strongly influenced by Bob Dylan's back-up group The Band, and upon his return to the UK formed the "supergroup" Blind Faith which included Stevie Winwood and Ginger Baker. An eponymous album featuring rather controversial cover artwork in the form of a naked young girl holding a phallic model air-plane and an extensive US tour followed before the group dissolved after just over a year.

The end of 1969 marked Clapton's return to collaboration, and after appearing with John Lennon and Yoko Ono as a member of the Plastic Ono Band in Toronto in September, he began rehearsing with the American group Delaney & Bonnie & Friends with the view to an upcoming tour together. The loosely constructed band founded by Delaney and Bonnie Bramlett featured a revolving spectrum of seminal artists including Rita Coolidge, Bobby Keyes, George Harrison, Dave Mason, Carl Radle, Leon Russell, Stephen Stills, and Bobby Whitlock. Clapton said of the European and American tour, "This is the first tour I've ever been on in my life— and I've been on a good few I can tell you— where everybody has had a good time." After the tour Eric recorded his first solo effort, *Eric Clapton*, which was produced by Delaney Bramlett. Bramlett and Clapton's joint appreciation and understanding of the blues made for a sympathetic partnership; as Delaney put it, "The only difference was that I had been raised on this music, while Eric had raised himself on it." Of Delaney, Eric says, "He was the first person to instill in me a sense of purpose." The classic song "Let It Rain" remains a testimony to the two musicians' common creativity.

1970 saw the formation of Derek and the Dominos and the subsequent release of what is very often regarded as Eric Clapton's finest album, *Layla and Other Assorted Love Songs*. Duane Allman and a variety of Delaney & Bonnie & Friends musicians were part of The Dominos, and the album showcased many Clapton favorites including "Bell Bottom Blues," "Have You Ever Loved a Woman," and, of course, "Layla." The inspiration behind Clapton's heartfelt writing was George Harrison's wife, Patti, who Clapton would later marry. "To have ownership of something that powerful is something I'll never be able to get used to," said Eric of "Layla." "It still knocks me out when I play it."

Clapton spent the next three years in a sort of semi-retirement due to his heroin addiction. Sporadic musical appearances—such as George Harrison's 1971 Concert for Bangladesh and a "comeback" concert at The Rainbow Theatre in London in 1973 organized by Pete Townshend—as well as session work with Bobby Keyes, Stephen Stills, Howlin' Wolf, Dr. John, Duane Allman, and Stevie Wonder peppered this difficult time.

Clapton's true comeback commenced at a party his long-time manager Robert Stigwood organized at the China Garden restaurant in London's Soho in April 1974. In attendance were Elton John, Pete Townshend, and Ronnie Wood, among others. At the celebration Clapton announced, "I'm feeling very well. I'm really happy." Jumping right back into his customary frenetic touring and recording pace, Eric Clapton and His Band recorded the album *461 Ocean Boulevard* in Miami and spent the summer of 1974 touring the States. *461* includes a cover of Bob Marley's "I Shot the Sheriff" which became a number one hit in the U.S. and gave reggae music a much more prominent position in the American music scene. Clapton recalls his subsequent meeting with Marley during his short UK tour with The Wailers: "I walked into the dressing room that I couldn't see the

other side of because of the smoke. I sat and talked to Bob... he was so warm. A beautiful man."

Kingston, Jamaica was the chosen spot to record yet another album, *There's One In Every Crowd*, released in April 1975. This was an eclectic record combining reggae, country blues, and gospel influences and may be viewed as a vehicle for Eric to escape the "Clapton Is God" guitar-hero status he had secured in the sixties. RSO Records, however, were not as eager to waylay Clapton's strength as a soloist, and neither were the public, hence the release in August 1975 of the album *E.C. Was Here*, a compilation of live tracks showcasing Clapton's guitar-based works.

That same year Clapton was encouraged to become a tax exile and established residency in the Bahamas. Many public appearances with his then-girlfriend Patti Harrison, studio and jam sessions with the likes of The Rolling Stones and Bob Dylan, and his usual unrelentless tour schedule filled the year. The album *No Reason to Cry* was recorded in early 1976 at Malibu California's Shangri-La Studios (once a bordello) and featured guest appearances from The Band, Bob Dylan, Ronnie Wood, and Robbie Robertson. In September Eric and Patti joined the celebration of Buddy Holly's 40th birthday anniversary at a star-studded party, and that evening Clapton composed what was to become one of his most popular songs, "Wonderful Tonight." Of the tune Clapton says, "The songs you write very quickly are always the best."

Eric's next album, which he dubbed "lightweight," was *Slowhand*, a big commercial success opening with the consummate riff of "Cocaine." Yet another year of near-constant touring followed, until Clapton again entered the studio to record his November 1978 album *Backless*. The album was named as a tribute of sorts to Bob Dylan, who Clapton said "knew exactly what was going on around him all the time... you had to focus all your attention on him, and if you didn't, he knew it, and he'd turn around and look at you and you'd get daggers." Muddy Waters was the support act for the album's tour. Albert Lee then joined Clapton and Carl Radle in March 1979

for the Irish and U.S. leg of the tour, adding yet another dimension to Clapton's sound with his guitar and vocals.

On March 27th, Eric married Patti Harrison in Tucson, Arizona, and in May they flew back to the UK to celebrate their wedding at Eric's home along with George Harrison, Paul McCartney, Ringo Starr, and some 200 other guests.

Shortly after the release of *Backless*, Clapton fired the American band which had been with him for almost five years in search of a fresh sound and approach. The resulting group made up of experienced English musicians released a live album entitled *Just One Night* which was recorded at the Budokan in Tokyo in December 1979. Eric was reluctant to release the album, as he felt that live performances were "something that should only happen once." The new band then returned to the studio and released an album which saw the return of Clapton's guitar entitled *Another Ticket* in February of 1981. The tour in support of the record was cut short after just a few U.S. shows as Eric was rushed off stage and to the hospital due to an acute ulcer. Six months of recovery followed, and close to fifty concerts had to be canceled.

Clapton spent the majority of 1982 coming to terms with the fact that he had an alcohol problem, and, with the help of Alcoholics Anonymous, he managed to kick the habit. While hospitalized for his ulcers he was told that he needed to curtail his drinking, and as Eric said, "I think that was the first time anyone had ever said something like that to me... I had to go further down that road to complete insanity before I stopped." But stop he did, and in February of 1983 he released the album *Money and Cigarettes*. After firing the original line-up and starting afresh with a new band, Clapton found the new rhythm section to be a great motivation: "If I wanted to get in on it, I had to work... And that's when I decided I was getting back to where I should be."

A host of live performances, including the star-studded ARMS Benefit concerts at London's Royal Albert Hall, filled the next year. In 1984 Clapton contributed to every track on Roger Waters' *Pros and Cons of Hitch-Hiking* LP and went on tour with Waters in support of the album. The next two years saw Clapton playing at his best yet, and two more solo albums were released

within the space of fifteen months; both *Behind the Sun* and the hugely successful *August* were produced by Phil Collins. The latter album was named in honor of the birth of Clapton's son Conor that very month. Sandwiched between the two albums' release dates was the momentous Live Aid Concert in July of 1985; Clapton performed "White Room," "She's Waiting," and "Layla."

On-stage jamming with a roster of top musicians highlighted the next few years as Clapton joined up with Dire Straits, Phil Collins, The Rolling Stones, Robert Cray, Prince, Keith Richards, Lionel Ritchie, Buddy Guy, Jeff Beck, and Sting. Eric also recorded tracks for several film soundtracks including *The Color of Money*, *Lethal Weapon*, and *Buster*. In November of 1989 the *Journeyman* album was released; of the album Clapton said, "I was very firm in making sure this record was for me." His now-customary gig at the beginning of each year at London's Royal Albert Hall was booked for a record-breaking eighteen nights in January of 1990. This was a milestone quickly passed, as the next year Clapton topped his own record with two dozen nights at the famous venue, prompting the December 1991 release of the live double album *24 Nights*.

On August 26, 1990 Stevie Ray Vaughan, along with Clapton's agent and members of his crew, died when the helicopter they were in (one of a convoy transporting Eric and band from that evening's gig) crashed. Eric and his entourage, after much deliberation, decided to carry on with the tour. As Clapton worded it, "it was the best tribute I thought we could make… it was in honor of their memory."

Tragically, less than a year later Eric's young son Conor died after falling out of a window in New York. After this terrible accident, Clapton said, "My soul went dead to music." Slowly turning back to music to begin the "healing process," Eric wrote the heart-wrenching song "Tears In Heaven" which was featured on the *Rush* film soundtrack.

Clapton ended 1991 with a brief Japanese tour with George Harrison. He then began the New Year by recording and filming a concert for MTV's "Unplugged" series, followed by his traditional run at the Albert Hall. Later that year he toured incorporating quite a few double bills with Elton John. The *Unplugged* album was released in August of '92 and soon became Eric's best-selling record ever, earning him several Grammy awards. "There's not much I can say about these songs," Eric said, "except that they helped me through a very, very hard patch in my life."

In January 1993 Cream got back together for one night at the Rock'n'Roll Hall of Fame awards. Clapton filled out the year with his usual combination of live performance and session work, this time recording with artists as diverse as Kate Bush and Ray Charles. At the end of the year *Stone Free—A Tribute to Jimi Hendrix* was released on which Clapton covered the title track.

Eric Clapton's most recent album has seen him come full circle. On *From the Cradle*, an all-blues recording released in September 1994, Clapton returned to the music which captured his emotions and jump-started his musical career many years before. In an attempt to recreate the original recordings as faithfully as he could, Clapton discovered that "it still came out as me which is the beauty of the whole exercise."

68

Discography

THE YARDBIRDS

Five Live Yardbirds
Too Much Monkey Business/Got Love If You Want It/ Smokestack Lightning/Good Morning Little Schoolgirl/ Respectable/Five Long Years/Pretty Girl/Louise/I'm A Man/Here 'Tis
UK: Columbia 33SX 1677; Feb 1965
US: Rhino R2-70189

JOHN MAYALL'S BLUESBREAKERS

John Mayall's Bluesbreakers With Eric Clapton
All Your Love/Hideaway/Little Girl/Another Man/Double Crossin' Time/What'd I Say/Key To Love/Parchman Farm/Have You Heard/Ramblin' On My Mind/Steppin' Out/It Ain't Right
UK: Decca SKL4804; Jul 1966
US: Deram 800086-2

CREAM

Fresh Cream
Wrapping Paper/I Feel Free/The Coffee Song/N.S.U./Sleepy Time Time/Dreaming/Sweet Wine/Spoonful/Cat's Squirrel/Four Until Late/Rollin' And Tumblin'/I'm So Glad/Toad
UK: Reaction 593001; Dec 1966
US: Polydor 827576-2

Disraeli Gears
Strange Brew/Sunshine Of Your Love/World Of Pain/Dance The Night Away/Blue Condition/Tales Of Brave Ulysses/Swlabr/We're Going Wrong/Outside Woman Blues/Take It Back/Mother's Lament
UK: Reaction 593003; Nov 1967
US: Polydor 823636-2

Wheels Of Fire
Disc One—In The Studio: White Room/Sitting On Top Of The World/Passing The Time/As You Said/Pressed Rat And Warthog/Politician/Those Were The Days/Born Under A Bad Sign/Deserted Cities Of The Heart/Anyone For Tennis
Disc Two—Live at the Fillmore: Crossroads/Spoonful / Traintime/Toad
UK: Polydor 583031; Aug 1968
US: Polydor 827578-2

Goodbye Cream
I'm So Glad/Politician/Sitting On Top Of The World/Badge/ Doing That Scrapyard Thing/What A Bringdown
UK: Polydor 583053; Mar 1969
US: Polydor 823660-2

Live Cream
N.S.U./Sleepy Time Time/Sweet Wine/Rollin' And Tumblin'/ Lawdy Mama
UK: Polydor 2383016; Jun 1970
US: Polydor 827577-2

Live Cream Volume II
Deserted Cities Of The Heart/White Room/Politician/Tales Of Brave Ulysses/Sunshine Of Your Love/Steppin' Out
UK: Polydor 2383119; Jul 1972
US: Polydor 823661-2

BLIND FAITH

Blind Faith
Had To Cry Today/Can't Find My Way Home/Well All Right/Presence Of The Lord/Sea Of Joy/Do What You Like
UK: Polydor 583059; Aug 1969
US: Polydor 825094-2

DELANEY & BONNIE & FRIENDS

Delaney & Bonnie & Friends On Tour With Eric Clapton
Things Get Better/Poor Elijah —Tribute to Johnson (Medley)/Only You Know And I Know/I Don't Want To Discuss it/That's What My Man Is For/Where There's A Will, There's A Way/Coming Home/Little Richard Medley
ATCO 33326-2; 1970

DEREK AND THE DOMINOS

Layla and Other Assorted Love Songs
I Looked Away/Bell Bottom Blues/Keep On Growing/Nobody Knows You When You're Down And Out/I Am Yours/Anyday/Key To The Highway/Tell The Truth/Why Does Love Got To Be So Sad?/Have You Ever Loved A Woman/Little Wing/It's Too Late/Layla/Thorn Tree In The Garden
UK: Polydor Super 2625005; Dec 1970
US: Polydor 847090-2

Derek and the Dominos in Concert
Why Does Love Got To Be So Sad/Got To Get Better In A Little While/Let It Rain/Presence Of The Lord/Tell The Truth/Bottle Of Red Wine/Roll It Over/Blues Power/Have You Ever Loved A Woman
UK: USRSO 2659020; Mar 1973
US: Polydor 831416-2

Layla 20th Anniversary Edition
Disc One—Layla: I Looked Away/Bell Bottom Blues/Keep On Growing/Nobody Knows You When You're Down And Out/I Am Yours/Anyday/Key To The Highway/Tell The Truth/Why Does Love Got To Be So Sad?/Have You Ever Loved A Woman/Little Wing/It's Too Late/Layla/Thorn Tree In The Garden
Disc Two—The Jams
Disc Three—Have You Ever Loved A Woman (Alternate Master 1)/Have You Ever Loved A Woman (Alternate Master 2)/Tell The Truth (Jam 1)/Tell The Truth (Jam 2)/Mean Old World (Rehearsal)/Mean Old World (Band Version) /Mean Old World (Duet Version)/It Hurts Me Too (Jam)/Tender Love (Incomplete Master)/It's Too Late (Alternate Master)
Polydor Box Set 847 083 2; Dec 1990

Derek and the Dominos Live at the Fillmore
Why Does Love Got To Be So Sad/Key To The Highway/Tell The Truth/Nobody Knows You When You're Down And Out/Little Wing/Let It Rain/Crossroads
Polydor 521682; Feb 1994

ERIC CLAPTON

Eric Clapton
Slunky/Bad Boy/Lonesome And A Long Way From Home/After Midnight/Easy Now/Blues Power/Bottle Of Red Wine/Lovin' You Lovin' Me/Told You For The Last Time/Don't Know Why/Let It Rain
UK: Polydor Super 3383021; Aug 1970
US: Polydor 825093-2

Rainbow Concert
Badge/Roll It Over/Presence Of The Lord/Pearly Queen/After Midnight/Little Wing
UK: RSO 2394116; Sep 1973
US: Polydor 831320-2

461 Ocean Boulevard
Motherless Children/Willie And The Hand Jive/Get Ready/I Shot The Sheriff/I Can't Hold Out/Please Be With Me/Let It Grow/Steady Rollin' Man/Mainline Florida/Give Me Strength
UK: RSO 2479118; Aug 1974
US: Polydor 811697-2

There's One In Every Crowd
We've Been Told (Jesus Coming Soon)/Swing Low Sweet Chariot/Little Rachel/Don't Blame Me/The Sky Is Crying/Singin' The Blues/Better Make It Through Today/Pretty Blue Eyes/High/Opposites
UK: RSO 2479132; Apr 1975
US: Polydor 829649-2

E.C. Was Here
Have You Ever Loved A Woman/Presence Of The Lord/Drifting Blues/Can't Find My Way Home/Ramblin' On My Mind/Further On Up The Road
UK: RSO 2394160; Aug 1975
US: Polydor 831519-2

No Reason To Cry
Beautiful Thing/Carnival/Sign Language/County Jail Blues/All Our Past Times/Hello Old Friend/Double Trouble/Innocent Times/Hungry/Black Summer Rain/Last Night
UK: RSO 2394160; Aug 1976
US: Polydor 813582-2

Slowhand
Cocaine/Wonderful Tonight/Lay Down Sally/Next Time You See Her/We're All The Way/The Core/May You Never/Mean Old Frisco/Peaches And Diesel
UK: RSO 2479201; Nov 1977
US: Polydor 823276-2

Backless
Walk Out In The Rain/Watch Out For Lucy/I'll Make Love To You Anytime/Roll It/Tell Me That You Love Me/If I Don't Be There By Morning/Early In The Morning/Promises/Golden Ring/Tulsa Time
UK: RSO 2479221; Nov 1978
US: Polydor 813581-2

Just One Night
Tulsa Time/Early In The Morning/Lay Down Sally/Wonderful Tonight/If I Don't Be There By Morning/Worried Life Blues/All Our Past Times/After Midnight/Double Trouble/Setting Me Up/Blues Power/Ramblin' On My Mind/Have You Ever Loved A Woman/Cocaine/Further On Up The Road
UK: RSO 2479240; May 1980
US: Polydor 800093-2

Another Ticket
Something Special/Black Rose/Blow Wind Blow/Another Ticket/I Can't Stand It/Hold Me Lord/Floating Bridge/Catch Me If You Can/Rita Mae
UK: RSO 2479285; Feb 1981
US: Polydor 827579-2

Money and Cigarettes
Everybody Oughta Make A Change/The Shape You're In/Ain't Going Down/I've Got A Rock'n'Roll Heart/Man Overboard/Pretty Girl/Man In Love/Crosscut Saw/Slow Down Linda/Crazy Country Hop
UK: Duck 923773-2; Feb 1983
US: Warner Bros. 23773-2

Behind the Sun
She's Waiting/See What Love Can Do/Same Old Blues/Knock On Wood/Something's Happening/Forever Man/It All Depends/Tangled In Love/Never Make You Cry/Just Like A Prisoner/Behind The Sun
UK: Duck 925166-2; Mar 1985
US: Warner Bros. 25166-2

August
It's In The Way That You Use It/Run/Tearing Us Apart/Bad Influence/Walk Away/Hung Up On Your Love/Take A Chance/Hold On/Miss You/Holy Mother/Behind The Mask/Grand Illusion
UK: Duck 925476-2; Aug 1986
US: Warner Bros. 25476-2

Crossroads
Boom Boom/Honey In Your Hips/Baby What's Wrong/I Wish You Would/A Certain Girl/Good Morning Little Schoolgirl/I Ain't Got You/For Your Love/Got To Hurry/Lonely Years/Bernard Jenkins/Hideaway/All Your Love/Ramblin' On My Mind/Have You Ever Loved A Woman/Wrapping Paper/I Feel Free/Spoonful/Lawdy Mama/Strange Brew/Sunshine Of Your Love/Tales Of Brave Ulysses/Steppin' Out/Anyone For Tennis/White Room/ Crossroads/Badge/Presence Of The Lord/Can't Find My Way Home/ Sleeping In The Ground/Comin' Home/Blues Power/After Midnight/Let It Rain/Tell The Truth/Roll It Over/Layla/Mean Old World/Key To The Highway/Crossroads/Got To Get Better In A Little While/Evil/One More Chance/Mean Old Frisco/Snake Lake Blues/Let It Grow/Ain't That Lovin You/Motherless Children/I Shot The Sheriff/Better Make It Through Today/The Sky Is Crying/I Found A Love/(When Things Go Wrong) It Hurts Me Too/Watcha Gonna Do/Knockin' On Heaven's Door/Someone Like You/Hello Old Friend/Sign Language/Further On Up The Road/Lay Down Sally/Wonderful Tonight/Cocaine/Promises/If I Don't Be There By Morning/Double Trouble/I Can't Stand It/The Shape You're In/Heaven Is One Step Away/She's Waiting/Too Bad/Miss You/Wanna Make Love To You/After Midnight
Polydor 835261-2; Apr 1988

Journeyman
Pretending/Anything For Your Love/Bad Love/Running On Faith/Hard Times/Hound Dog/No Alibis/Run So Far/Old Love/Breaking Point/Lead Me On/Before You Accuse Me
UK: Duck 926074-2; Nov 1989
US: Reprise 26074-2

24 Nights
Badge/Running On Faith/White Room/Sunshine Of Your Love/Watch Yourself/Have You Ever Loved A Woman/Worried Life Blues/Hoodoo Man/Pretending/Bad Love/Old Love/Wonderful Tonight/Bell Bottom Blues/Hard Times/Edge Of Darkness
UK: Duck 759926420-2; Dec 1991
US: Reprise 26420-2

Unplugged
Signe/Before You Accuse Me/Hey Hey/Tears In Heaven/Lonely Stranger/Nobody Knows You When You're Down And Out/ Layla/Running On Faith/Walkin' Blues/Alberta/San Francisco Bay Blues/Malted Milk/Old Love/Rollin' & Tumblin'
UK: Duck 936245024-2; Aug 1992
US: Reprise 45024-2

The Cream of Eric Clapton
Layla/I Feel Free/Sunshine Of Your Love/Crossroads/Strange Brew/White Room/Bell Bottom Blues/Cocaine/I Shot The Sheriff/ After Midnight/Swing Low Sweet Chariot/Lay Down Sally/ Knockin' On Heaven's Door/Wonderful Tonight/Let It Grow/ Promises/I Can't Stand It
UK: Polydor 521 881-2; Jul 1994
US: Polydor 527116

From the Cradle
Blues Before Sunrise/Third Degree/Reconsider Baby/Hoochie Coochie Man/Five Long Years/I'm Tore Down/How Long Blues/Goin' Away Baby/Blues Leave Me Alone/Sinner's Prayer/Motherless Child/It Hurts Me Too/Someday After A While/Standin' Round Crying/Driftin'/Groaning The Blues
UK: Duck 936245735-2; Sep 1994
US: Reprise 45735-2

Eric Clapton's Rainbow Concert
Layla/Badge/Blues Power/Roll It Over/Little Wing/Bottle of Red Wine/After Midnight/Bell Bottom Blues/Presence Of The Lord/Tell The Truth/Pearly Queen/Key To The Highway/Let It Rain/Crossroads
US: Polydor 31452 7472-2; Jul 1995

from Unplugged

Alberta

New Words and New Music Adaptation by Huddie Ledbetter

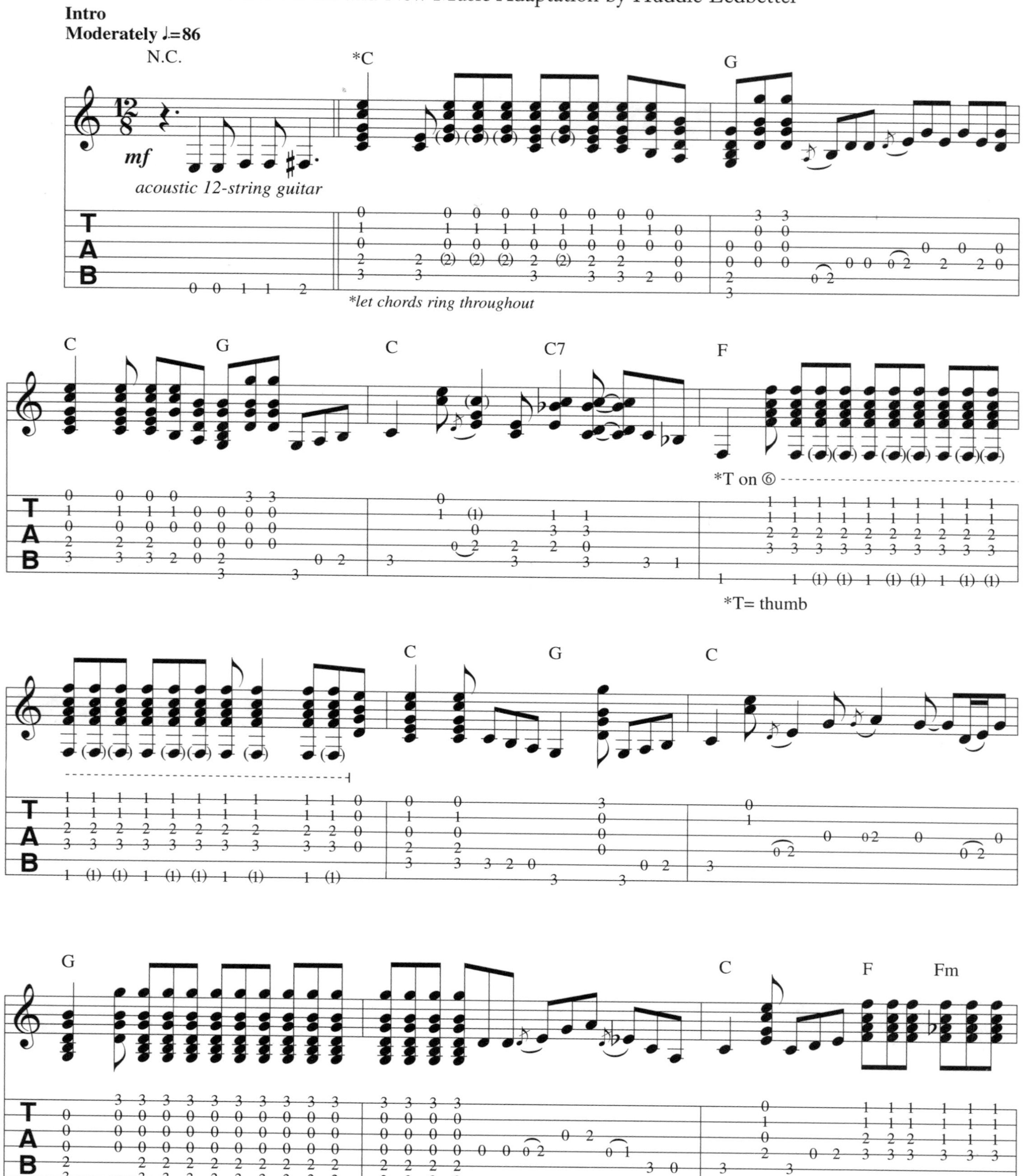

Additional lyrics

2. Alberta, Alberta, where'd you stay last night?
   Alberta, Alberta, where'd you stay last night?
   Come home this mornin', clothes don't fit you right.

3. *Instrumental*

4. Alberta, Alberta, girl you're on my mind.
   Alberta, Alberta, girl you're on my mind.
   Ain't had no lovin' in such a great, long time.

5. Alberta, Alberta, where you been so long?
   Alberta, Alberta, where you been so long?
   Ain't had no lovin' since you've been gone.

from John Mayall's Bluesbreakers with Eric Clapton

All Your Love
(I Miss Loving)
by Otis Rush

Am
>B R
Em
Dm
Am
hold bend
hold bend
B
B
B B
B R
Verse 1
N.C.
Am
guitar 2 with Rhythm figure 1
All the lov - in' - est lov - in',
all the kiss - in' - est kiss -
end Rhythm figure 1

Dm
in', all the lov - in' - est lov - in', ___
Am
all the kiss - in' - est kiss - in'. Be - fore I met you
Em
Dm
Am
ba - by, nev - er knew what I was miss - in'. ___
Verse 2
end Rhythm figure 1
with Rhythm figure 1 (first 11 bars only)
N.C.
Am
All your love, ___ pret - ty ba - by, that I got in store for

Dm
you; all your love, pret - ty ba - by,
B R
Am
that I got in store for you.
I love you, pret - ty
B
Em
Dm
Am
end Rhythm figure 1
ba - by.
Well, I say you love me too.
Guitar solo
N.C.
Am
let ring
let ring
Rhythm figure 2

Dm
let ring
Am
let ring
let ring
Em
Dm
Am

Medium blues shuffle ♩=120
N.C.
A7
end Rhythm figure 2
B
B
B
B R
D7
B
B hold bend
A7
B
E7
D7
A7
B
B hold bend
B
Chorus
N.C.
A7
All your lov-in', pret-ty ba - by, all your lov - in', pret - ty
by, hey hey, ba -
B

D7
ba - by,
by,
all your lov - in', pret - ty ba - by,
Yeah, yeah, yeah, yeah, yeah, ba - by,

A7
all your lov - in', pret - ty ba - by.
oh, oh, ba - by.
Just be - fore I met you,

E7
D7
1. A7
ba - by,
I nev - er knew what I was miss - in'.

Moderate blues rhumba ♩=108
N.C
2.
A
N.C.
Hey, hey, ba - miss-in'.
Am
with Rhythm figure 1 (first 8 bars only)
A.H.
Dm
end Rhythm figure 1
Em
Am
N.C.
(drums)
rit.

from Wheels Of Fire

Born Under A Bad Sign

by William Bell and Booker T. Jones

Moderately

*Chord symbol reflects suggested tonality

Chorus

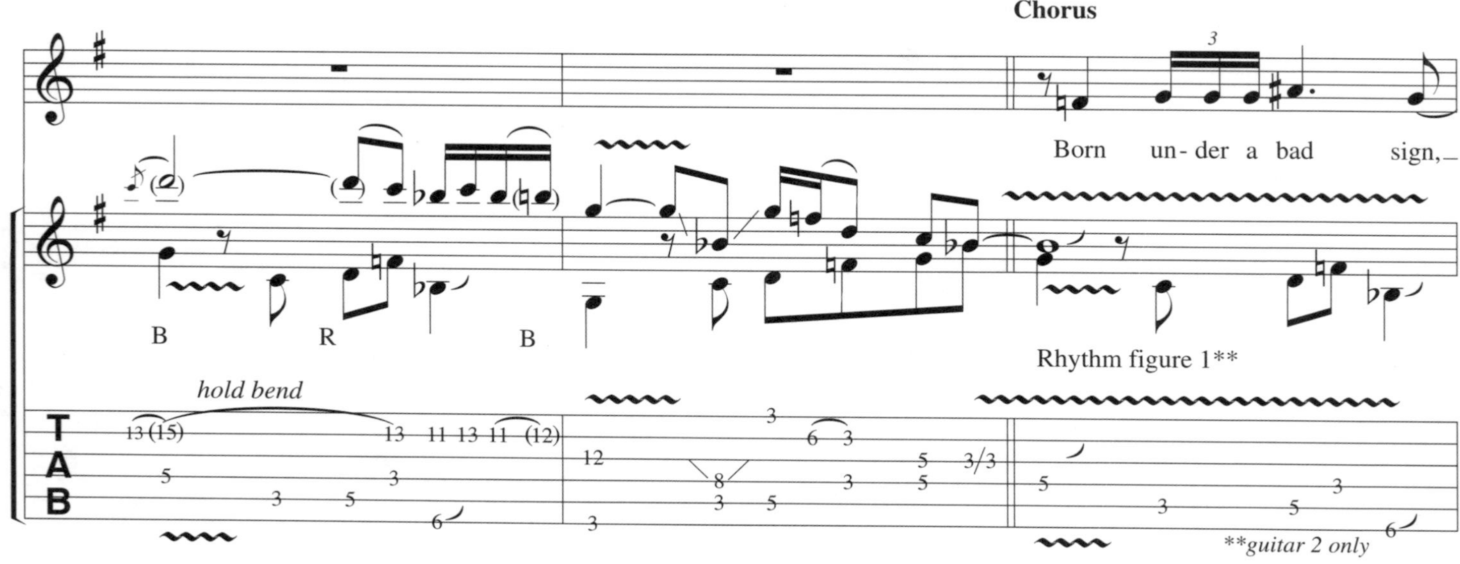

D7♯9
E♭ D D♭ C7
If it was-n't for bad luck,
I would-n't have no luck
(G7)
at all.
B let ring
B
Verse 1
Bad luck and trou - ble's my on - ly friend,
I've been down ev - er since
Rhythm figure 2**
guitar 1 tacet
**guitar 2 only
I was ten.
Born un-der a bad sign,
guitar 1

I've been down since I be-gan to crawl.
B
let ring
D7#9
E♭
D7
D♭7
C7
If it was-n't for bad luck,
I would-n't have no luck at
B
end Rhythm figure 2
(G7)
all.
Verse 2
guitar 2 Rhythm figure 2 simile
No wine and wom - en,
It's all I crave,
guitar 1

big, bad wom-an, a-gon-na car-ry me-a a-to my grave.

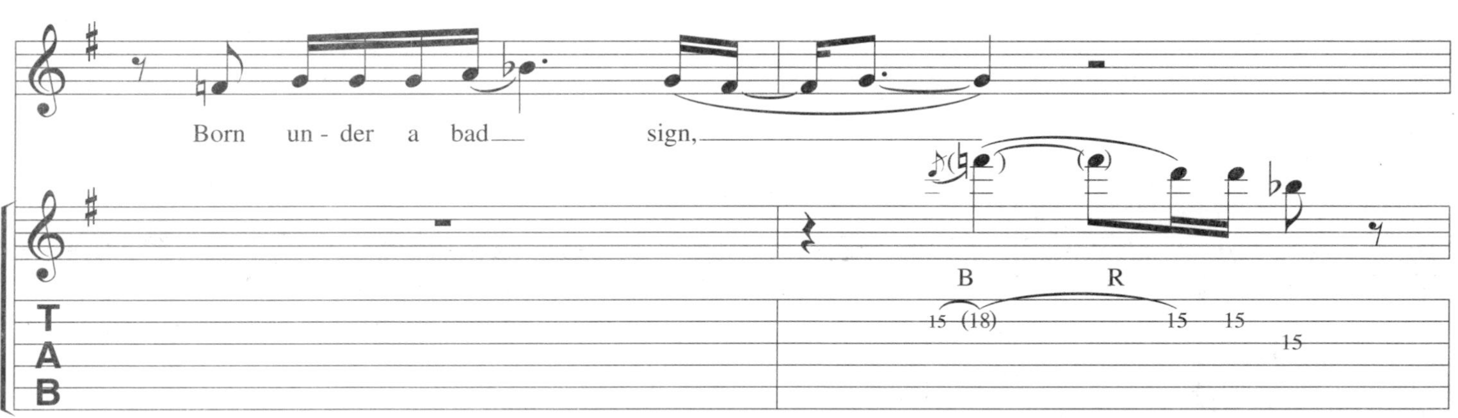
Born un-der a bad sign,
B R
T
A
B
15 (18) 15 15 15

I've been down since I be-gan to crawl.
B B
T
A
B
17 15 6 (7) 6 (7) 6 7 5

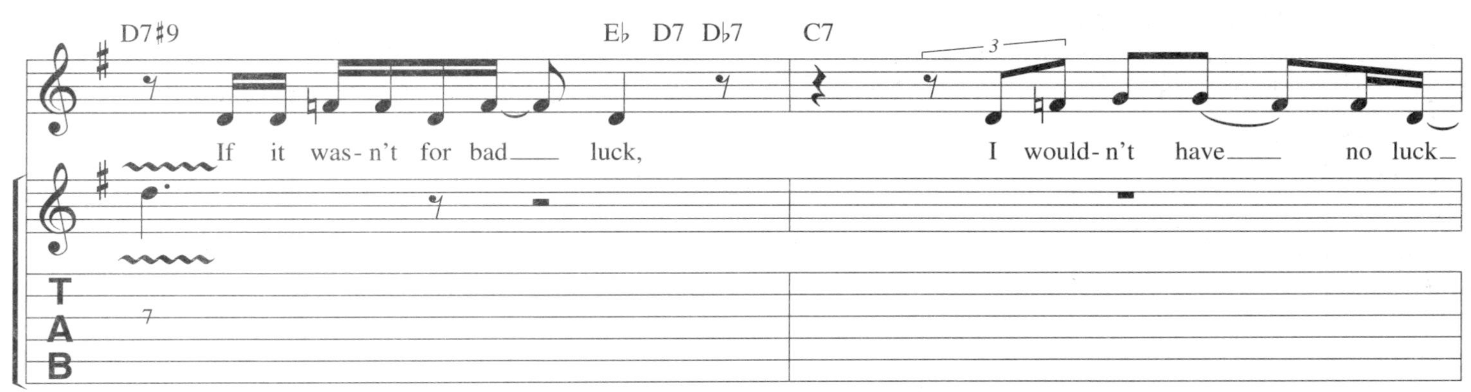
D7♯9
E♭ D7 D♭7
C7
If it was-n't for bad luck, I would-n't have no luck
T
A
B
7

guitar 2 Rhythm figure 1 (four times) simile
(G5)
at all.
let ring
B
Guitar solo
B hold bend R
let ring
let ring
B
B
B
B
B
B
guitar 1
B
B B R
guitar 2

loco
D7♯9
E♭
D
D♭
C7
C7♯9
B
C
D♭
B
B R
P.M.
D7
D7♯9
E♭
D
D♭ C7
B R
B R
B B
B R
let ring
(G7)

Verse 3

guitar 2 Rhythm figure 1 (1st eight bars only) *simile*

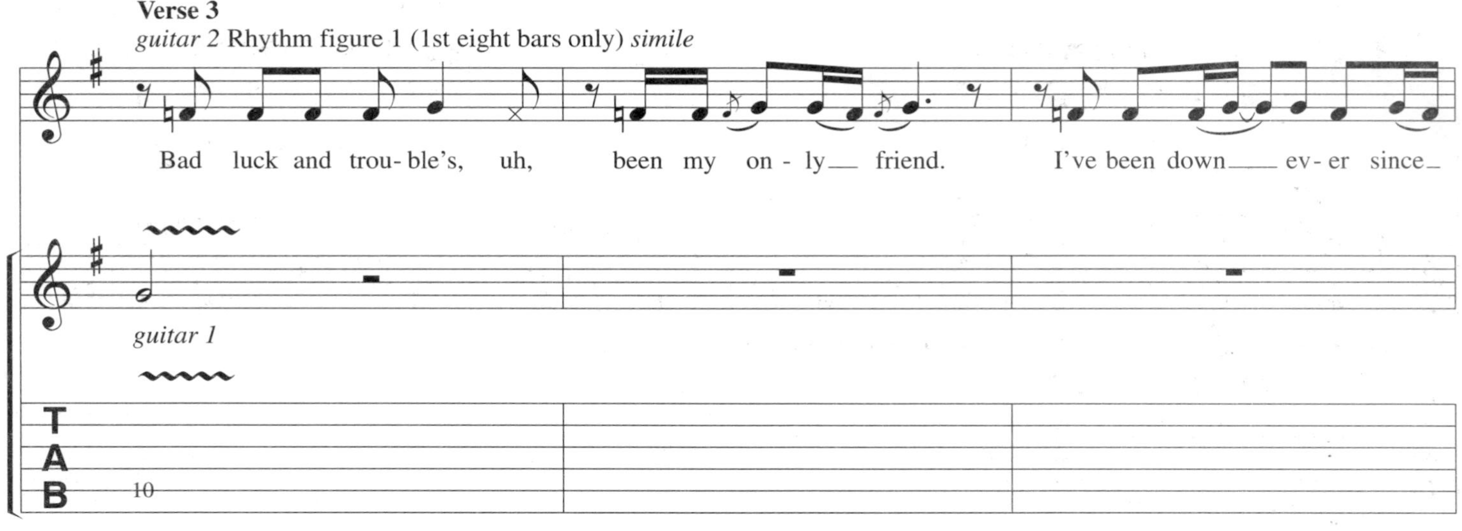

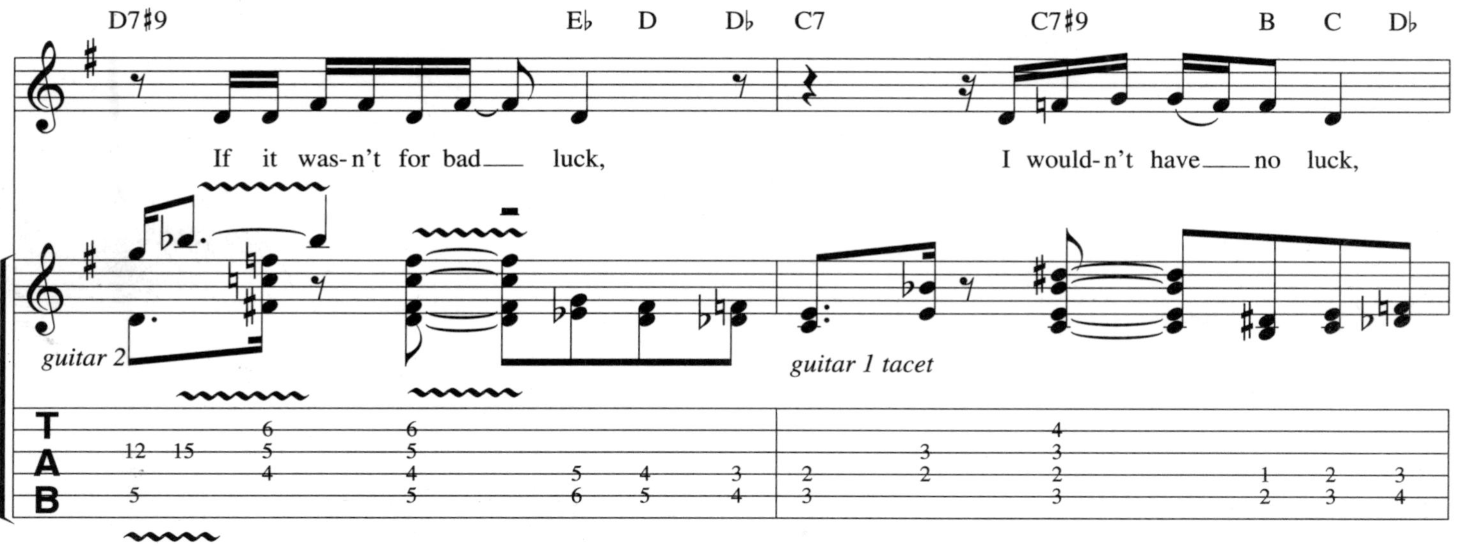

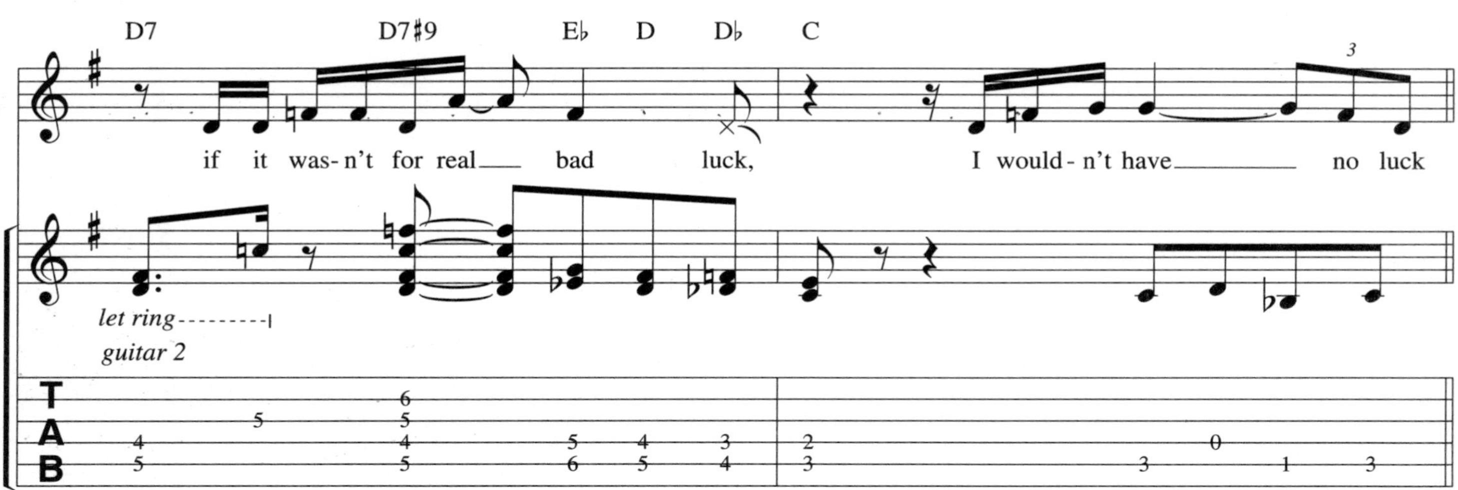

Outro

guitar 2 Rhythm figure 1 (until fade) *simile*

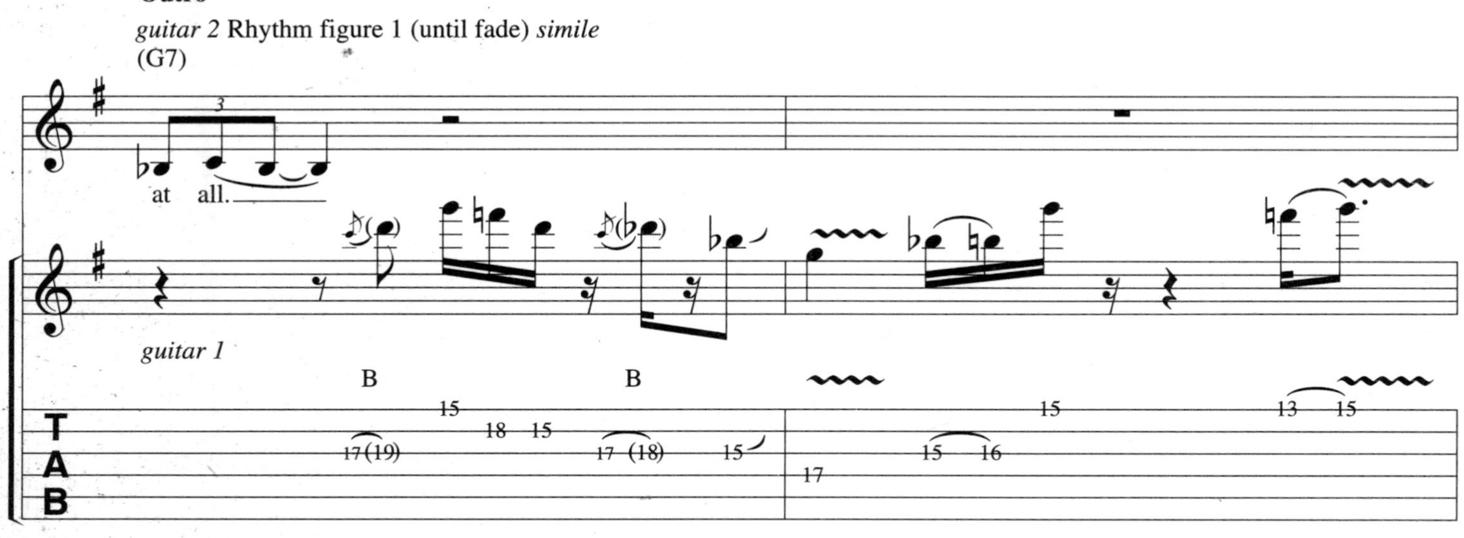

Born under a bad sign.
8
B
B B
loco
Born under a bad sign.
B
B
begin fade
B
B R
B R
let ring
8
fade out
B
B

from Layla And Other Assorted Love Songs

Anyday

Words and Music by Eric Clapton and Bobby Whitlock

1. I
Riff A
end Riff A
rakes
*hold first note of each rake for full duration of second note of rake
Verse
Riff A (four times) simile
A
A/G
D/F♯
F
heard you talk - in' and I thought I heard you say yeah,
3. See Additional lyrics
Rhythm figure 2
"Please leave me a - lone.
end Rhythm figure 2
Noth-ing in this world can make me stay,

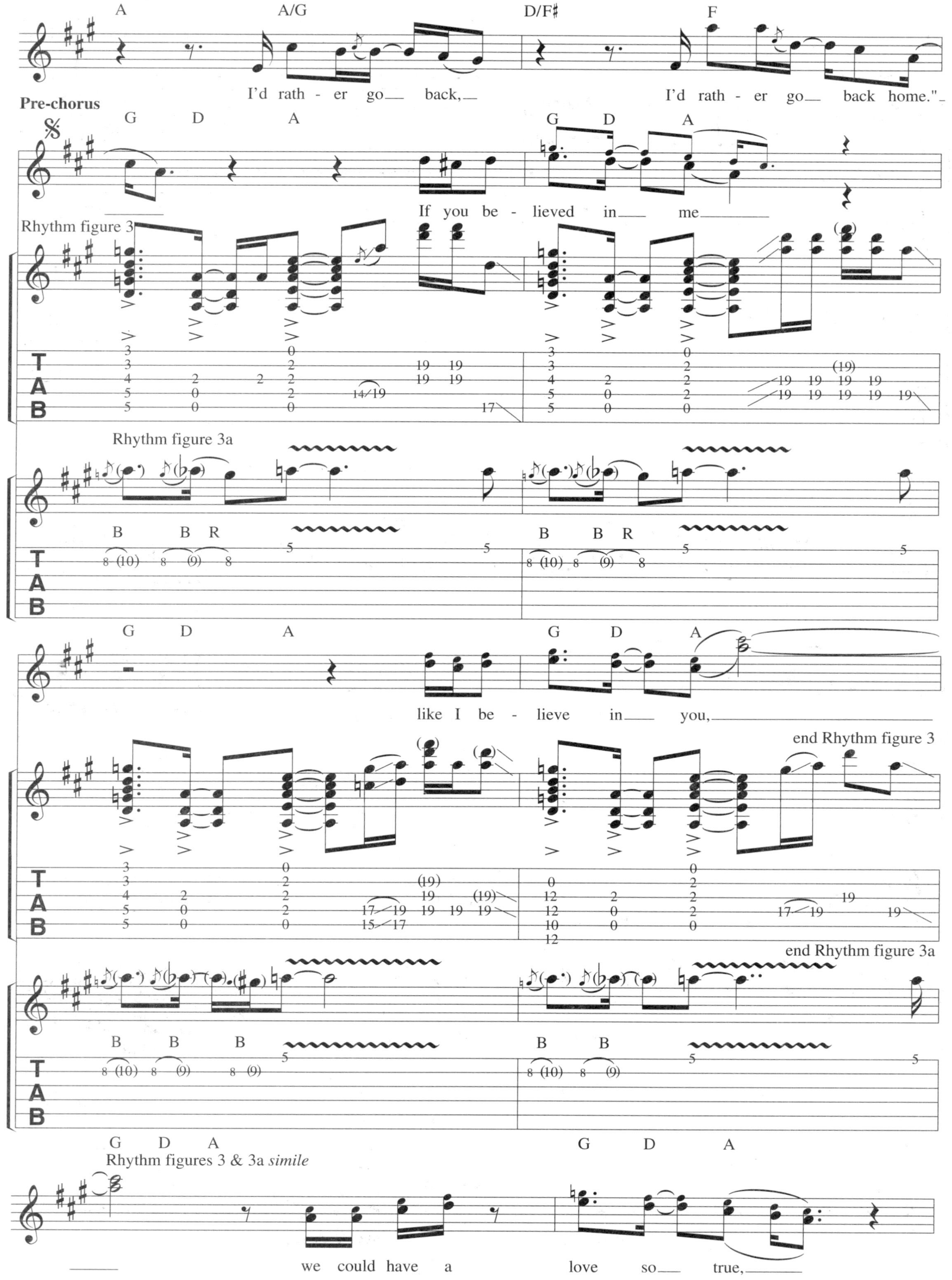
A A/G D/F♯ F
I'd rath - er go back, I'd rath - er go back home."
Pre-chorus
G D A G D A
If you be - lieved in me
Rhythm figure 3
Rhythm figure 3a
B B R B B R
G D A G D A
like I be - lieve in you,
end Rhythm figure 3
end Rhythm figure 3a
B B B B B
G D A G D A
Rhythm figures 3 & 3a *simile*
we could have a love so true,

G D A
G D A
end Rhythm figures 3 & 3a
we would go on
end - less - ly.
And I know
Chorus
D
A
G
guitar 2 Rhythm figure 4a
any day,
any day,
I - will see you smile.
guitar 1 Rhythm figure 4
guitar 3 Rhythm figure 4b
⑥open
D
D
A
G
B B B R

D
A
G
Any-way,
an-y-way,
on-ly for a lit-tle while.
⑥open
D
D
A
G
to Coda
end Rhythm figure 4a
end Rhythm figure 4
B
B R B hold bend R
end Rhythm figure 4b
Rhythm figures 1 & 1a simile
to Coda
Well,

Verse 2
A A/G D/F♯ Fsus2
Rhythm figure 2 (two times) & Riff A (four times)
some - day ba - by I know you're gon - na need me, huh
A A/G D/F♯ F A A/G
when this old world has got you down. Yeah yeah. I'll be right here, so
D/F♯ F A A/G D/F♯ F
D.S. al Coda
wom-an call me, Lord and I'll nev-er, ev - er, ev-er let you down!
Coda
Guitar solo
Rhythm figure 2 (2 times)
(A5)
with last bar of Rhythm figures 1 & 1a
A A/G D/F♯ F
guitar 3
hold bend
B R B R
T
A
B
A A/G D/F♯ F
B R B
hold bend
B R
A A/G D/F♯ F
B B B R B B

from Crossroads

Boom Boom

by John Lee Hooker

E N.C.
B A/C♯
T A B
B N.C.
E A6/E E
N.C.
E A6/E E N.C.
Boom, boom, boom, boom,
boom,
I'm gon - na shoot 'cha right
you know I like it like
E A6/E E N.C. A D6/A A
down.
that.
Knock ya off your feet,
With your ba - by talk,
N.C. E A6/E E
take you home with me.
oh, and the way that you walk.

N.C.
B
E6/B
B
Put you in my house.
You know it knocks me right down.
N.C.
E
A6/E
E
Boom, boom, boom, boom.
Knocks me off of my feet.
N.C.
E
A6/E
E
N.C.
Boom, boom, boom, boom.
Yeah, yeah, yeah,
E
A6/E
E
N.C.
A
D6/A
A
yeah.
I love to see you strut,
Oh, oh, oh, oh,
N.C.
E
A6/E
E
when you're walk - in' to me.
how, how, how, how.
N.C.
B
E6/B
B
When you're talk - in' to me,
Yeah, yeah, yeah, yeah.
N.C.
E
A6/E
E
B7/E
that knocks me out.
Now, now, now, now.
Yeah, let's go!

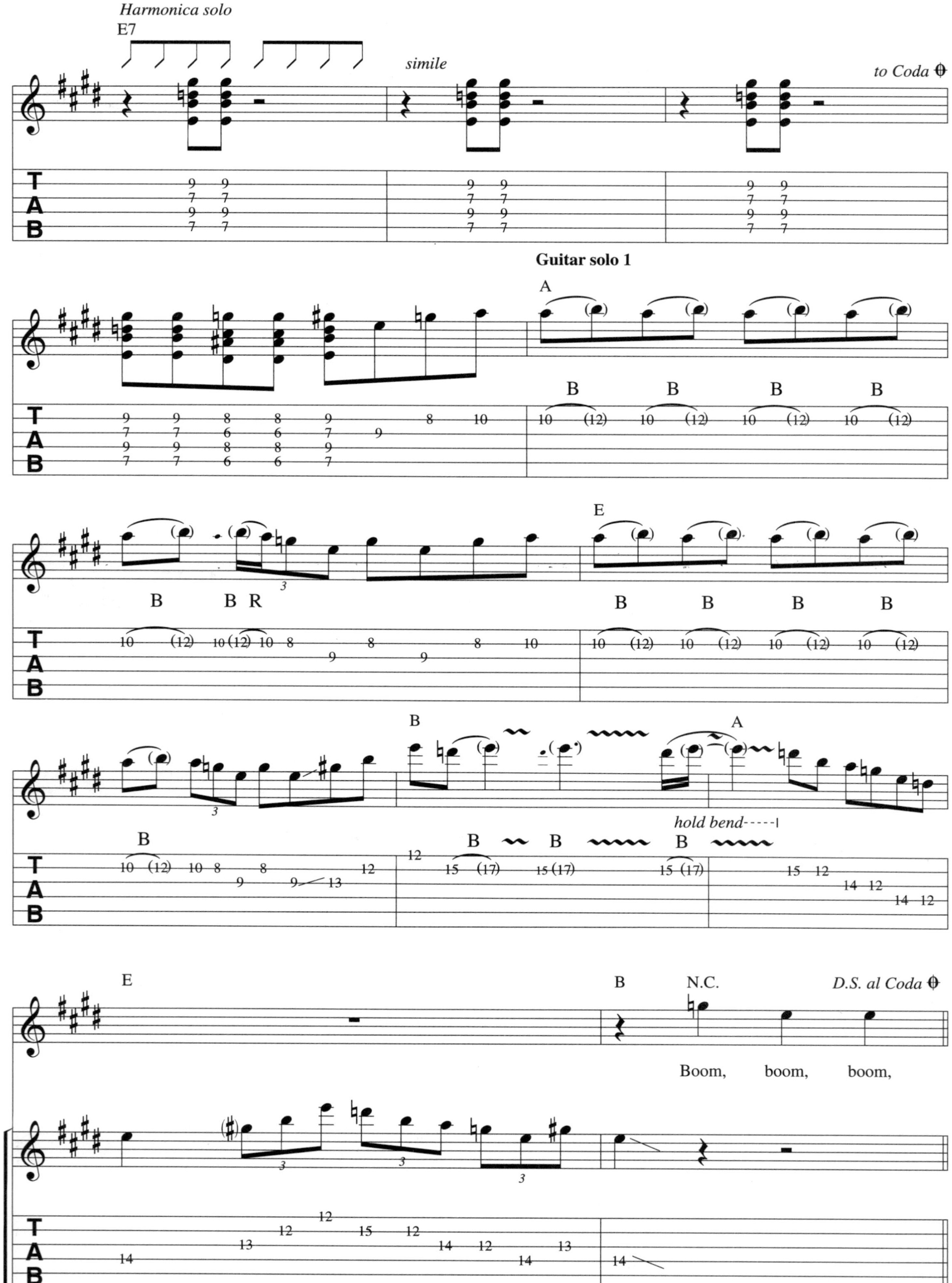
Harmonica solo
E7
simile
to Coda
Guitar solo 1
A
B
B R
E
hold bend
N.C.
D.S. al Coda
Boom, boom, boom,

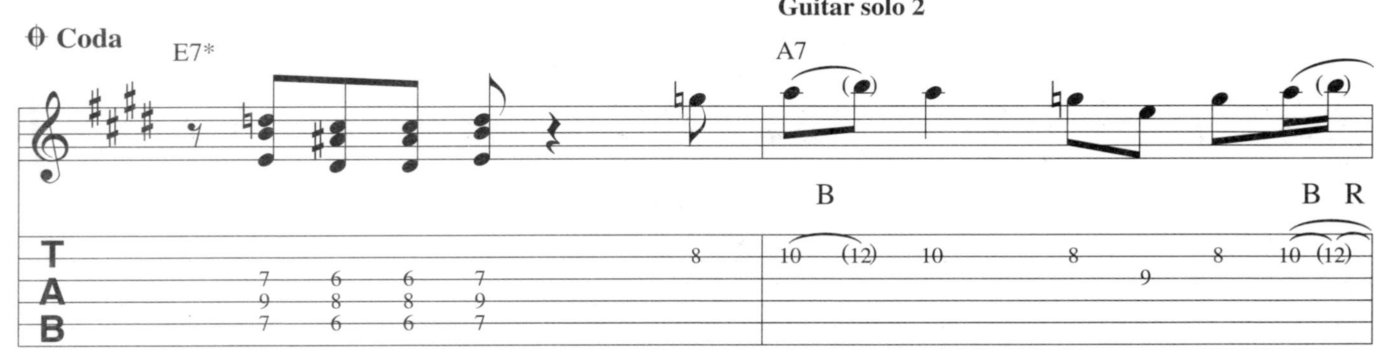
Coda
Guitar solo 2
E7*
A7
B
B R
T
A
B
*Rhythm guitar continues simile to end

E7
T
A
B

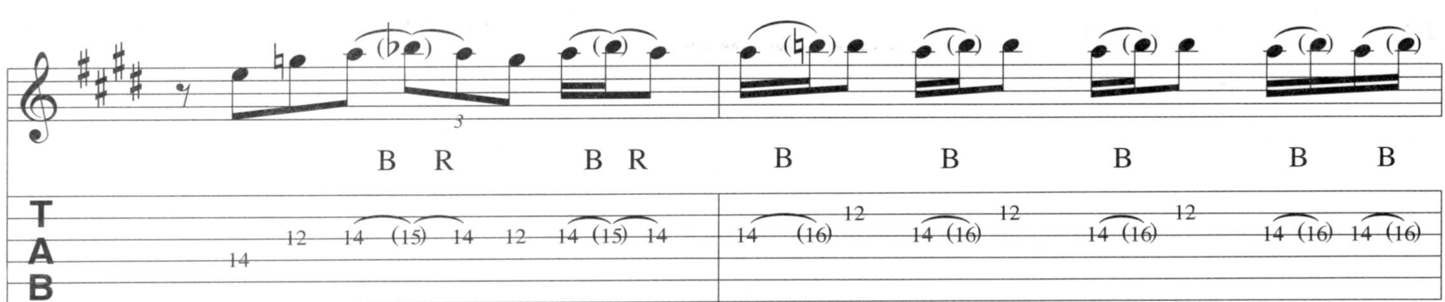
B R
B R
B
B
B
B B
T
A
B

A
B
B
B
B
T
A
B

Straight 4 feel
E
E6
E9
B
T
A
B

released as a single in December 1969

Comin' Home

Words and Music by Bonnie Sheridan and Eric Clapton

Dsus D
A
to Coda
D
B B B R
B R
Dsus
1.,2.,3.
Dsus D
4.
A D
1st time only
B R
B R
let ring

Verse
A
Been out on the road 'bout six months
Hitch hik in' on the turn - pike all day long.
Riff 1
end Riff 1
Rhythm figure 1*
B
let ring
B
end Rhythm figure 1
with fingers
B
B
*Rhythm figure 1 includes guitars 2&3
guitar 1 Riff A (six times)
guitars 2&3 with Rhythm figure 1 (three times)
too long. I want you so
No - bod - y seemed to no -
bad, I can hard - ly stand it.
tice; just pass me o - ver.
I'm so tired, and I'm all a - lone.
To keep from go - in' cra - zy, I got - ta sing my song.
We'll soon be to - geth - er,
Got a-whole lot of lov - in'.
guitars 2&3 with Rhythm figure 1
(first two measures only)
1.
and that's it. I'm com - in' home to your
and ba - by that's why I'm com - in' home

love.
*guitars 2&3
guitar 2
guitar 1
B R
*note held from previous measure
A
D
A
guitar 3 with slide
guitar 1
guitar 2
Dsus
D
A
D
B R

2.
A
guitar 2
Guitar solo
E5
to your love.
let ring
B R B R
*guitar 3 holds from previous measure
guitar 3 tacet
Rhythm figure 2
end Rhythm figure 2
guitar 2 Rhythm figure 2 (two times) simile

guitar 1
guitar 3 with slide

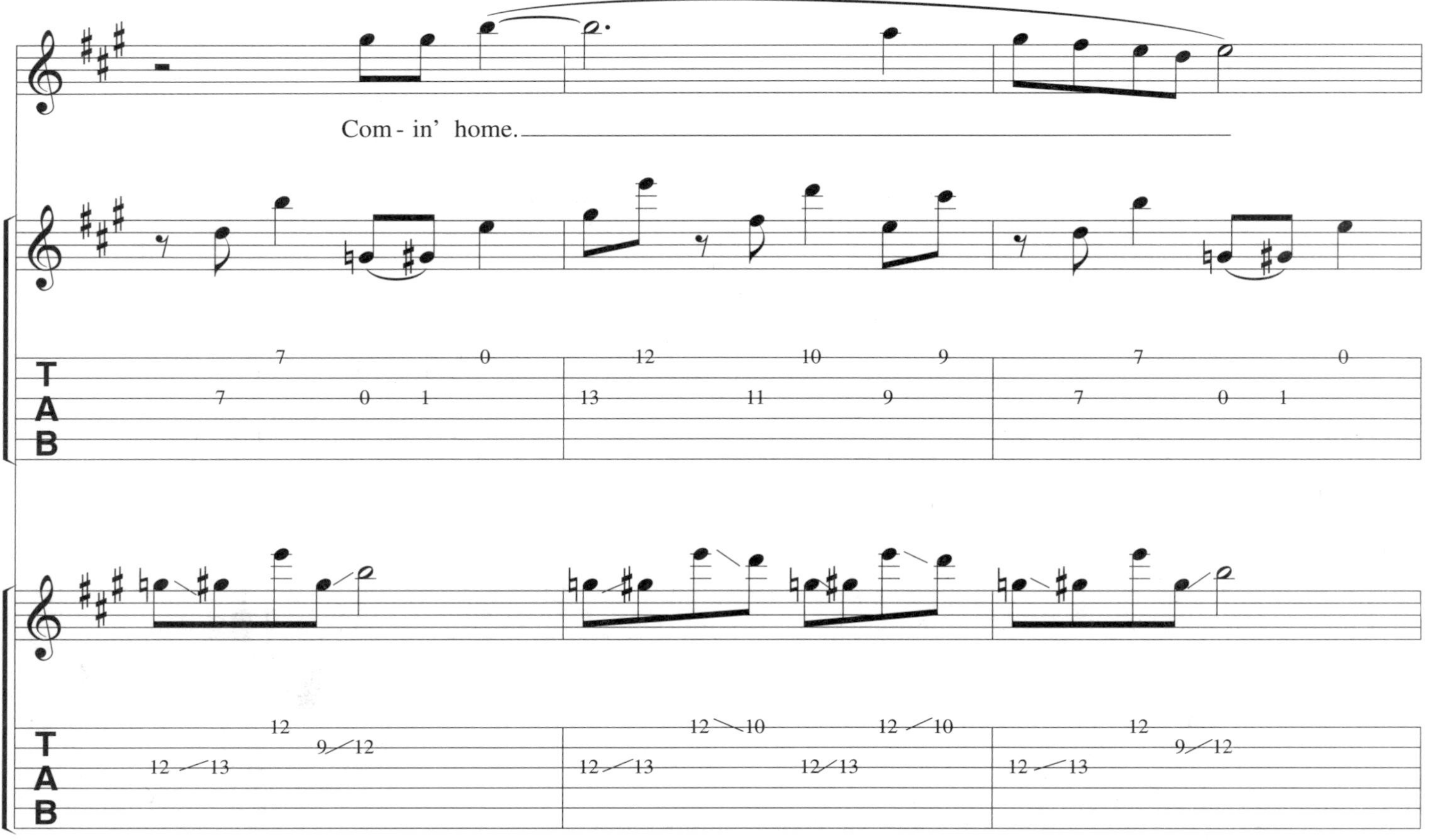
Com - in' home.

D.S. al Coda
Yeah!
with fingers

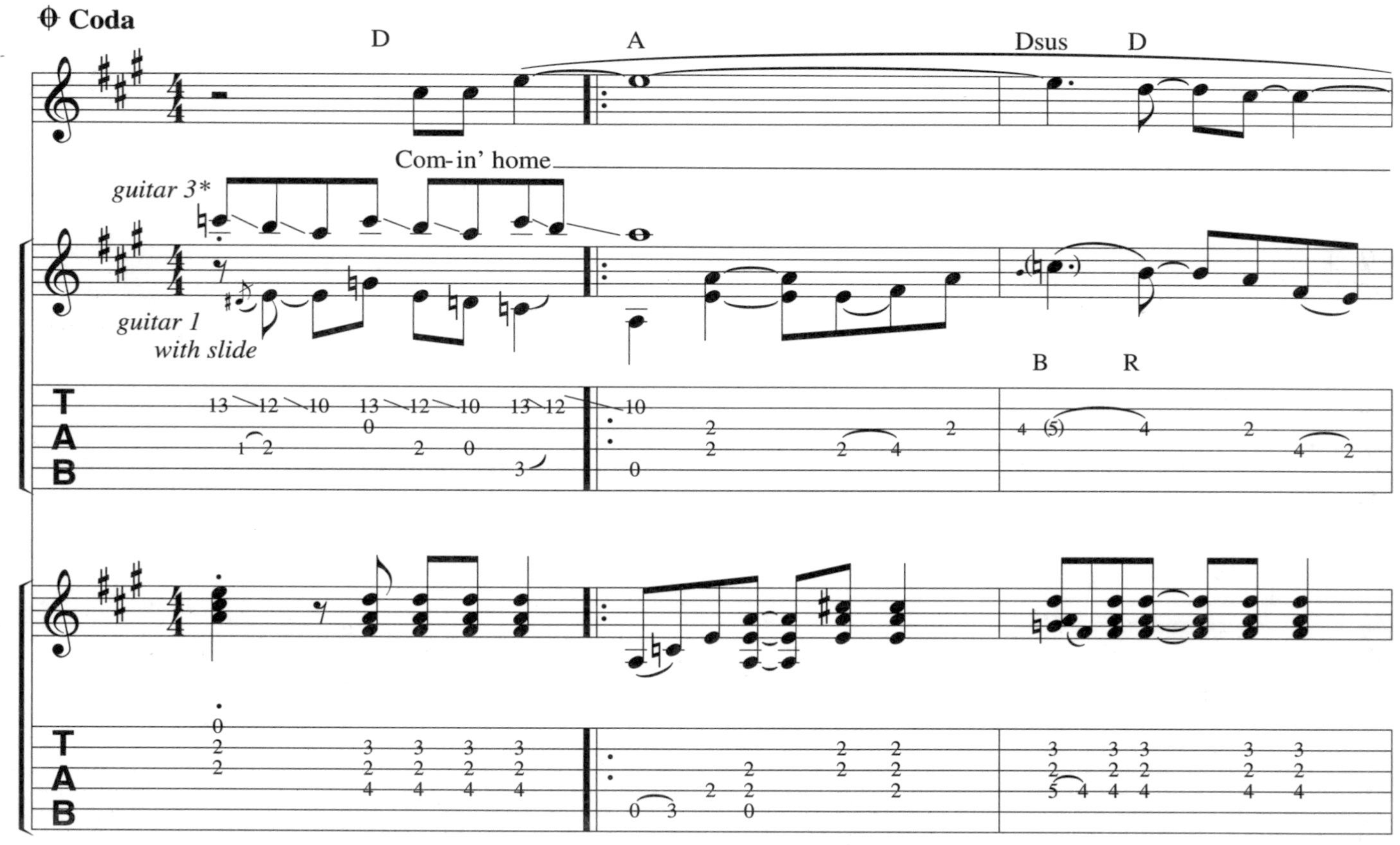
Coda
D
A
Dsus
D
Com-in' home
guitar 3*
guitar 1
with slide

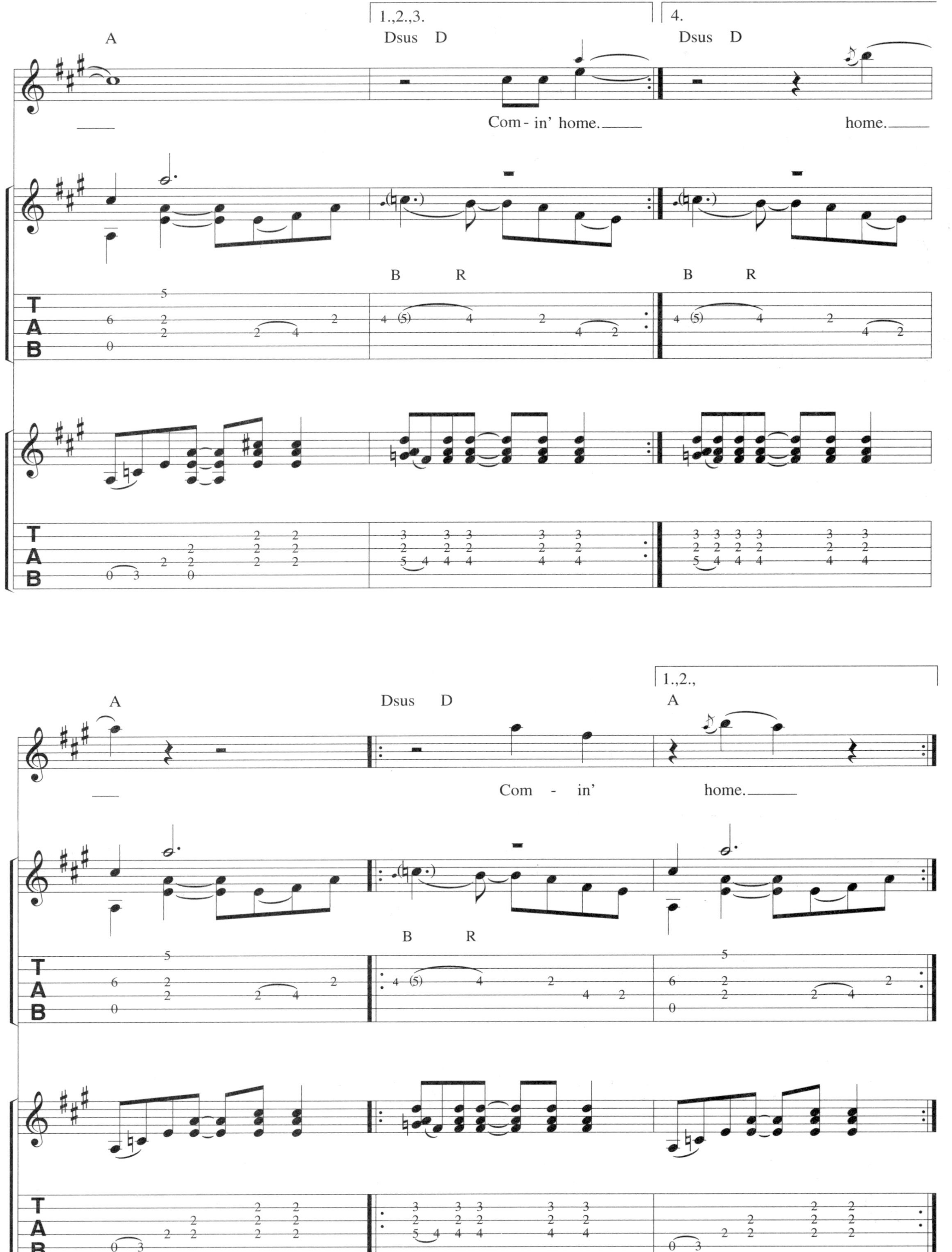

1.,2.,3.
4.
A
Dsus D
Dsus D
Com - in' home.
home.
B R
B R
T
A
B
1.,2.,
A
Dsus D
A
Com - in' home.
B R

3. Dsus D A Dsus D

Com - in home. Babe, I'm com - in'

B R B R

A D *repeat and fade*

Com - in' home.

B R

from From The Cradle

I'm Tore Down

by Sonny Thompson

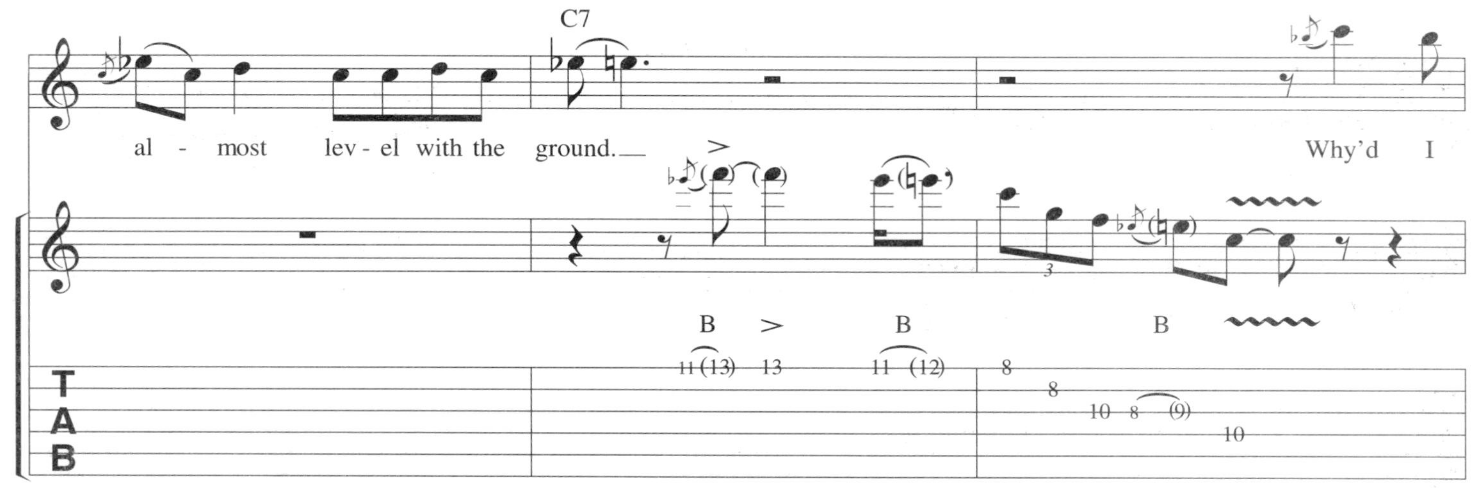
C7
al - most lev - el with the ground.
Why'd I
B
B
B
T
A
B
11 (13) 13
11 (12)
8
8
10 8 (9)
10

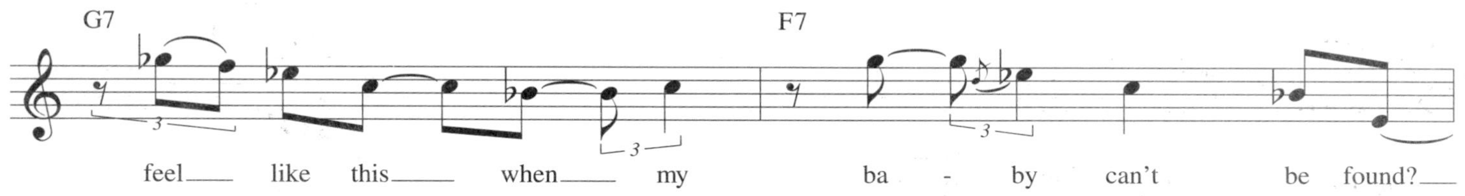
G7
F7
feel like this when my ba - by can't be found?

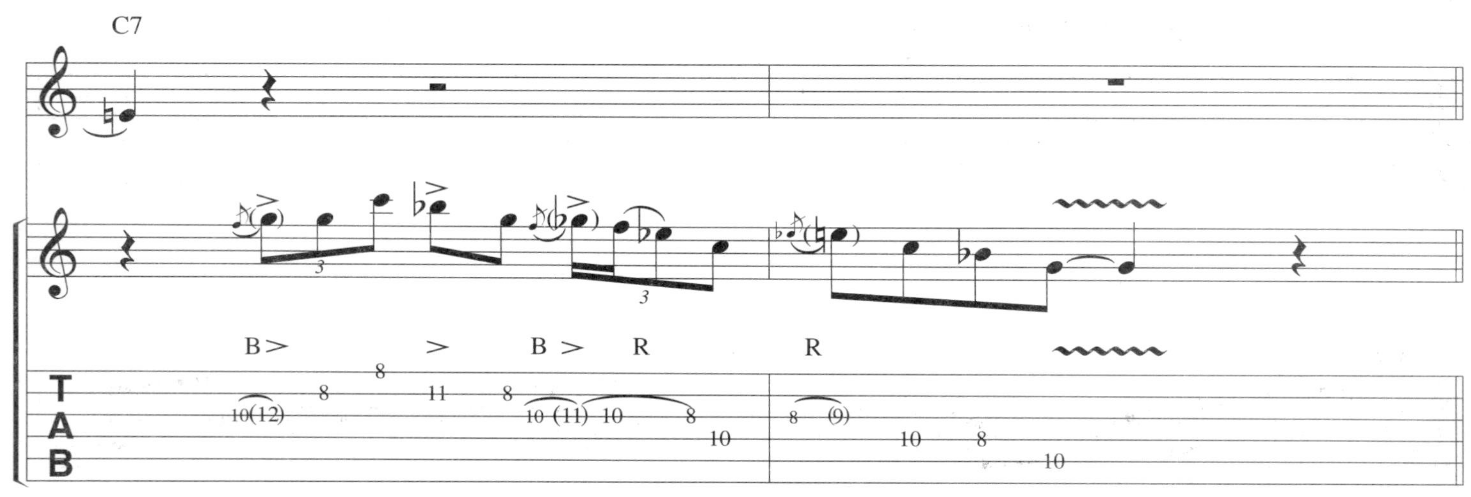
C7
B
B
R
R
T
A
B
10(12) 8 8 11 8 10 (11) 10 8 10
8 (9) 10 8 10

C7
1. Went to the riv - er, to jump in. My ba - by showed up and said,
guitars 1 and 2
T
A
B
8 10 10 10 10
8 8 9 8
8

N.C. F7

guitar 2 continues shuffle rhythm simile

"I will tell you when." Well, I'm tore down, al - most lev - el with the

C7

ground.___ Why'd___ I

hold bend

G7 F7

feel___ like this___ when___ my ba - by can't be found?___

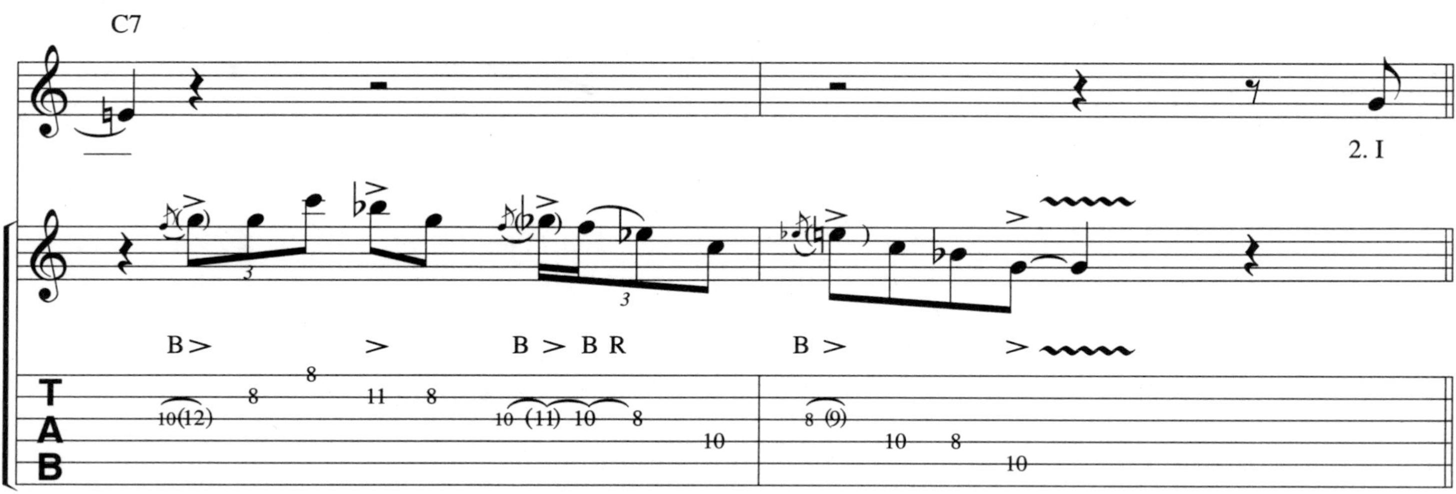

C7
D♭7
C7
love you babe with all my heart and soul. Love like mine will
3. Love you ba - by with all my might. Love like mine is
guitars 1 and 2
let ring

D♭7
C7
nev - er grow old. Love you in the morn - ing and in the
out - ta sight. I'll lie for you if you

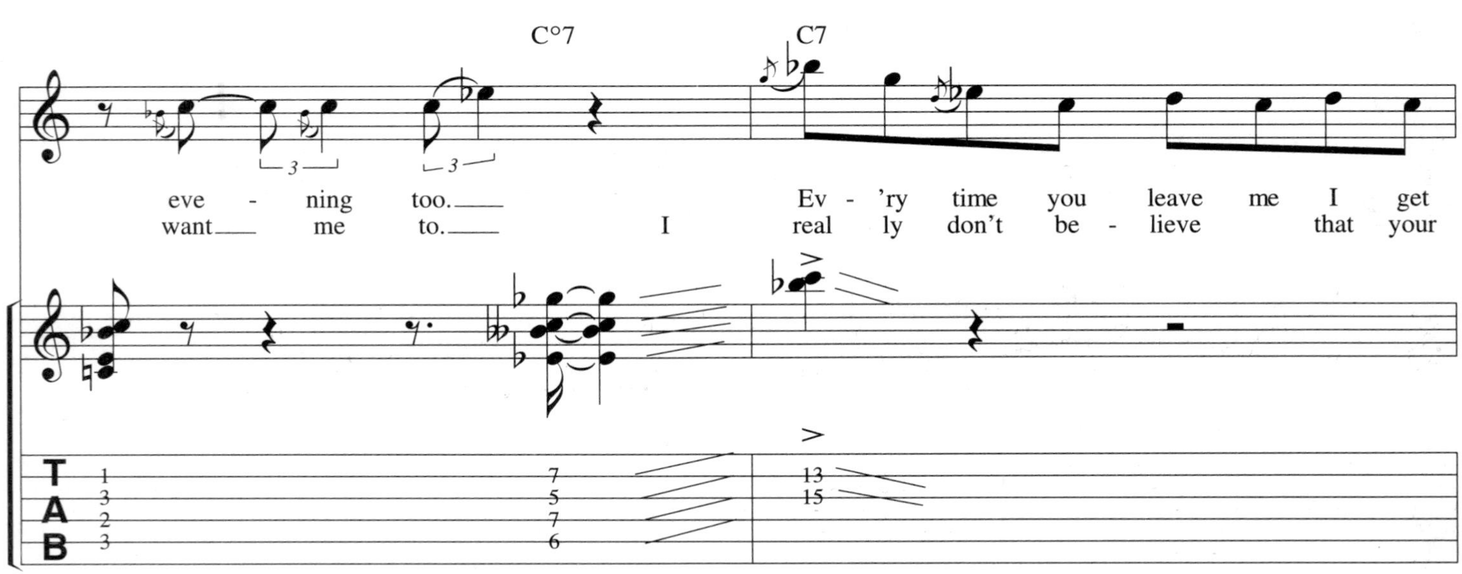
C°7
C7
eve - ning too. Ev - 'ry time you leave me I get
want me to. I real ly don't be - lieve that your

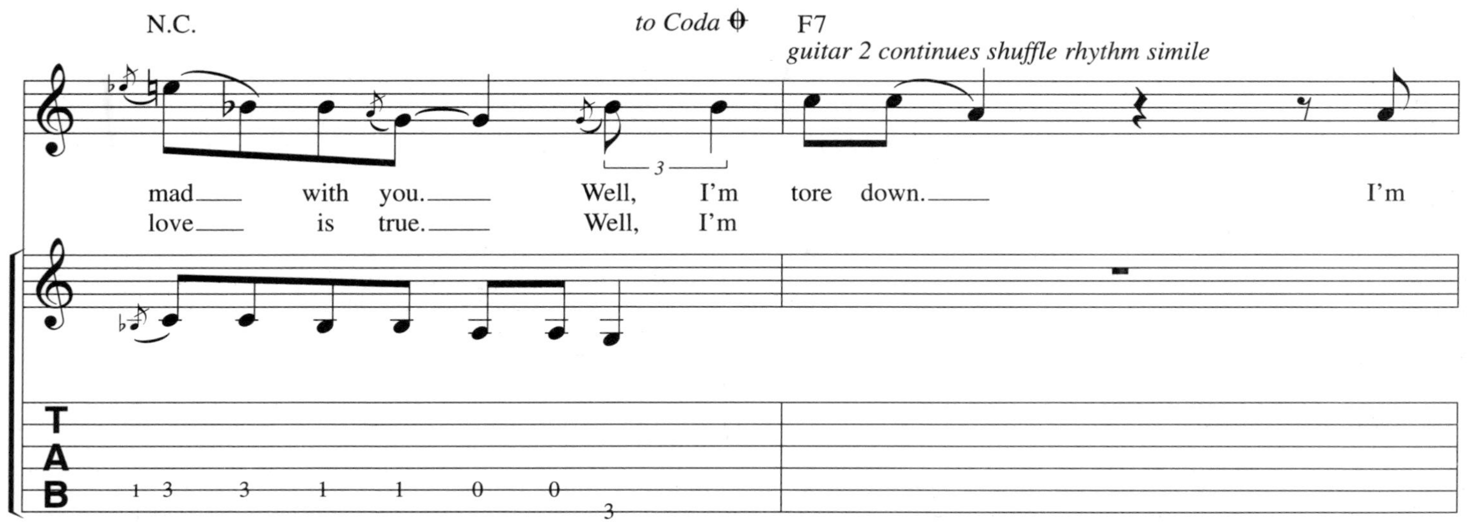
N.C.
to Coda
F7
guitar 2 continues shuffle rhythm simile
mad with you. Well, I'm tore down. I'm
love is true. Well, I'm
T
A
B
1 3 3 1 1 0 0 3

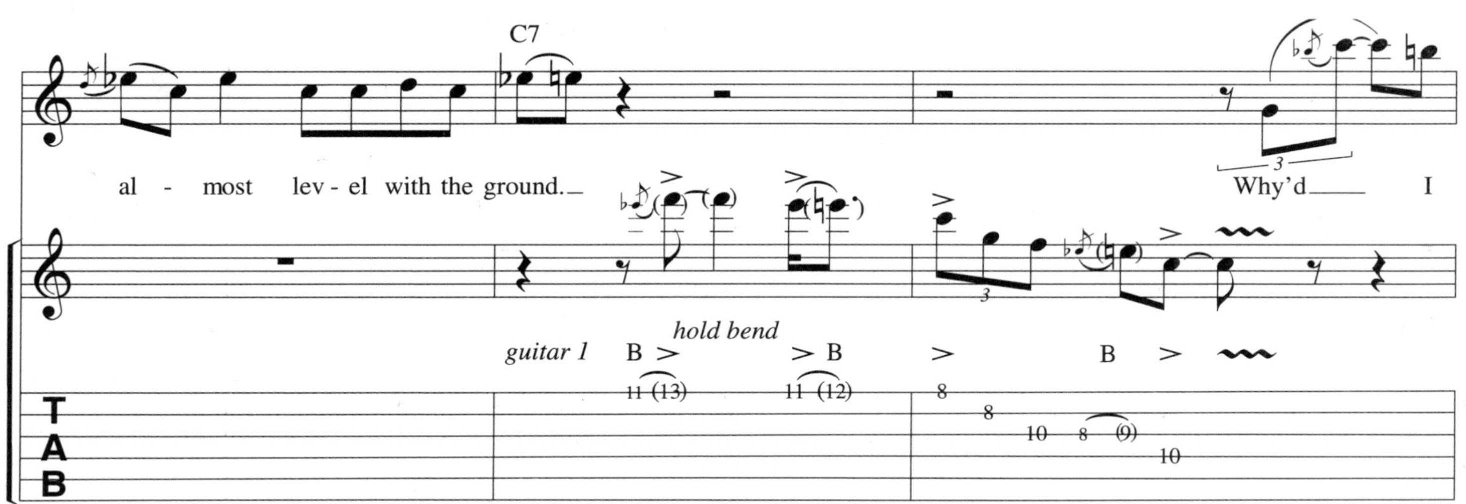
C7
al - most lev - el with the ground. Why'd I
guitar 1
hold bend
B
B
B
11 (13) 11 (12) 8 8 10 8 (9) 10
T
A
B

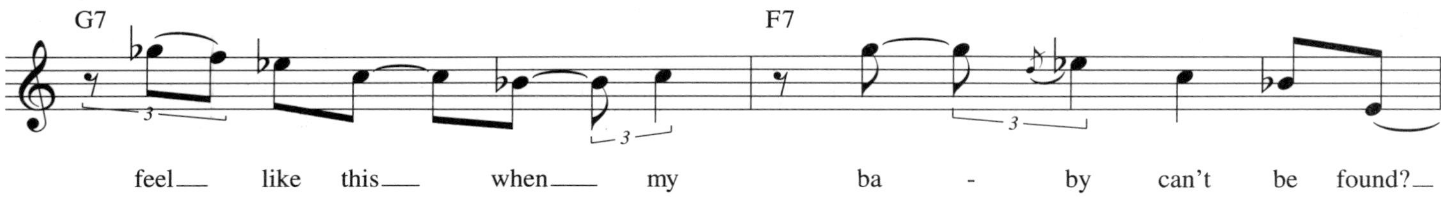
G7
F7
feel like this when my ba - by can't be found?

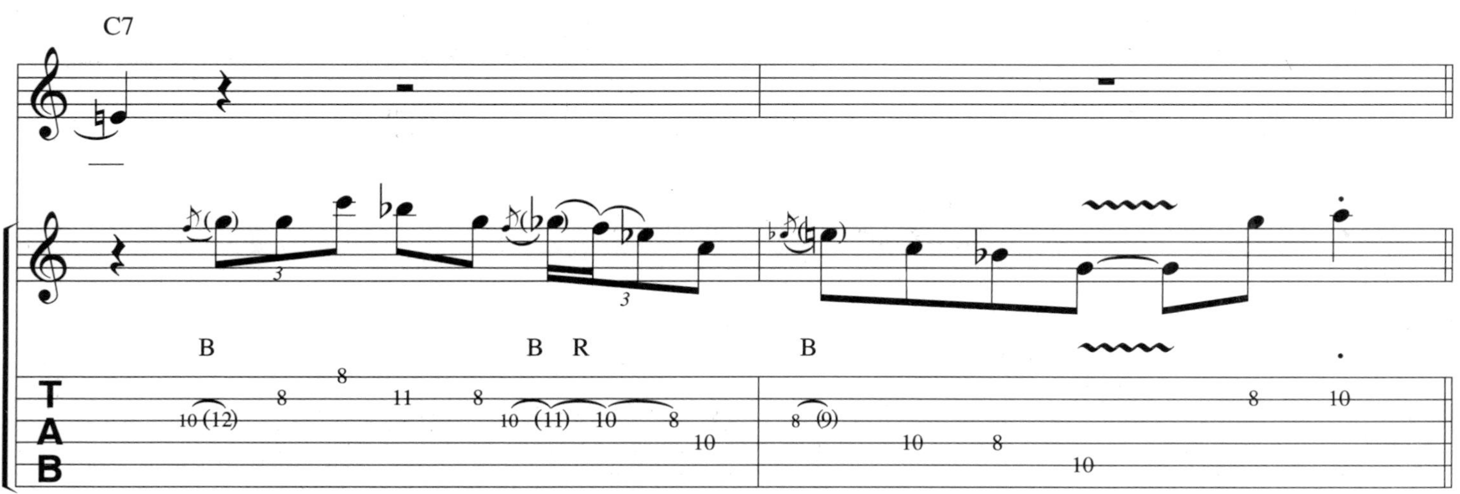
C7
B
B R
B
T
A
B
10 (12) 8 8 11 8 10 (11) 10 8 10 8 (9) 10 8 10 8 10

Guitar solo

C7*
guitar 1
*guitar 2 plays ad lib shuffle pattern
F7
C7
G7
F7
C7
B
R

F7 guitar 2 continues shuffle rhythm simile
loco
B R
C7
B
G7
F7
B
C7
D.S. al Coda
Coda
guitar 2 continues shuffle rhythm simile
F7
C7
tore down.
I'm al - most lev - el with the ground.
B
B
G7
Why'd I feel like this when my
B

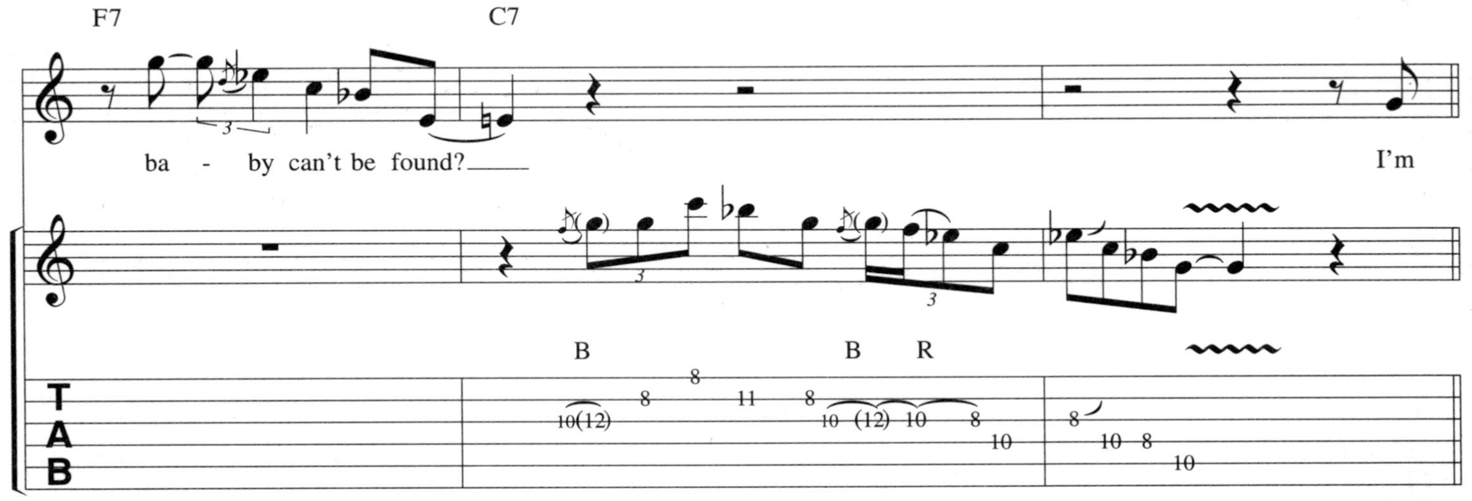
F7
C7
ba - by can't be found?
I'm
B
B R

C7
tore down.
al - most lev - el with the ground.
B
B

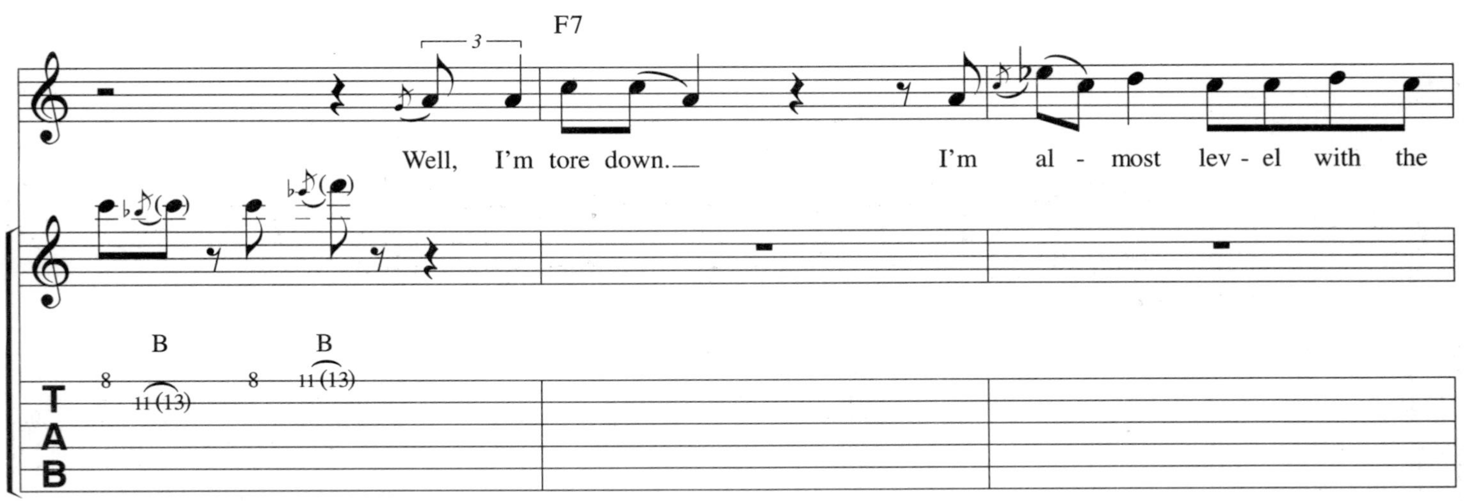
F7
Well, I'm tore down.
I'm al - most lev - el with the
B
B

C7
G7
ground.
Why'd I feel like this when my
B hold bend B
B
T
A
B

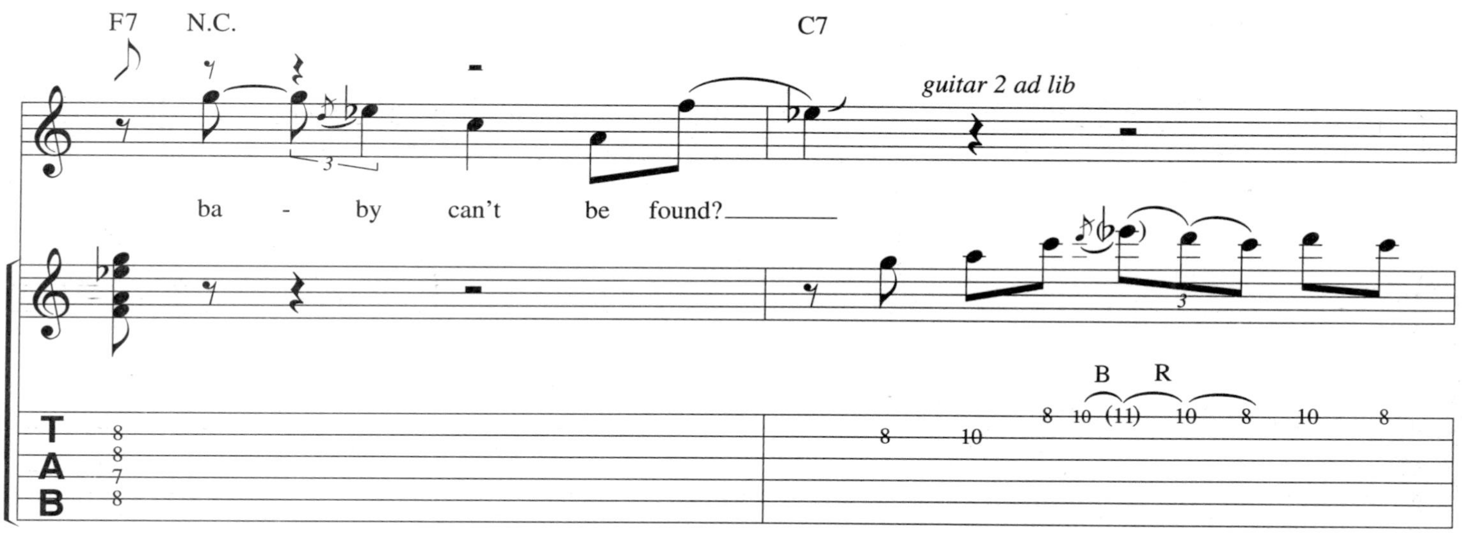
F7 N.C.
C7
guitar 2 ad lib
ba - by can't be found?
B R
T
A
B

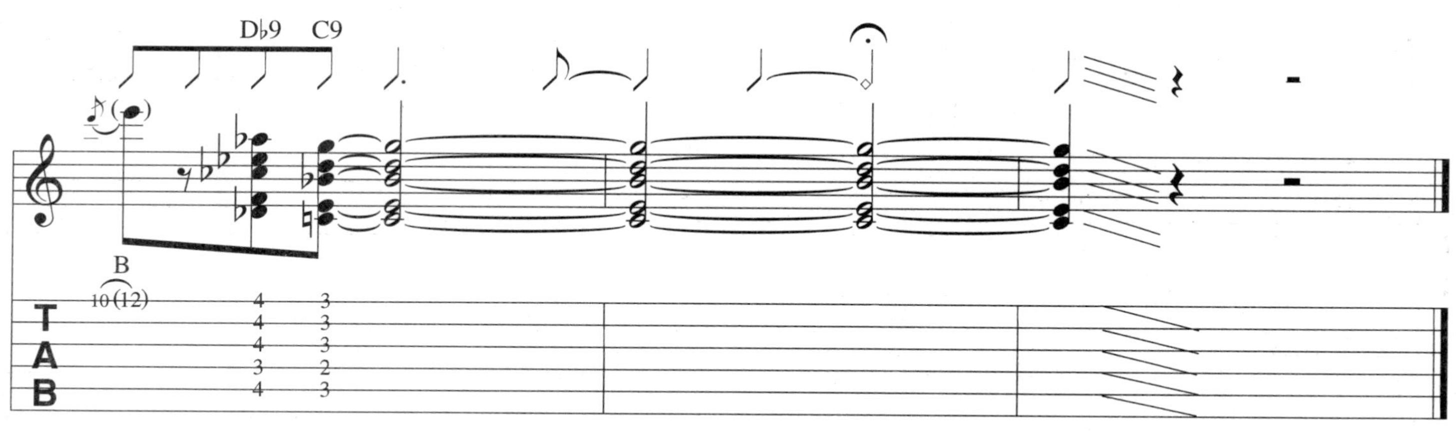
D♭9 C9
B
T
A
B

from Wheels Of Fire

Crossroads

by Robert Johnson

A
B
D
hold bend
hold bend
A
E
D

D.S. (third verse) al Coda
Coda
Guitar solo 2

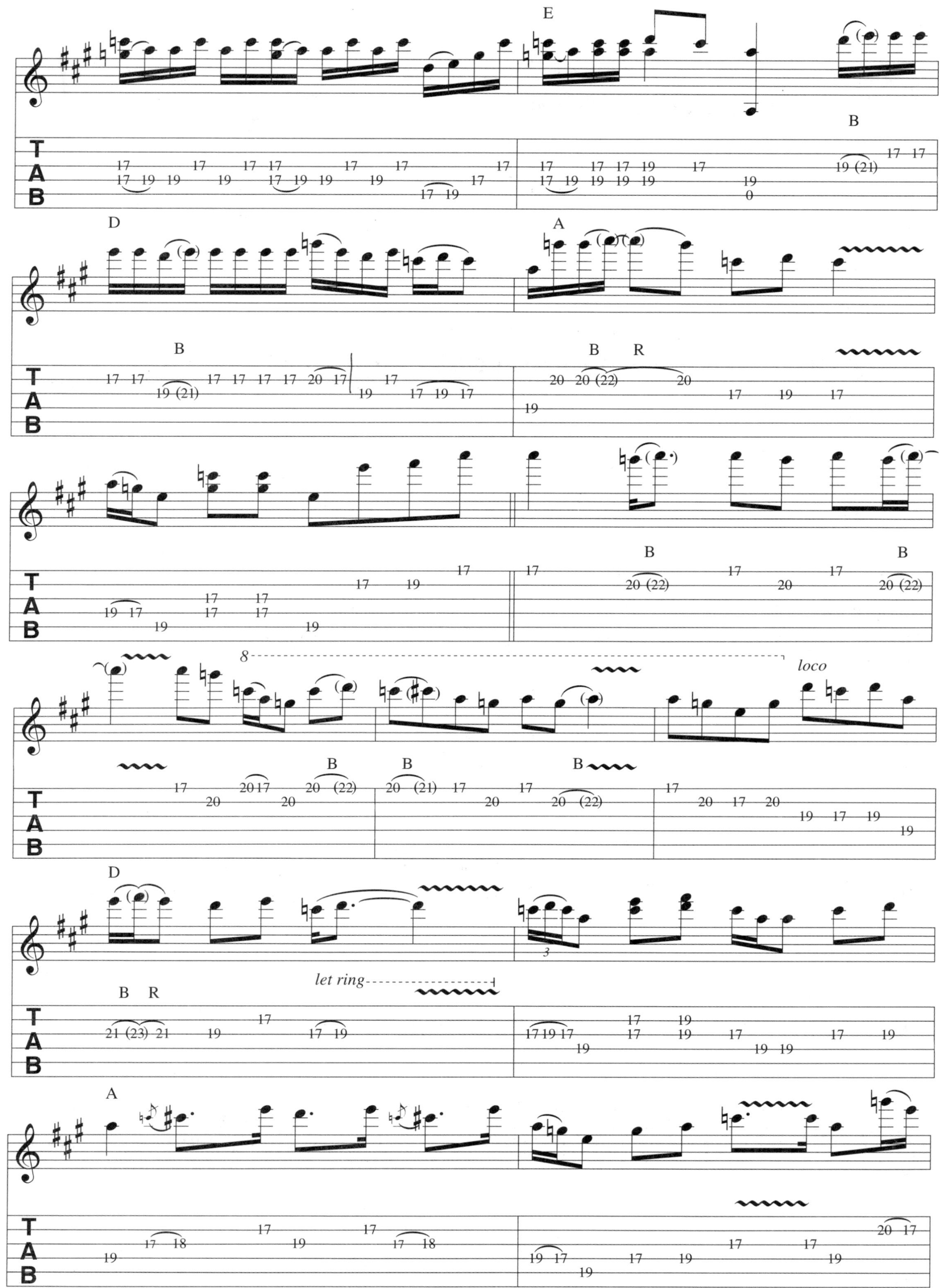

E
B
D
B
A
B R
B
B
8
loco
B
B
B
D
B R
let ring
A

E
D
hold bend
B
B R
A
B
B
B
B
B B B B B B B B B
B hold bend
D
B
B
B
B R

A
B
B
E
D
B
B
A
B
B R
loco
D.S.S. al Coda ΦΦ
ΦΦ Coda
D
N.C.
-lieve I'm sink - in' down.
B
A

from From The Cradle

Five Long Years

by Eddie Boyd

*Chord symbols reflect suggested tonality.

D7
T
A
B
A7

E9
let ring
D7

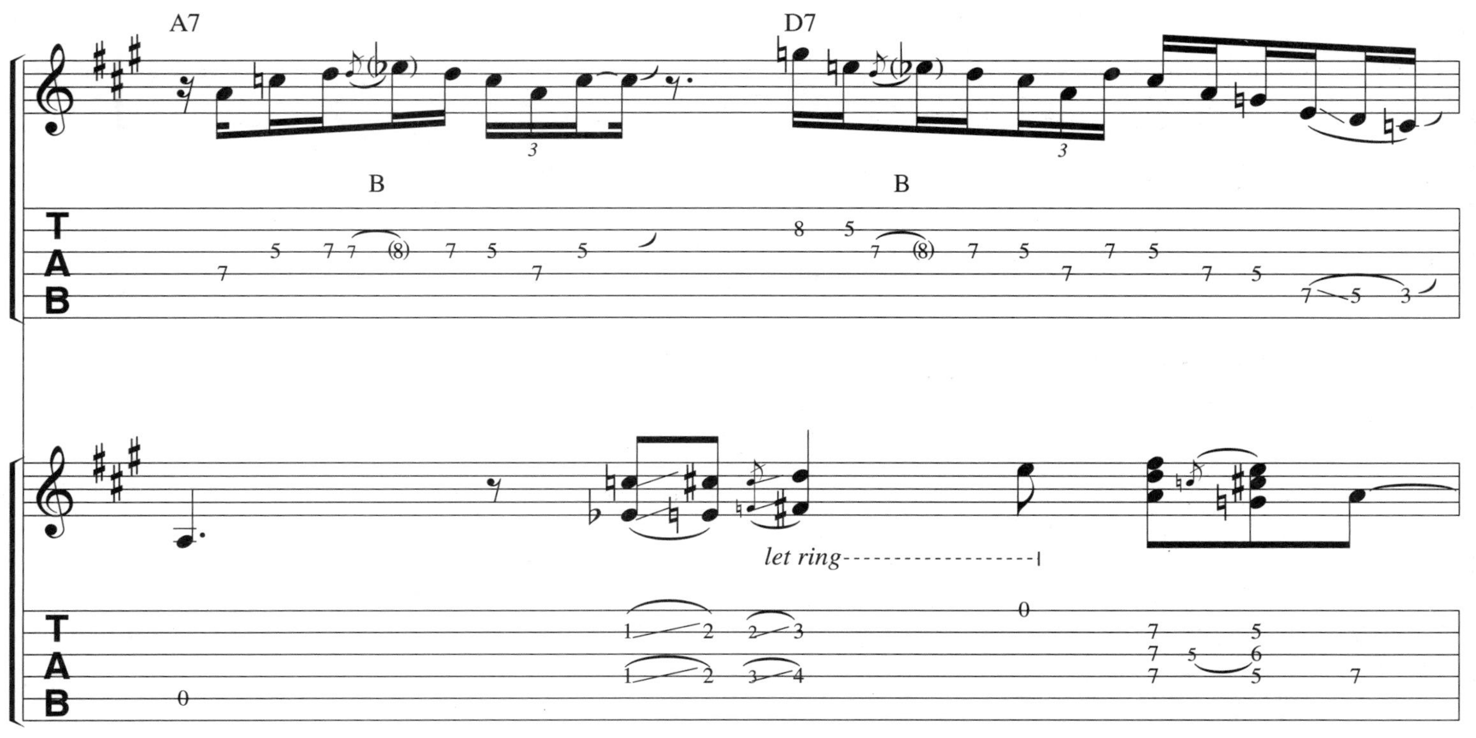

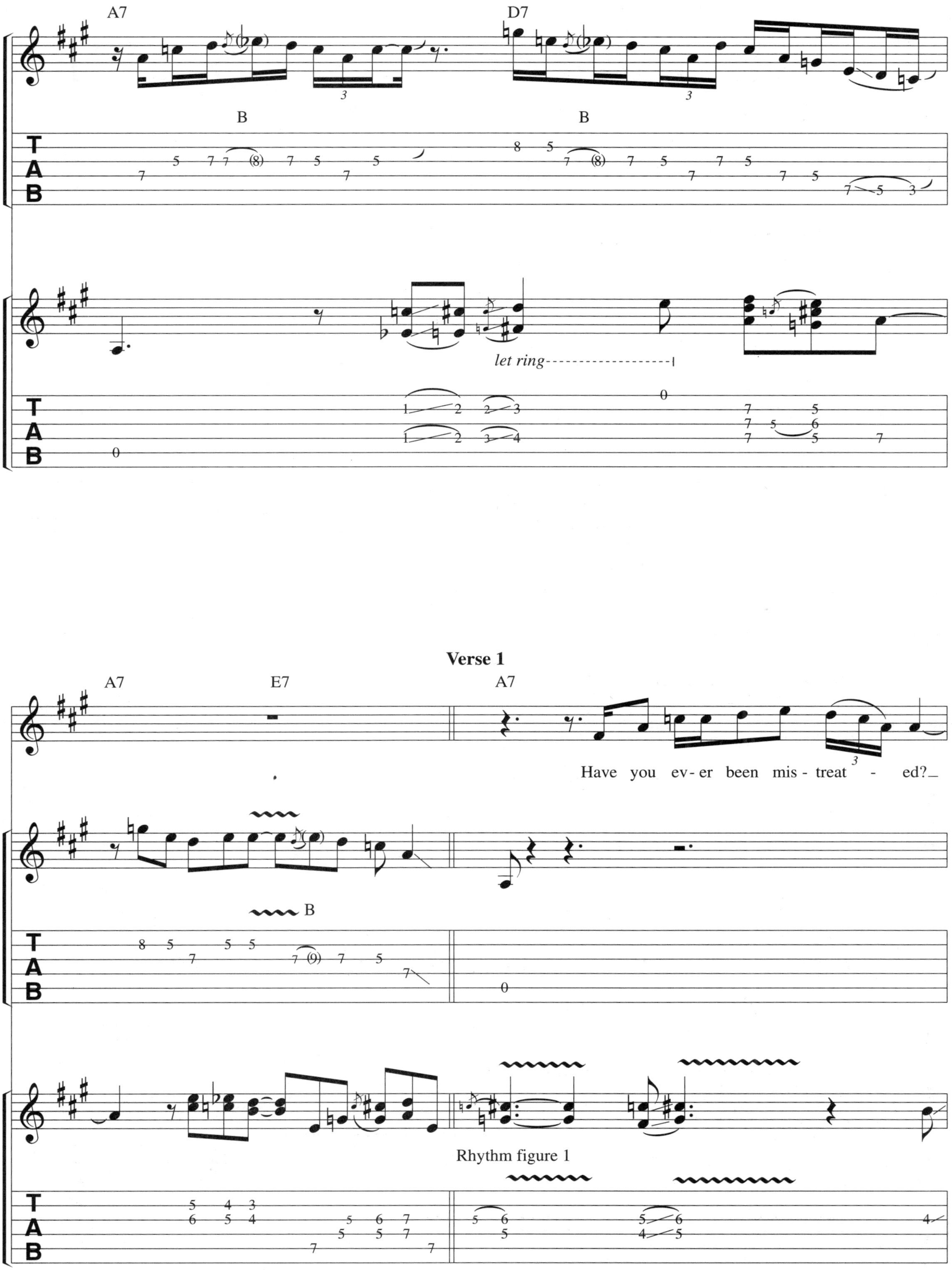

Verse 1

A7 E7 A7

Have you ever been mis-treat - ed?

B

Rhythm figure 1

D7
A7
E7
You know just what I'm talk - in' a-
B
A7
D7
bout.
Have you ev - er been mis - treat -
B

A7
E7
— ed?
You know — just what I'm talk - in' a -
B
B R
T
A
B
A7
E9
bout.
I've worked five — long — years for the
B R

D9
A7
D7
one wom - an.
She had the nerve to
B R
let ring
Verse 2
guitar 2 with Rhythm figure 1
A7
E7
A7
put me out.
I got a job in a steel mill,
guitar 1
end Rhythm figure 1

D7
A7
E7
shuck- in' steel like a slave.
Five long years ev- 'ry Fri - day I come
A7
D7
straight home with all my pay.
Have you ev- er been mis-
treat - ed?
A7
E7
You know just what I'm talk -

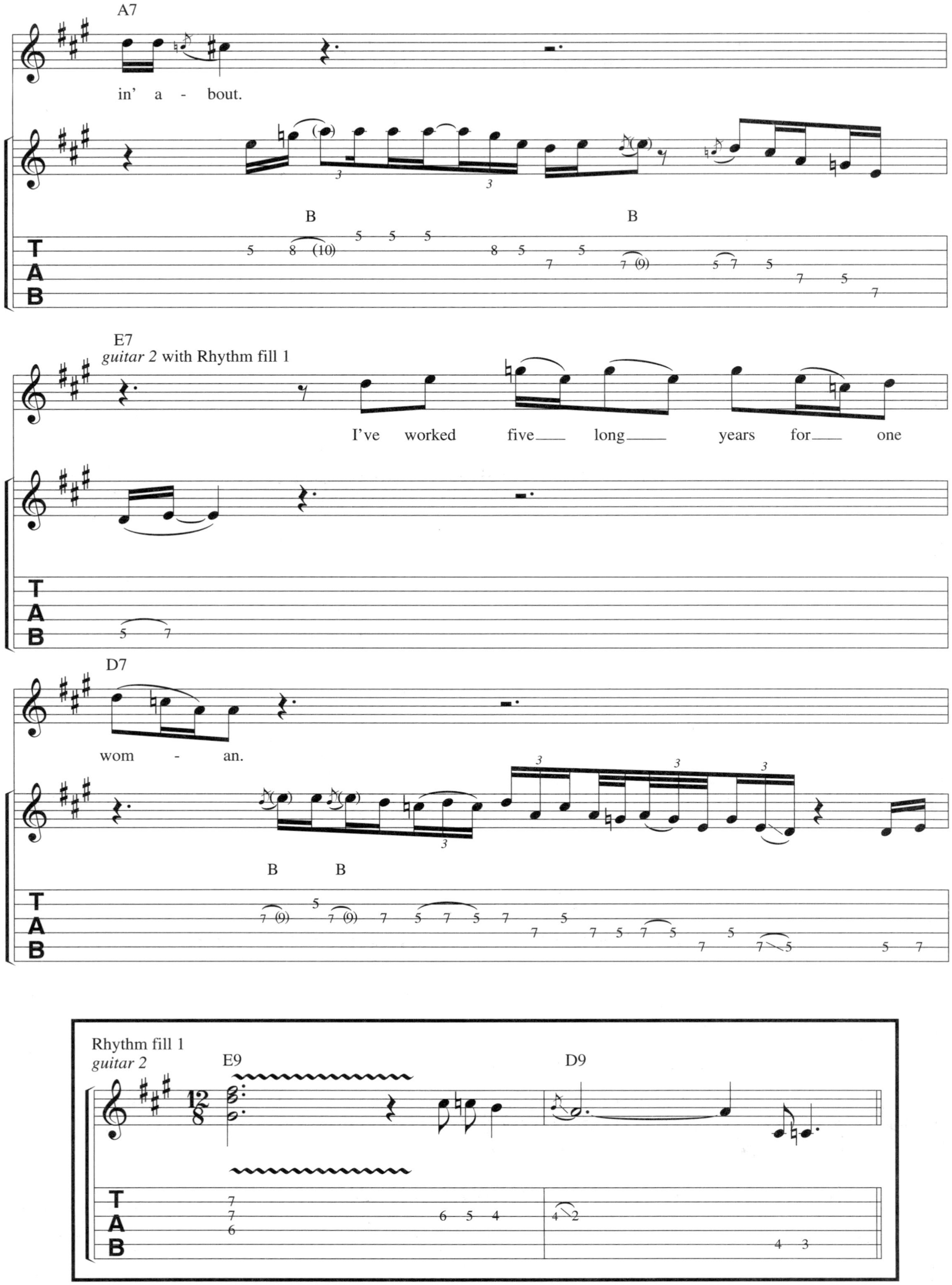

A7

in' a - bout.

B B

E7

guitar 2 with Rhythm fill 1

I've worked five long years for one

D7

wom - an.

B B

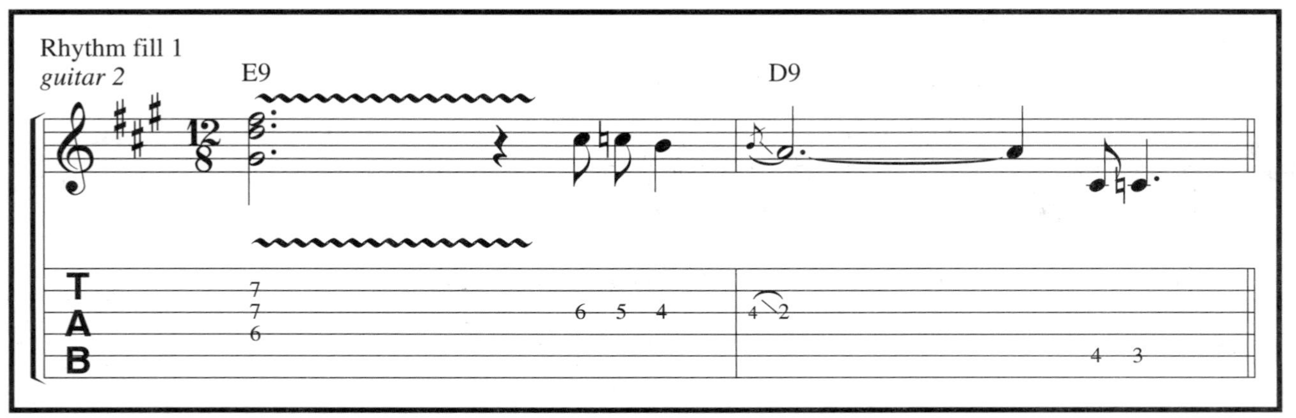

A7
D7
A7
E7
She had the nerve ——— to put me out.
B
8 5 7 5 5 10 8 10 (12)
5 7 5 7 7

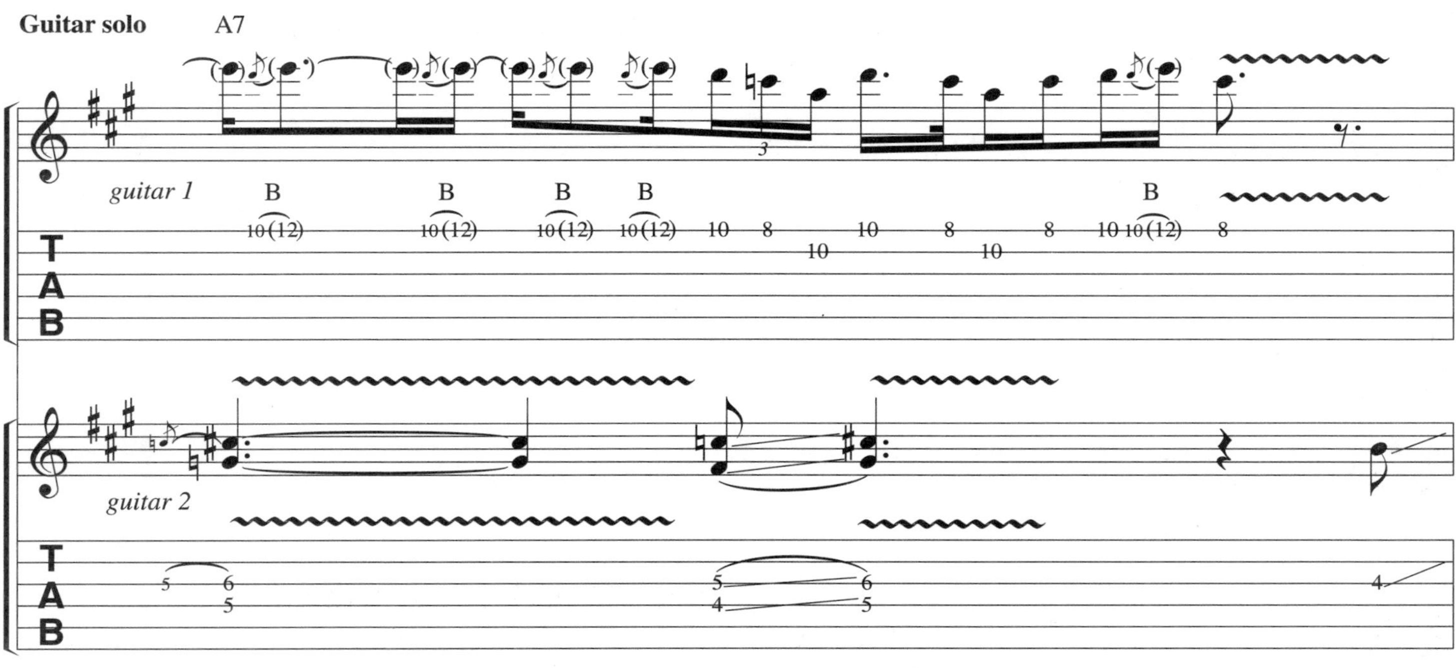
Guitar solo
A7
guitar 1
B
B
B
B
B
guitar 2

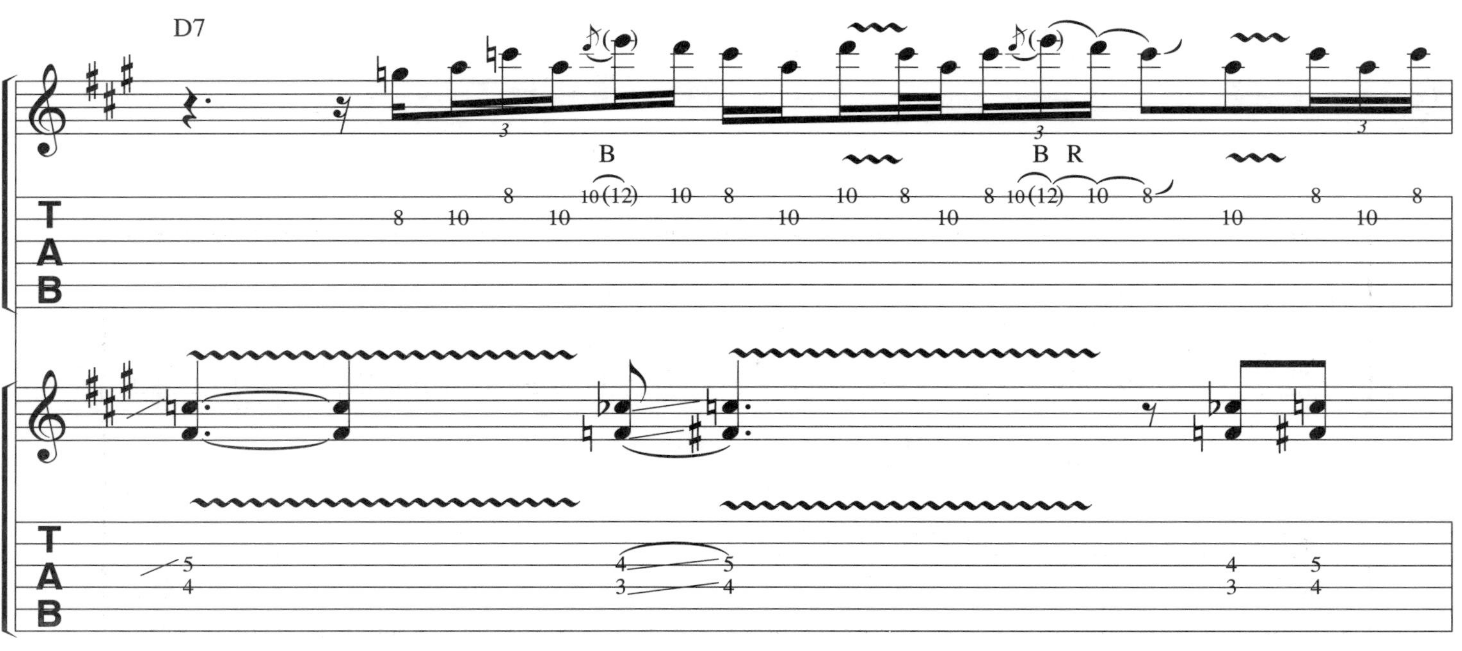
D7
B
B R

A7
E7
A7
D7
B R
B
TAB

A7
E7
A7

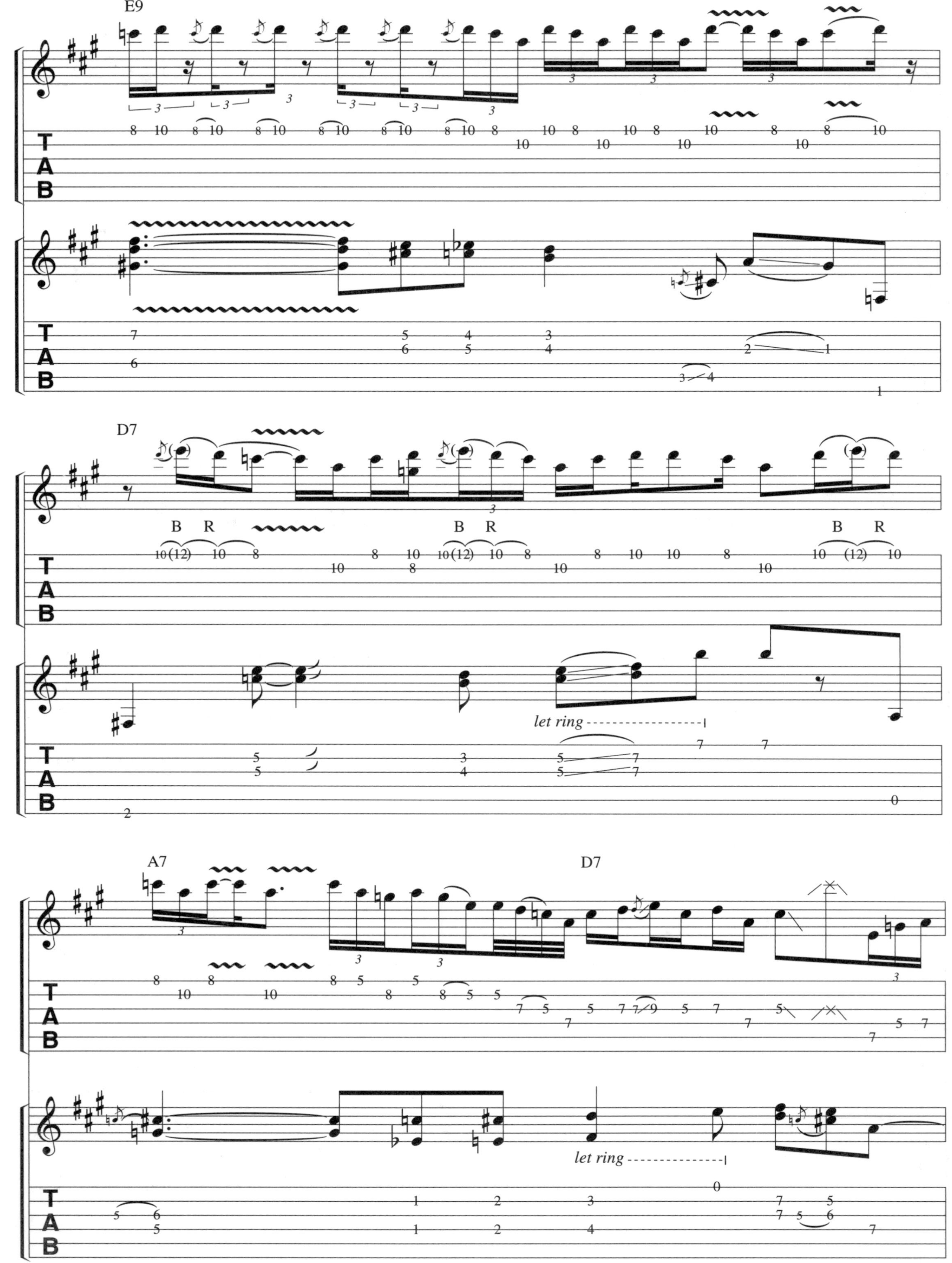
E9
D7
B R
let ring
A7
D7

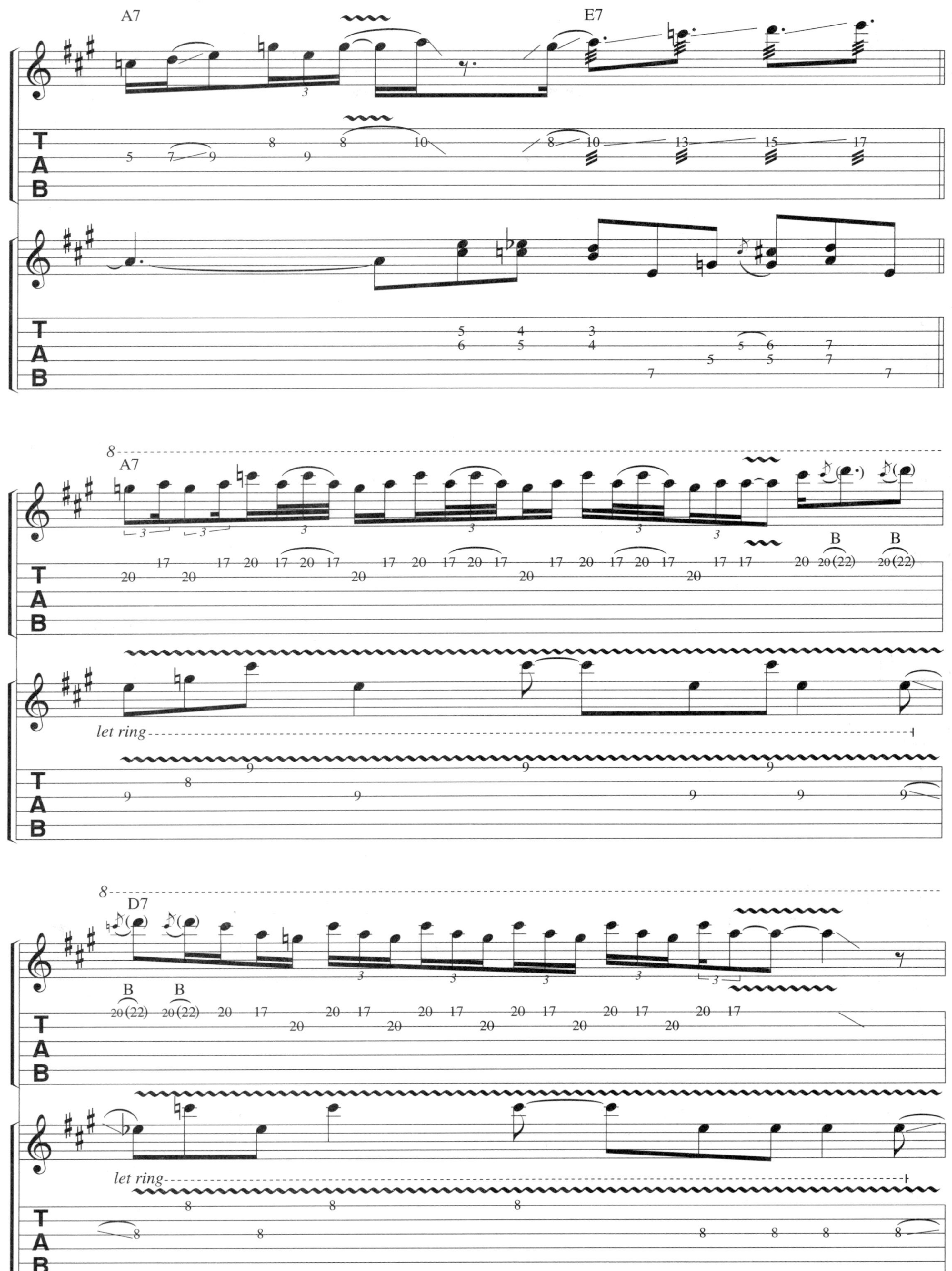
A7
E7
3
8
let ring
D7
B

A7
let ring
let ring
D7

A7
E7
let ring
A7
let ring

8
loco
E9
3
B
TAB
D9
B B B B
B
let ring
A7
D7
B R
B R
B
let ring

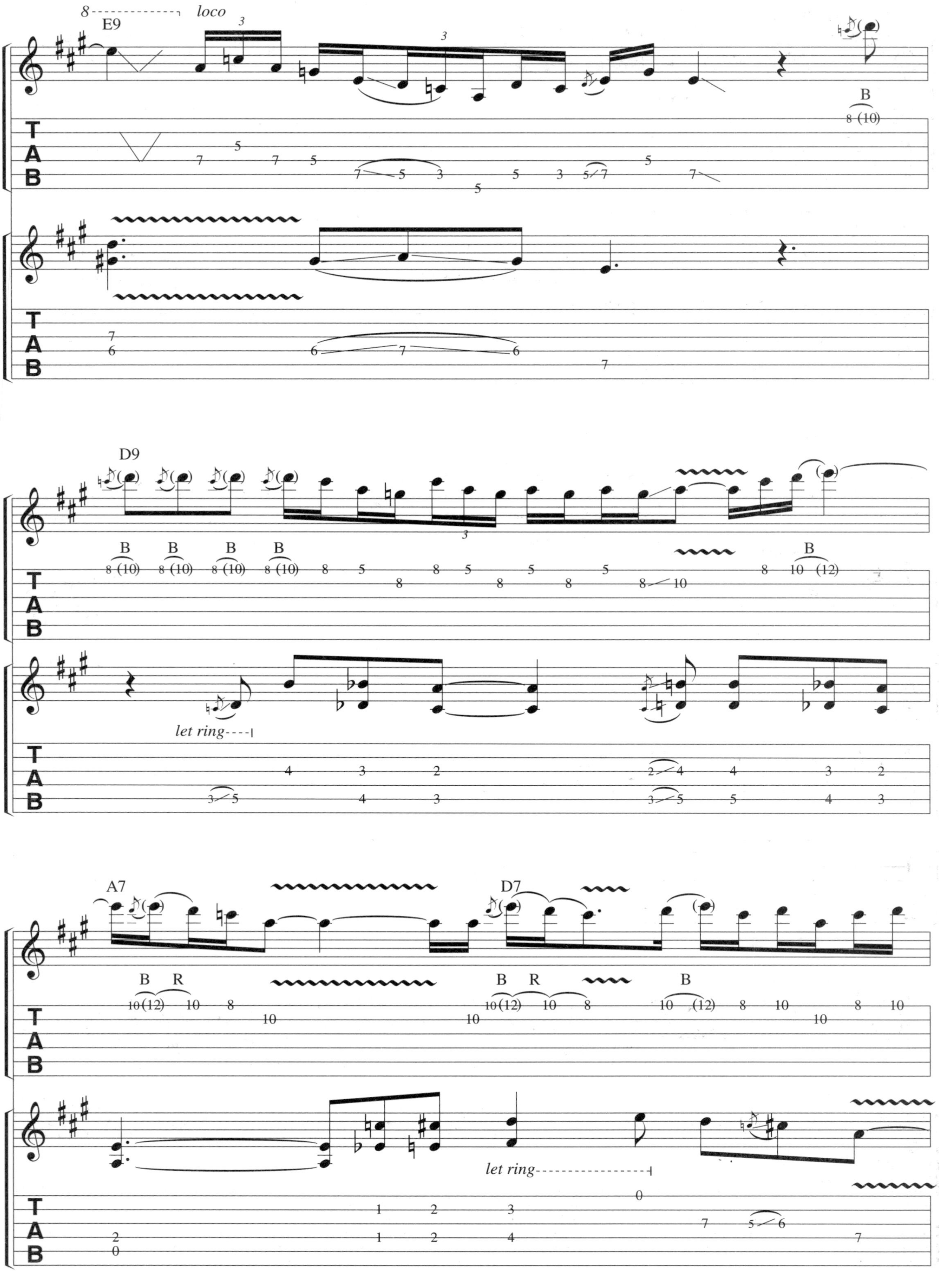

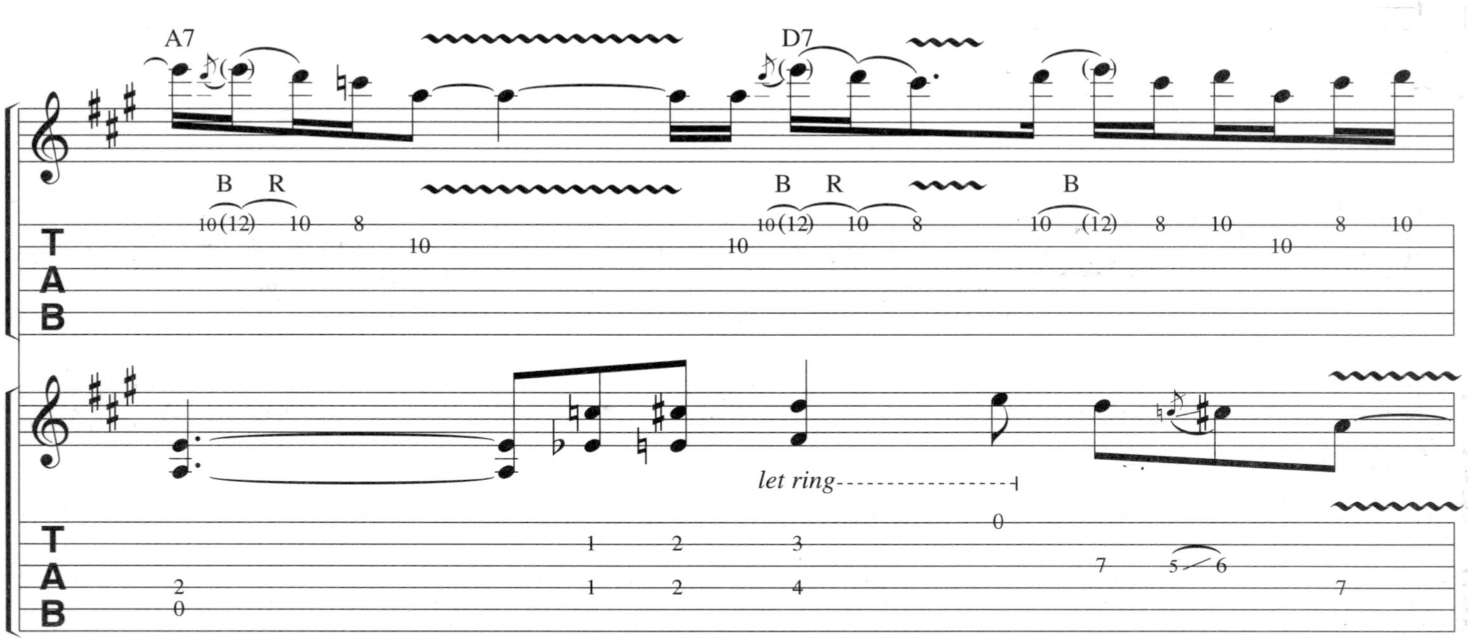

A7 E7

Verse 3

A7 D7

I've fi-nal-ly learned my les - son, should 'a' long time a-go.

B R

A7

guitar 2 tacet

The next wom-an that I mar-ry, she gon-na work and bring me the gold.

guitar 1

D7
Have you ev - er been mis - treat - ed?

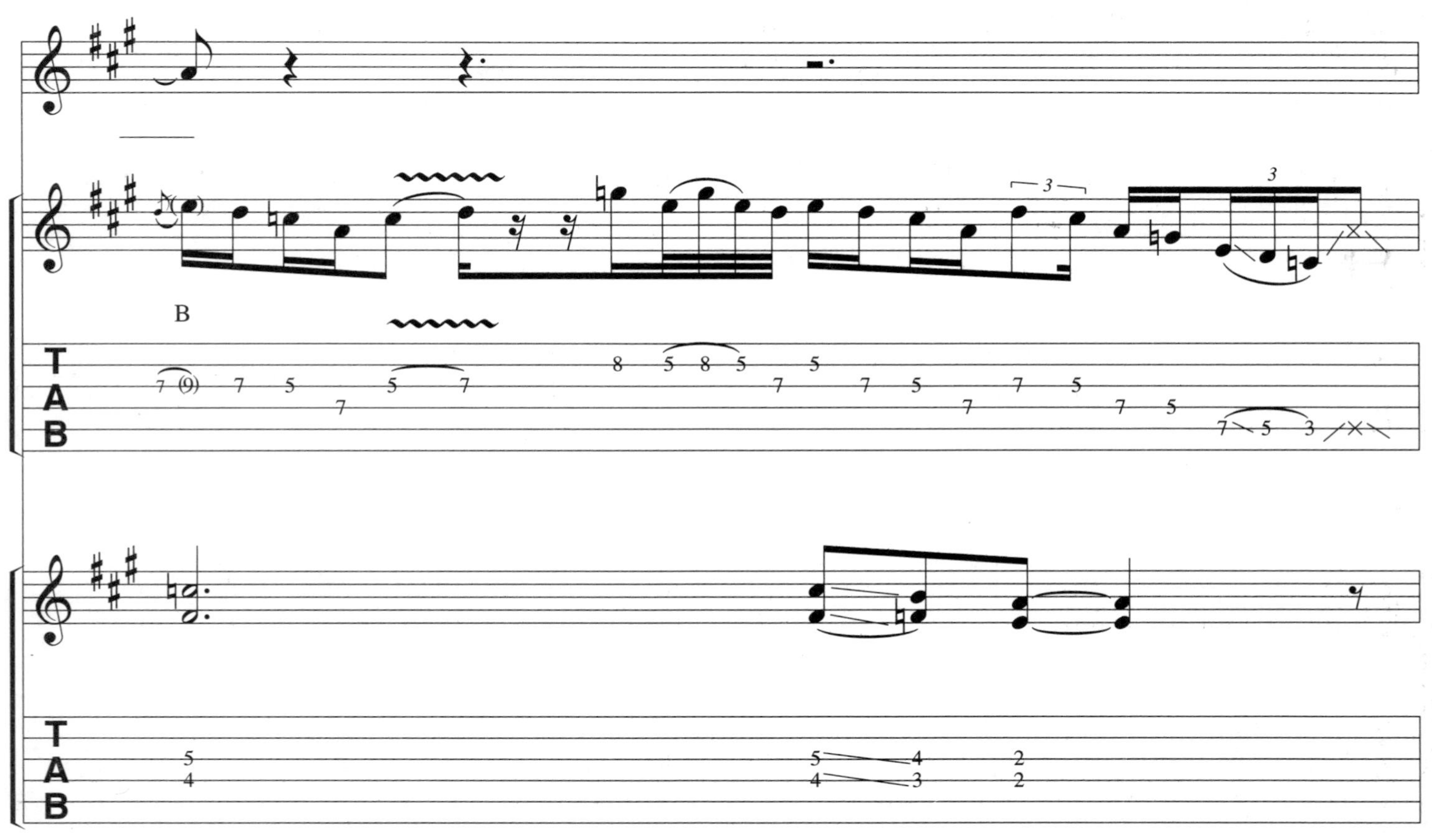
B

A7 E7

You know ___ just what I'm talk - in' a - bout. ___

A7 F9

B B B R

E9
It's been five long years for one wom - an.
T
A
B
Freely
D9
guitar 1 tacet
rit.
she had the nerve, she had the nerve, she had the nerve, she had the nerve to put me
guitar 2
A tempo
A7
D7
A7
B♭9
A9
out.
guitar 1
B
B R
B
B
guitar 2

from From The Cradle

It Hurts Me Too

by Mel London

⑥open
⑥4fr ⑤2fr ⑤open
⑥3fr ⑤open ④open
D D5 D/C E7/B B♭6 D/A D5 F F♯ A B D A end Rhythm figure 1
1. You said you was
let ring
% Verse
D5 D6 D5 D6 D5 D6 D5 D6 D5
guitar 1
guitar 2 with Rhythm figure 1 simile
hurt-in', al - most lost your mind. Out on the man you
2., 3., 4. See additional lyrics
G5 G6 G5 G6 G5 G6 G5 G6 G G5 G
love, he hurt you all the time. When things go
to Coda
D5 D6 D5 D6 A5 A6 G5 G6 D D/C E7/B B♭6
wrong, go wrong with you, it hurts me too.
guitar 1 with slide
let ring let ring let ring let ring

Guitar solo

guitar 2 Rhythm figure 1 *simile*

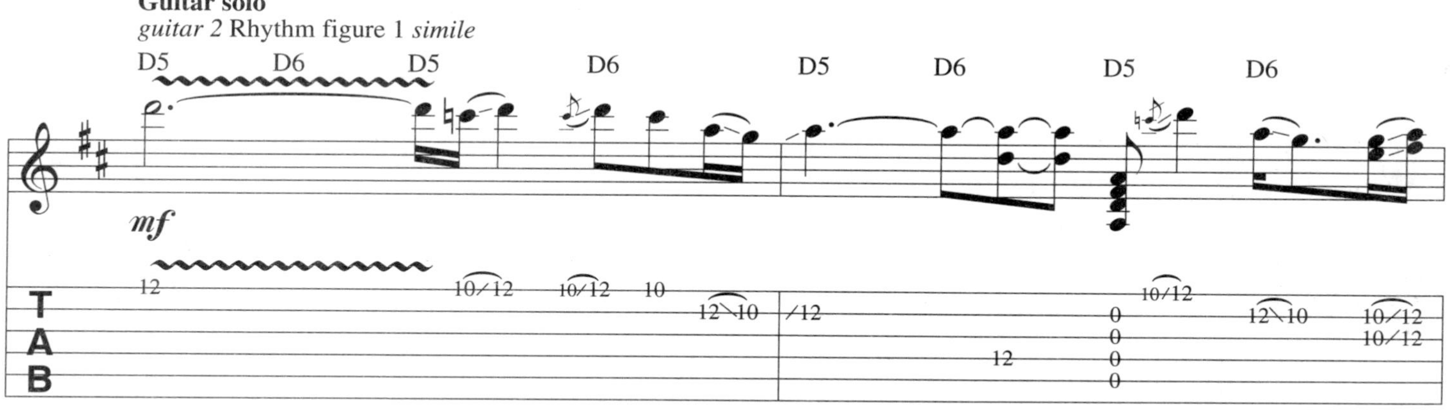

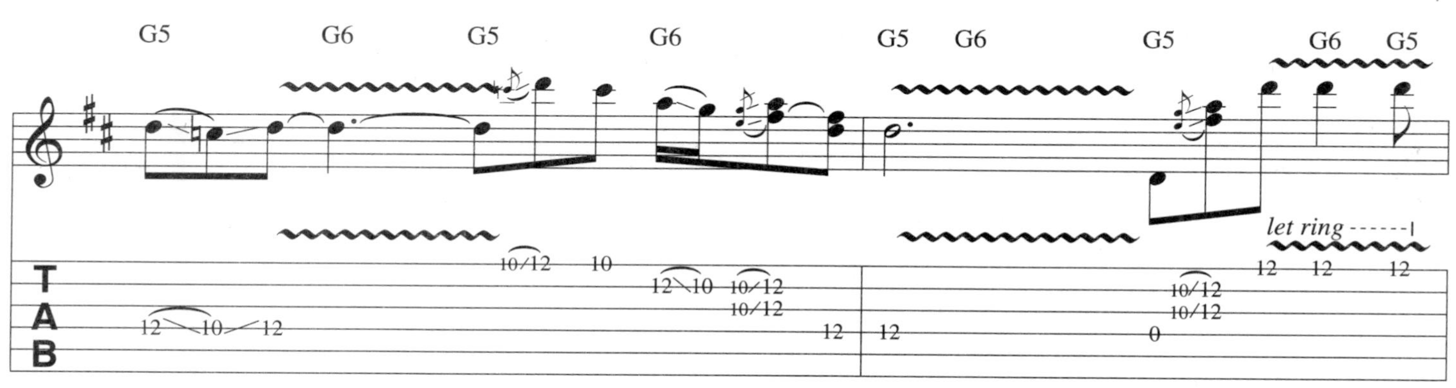

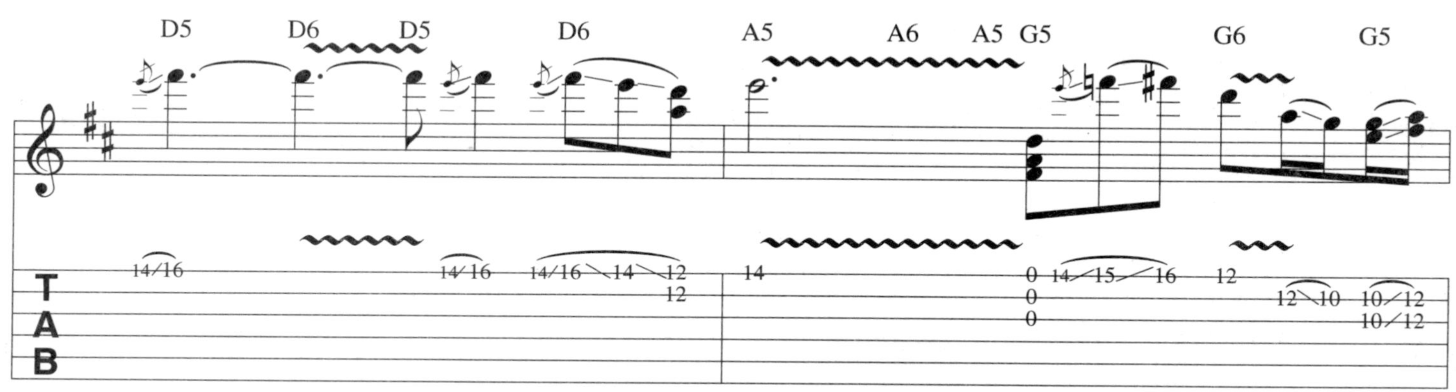

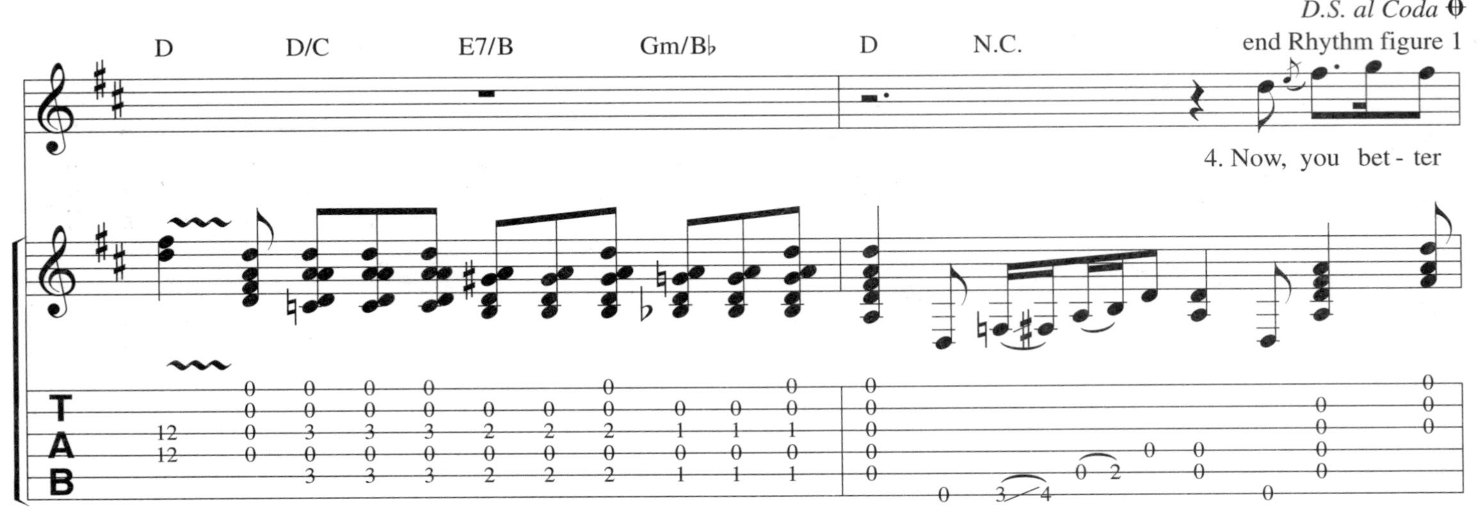
D.S. al Coda
D
D/C
E7/B
Gm/B♭
D
N.C.
end Rhythm figure 1
4. Now, you bet - ter

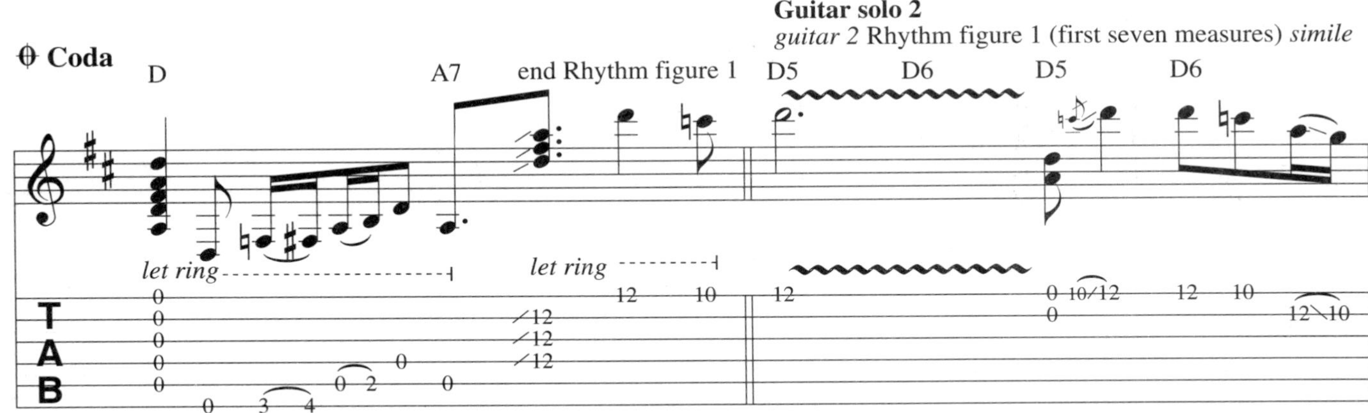
Coda
D
A7
end Rhythm figure 1
Guitar solo 2
guitar 2 Rhythm figure 1 (first seven measures) simile
D5
D6
D5
D6
let ring
let ring

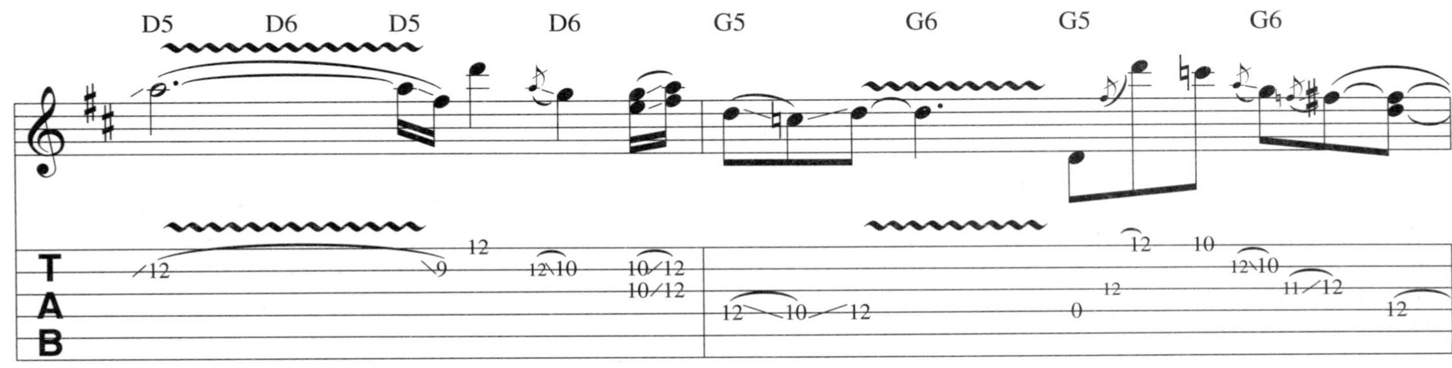
D5
D6
D5
D6
G5
G6
G5
G6

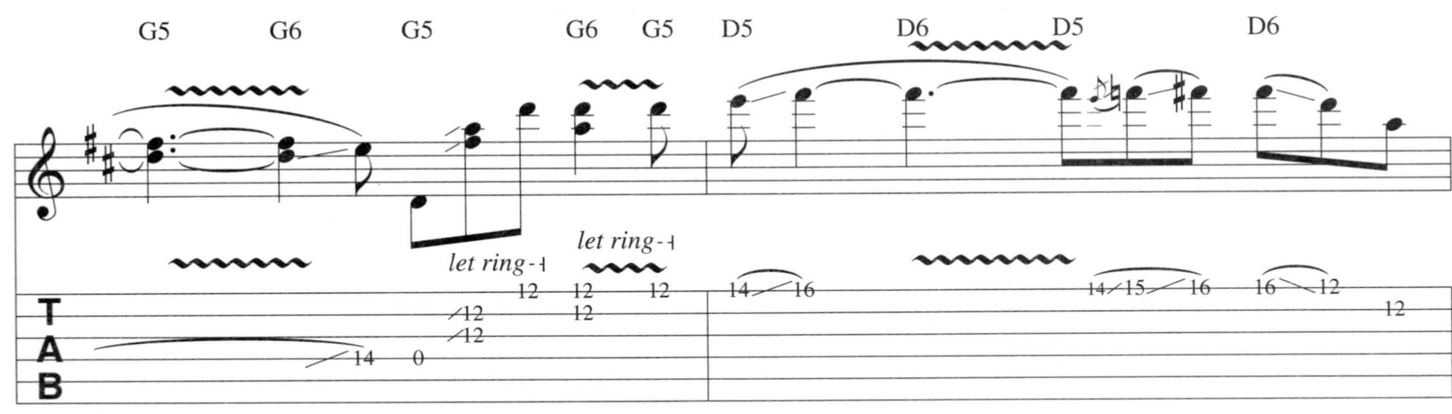
G5
G6
G5
G6
G5
D5
D6
D5
D6
let ring
let ring

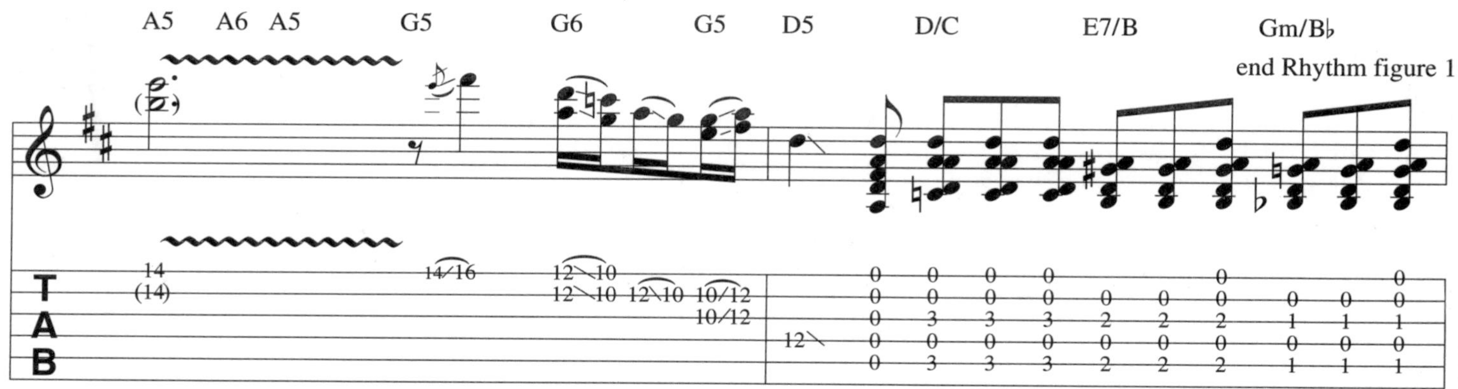

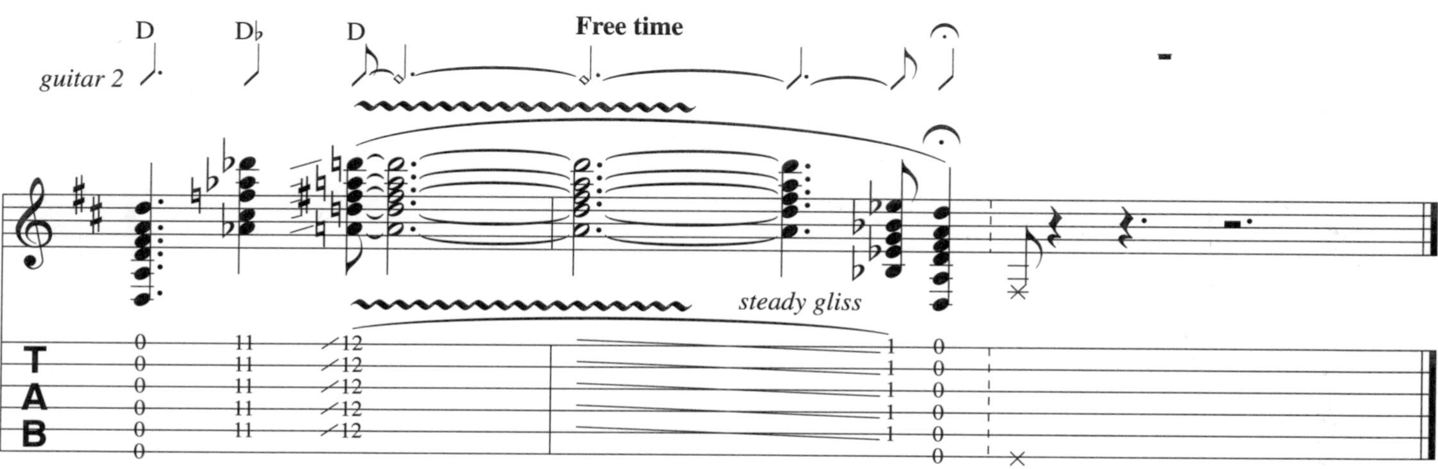

Additional lyrics

2. You love him more
When you should love him less.
I pick up behind him,
And take his mess.
When things go wrong,
Go wrong with you
It hurts me too.

3. He'll love another woman,
An' I love you.
Lord, you love him,
An' stick to him like glue.
When things go wrong,
Go wrong with you,
It hurts me too.

4. Now, you better leave him,
He better put you down.
Lord, I won't stand to see you
Pushed around.
When things go wrong,
Go wrong with you,
It hurts me too.

from Layla And Other Assorted Love Songs

I Looked Away

Words and Music by Eric Clapton and Bobby Whitlock

Chorus

C Dm G7

She took my hand and tried to make

Rhythm figure 2

let ring where possible

B B R B

E7 Am G F D7/F♯

me un - der - stand that she would al - ways be there.

let ring

P.H.

P.H.

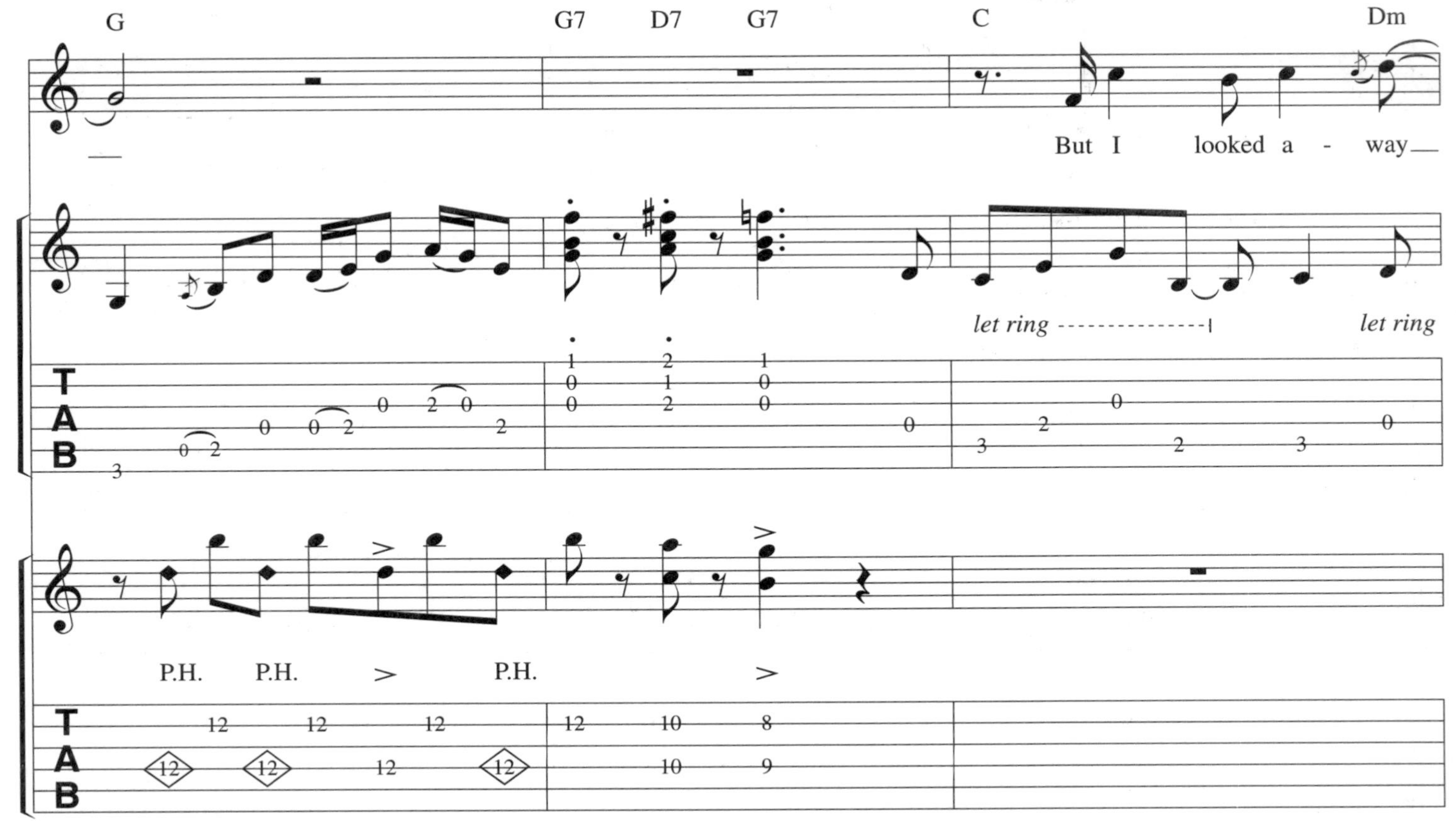

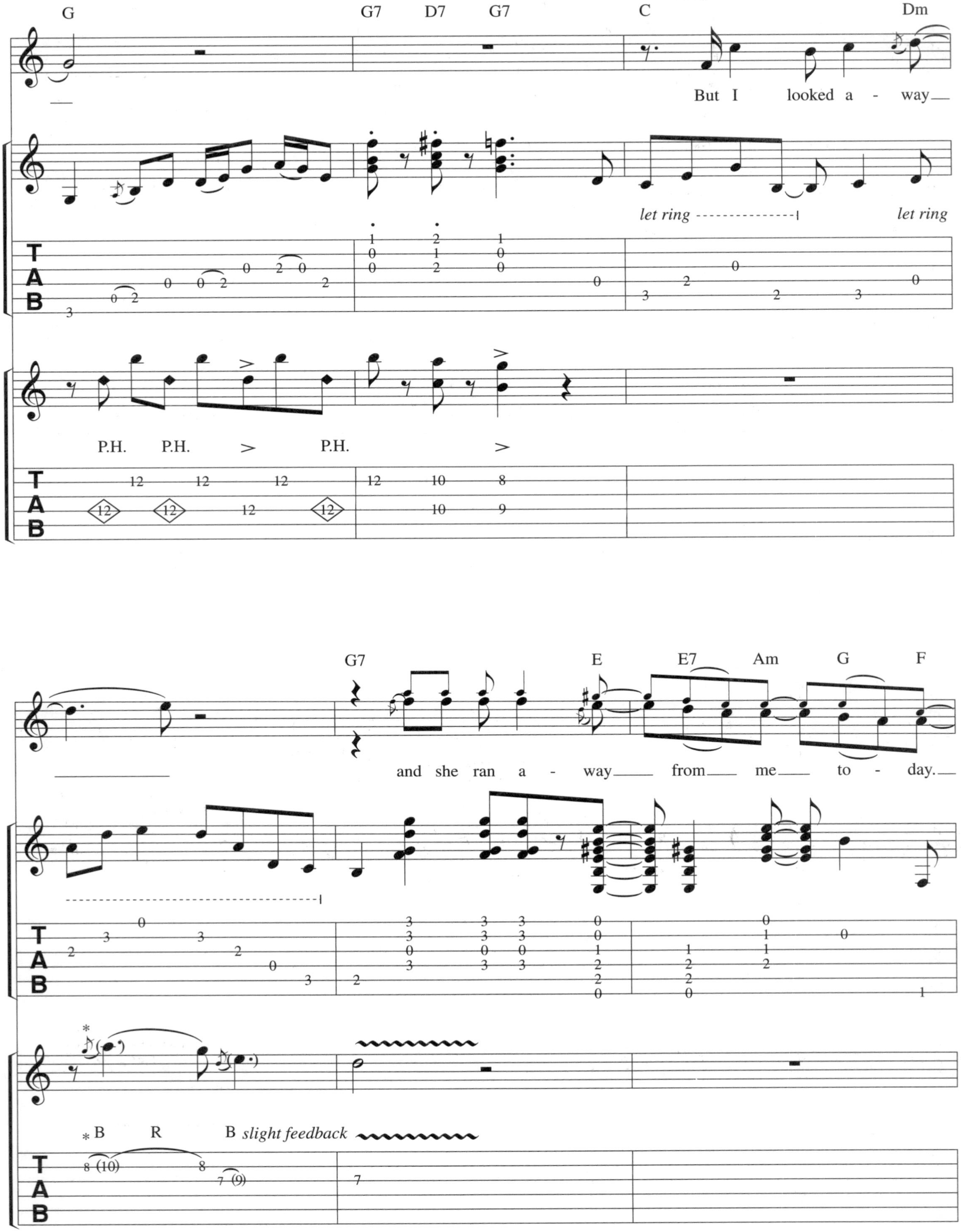

G7 E E7 Am G F

and she ran a - way from me to - day.

*B R B *slight feedback*

* *Pinched mute with R.H. thumb*

D7/F♯ G

— I'm such a lone - ly man.

N.H. B R B

Verse 1

E Am Fm9 B♭

— It came as no sur - prise — to me —

Yeah, yeah, —

B B B B B

Am Fm9 B♭ Am

that you'd leave me in mis - er - y, yeah, yeah. It seems like on - ly

now, now!

B R B *hold bend* R B R

Fm9 B♭/F Fm9 B♭/F Fm9 B♭/F Fm9 B♭/F

yes - ter - day She made a vow that she'd nev - er walk a - way.

(way.

end Rhythm figure 2

Chorus
guitar 1 Rhythm figure 2 *simile*

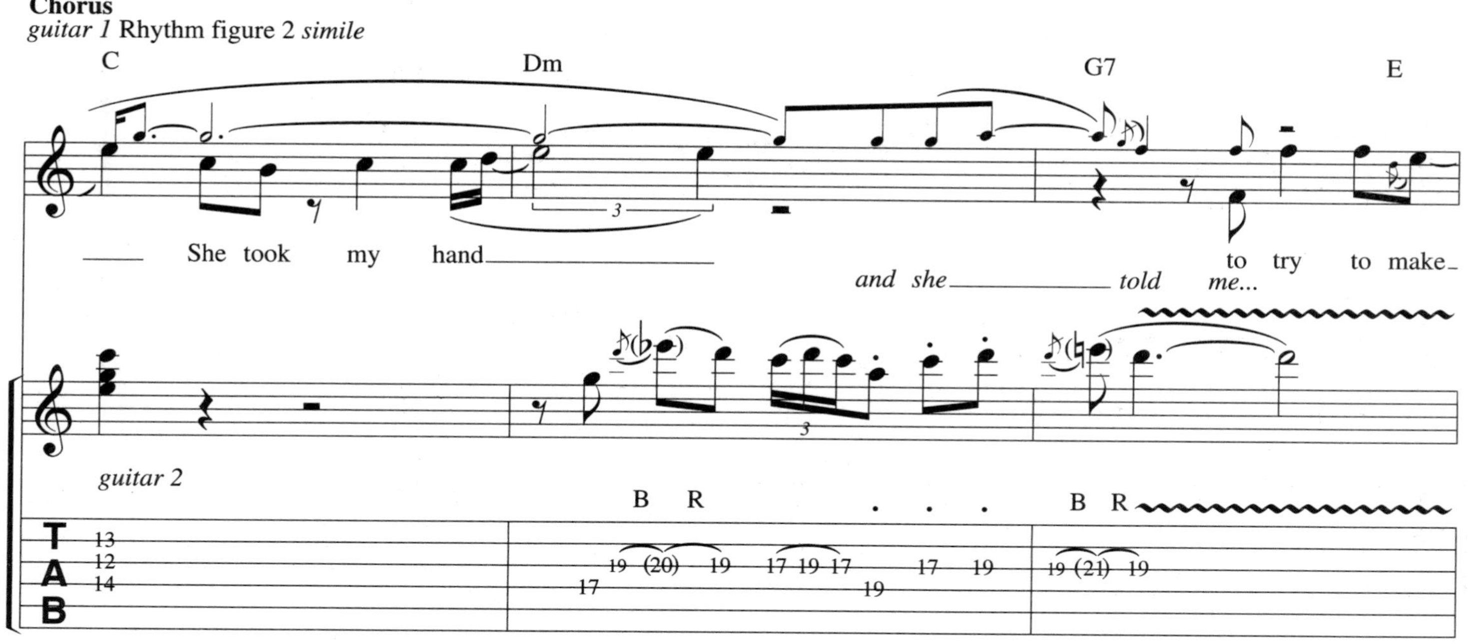

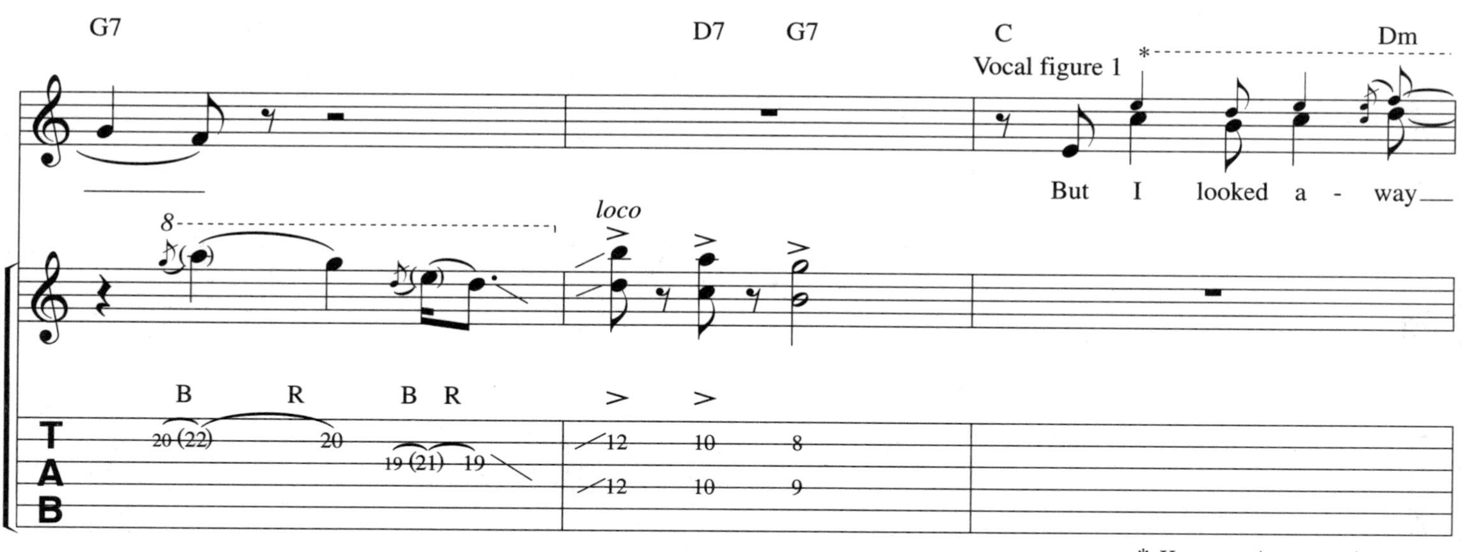

* Harmony (cue notes) out first time

G7 E E7 Am G F

then she ran a - way from me to - day.

B B R

TAB: 5 7 5 7/9 8 | 10(12) 10 | 10 (12) 10

D7/F♯ G7

end Vocal Figure 1

I'm such a lone - ly man.

let ring *let ring*

TAB: 10 10 10 10 | 12 12 12 12 12 12 12 12 12 12

Am
Fm9
B♭
Am
Fm9
to love an - oth - er man's - wom - an, ba - by.
I guess I'll
hold bend
B
R
8 (10)
5
8 (10)
8
5
B♭
F9
B♭/F
F9
B♭/F
F9
B♭/F
keep on sin - nin' and lov - in' ya, love
to my ver - y last
B R
Guitar solo 1
guitar 1 Rhythm figure 2 simile
C
Dm
G7
E
day.
guitar 2
guitar 3
* Use slight vibrato on each note for entire solo section (8 bars)
E7
Am
G
F
D7/F♯
B
hold bend
R
R
R

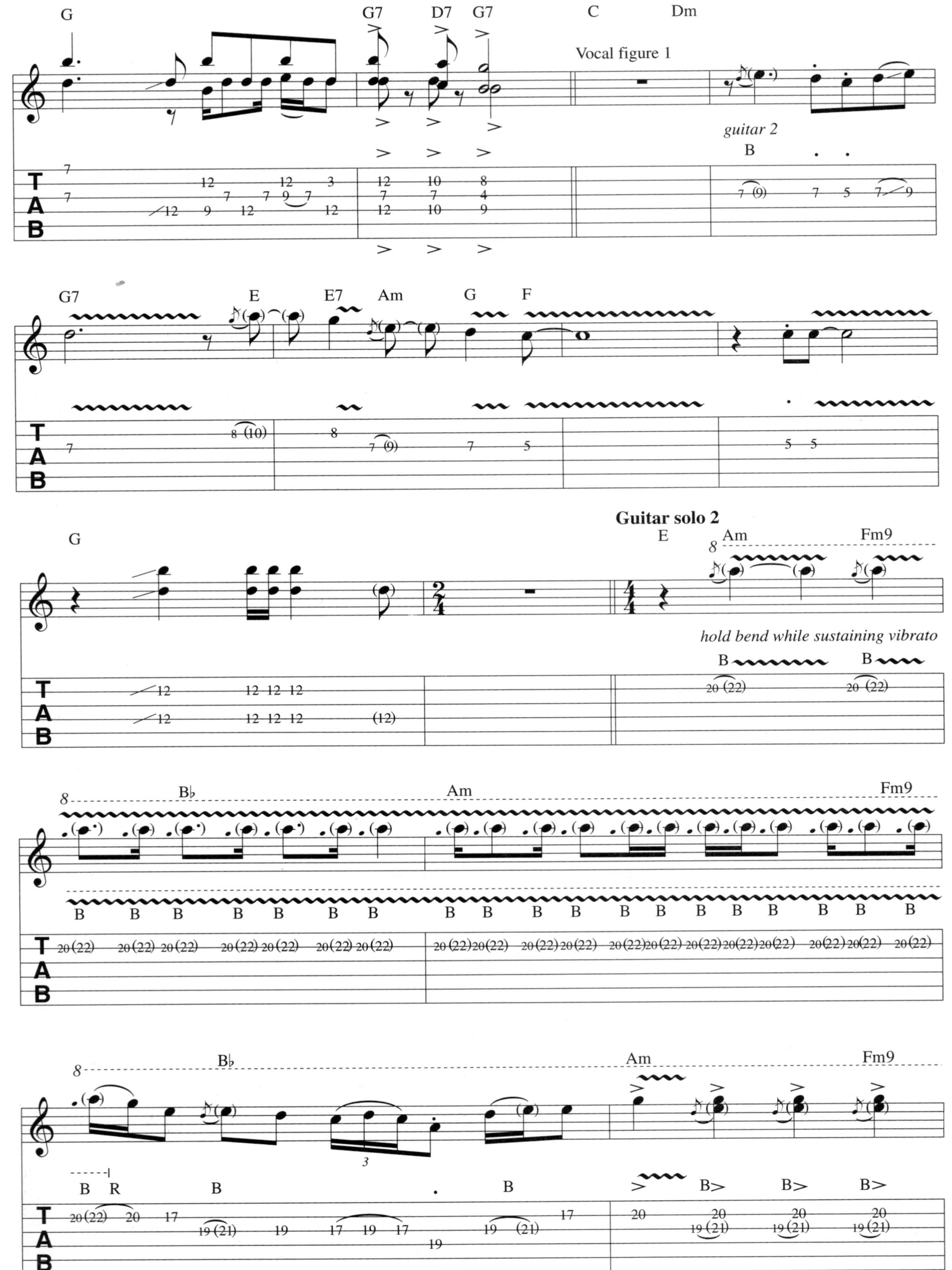
G
G7
D7
G7
C
Dm
Vocal figure 1
guitar 2
B
T
A
B
G7
E
E7
Am
G
F
G
Guitar solo 2
E
Am
Fm9
hold bend while sustaining vibrato
B
B
B♭
Am
Fm9
B♭
Am
Fm9
B
R
3

8
B♭
Fm9
B♭/F
Fm9
B♭/F
Fm9
B♭/F
B

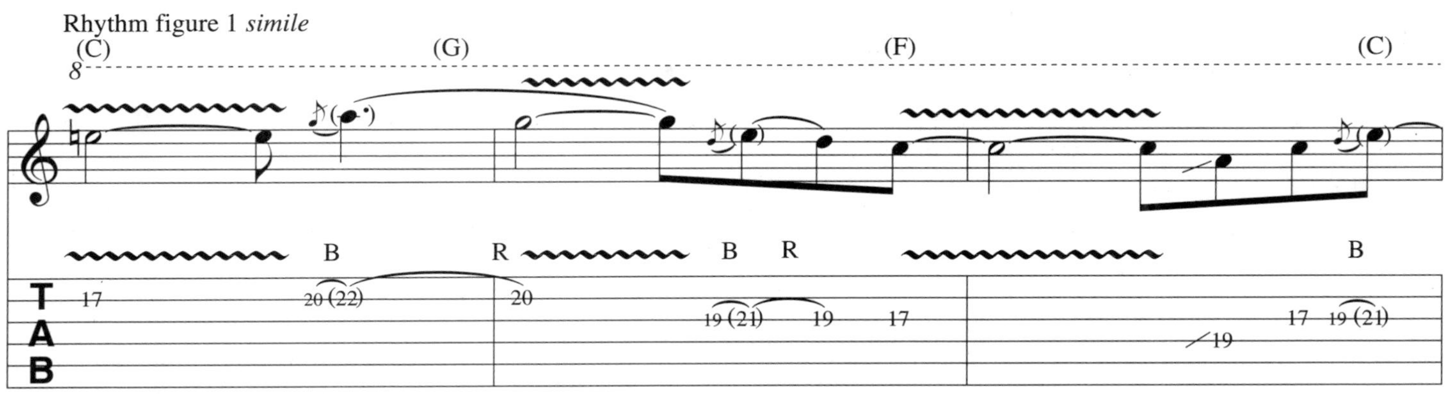
Rhythm figure 1 simile
(C)
(G)
(F)
(C)
B
R
B
R
B

8
(G)
C
loco
G
F
B

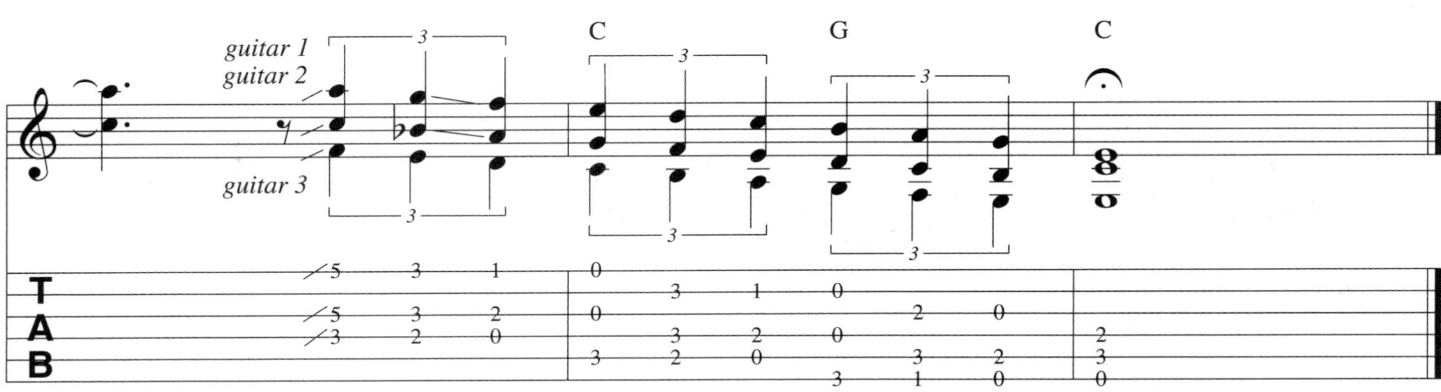
guitar 1
guitar 2
guitar 3
C
G
C

from Goodbye Cream

I'm So Glad

by Nehemiah "Skip" James

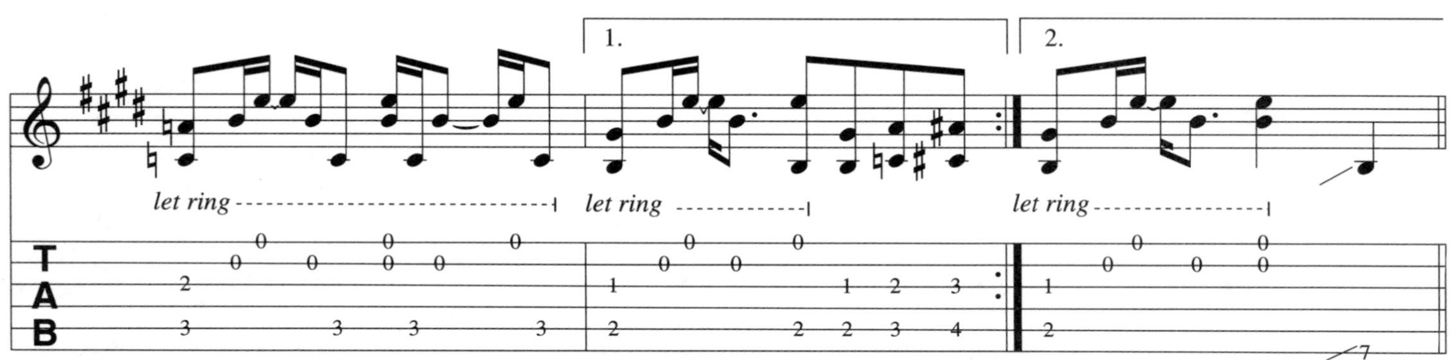

E
D5
E
Verse
glad, I'm glad, I'm glad.
1. Don't know what to do,
2. See additional lyrics
let ring
A/C♯
E7(no 3rd)
E
don't know what to do, don't know what to do.
Glad, glad, glad, glad.
let ring
let ring
let ring
A/C♯
E7(no 3rd)
A/C♯
Tired of weep - ing, tired of moan - ing, and I Tired of groan - in' for you.
Glad, glad, glad, glad,
let ring
let ring
Chorus
⑥open
E
E
E
D5
D
E5
I'm so glad, I'm so glad, I'm
glad.
let ring

D5
E5
E7
glad, I'm glad, I'm glad.
⑥open
E
D5
D
I'm so glad, I'm so glad, I'm glad, I'm glad, I'm
1.
2.
E5
glad.
Guitar solo
*E
U.B.
B
let ring
*Chord progression implied by bass guitar throughout

TAB

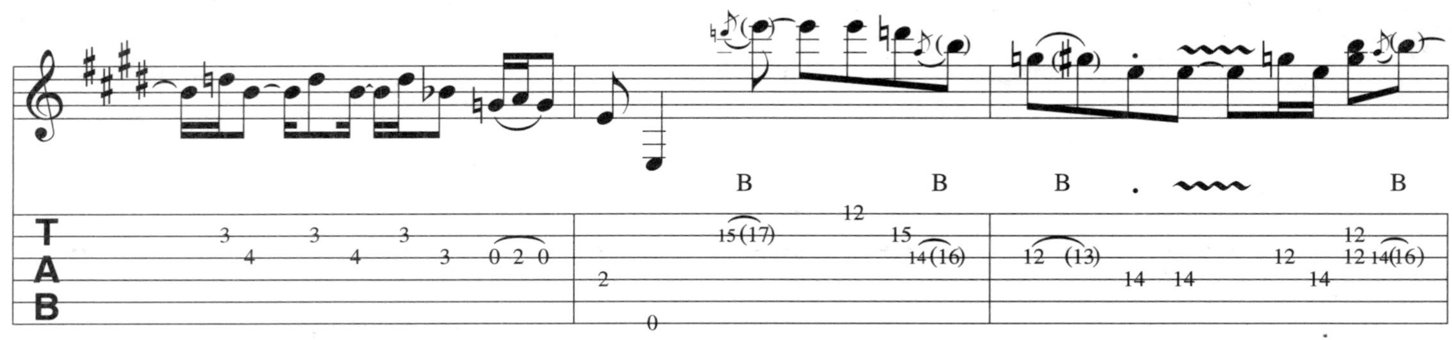
B B B B
TAB

B R B R
TAB

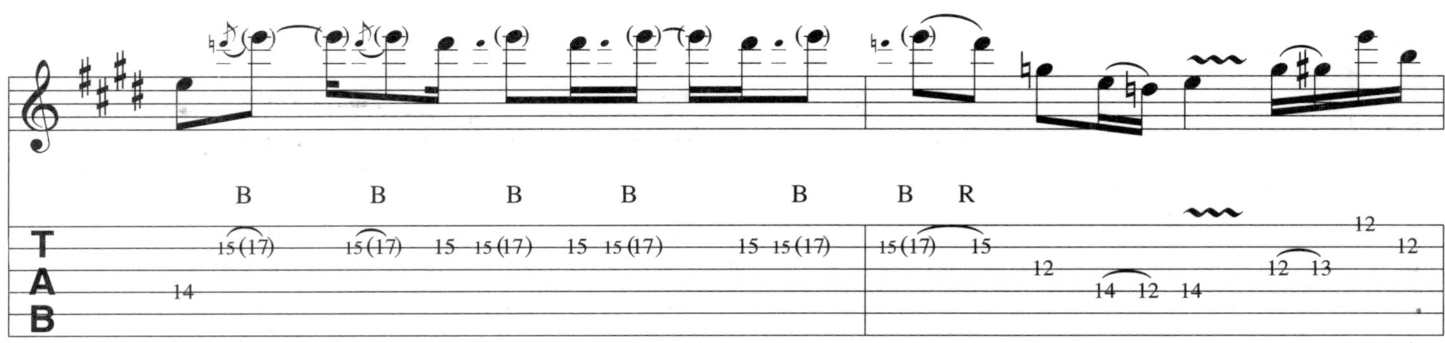
B B B B B B R
TAB

TAB

let ring

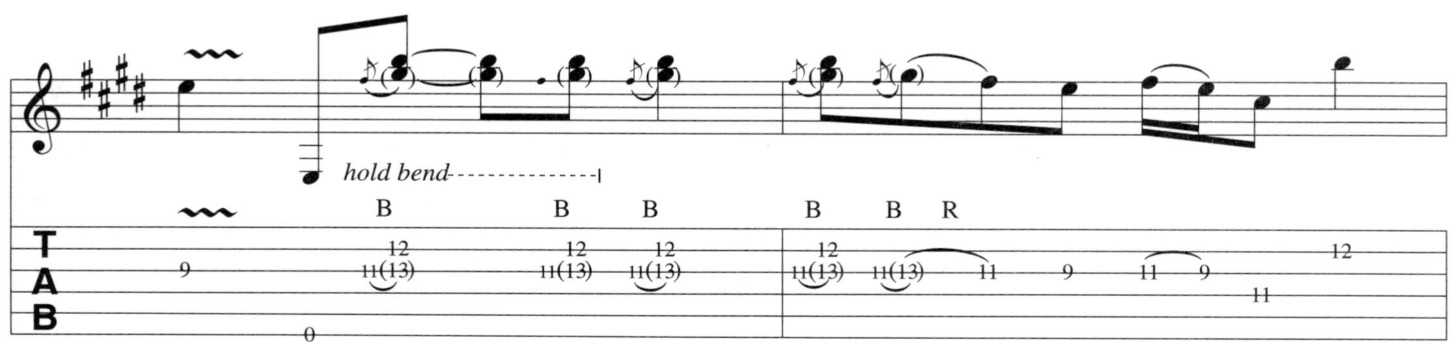
hold bend
B B B B B R

B R
hold bend
B B R

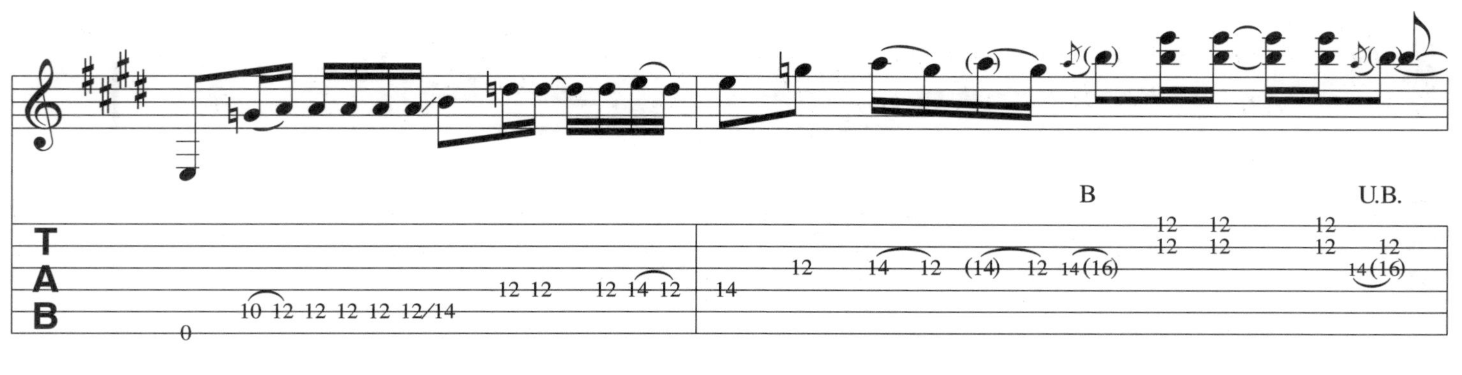
B
U.B.

U.B.
U.B.
U.B.

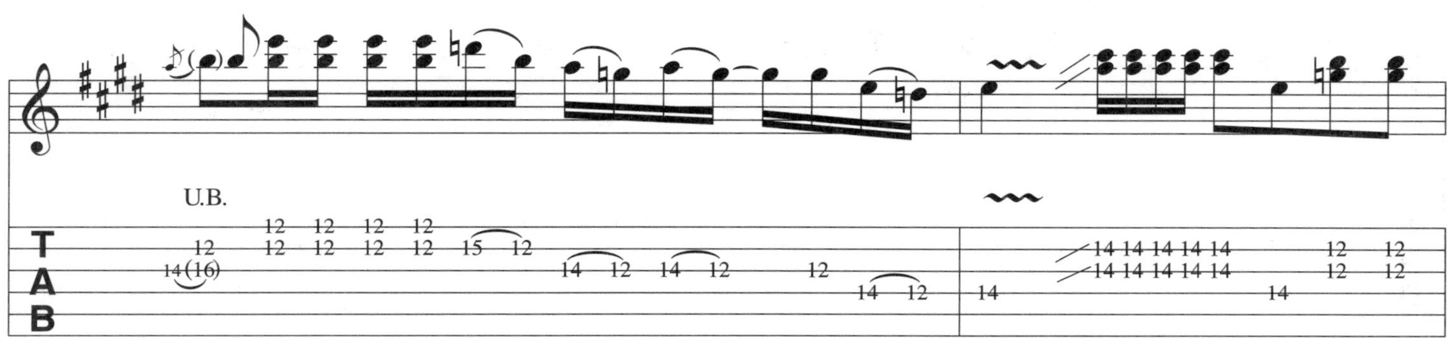
U.B.

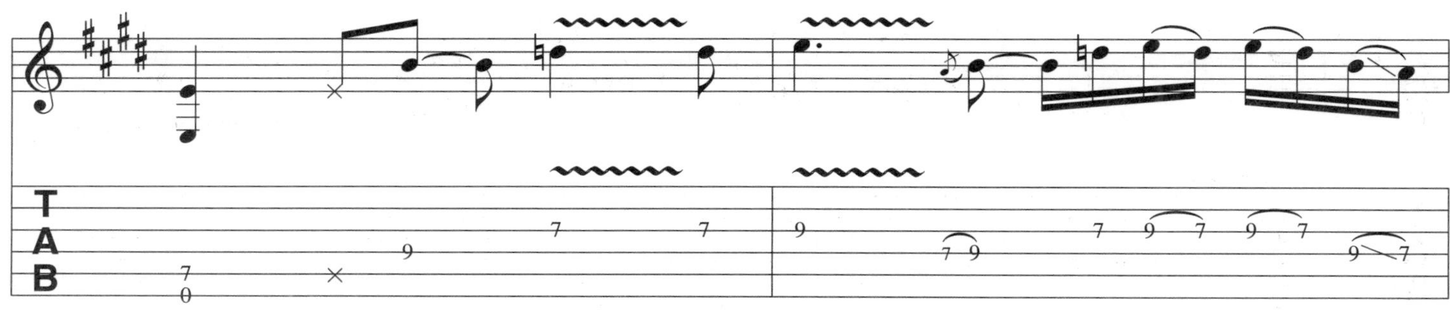

B
B

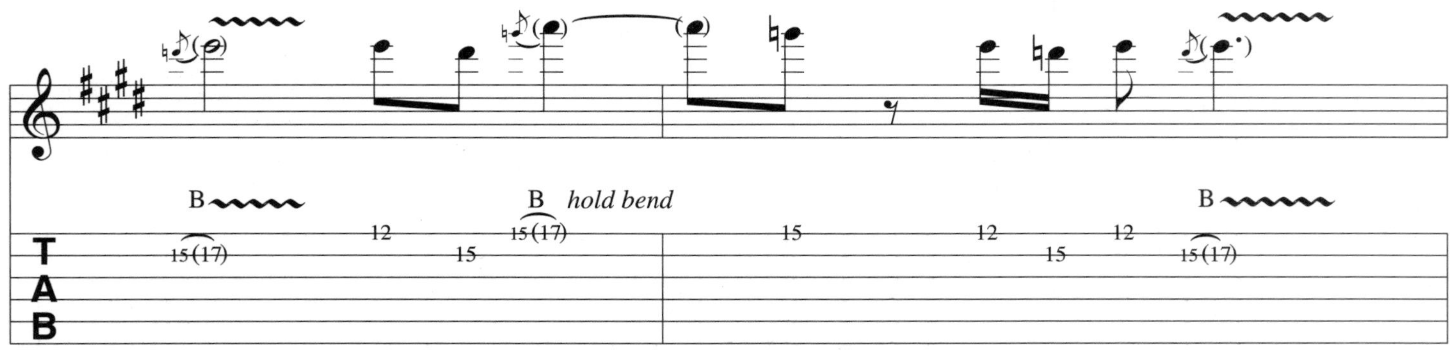
B
B hold bend
B

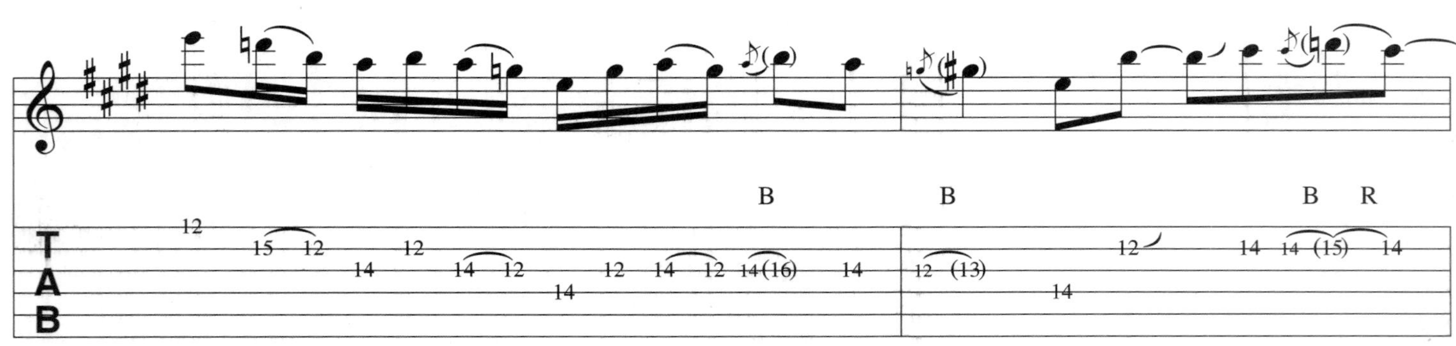
B
B
B R

B R
TAB
B
B R B R
B R

B R

U.B.
U.B.
B
B

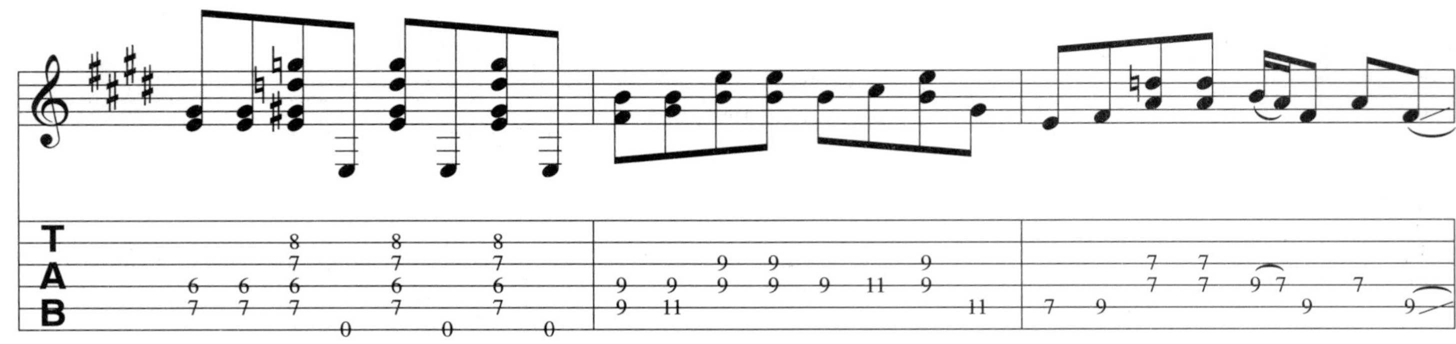

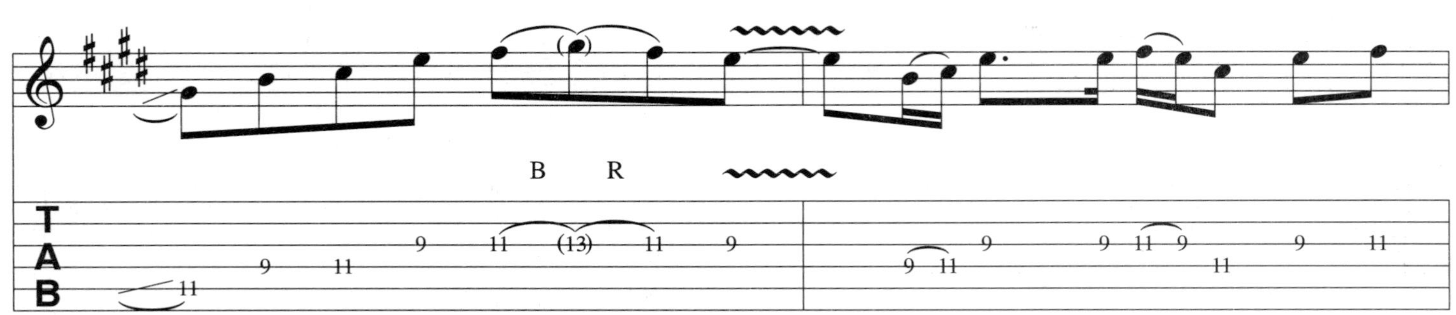
B R

hold bend
B B B B R

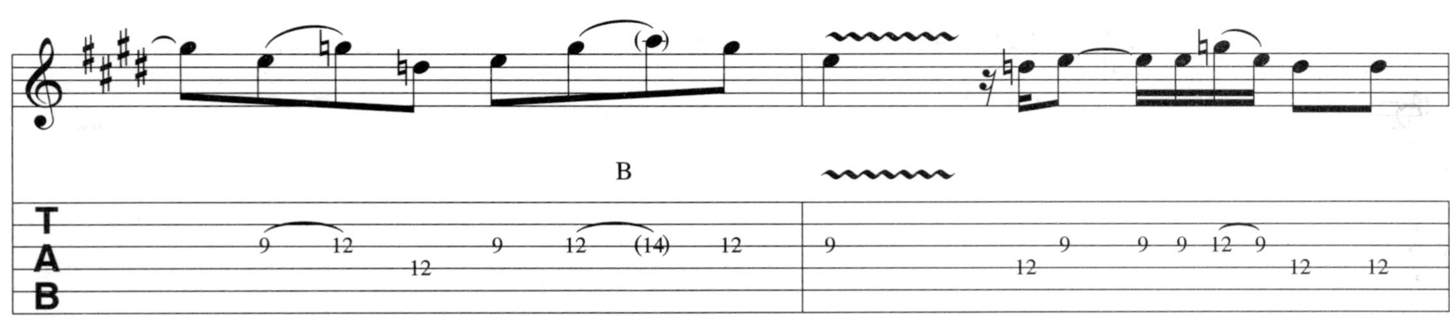
B

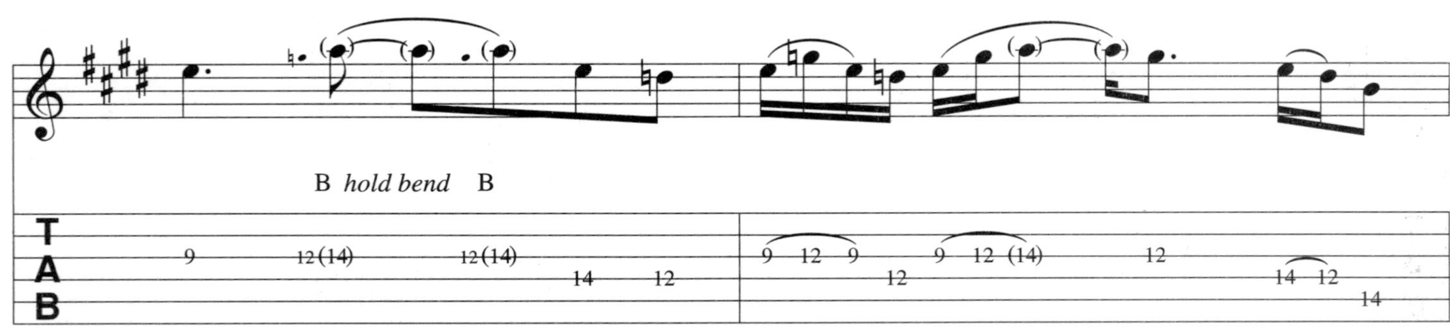
B hold bend B

let ring

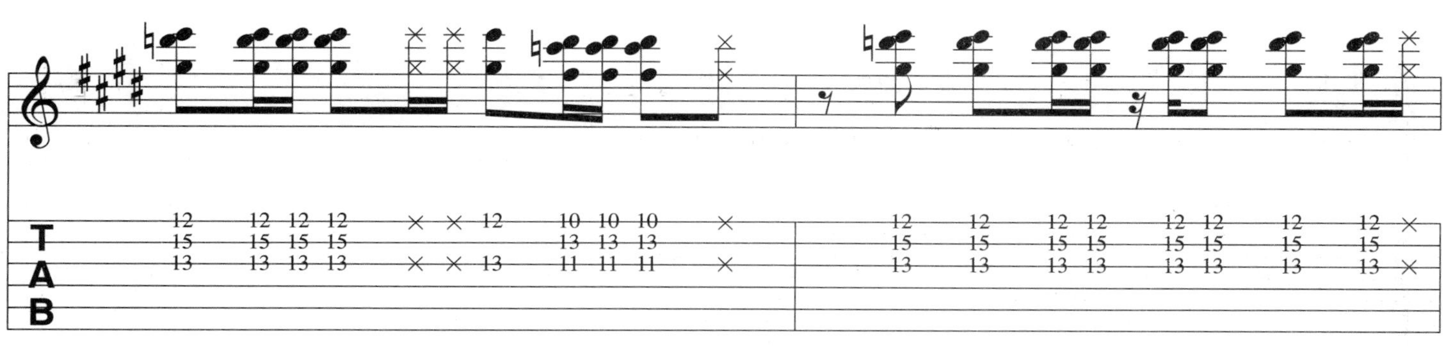

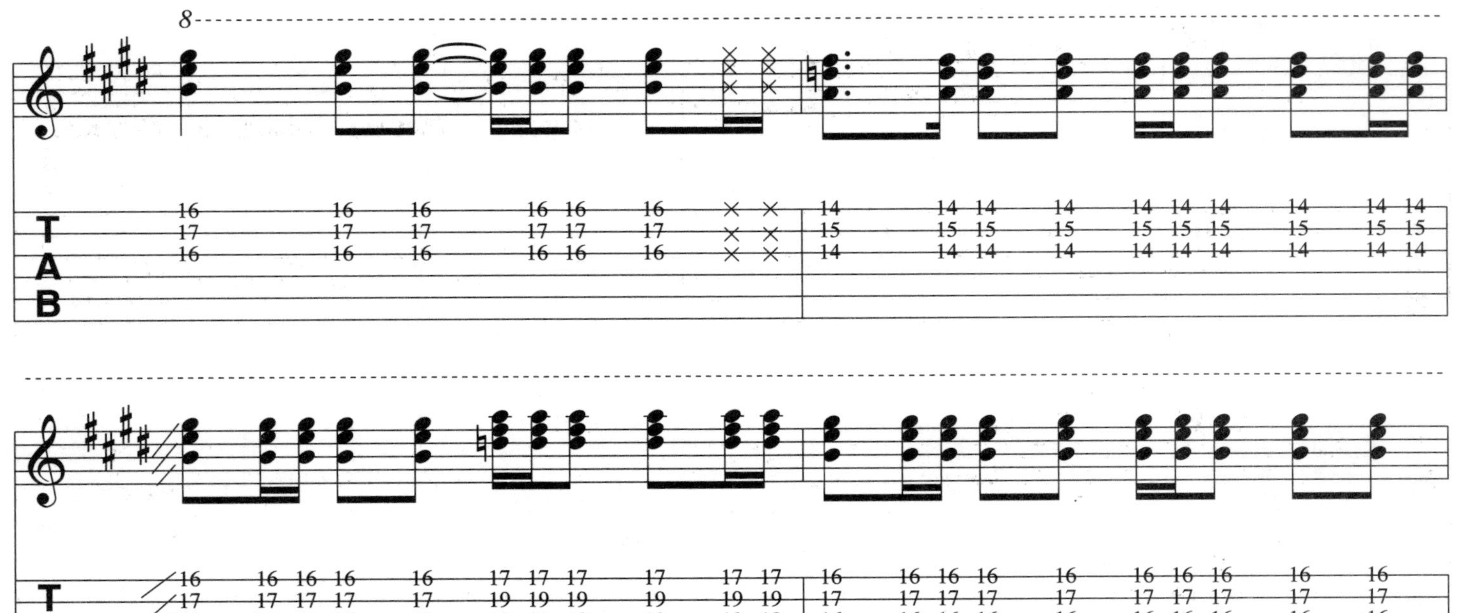
8
T
A
B

T
A
B

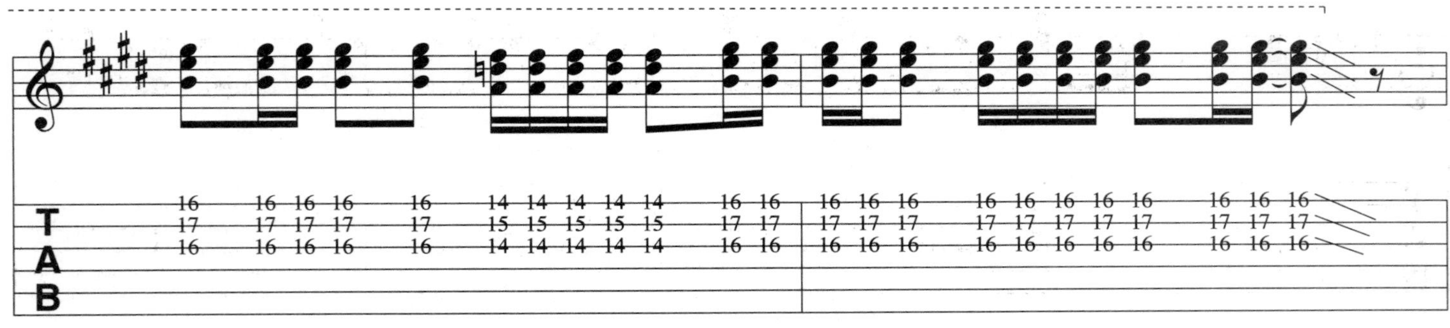
let ring
T
A
B

loco
B
R
B
R
T
A
B

let ring

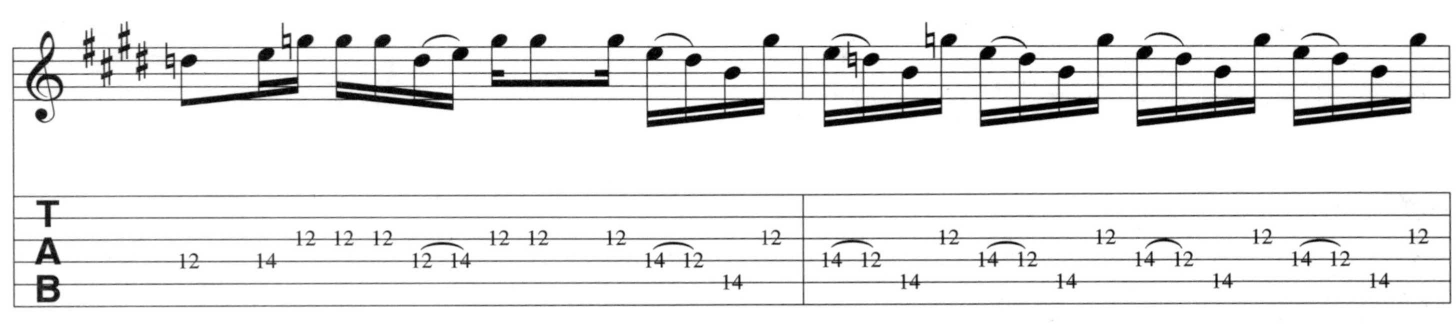

B
B
B

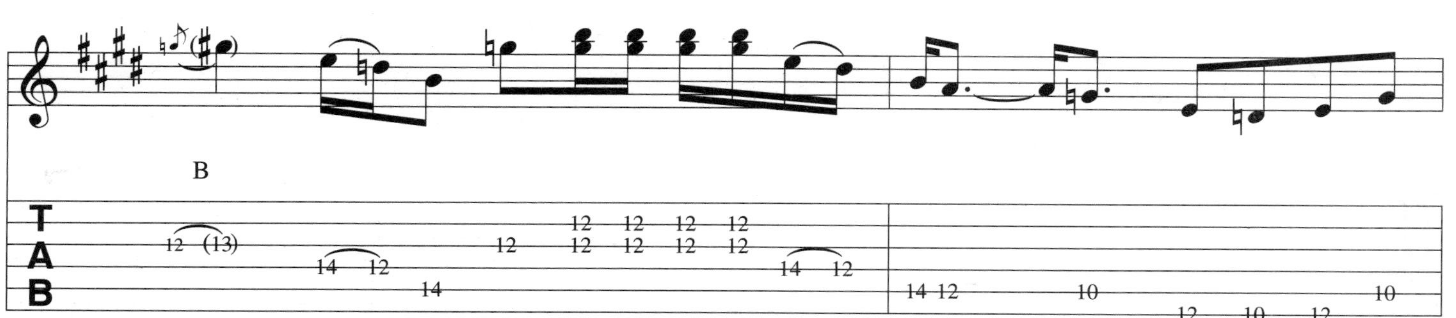

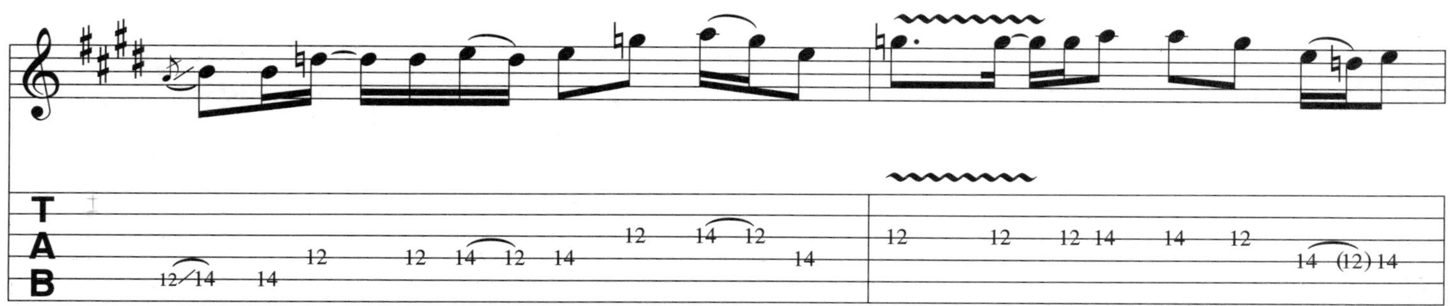

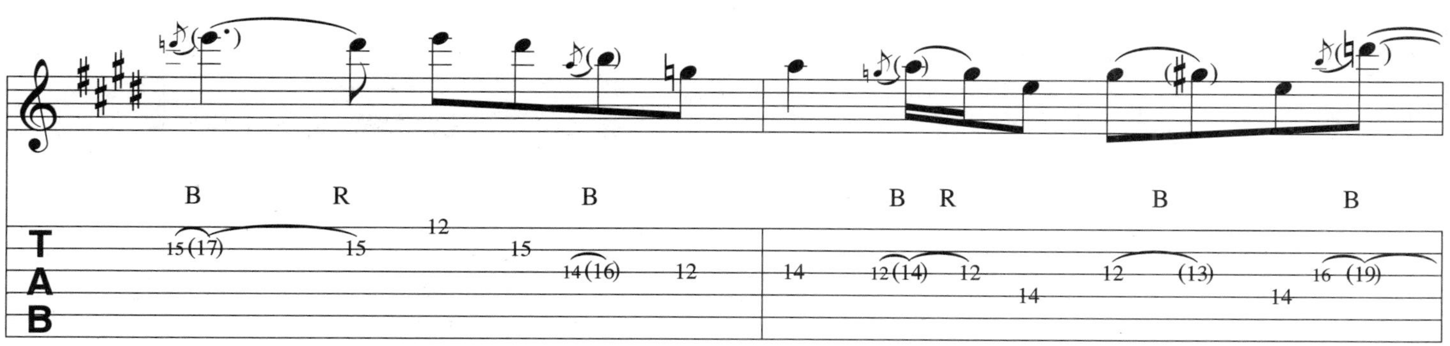

B

T
A
B
B
R
B
B

T
A
B

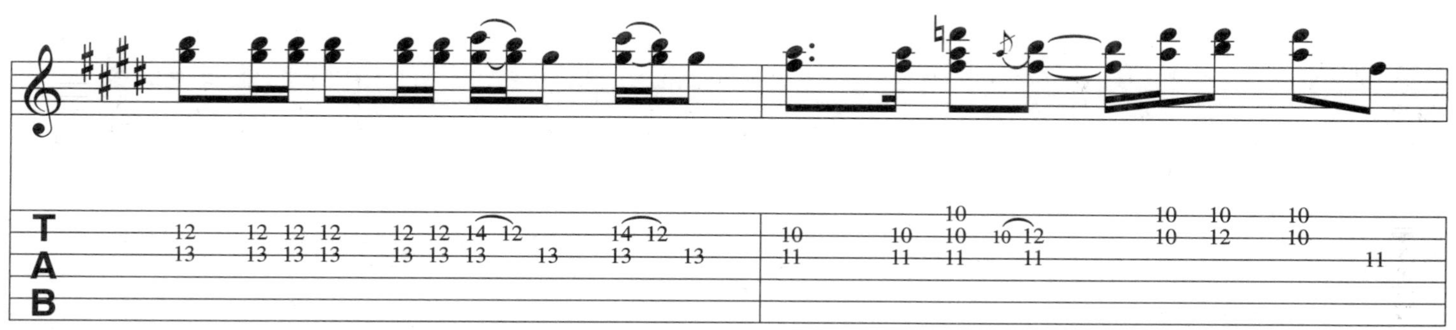

hold bend
U.B.
U.B.
U.B.
U.B.

U.B.
U.B.
B
B

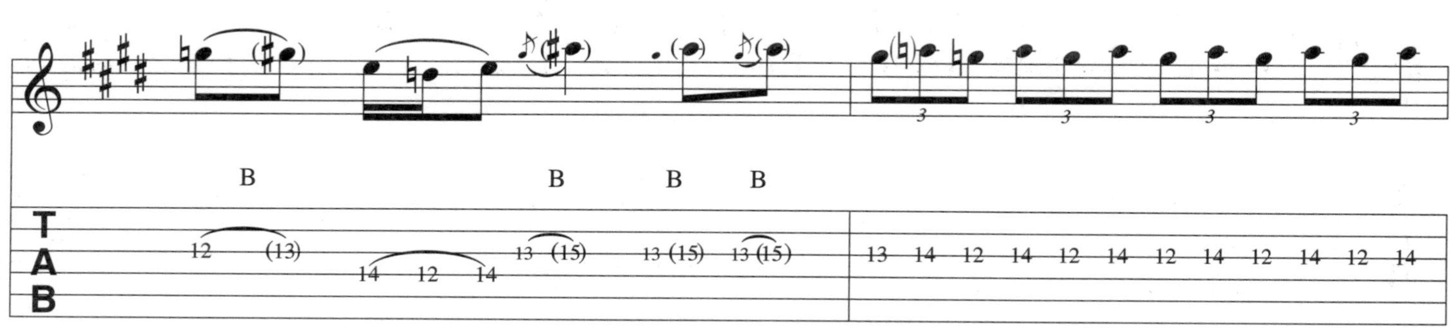
B
B
B
B

B
U.B. hold bend

mf
let ring
Chorus
⑥open
E
E
D5
④open
D
P.M.
E5
I'm so glad,
I'm so glad, I'm
glad, I'm glad, I'm glad.
glad.

⑥open
E
E
D5
④open
D
D5
④open
D
P.M.
P.M.
I'm so glad, I'm so glad, I'm
E
④open
D5 D D5 E5
E
⑥open ⑥5fr ⑥7fr
E A B
glad, I'm glad, I'm glad.
E5
D5
E5
I'm so glad, I'm so glad, I'm
I'm so glad. I'm so
D5
E5
E
glad, I'm glad, I'm glad.
glad, glad, I'm
E5 D
D5
I'm so glad, I'm so glad, I'm
I'm so glad, I'm so
E
D
E5
⑥12fr ⑥10fr ⑥open
E D E E
glad, I'm glad, I'm glad.
glad.
D5
④open
D
I'm so glad, I'm so glad, I'm

Additional lyrics

Tired of weepin', tired of moanin', tired of groanin' for you.
Don't know what to do, don't know what to do,
I don't know what to do, yeah!

from From The Cradle

I'm Your Hoochie Coochie Man

(Hoochie Coochie Man)

by Willie Dixon

1. ⑤open
A A7
guitars 1&2
to Coda
And then the world want to know what's this all a-bout?" But you know I'm here,
and then the world will know the
D7*
ev - 'ry-bod-y knows I'm here.
guitar 1
B B
*Chord symbols reflect suggested harmony.
guitar 2 plays ad lib rhythm.
A7
Well, I'm the
E7
D7
Hoo - chie Coo-chie man, ev - 'ry-bod - y knows I'm here.
let ring

A7
E7
2.
⑤open
A
A7
D7
guitar 2
continue ad lib rhythm
Hoo - chie Coo-chie man, but you know I'm here.
guitar 1
B
A7
ev - 'ry-bod - y knows I'm here.
B
E7
Well, I'm the Hoo - chie Coo- chie man,
let ring

D7
A7
ev - 'ry-bod-y knows I'm here.
harmonica solo
E7
A7
let ring
D7
A7
let ring
let ring
D7
let ring

A7
E7
D7
let ring
A7
B
E7
D.S. al Coda
Coda
A7 A5 A7 A5 A7 A5 A7 A5 D7
continue ad lib rhythm
don't you mess with me 'cause you know I'm here,
B
A7
ev - 'ry-bod - y knows I'm here.

Additional lyrics

3. On the seventh hour, on the seventh day,
On the seventh month, the seventh doctor say,
"You were born for good luck, that you'll see"
I got seven hundred dollars.
Don't you mess with me, 'cause you know I'm here.

from Eric Clapton

Let It Rain

Words and Music by Bonnie Sheridan and Eric Clapton

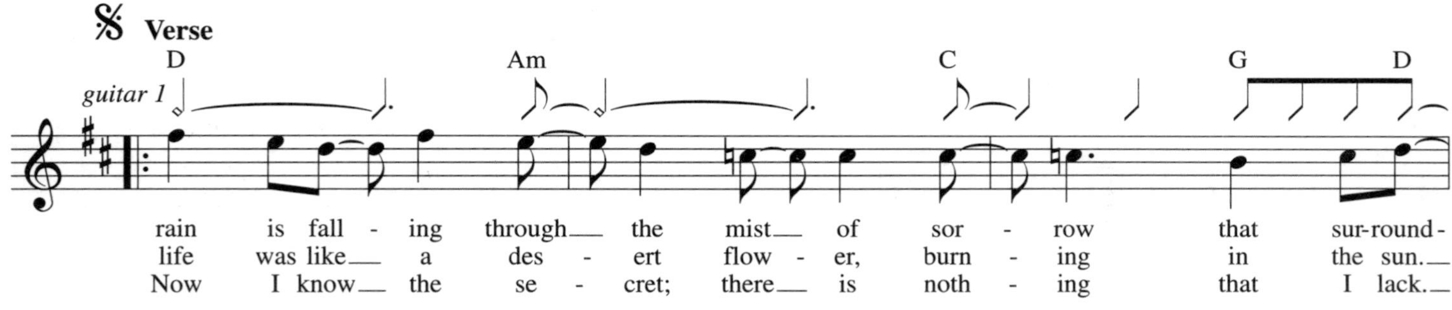

G
D
Chorus
Am
guitar 3
that may sur - round me.
was sad and done.
to give it back.
Let it rain;
let it rain.
guitar 1
guitar 2
Rhythm Fill 1
end Rhythm Fill 1
T
A
B
2
3
2
4
0
1
D
Am
C
G
D
with Rhythm Fill 1
Let your love rain down on me.
Let it rain;
Am
D
Am
to Coda
1.
C
G
D
with Rhythm fill 1 (two times)
let it rain.
Let it rain,
rain, rain.
2.
C
G
ritard
A
G/A
guitars 1 & 2 with Rhythm figure 1
My
rain,
rain.
A
G/A
A

Interlude
F♯m
F♯m/E♯
B
R
T
A
B
10
11
12
12
(14)
12
10

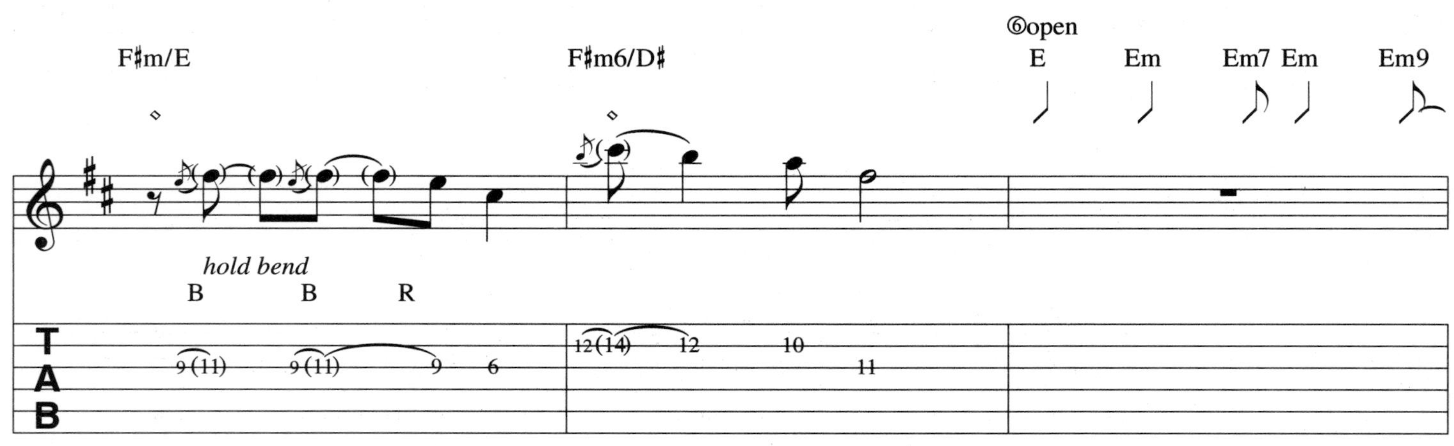
F♯m/E
F♯m6/D♯
⑥open
E
Em
Em7
Em
Em9
hold bend
B
B
R
9 (11)
9 (11)
9
6
12 (14)
12
10
11

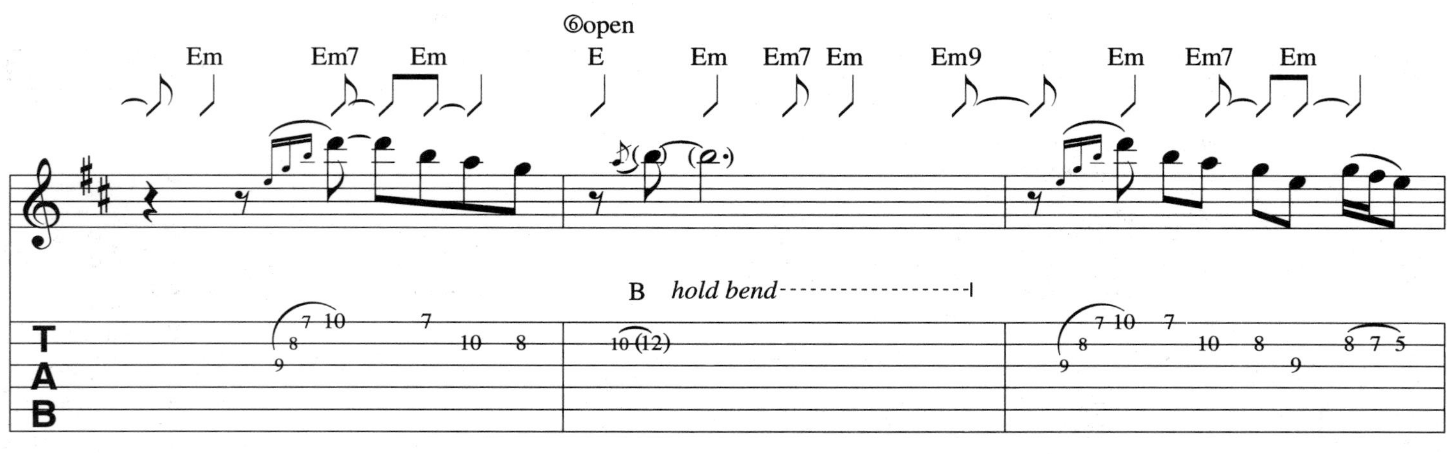
Em
Em7
Em
⑥open
E
Em
Em7
Em
Em9
Em
Em7
Em
B
hold bend
7
10
7
8
10
8
9
10 (12)
7
10
7
8
10
8
9
8
7
5
9
9

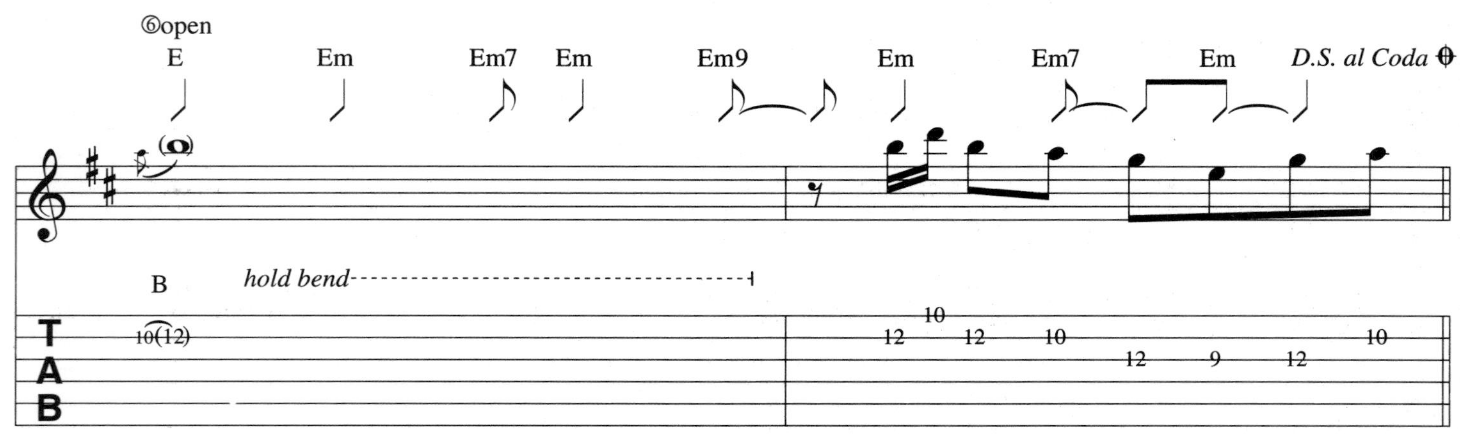
⑥open
E
Em
Em7
Em
Em9
Em
Em7
Em
D.S. al Coda
B
hold bend
10 (12)
10
12
12
10
12
9
12
10

Coda
guitar 3
Am
C
G
D
with Rhythm Fill 1
let it rain,
rain,
rain.
Let it rain;
Am
D
Am
C
G
D
with Rhythm fill 1 (two times)
let it rain.
Let your love
rain
down
on me.
Am
D
Am
C
G
with Rhythm fill 1 (two times)
Let it rain;
let it rain,
Let it rain
rain,
A
G/A
A
rain. (1st time only)
Rhythm figure 2
end Rhythm figure 2
T
A
B
Guitar solo 1
guitars 1 and 2 Rhythm figure 2 simile
A
G/A
guitar 3
B
T
A
B

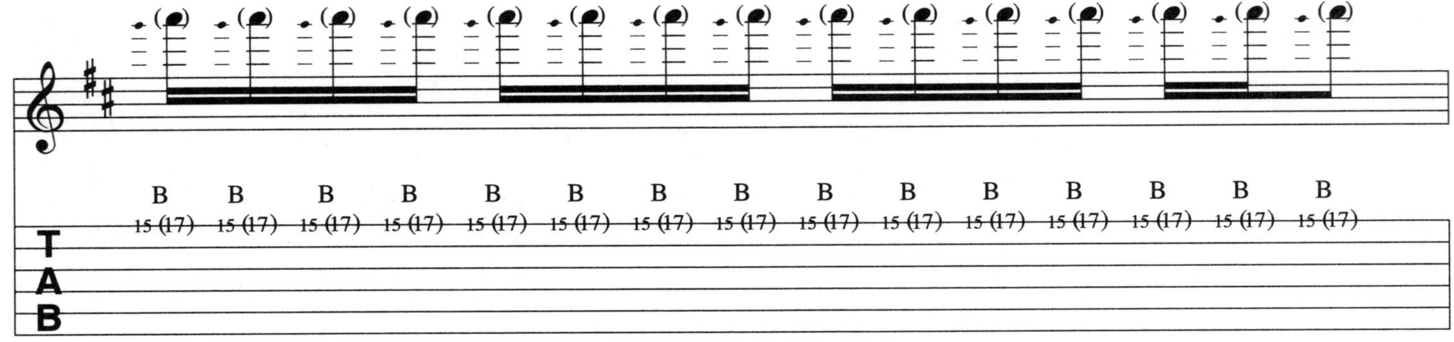

A
hold bend

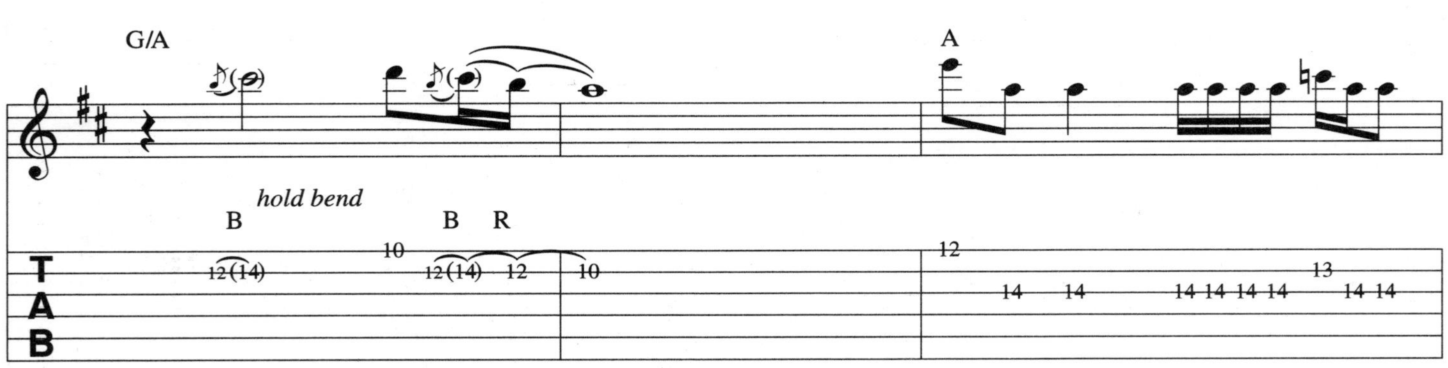
G/A
A
hold bend

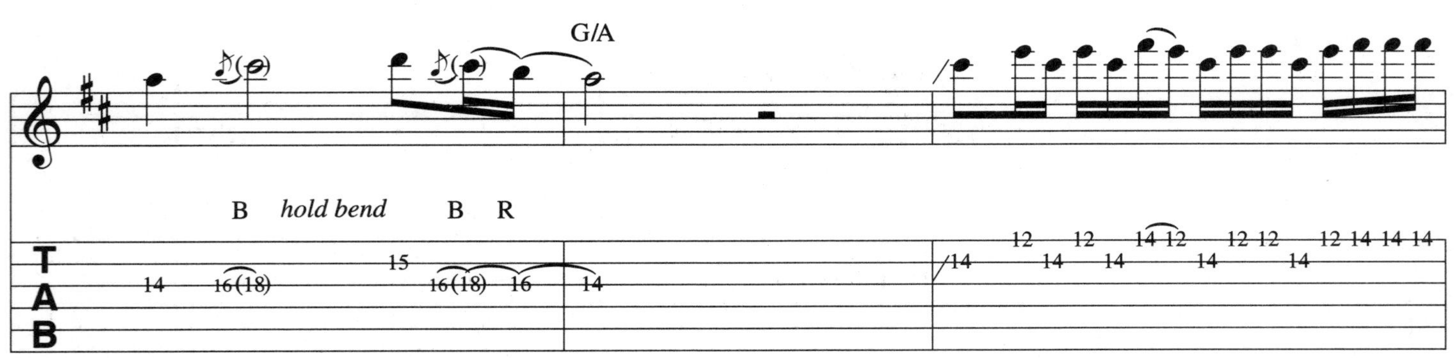
G/A
hold bend

A
G/A
A
G/A
A
let ring
G/A
A

keyboard solo
9
G/A
Guitar solo 2
8
A
G/A
A
G/A

A
B B R
G/A
B R
A
let ring
B B hold bend B R
G/A
let ring
B B hold bend
B
A
let ring
B B B B

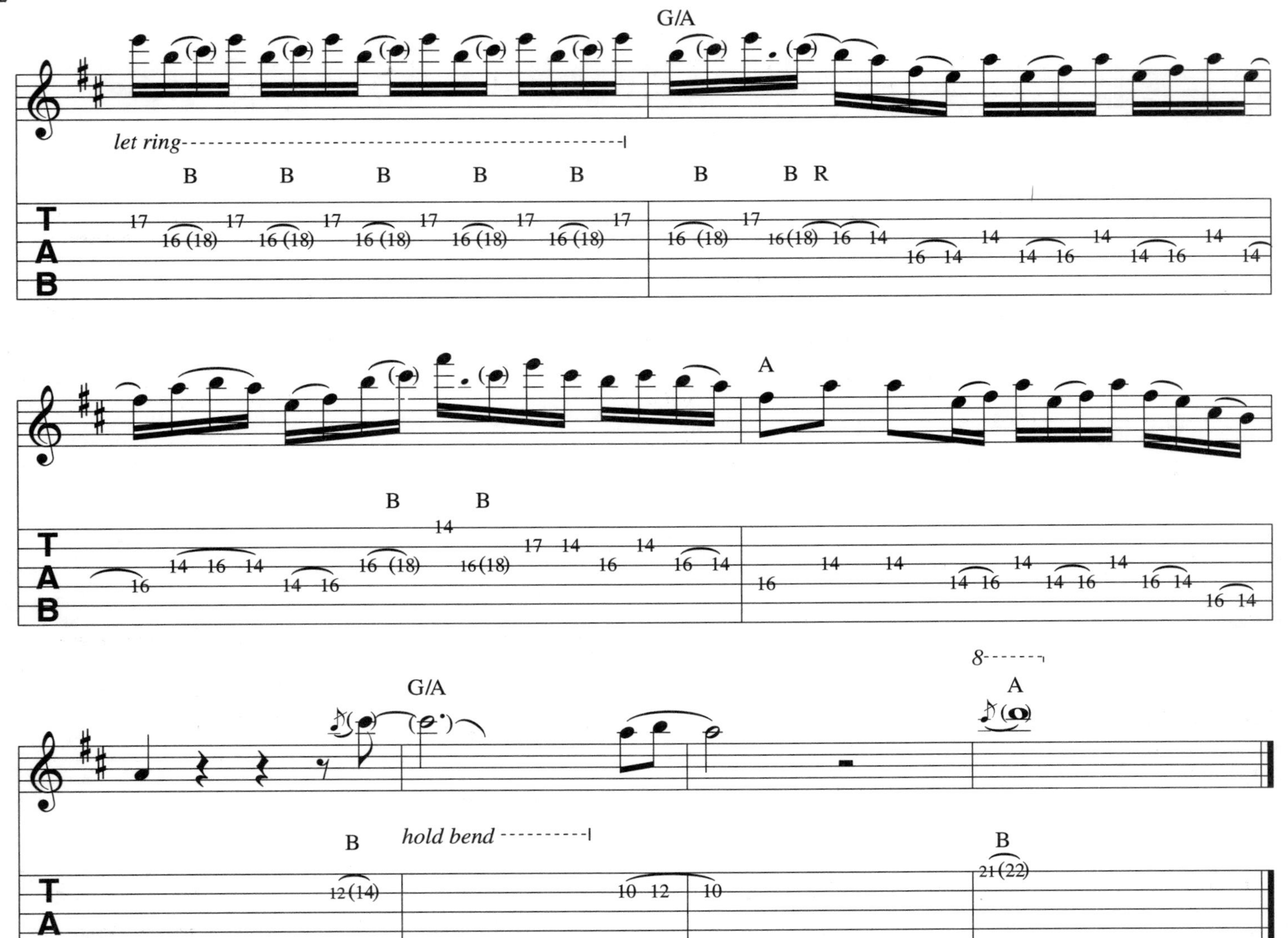
G/A
let ring
B
B
B
B
B
B
B R
T
A
B
17
16 (18)
17
16 (18)
17
16 (18)
17
16 (18)
17
16 (18)
17
16 (18)
17
16 (18) 16 14
16 14
14
14 16
14
14 16
14
14
A
B
B
14
17 14
14
16
14 16 14
14 16
16 (18)
16 (18)
16
16 14
16
14
14
14 16
14
14 16
14
16 14
16 14
8
G/A
A
hold bend
B
B
12 (14)
10 12
10
21 (22)
12

from Backless

If I Don't Be There By Morning

Words and Music by Bob Dylan

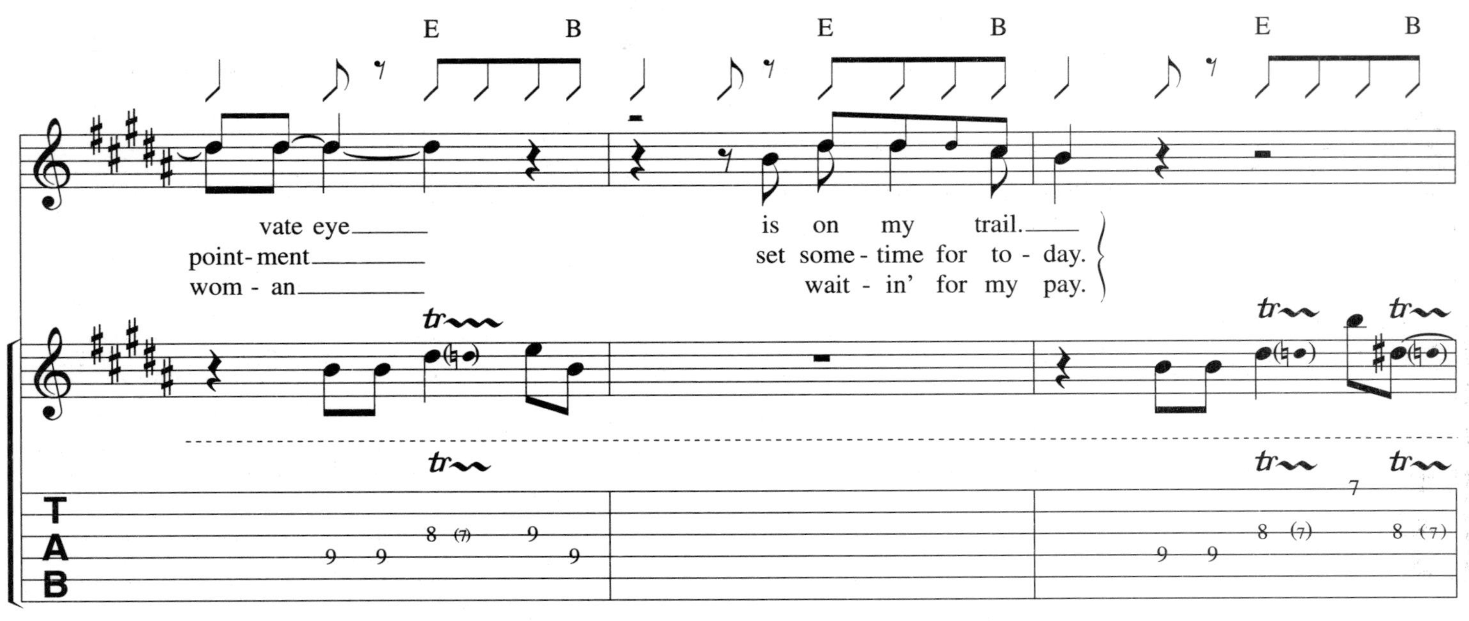
E
B
E
B
E
B
vate eye
is on my trail.
point-ment
set some-time for to-day.
wom-an
wait-in' for my pay.
tr
T
A
B

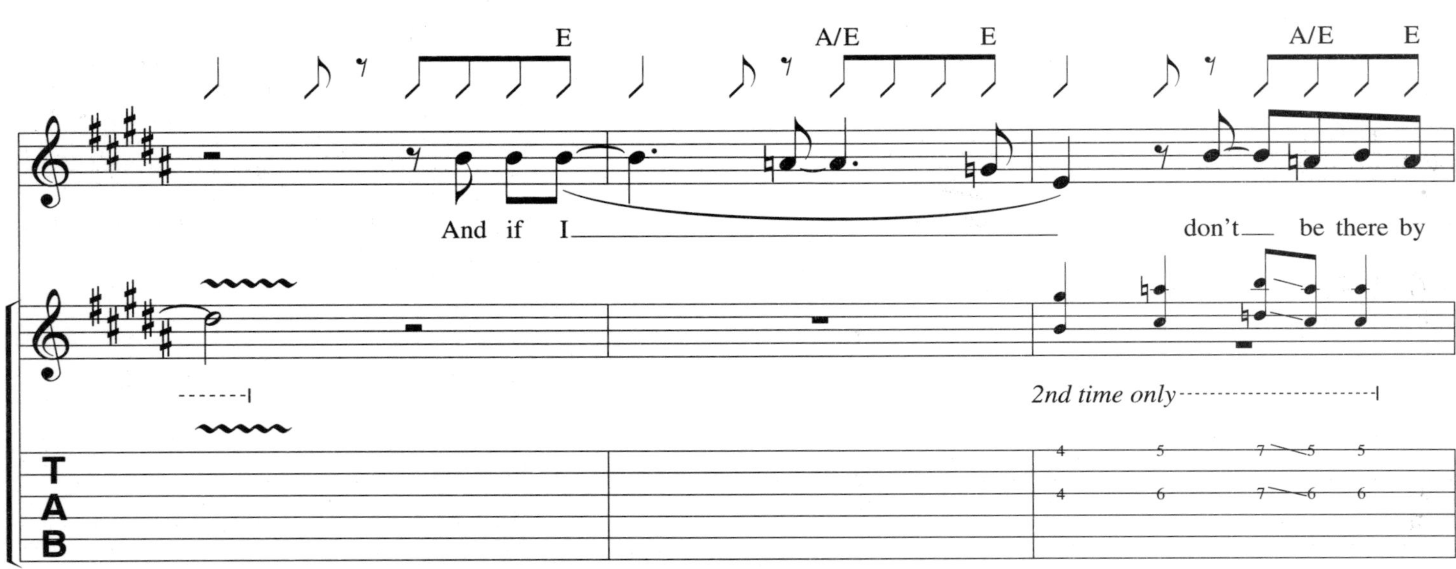
E
A/E
E
A/E
E
And if I
don't be there by
2nd time only
T
A
B

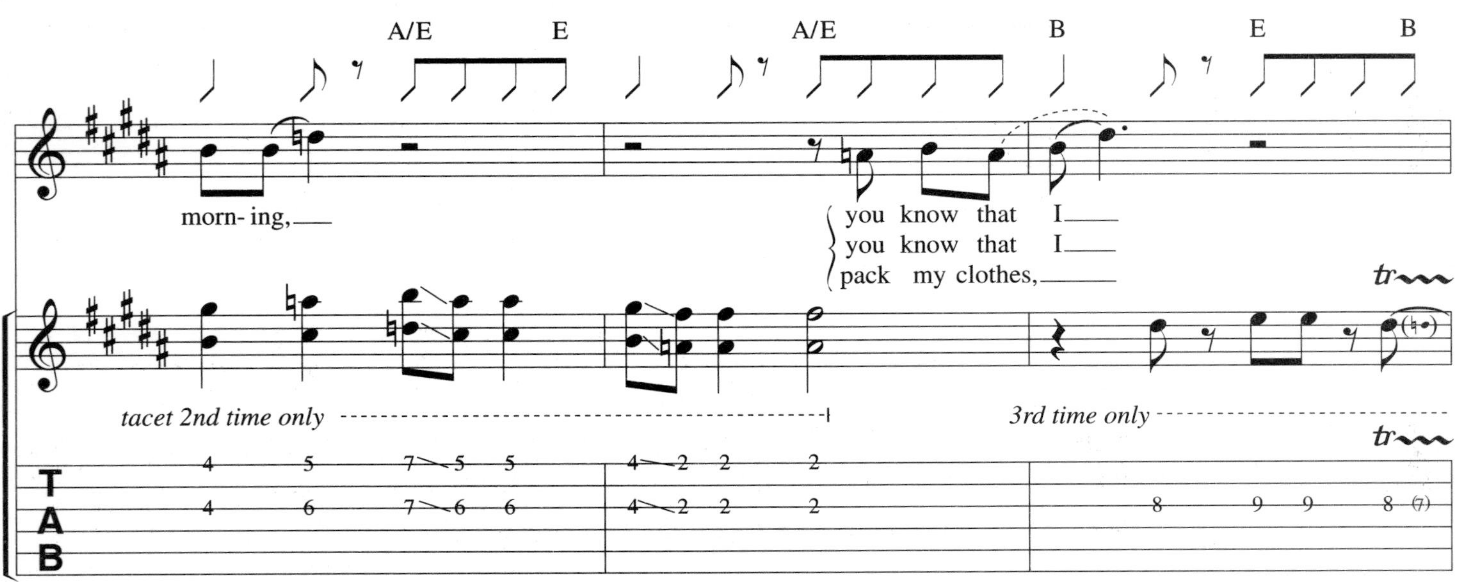
A/E
E
A/E
B
E
B
morn-ing,
you know that I
you know that I
pack my clothes,
tacet 2nd time only
3rd time only
tr
T
A
B

E
B
E
B
must have spent the night in jail.
must have gone the oth - er way
get down on your knees and pray.
tr
tr
T
A
B
9
8
(7)
1.
E
B
2.
E
B
Bridge
D♯m7
I been run-
Find-ing my way back to you,
T
A
B
7
9
7
9
G♯m7
E
A
girl, lone-ly and blue and mis-treat-ed, too.
D♯m7
G♯m7
Some-times I think of you, girl. Is it true

to Coda
C♯m7
F♯7
that you think of me too?
B B B B B B B
9(11) 9(11) 9(11) 9(11) 9(11) 9 (10) 9(10)
Guitar solo 1
B
E
B
let ring
B R B
let ring
T
A
B

E
A/E
E
A/E
E
A/E
E
B
B
E
B
E
B
B
D.S. (take second ending) al Coda
E
B
E
B
I got a
B
Coda
F♯7
B
E
B
I left my wom- an
tr
B
tr

E B E B E B
with a twen- ty dol- lar bill. I left her
E B E B E B
wait-ing. I hope she's wait-ing for me still.
E A/E E A/E E
And if I don't be there by
A/E E A/E E B E B
morn- ing, I know that I,
let ring
tr
TAB

E B
I nev - er will.
B R
9 (11) 9
tr
Guitar solo 2
A/E

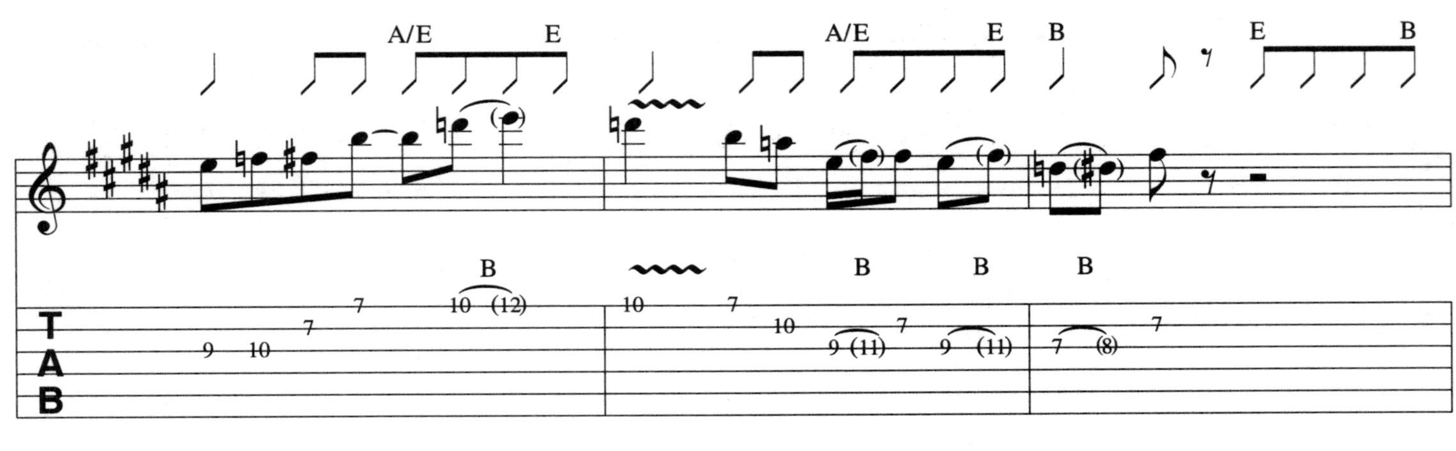
A/E
E
A/E
E
B
E
B
B
B
B
B
T
A
B

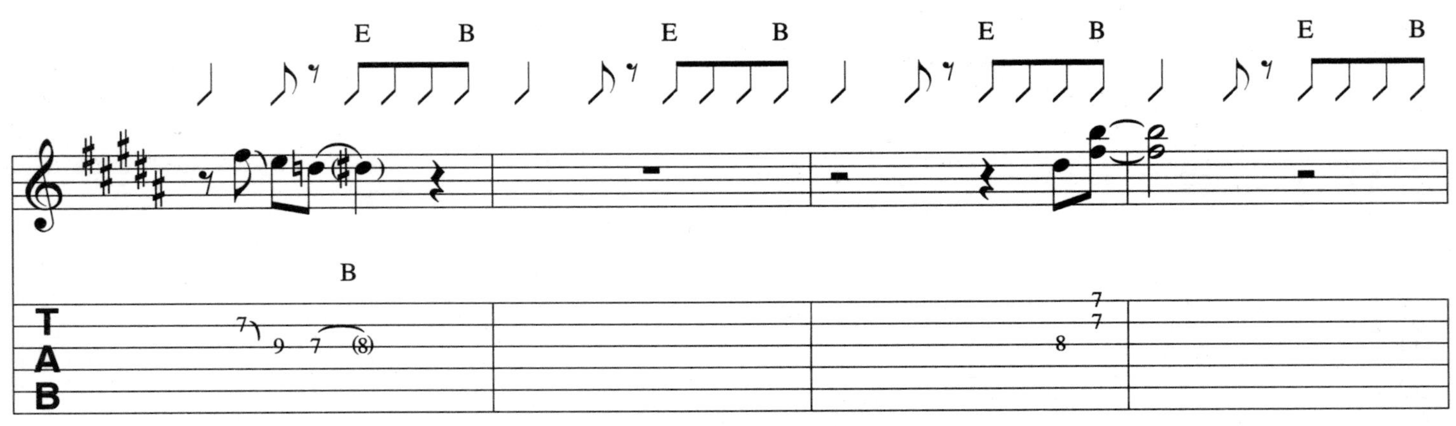
E
B
E
B
E
B
E
B
B
T
A
B

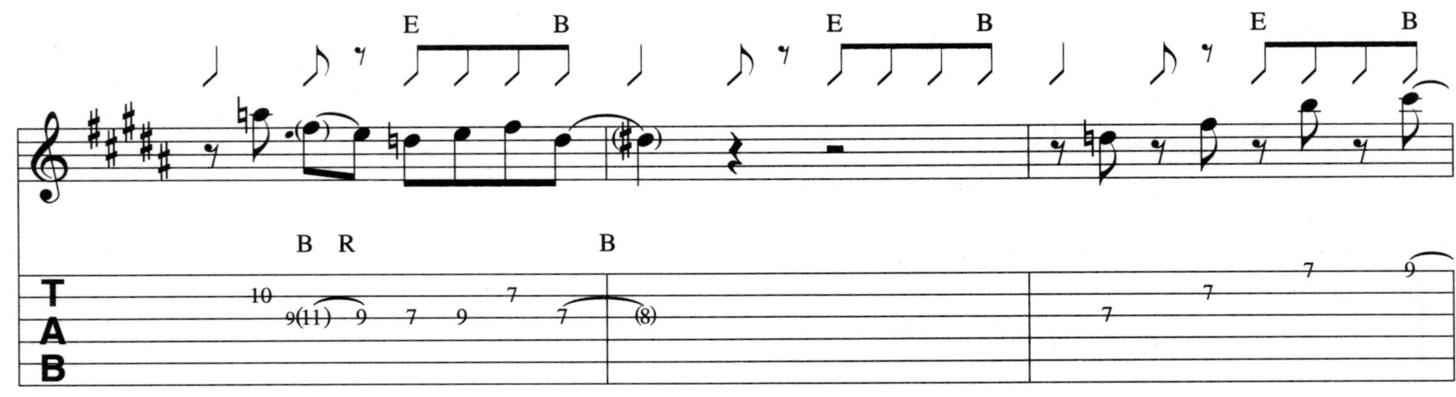
E
B
E
B
E
B
B R
B
T
A
B

E
B
E
B
E
B
B
T
A
B

E B E A/E E A/E
B R B R B R B R B B B R
TAB

E A/E E A/E B E B
B B
TAB

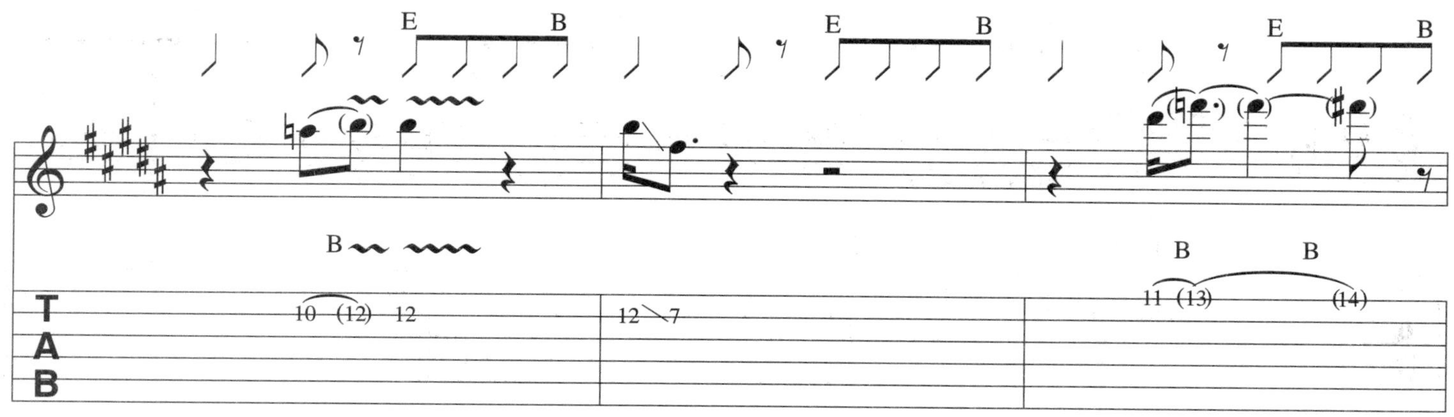
E B E B E B
B B B
TAB

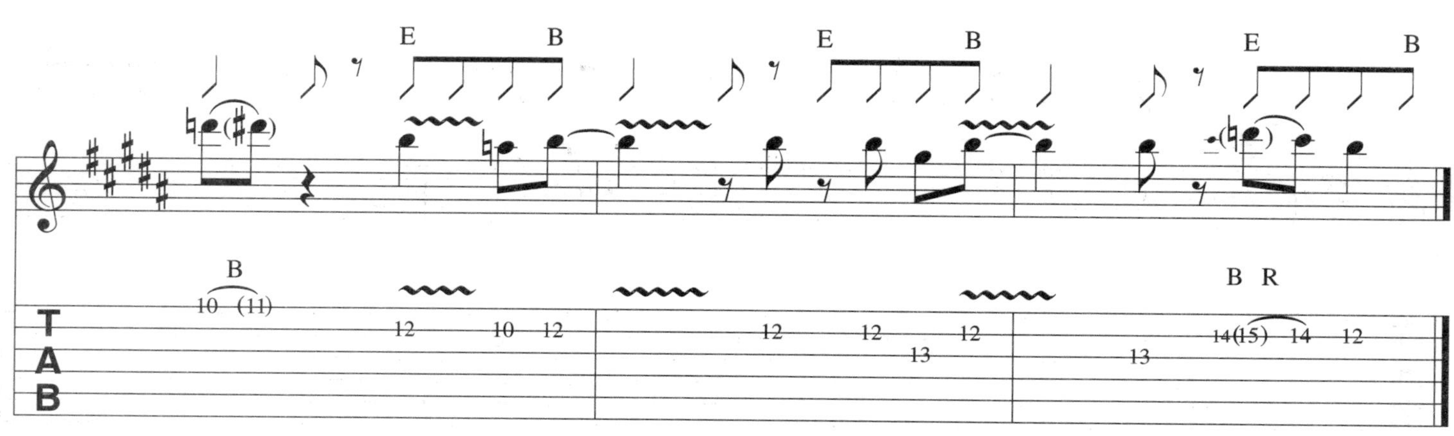
E B E B E B
B B R
TAB

from Layla And Other Assorted Love Songs

Keep On Growin'

Words and Music by Bobby Whitlock and Eric Clapton

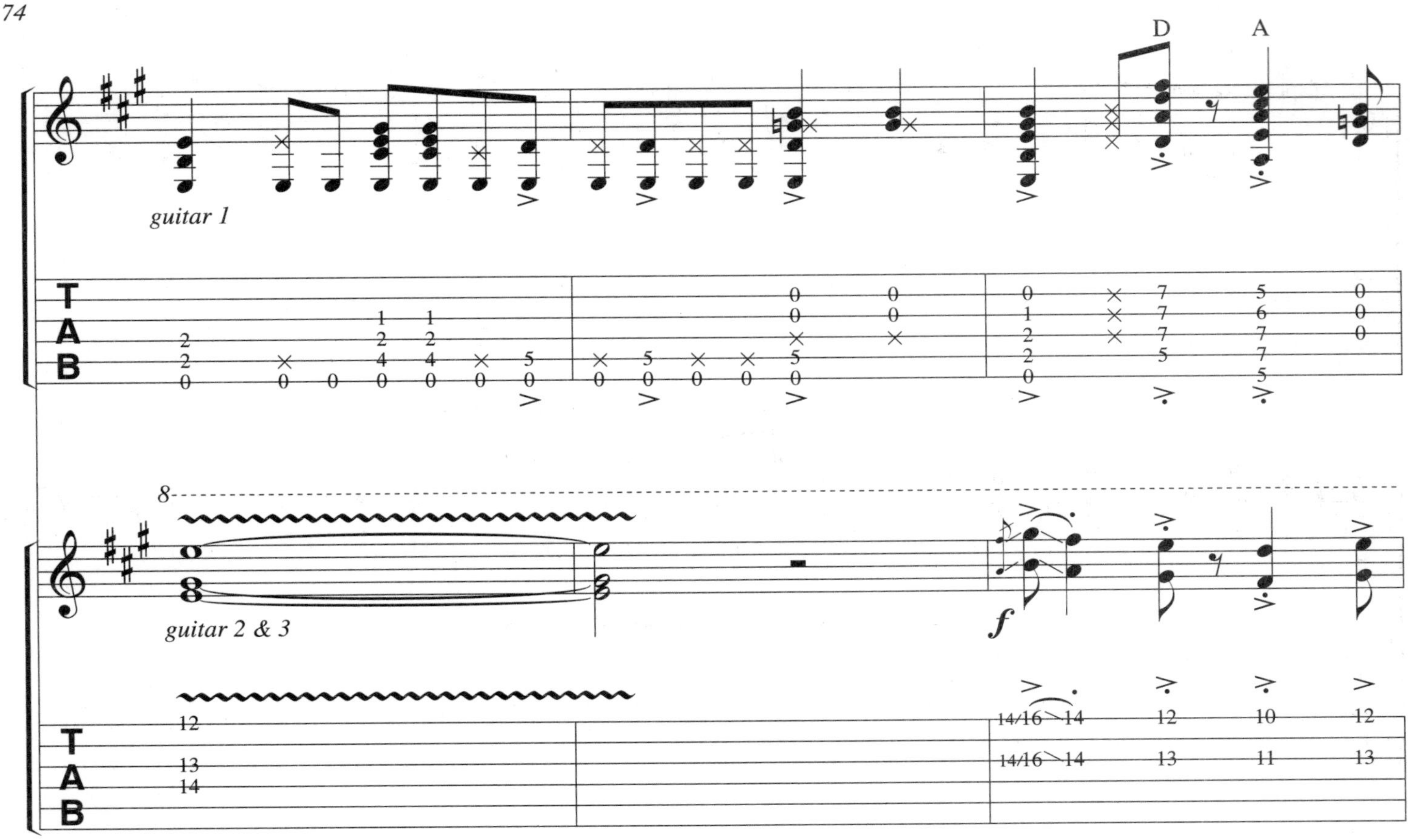

D A

guitar 1

guitar 2 & 3

E N.C.(A) D/A

Whoo!

Rhythm figure 1

Rhythm figure 1a

*guitar 3 plays cue notes

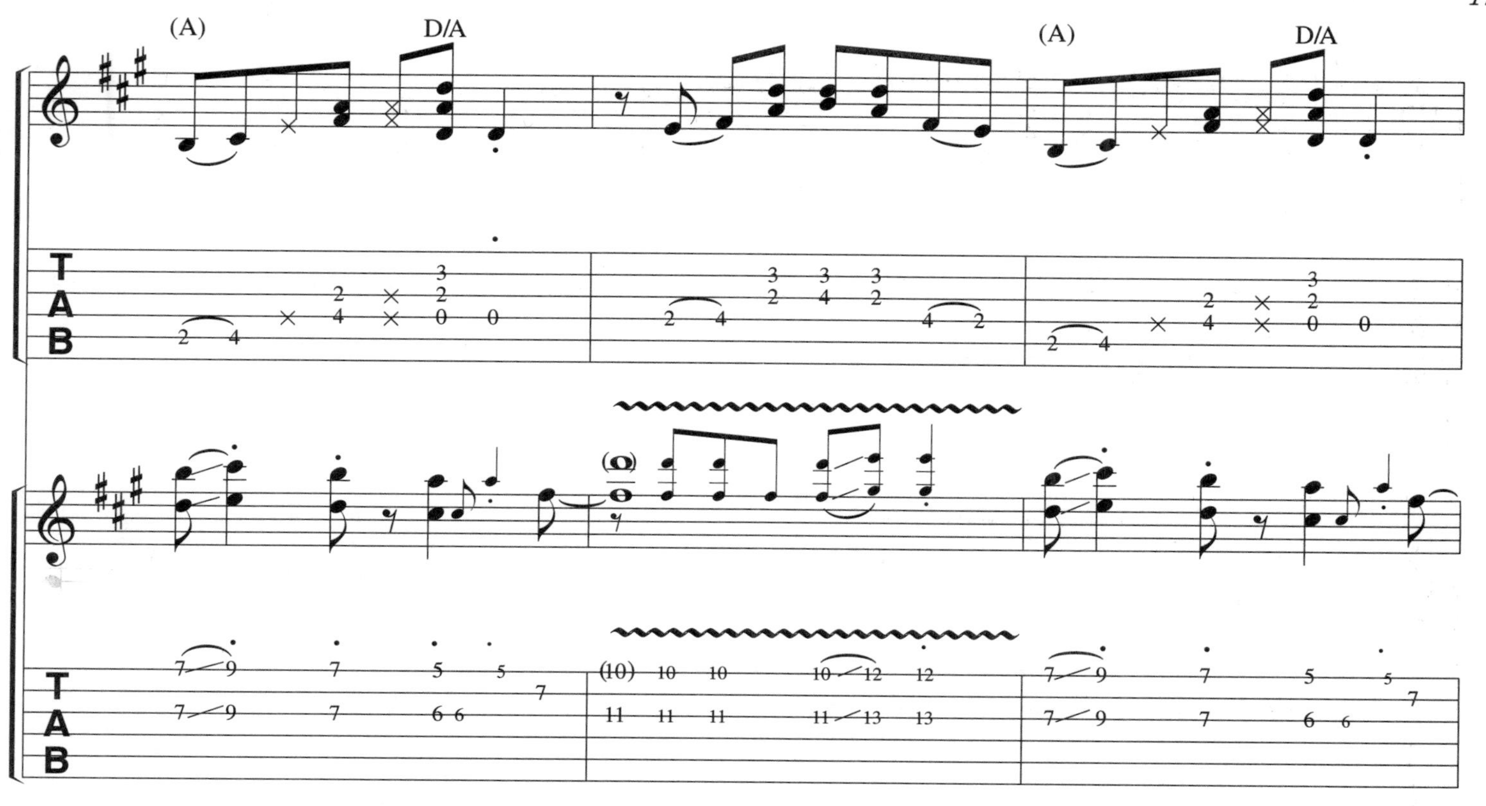

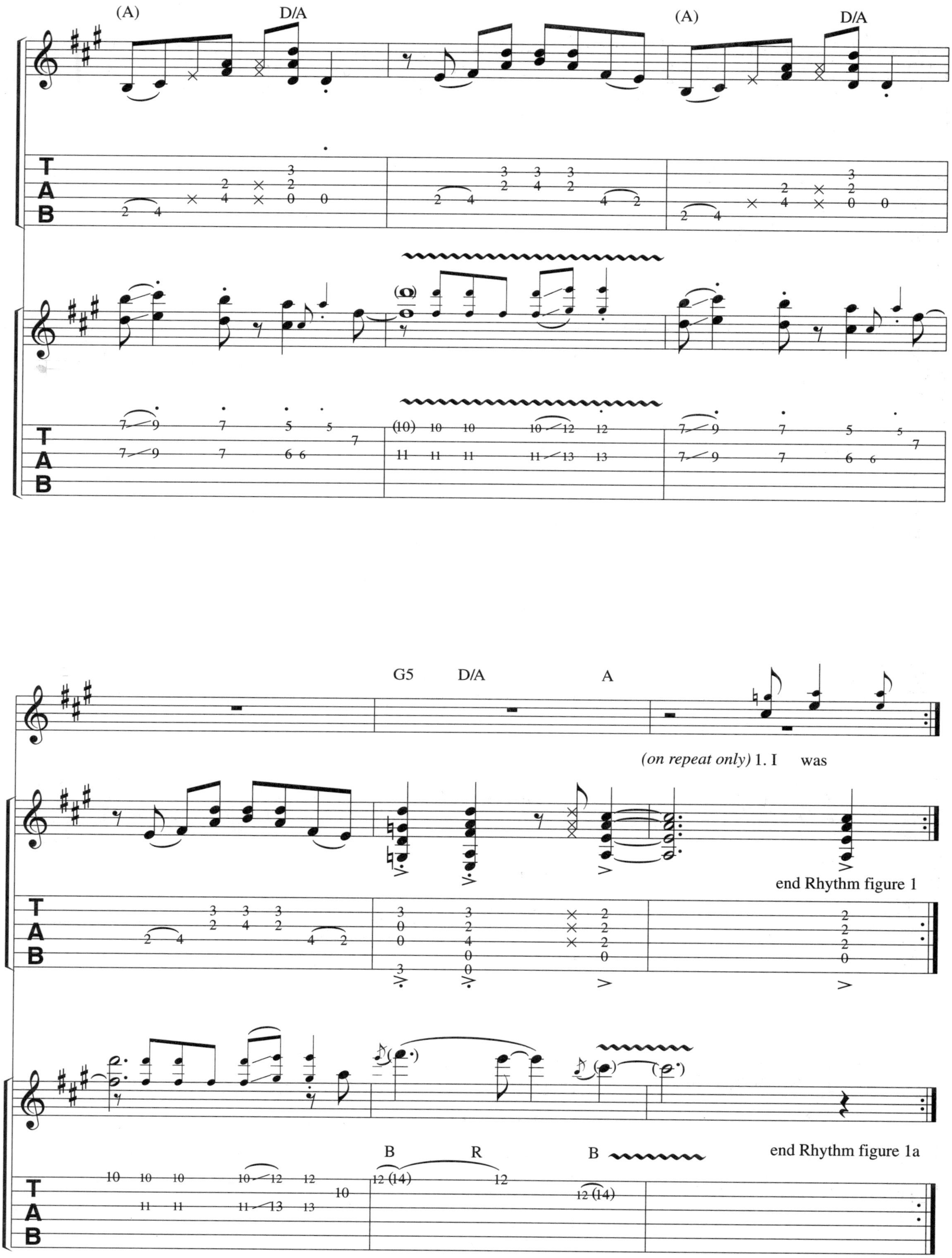
(A)
D/A
(A)
D/A
G5
D/A
A
(on repeat only) 1. I was
end Rhythm figure 1
B
R
B
end Rhythm figure 1a

Verse
⑤open
A
guitar 1 Rhythm figure 2
laugh - in',
(2.) stand - in',
play - in' in the streets.
look - in' in the face
I was un - know - ing,
of one who loved me,
I
guitars 2&3 Rhythm figure 2a
G5
D/A
end Rhythm figure 2
Rhythm figures 2 & 2a simile
did - n't know my fate.
feel ing so a - shamed.
Play - in'
Hop - in'
B hold bend
*guitar 2 cue notes on repeat
the game of love but nev - er real - ly show -
and pray - in', Lord that she could un - der - stand
to Coda
in',
me,
I thought that love could wait.
but I did - n't know her name.

Pre-chorus 1
guitar 1 Rhythm figure 3

D
F♯m
told me,
"Let me find a way.
Yes you did,
B B B B B B B B R
17(19) 17(19) 17 17(19) 17 17(19) 17 17(19) 17 17(19) 17(19) 17(19) 17 17
B
10 12(14) 12
⑤2fr./⑥open
B/E
4fr.
C♯/E
5fr.
D/E
7fr.
E
Aye, hey, yeah, yeah!"
Oh, yes you did.
B B R B B B
17(19) 17(19) 17 16(18) 17 17 17 16(18) 17 17 16(18) 16 11
B B R B B
12(14) 12 (13) 12 10 9 12 12 9 12(14) 12 12 12 15(17)

end Rhythm figure 3
end Vocal figure 1
B/E
C♯/E
D/E
E
Got to keep on
B
B R
Chorus 1
N.C.(A)
D/A
Rhythm figures 1&1a simile
grow - in',
a - keep on
(A)
D/A
grow - in',
a-keep on
grow - in'.
G5
D5
A
D.S. al Coda
2. I was
Coda
Pre-chorus 2
E
Vocal figure 1
guitar 1 Rhythm figure 3
D
A
guitar 2
hold bend
guitar 3

E
D
F♯m
B/E
C♯/E
D/E
E

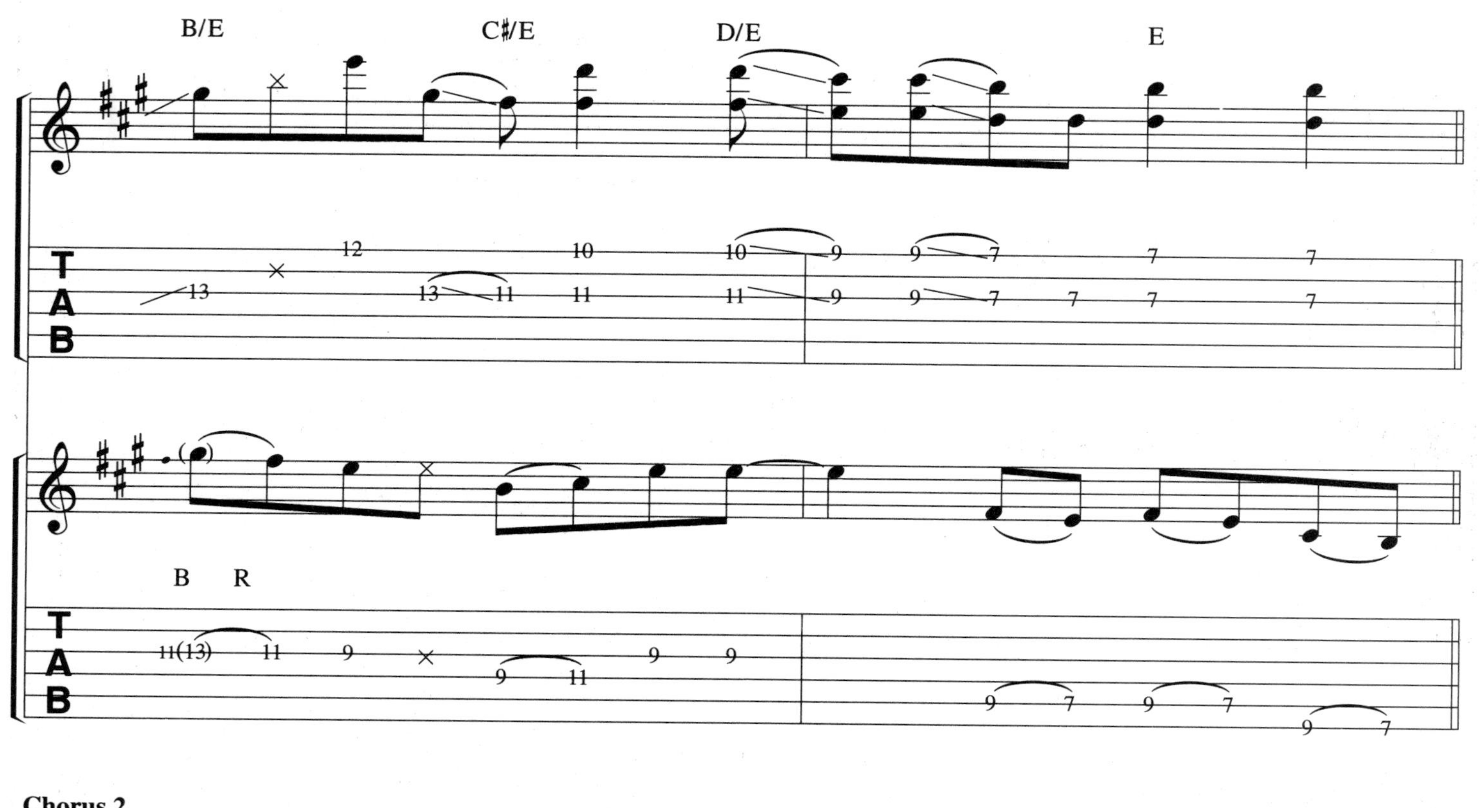

Chorus 2

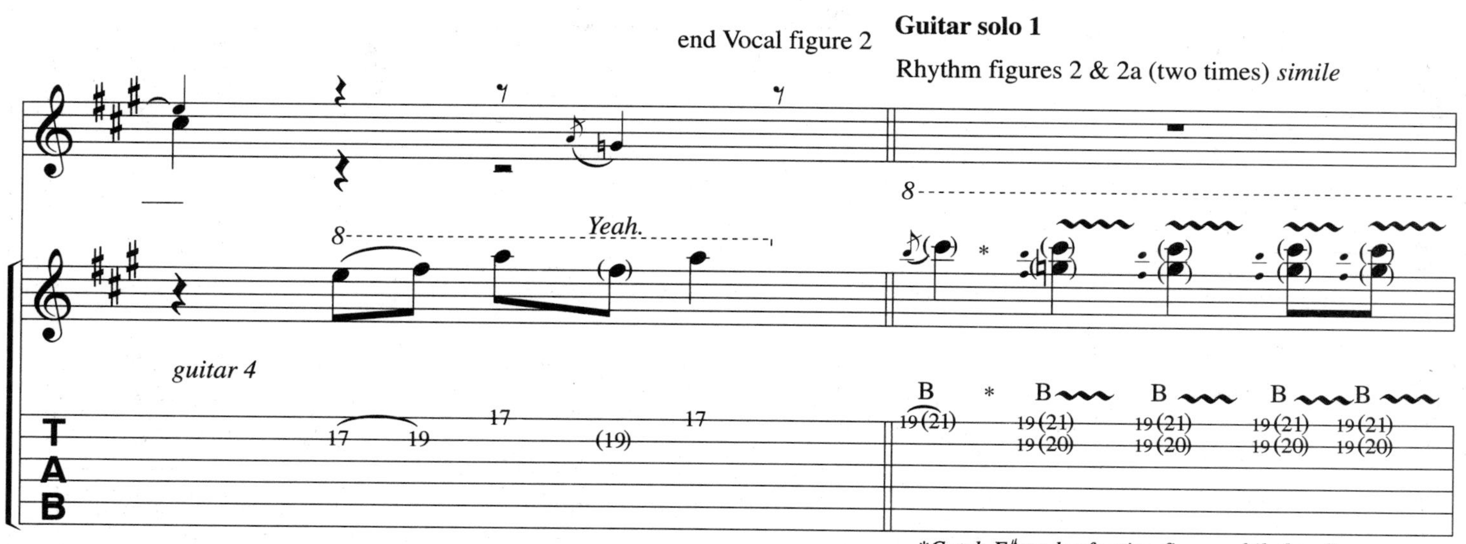

**Catch F♯ under fretting finger while bending B♮ (1st stg.), raising it's pitch approx. 1/2 step.*

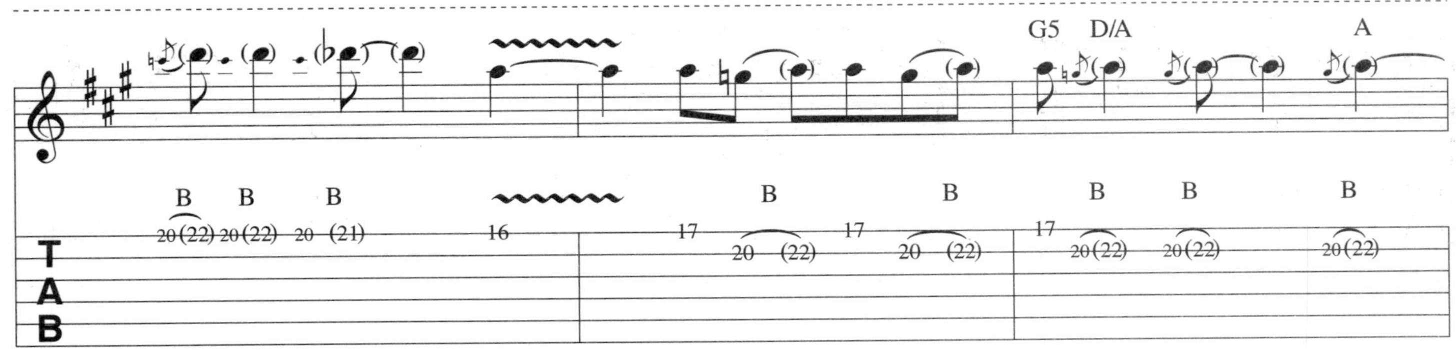
G5
D/A
A

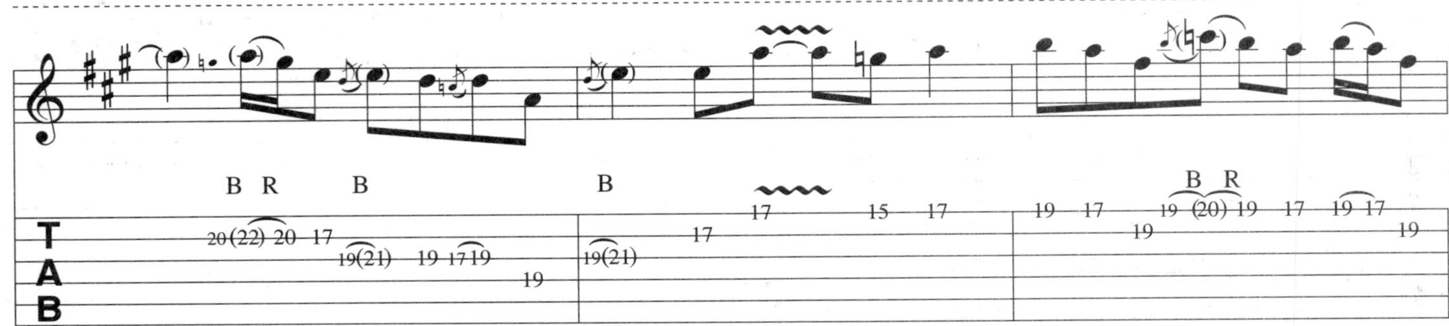

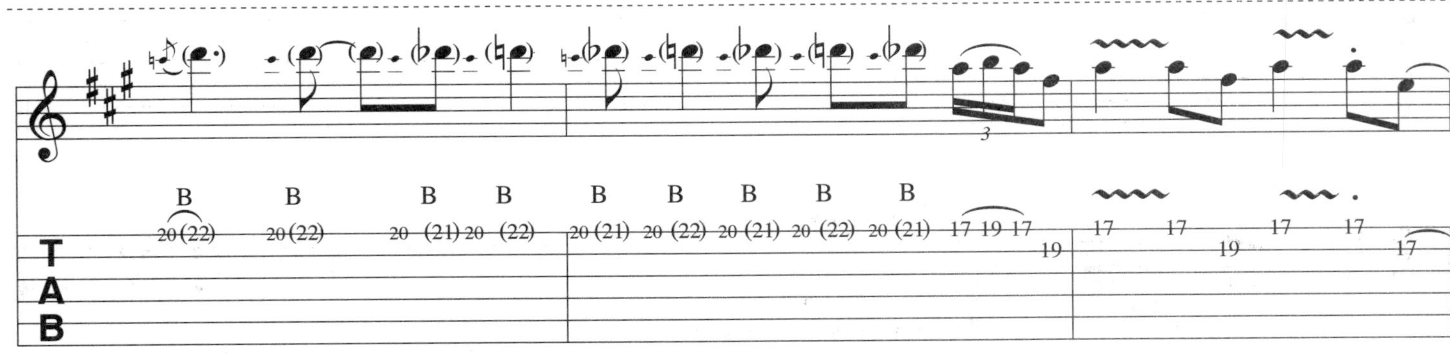

G5
D/A
A

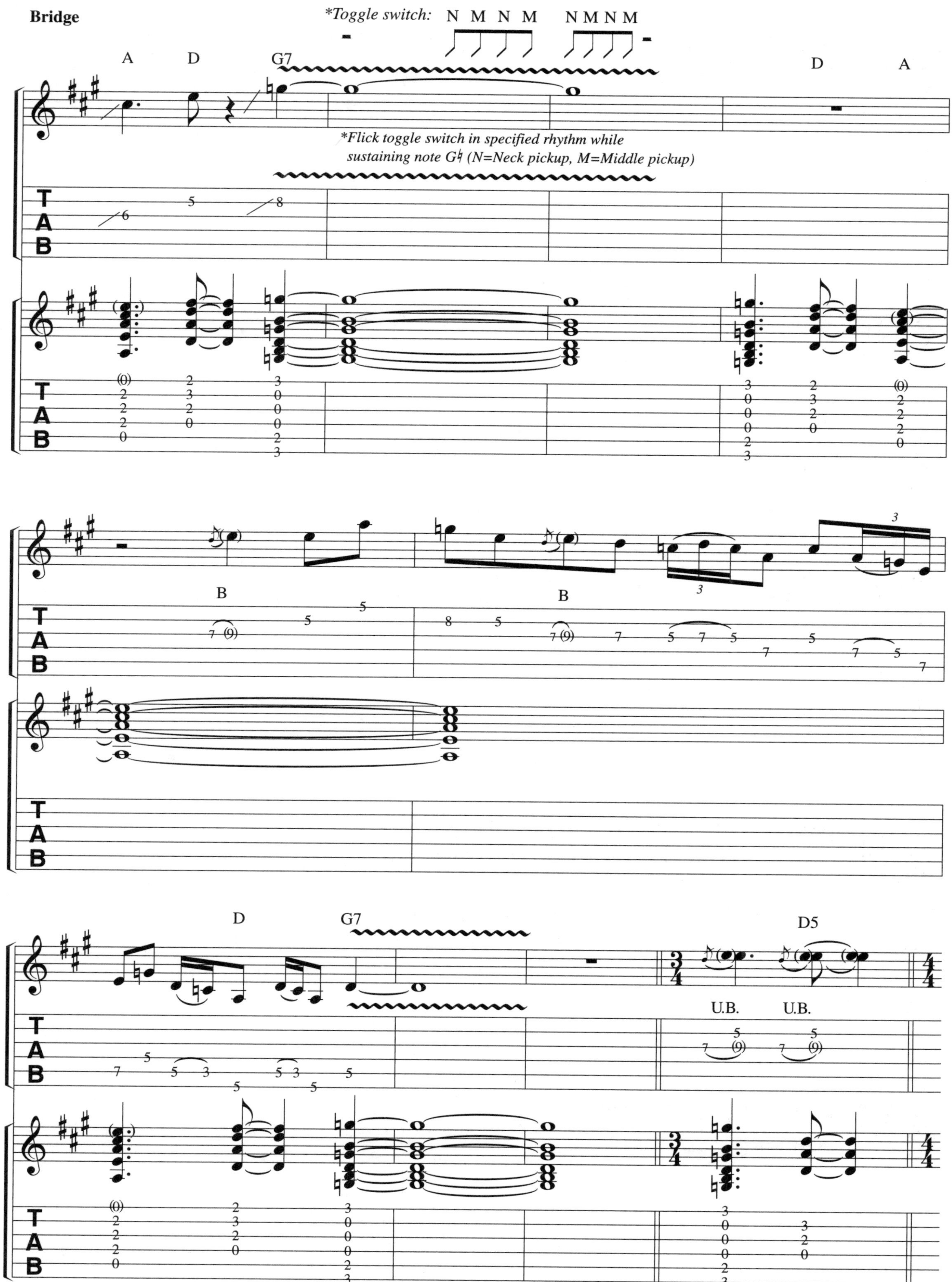
Bridge
*Toggle switch: N M N M N M N M
A
D
G7
D
A
*Flick toggle switch in specified rhythm while sustaining note G♮ (N=Neck pickup, M=Middle pickup)
B
B
D
G7
D5
U.B.
U.B.

E
guitar 1
guitar 2
U.B.
guitar 3
guitar 4
B
8
loco

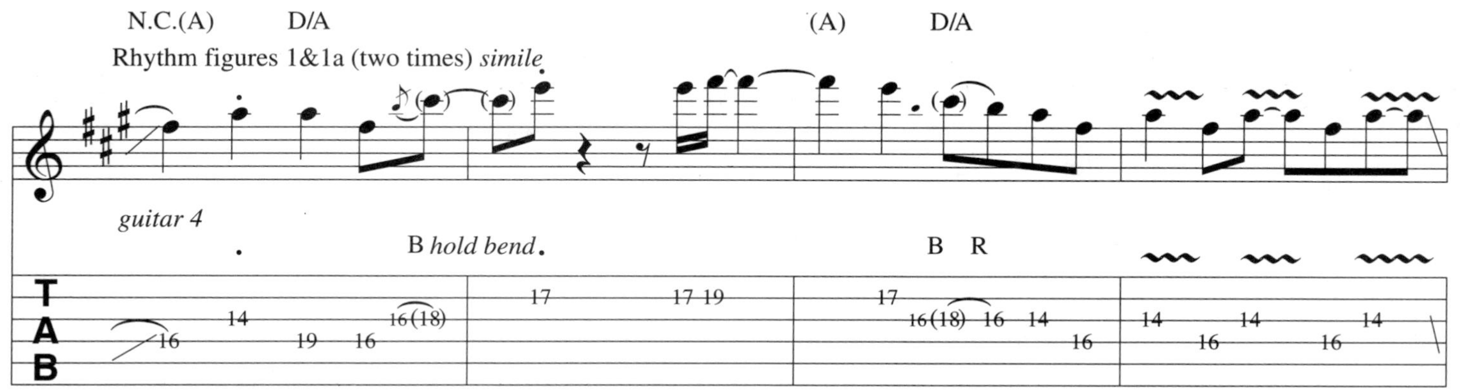
N.C.(A)
D/A
(A)
D/A
Rhythm figures 1&1a (two times) simile
guitar 4
B hold bend.
B R

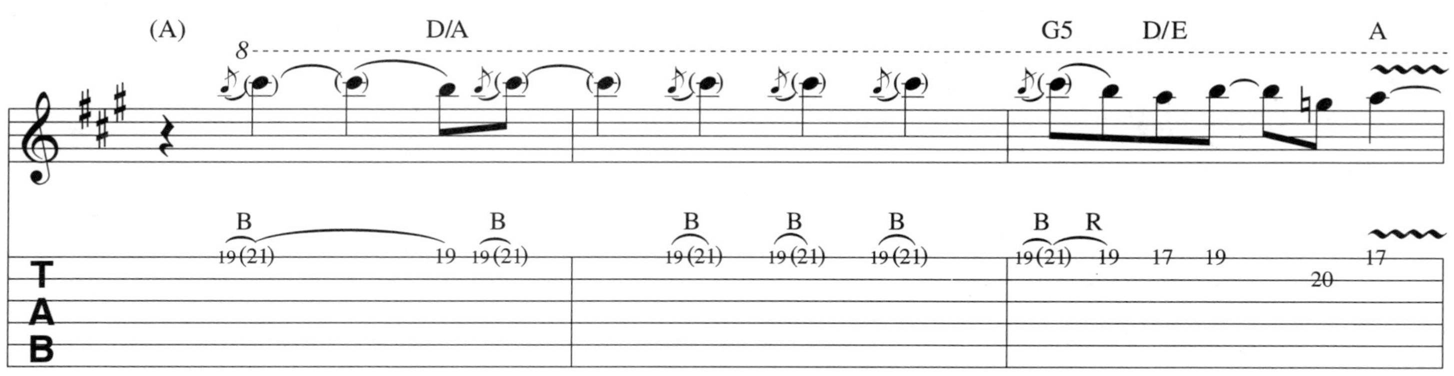
(A)
D/A
G5
D/E
A
B
B R

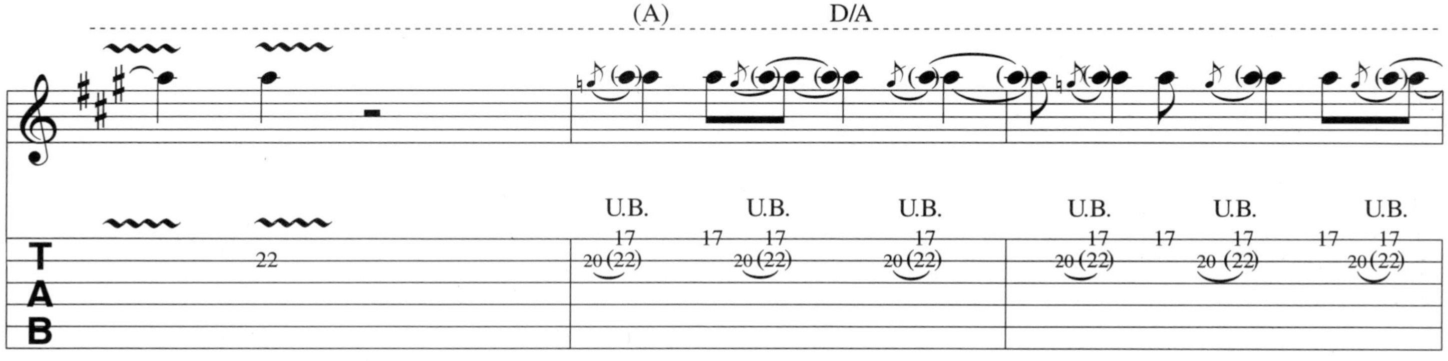
(A)
D/A
U.B.

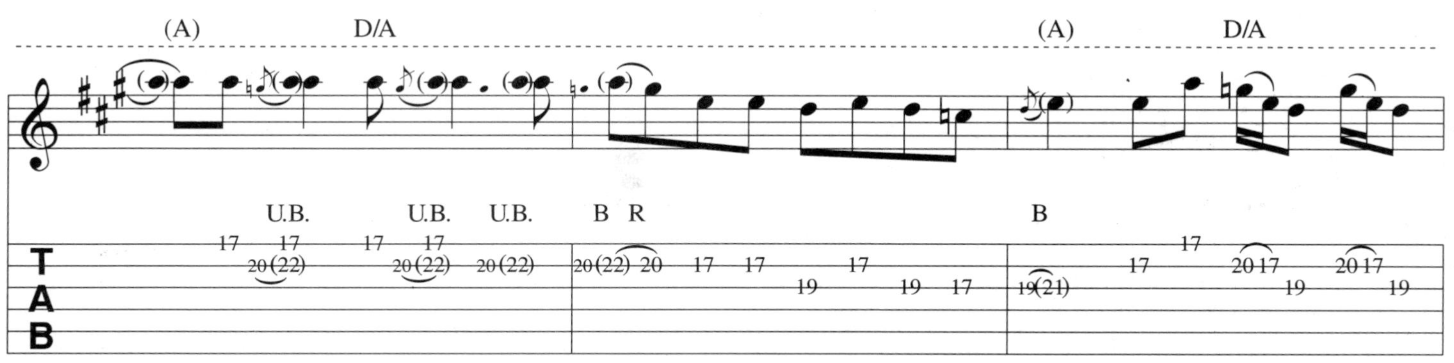
(A)
D/A
U.B.
B R
B

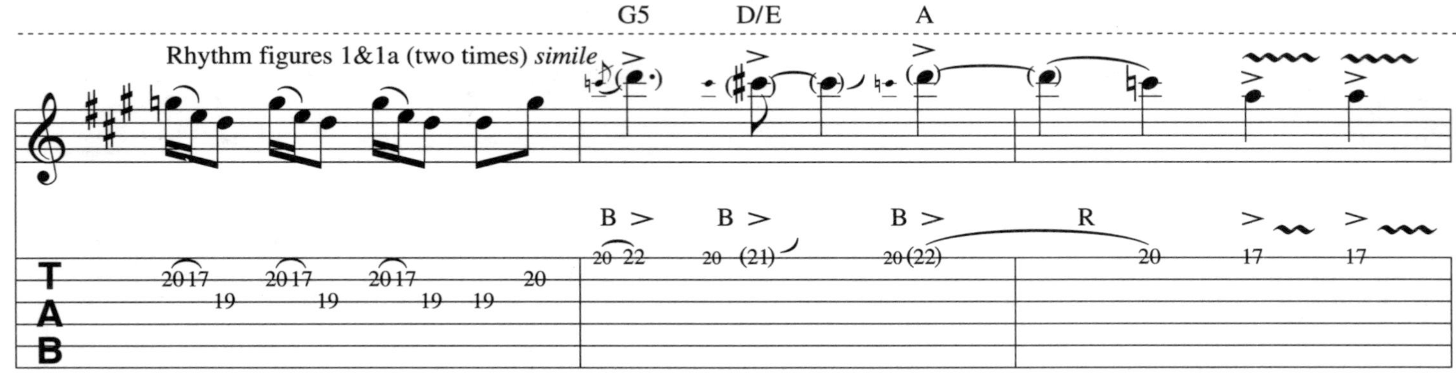
G5 D/E A
Rhythm figures 1&1a (two times) simile
B B B R
20 17 19 20 17 19 20 17 19 19 20
20 22 20 (21) 20 (22) 20 17 17

Verse 3

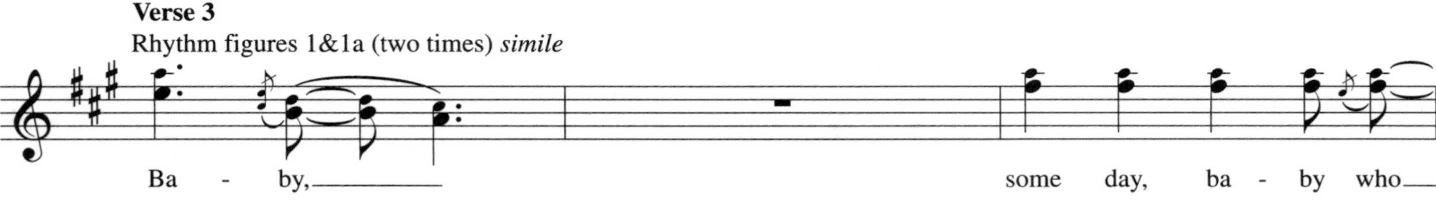
Rhythm figures 1&1a (two times) simile
Ba - by,
some day, ba - by who

knows where or when, Lord?

Just you wait and see. We'll be walk - ing

to - geth - er hand in hand, a - lone for - ev–

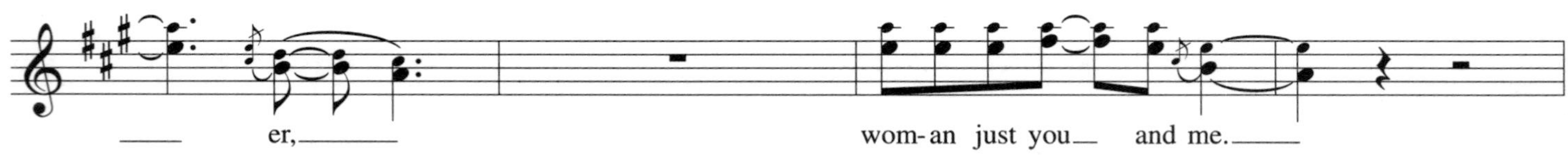
er,
wom-an just you and me.

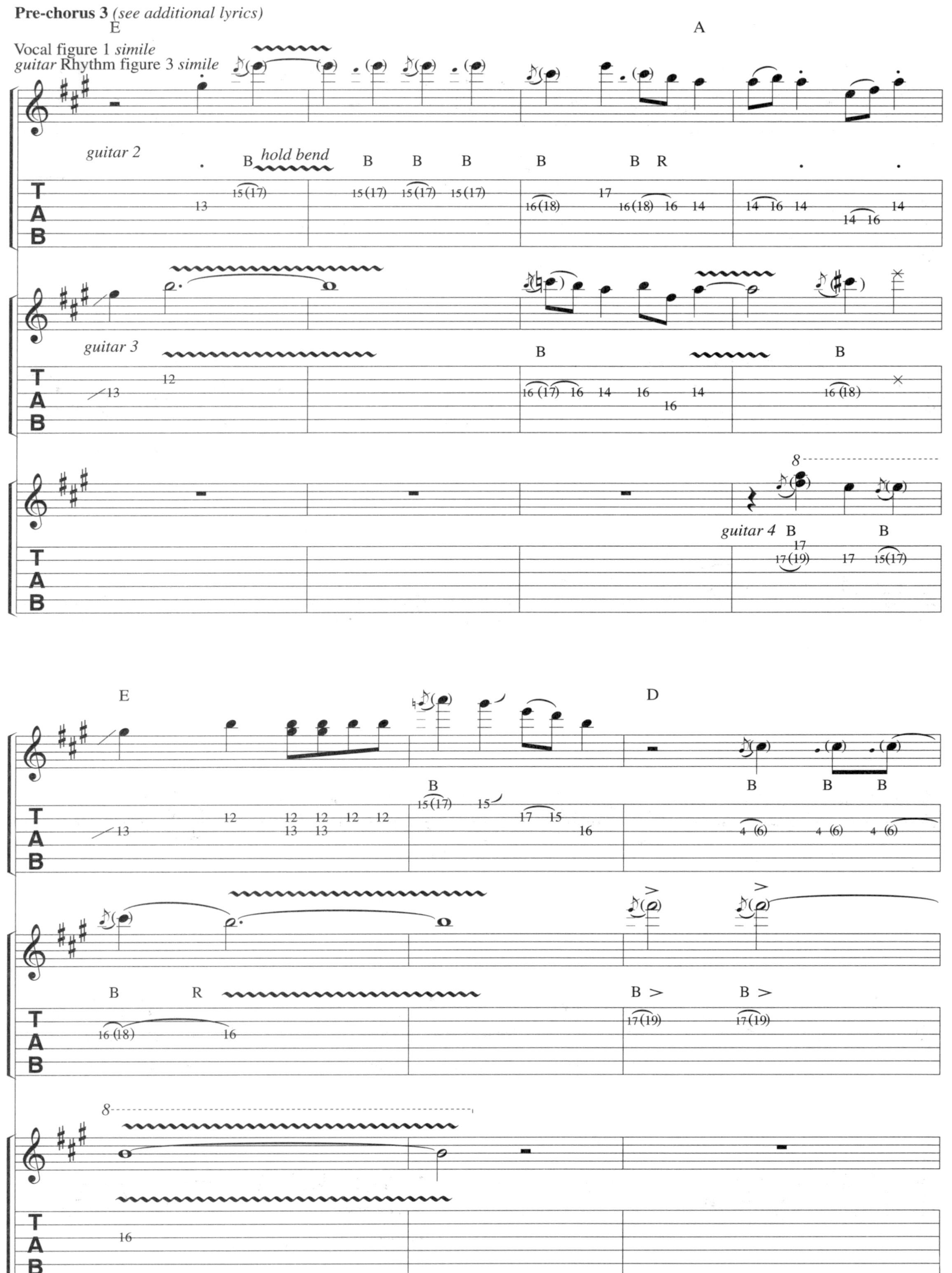
Pre-chorus 3 (see additional lyrics)
E
A
Vocal figure 1 simile
guitar Rhythm figure 3 simile
guitar 2
hold bend
B B B B B B R
guitar 3
B B
8
guitar 4 B B
E
D
B B B B
B R
B > B >
8

F♯m
B/E
C♯/E
D/E
E
B/E
C♯/E
D/E
E

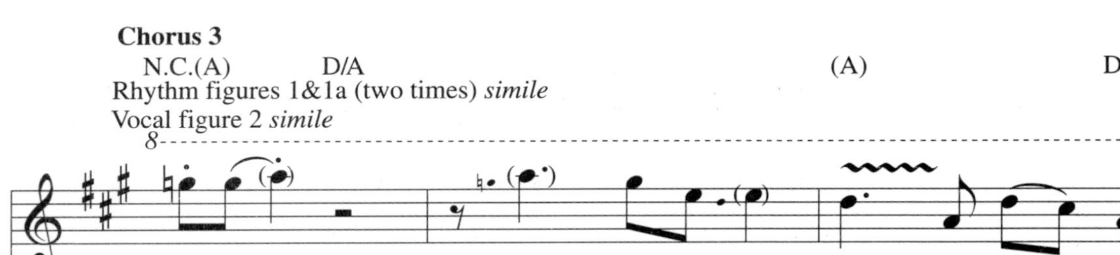
Chorus 3
N.C.(A)
D/A
(A)
D/A
Rhythm figures 1&1a (two times) simile
Vocal figure 2 simile

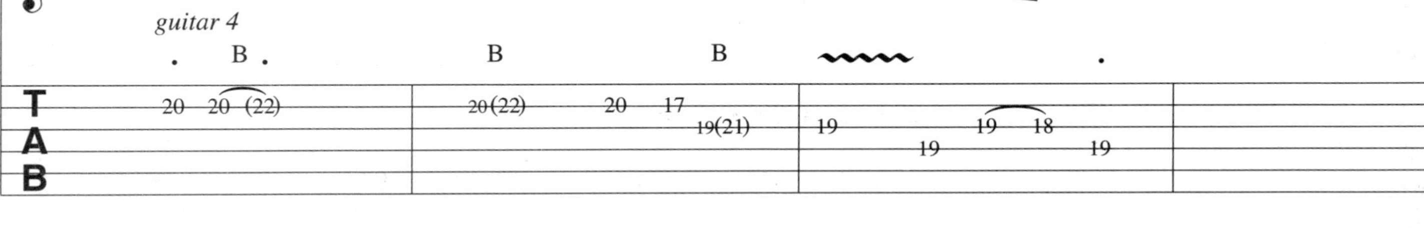
guitar 4

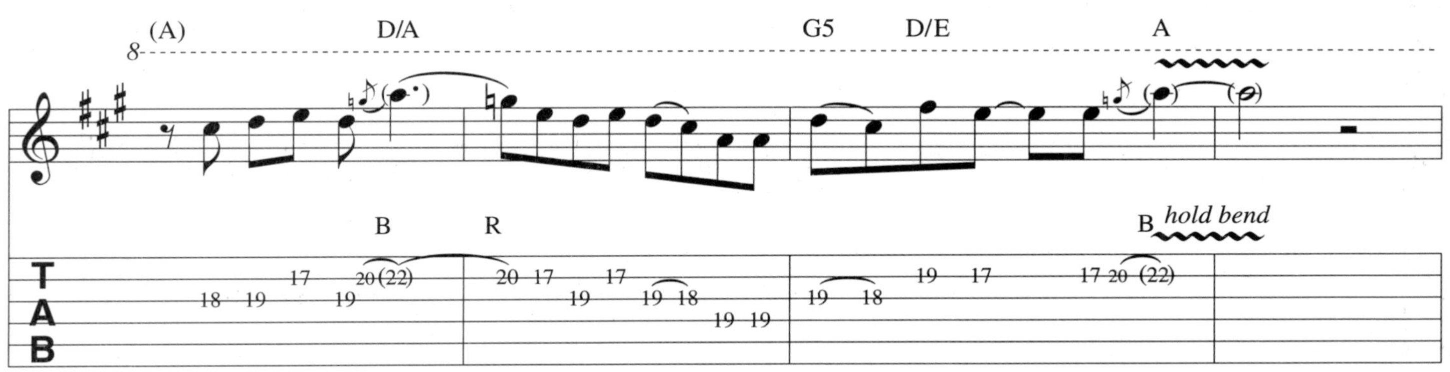
(A)
D/A
G5
D/E
A
hold bend

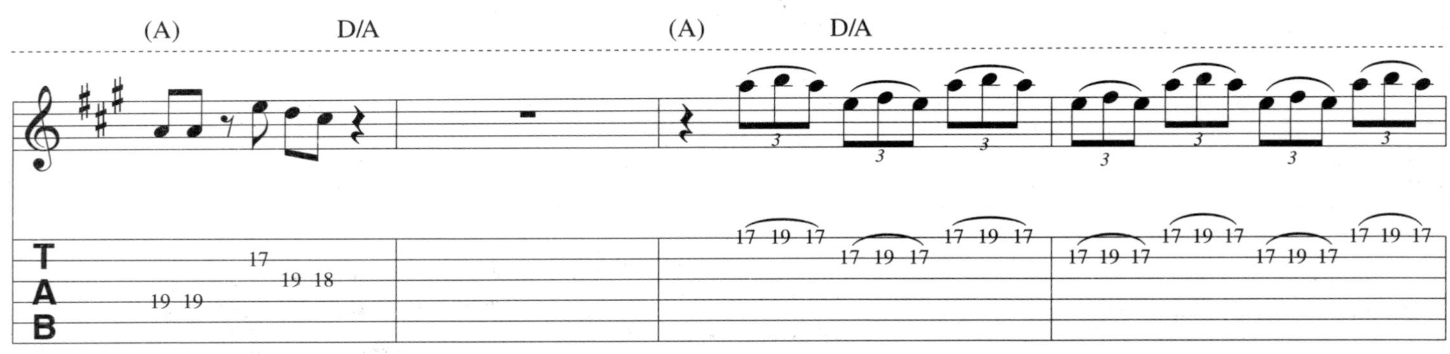
(A)
D/A
(A)
D/A

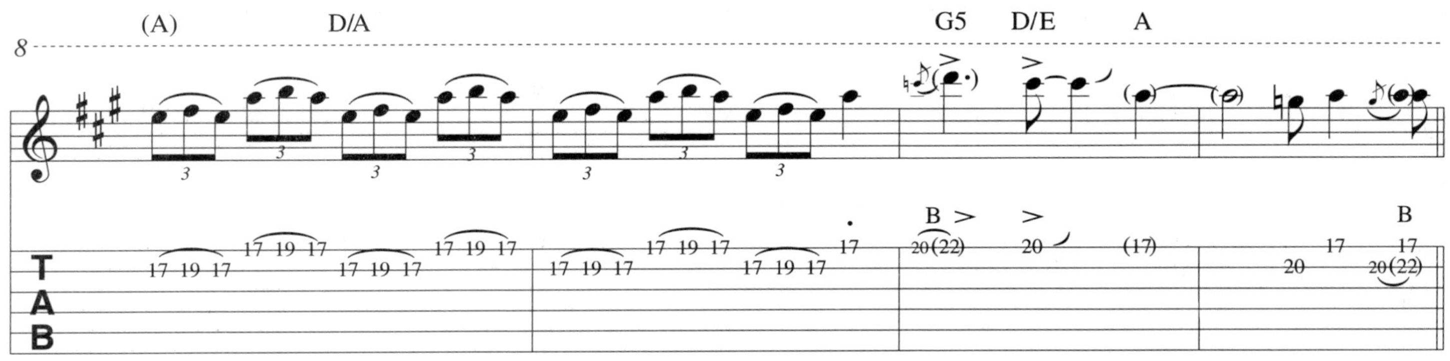
(A)
D/A
G5
D/E
A

Guitar solo 2
A
D
A
rhythm simile
guitar 2
hold bend
guitar 3
hold bend
guitar 4
D
A
D
U.B.

Additional lyrics

2nd Pre-chorus

She took my hand in hers
And told me I was wrong
She said, "You're gonna be all right, boy
Whoa, just as long"

3rd Pre-chorus

'Cause time's gonna change us, oh
And I know it's true
Our love's gonna keep on growin' and growin'
And here's all we got to do

from Crossroads

Knockin' On Heaven's Door

Words and Music by Bob Dylan

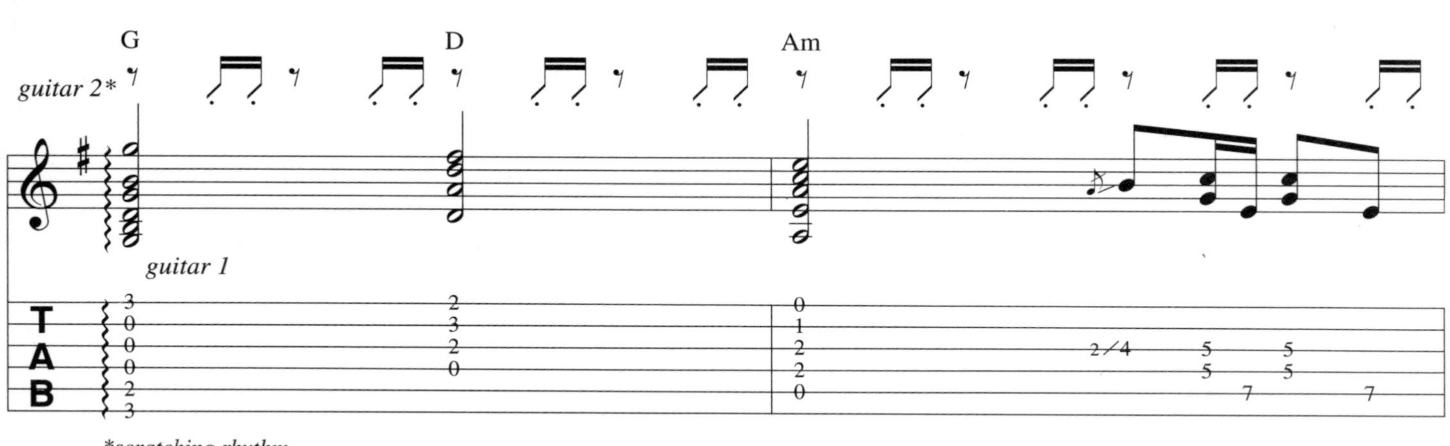

*scratching rhythm

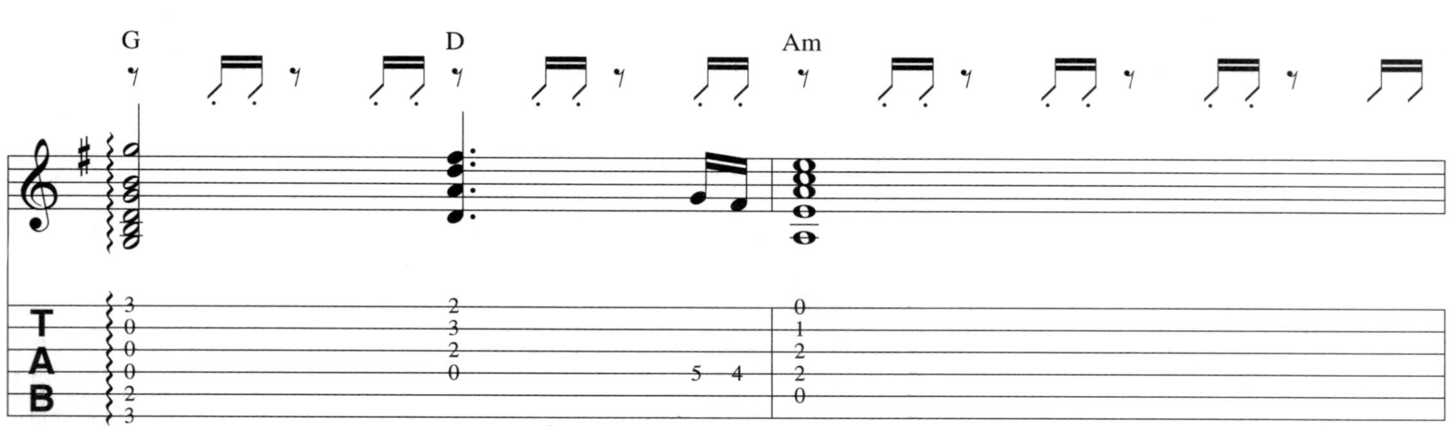

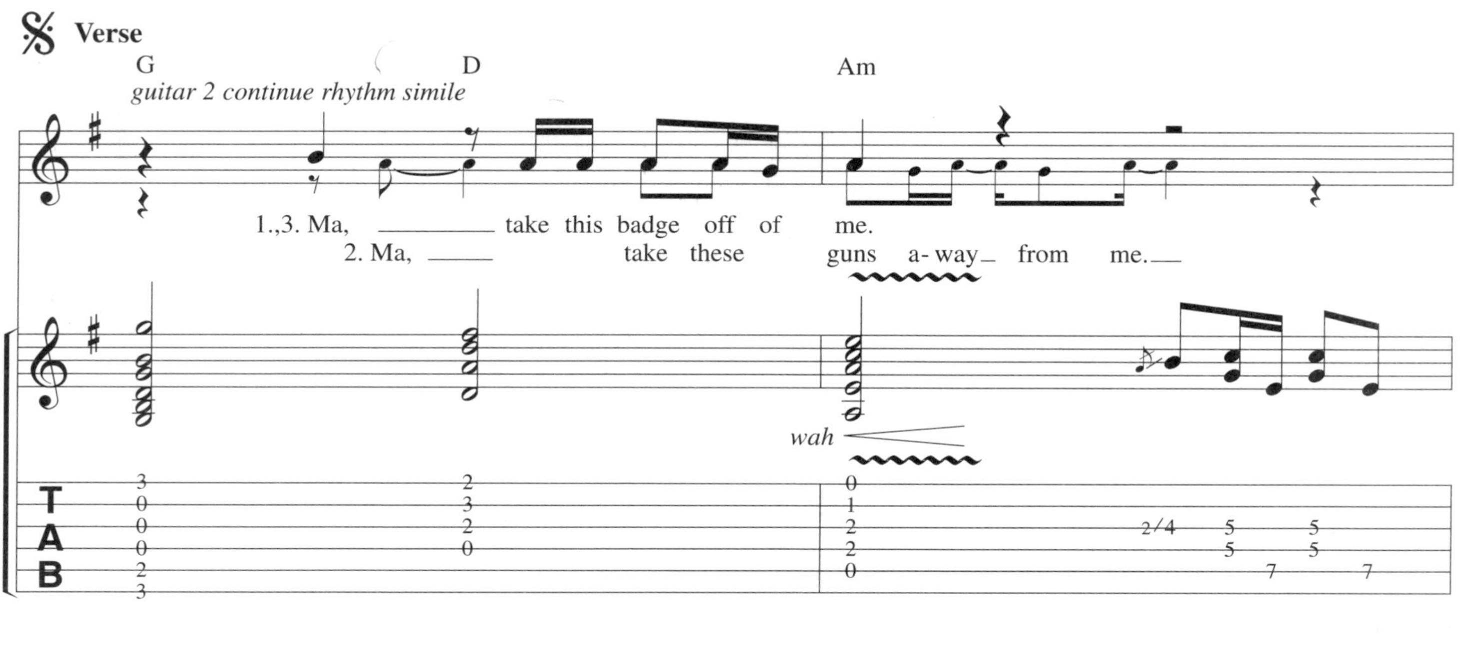

Verse
G
D
Am
guitar 2 continue rhythm simile
1.,3. Ma, take this badge off of me.
2. Ma, take these guns a-way from me.
wah
T
A
B

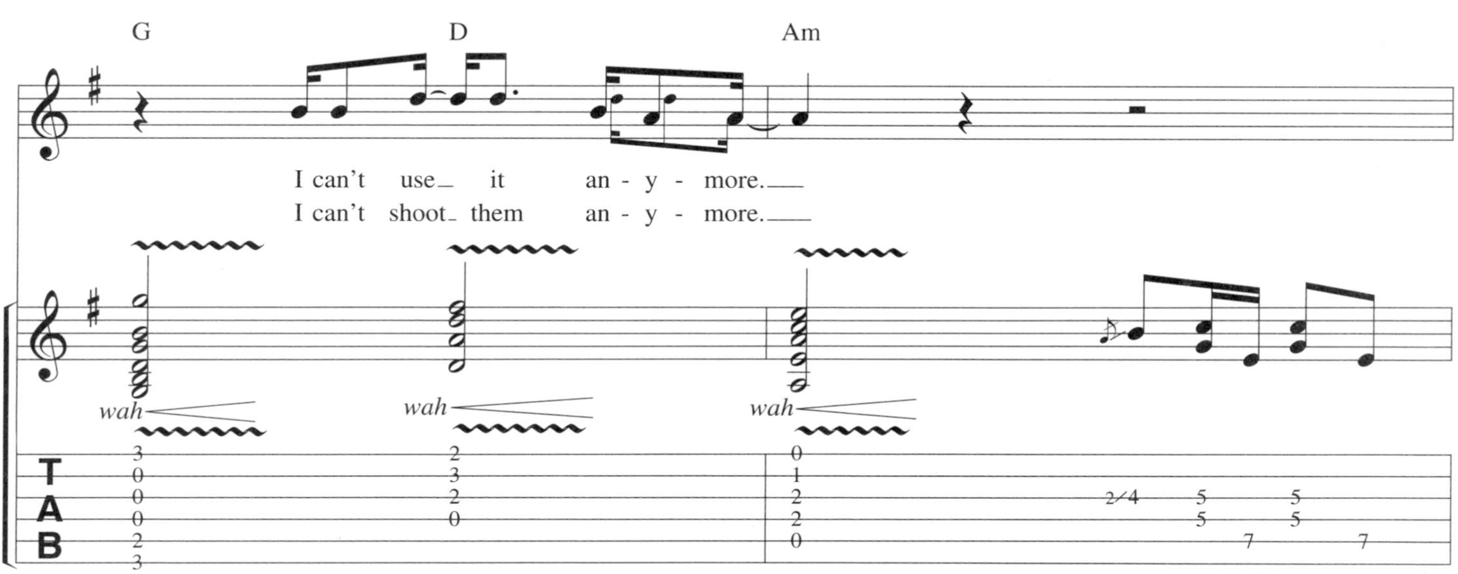

G
D
Am
I can't use it an - y - more.
I can't shoot them an - y - more.
wah
wah
wah

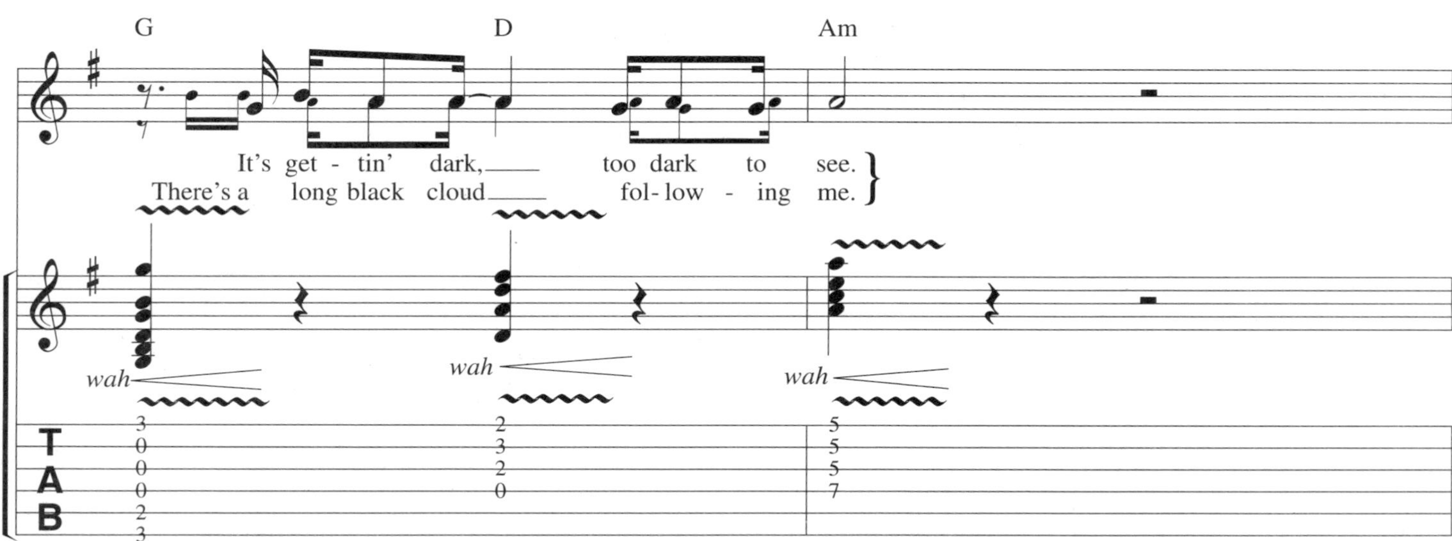

G
D
Am
It's get - tin' dark, too dark to see.
There's a long black cloud fol - low - ing me.
wah
wah
wah

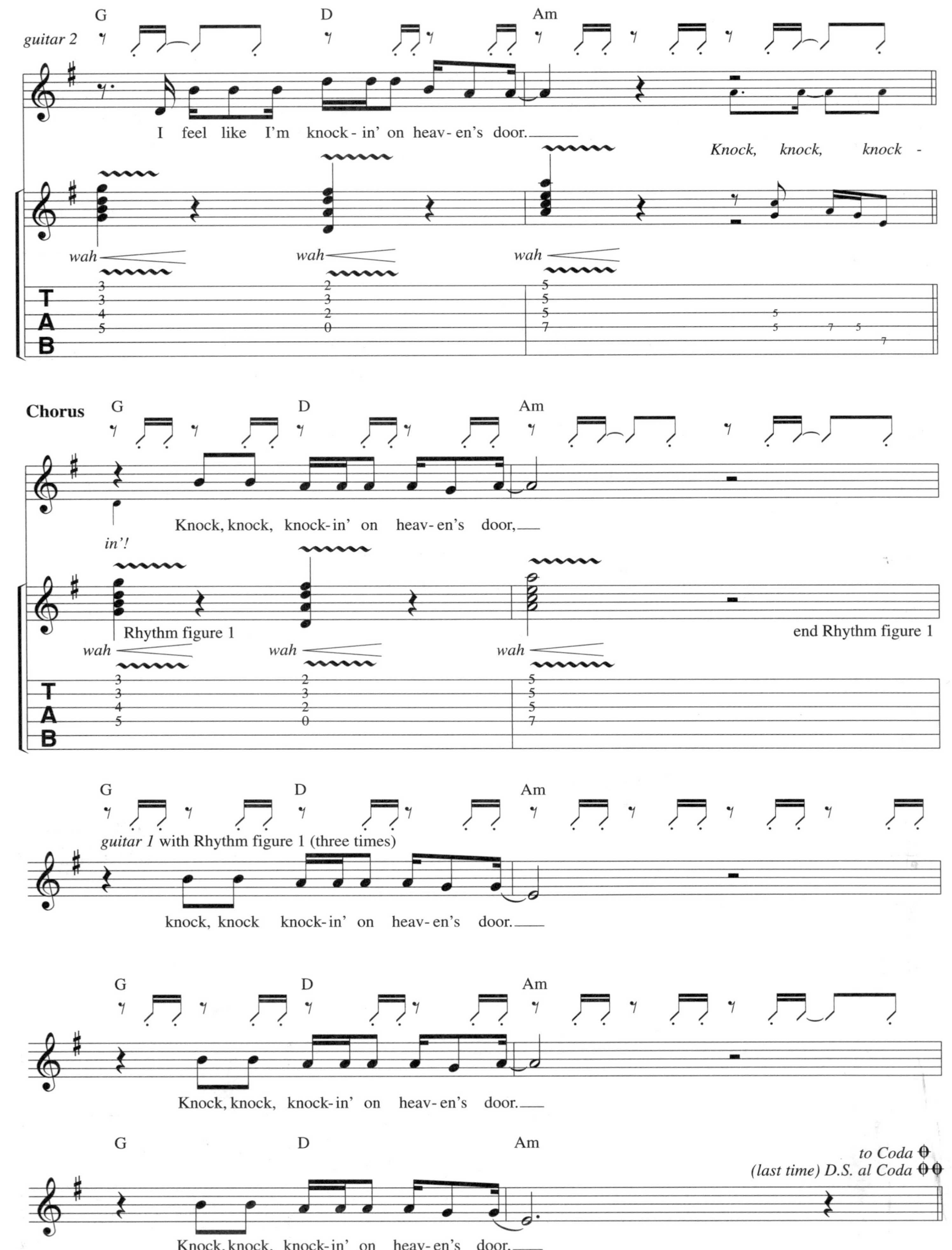
G
D
Am
guitar 2
I feel like I'm knock-in' on heav-en's door.
Knock, knock, knock-
wah
Chorus
Knock, knock, knock-in' on heav-en's door,
in'!
Rhythm figure 1
end Rhythm figure 1
guitar 1 with Rhythm figure 1 (three times)
knock, knock knock-in' on heav-en's door.
Knock, knock, knock-in' on heav-en's door.
to Coda
(last time) D.S. al Coda
Knock, knock, knock-in' on heav-en's door,

Coda
Guitar solo
guitars 1 and 2 continue simile
G D Am G D
guitar 3 with slide
Am G D Am
guitar 3 tacet
guitar 4
G D Am G D
guitar 3
guitar 4
Am G D Am
D.S. (first verse) to Coda
guitar 4 tacet
guitar 3
Coda
G D Am
play four times
G
Ooh, ooh, ooh, ooh!
3rd time
4th time

from Layla And Other Assorted Love Songs

Layla

Words and Music by Eric Clapton and Jim Gordon

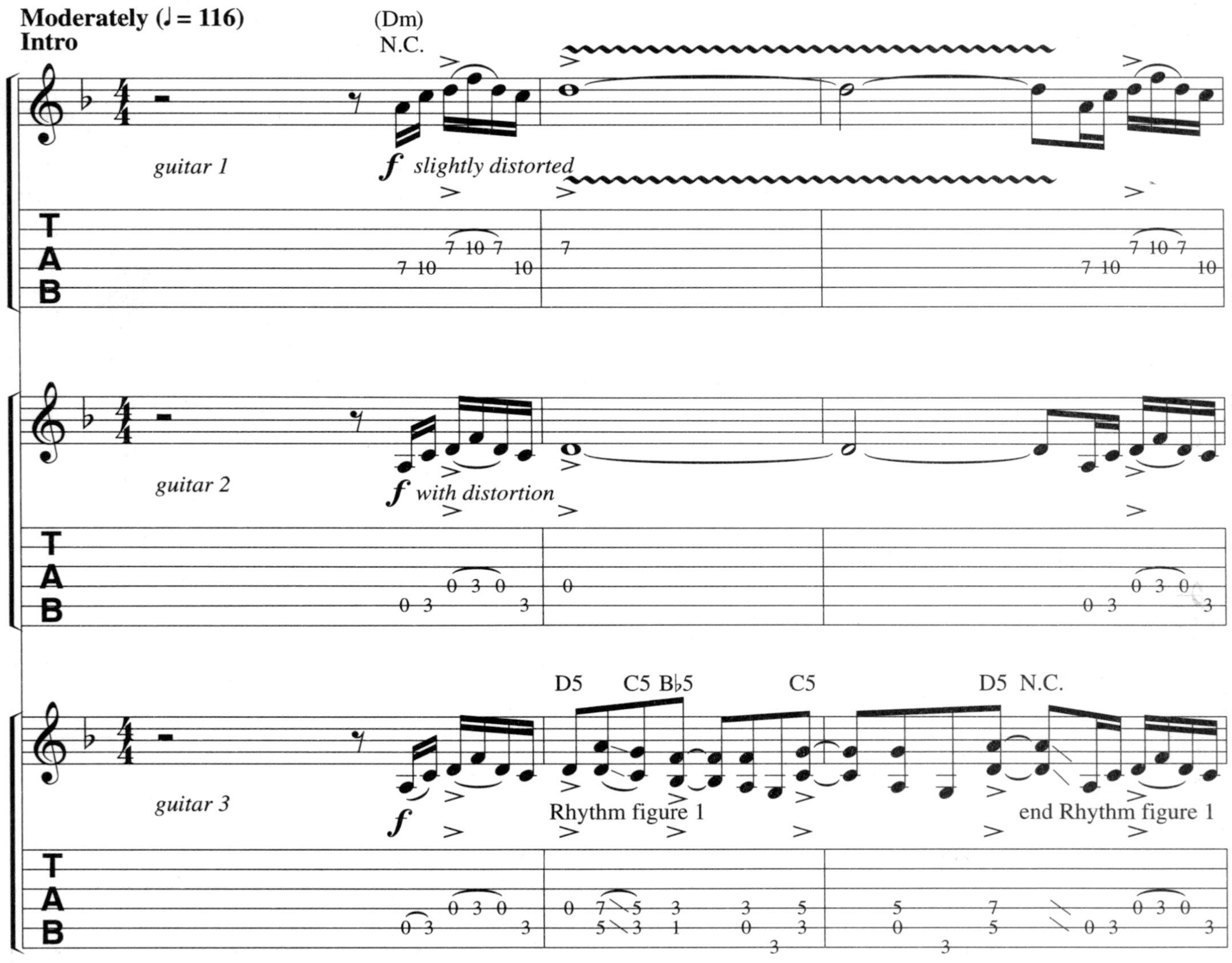

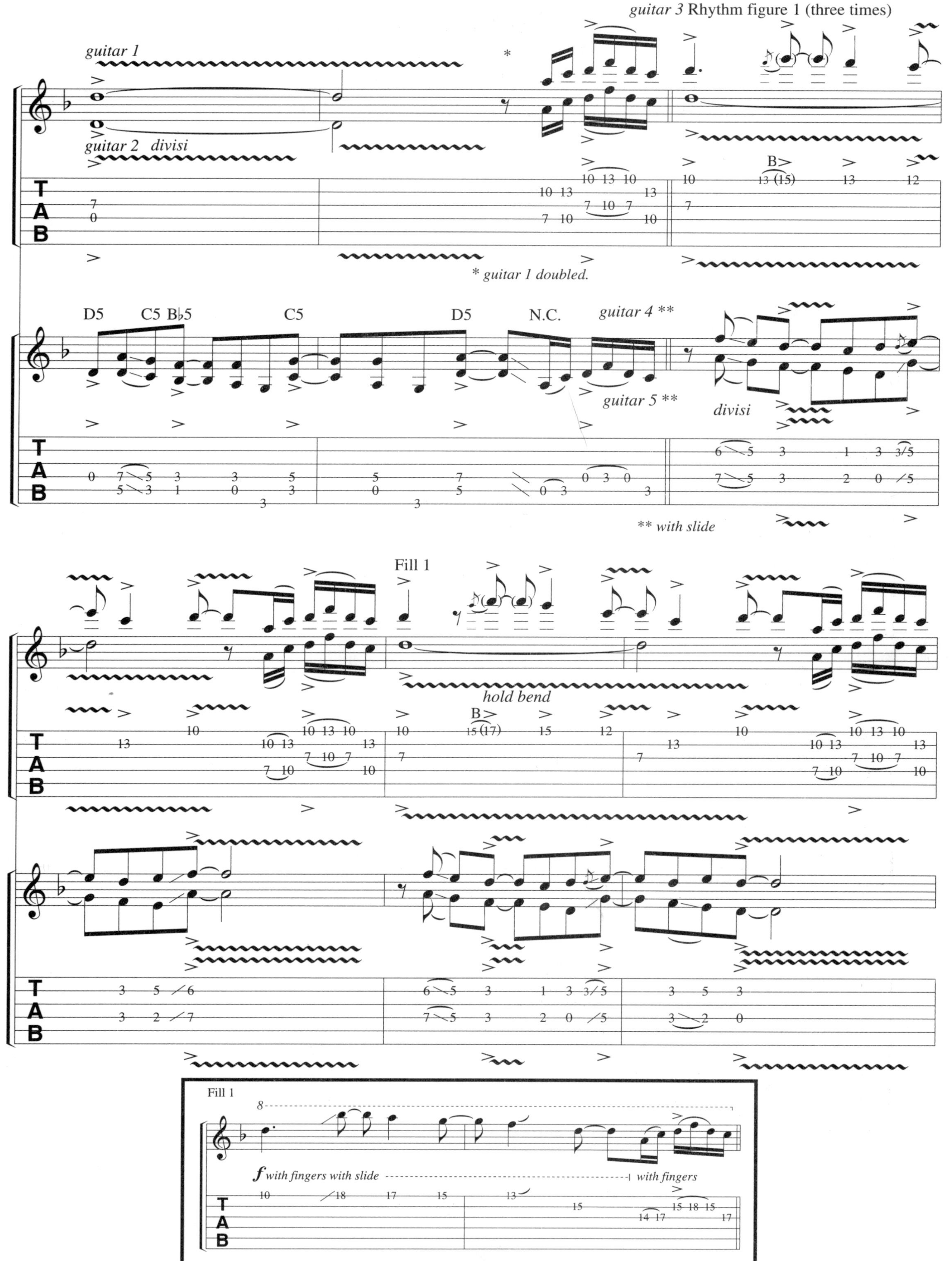
guitar 3 Rhythm figure 1 (three times)
guitar 1
guitar 2 divisi
* guitar 1 doubled.
D5
C5
B♭5
C5
D5
N.C.
guitar 4 **
guitar 5 **
divisi
** with slide
Fill 1
hold bend
Fill 1
f with fingers with slide
with fingers

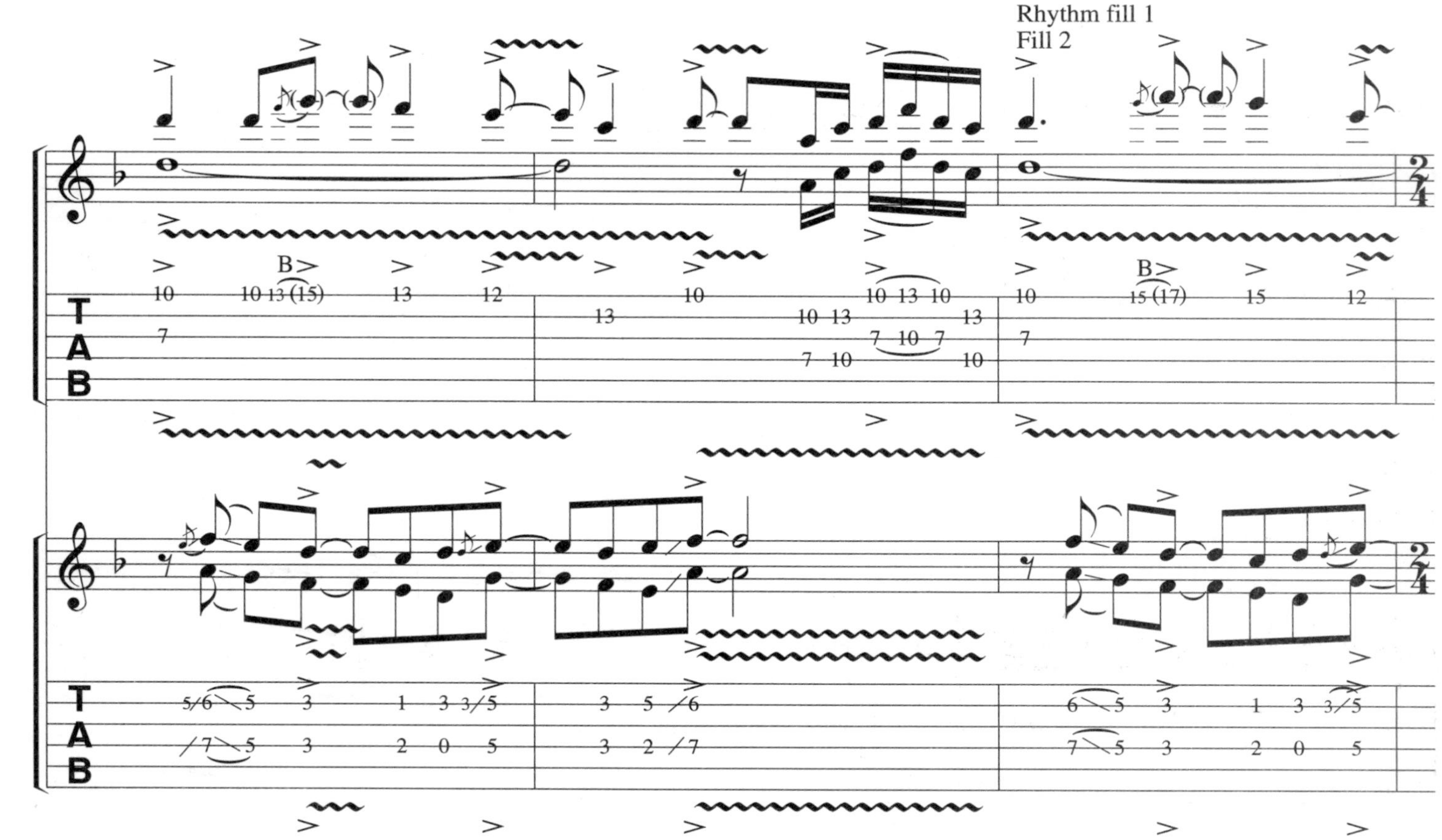

Rhythm fill 1
Fill 2

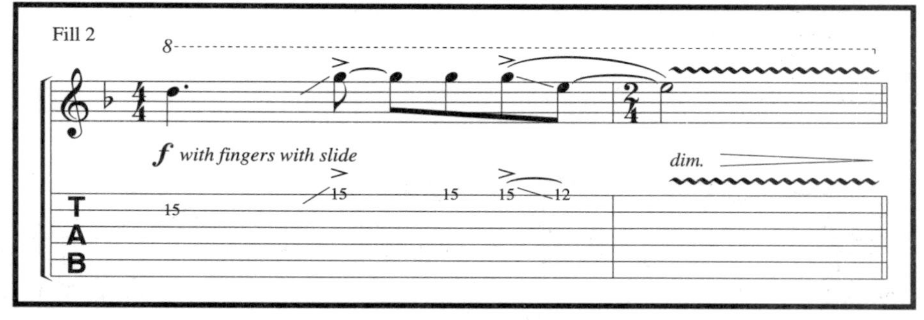

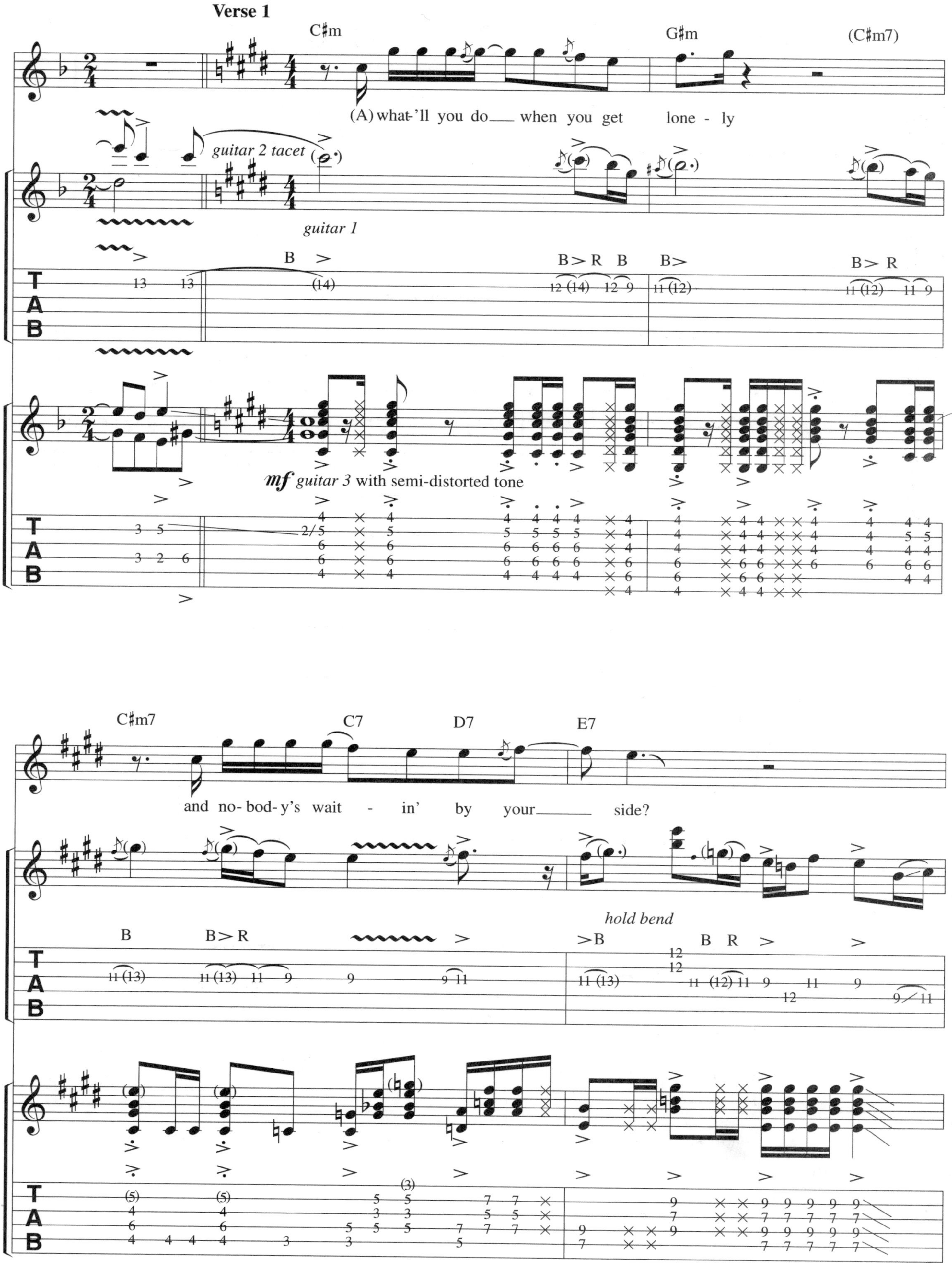

Verse 1

C♯m G♯m (C♯m7)

(A) what-'ll you do when you get lone - ly

guitar 2 tacet

guitar 1

mf guitar 3 with semi-distorted tone

F♯m
B
E
A
You been run - nin' and hid - ing much too long.
hold bend
B
B R
let ring
F♯m
B5
E
N.C.
You know it's just your fool - ish pride. Lay -
hold bend
B
B R
* Doubled sim. to intro

Chorus
guitar 3 Rhythm figure 1 (three times)
N.C. (Dm)
la, you got me on my knees Lay -
guitar 1
guitar 2 divisi
guitar 4
guitar 5 divisi
mf
la, I beg you dar - lin' please Lay -
dim.

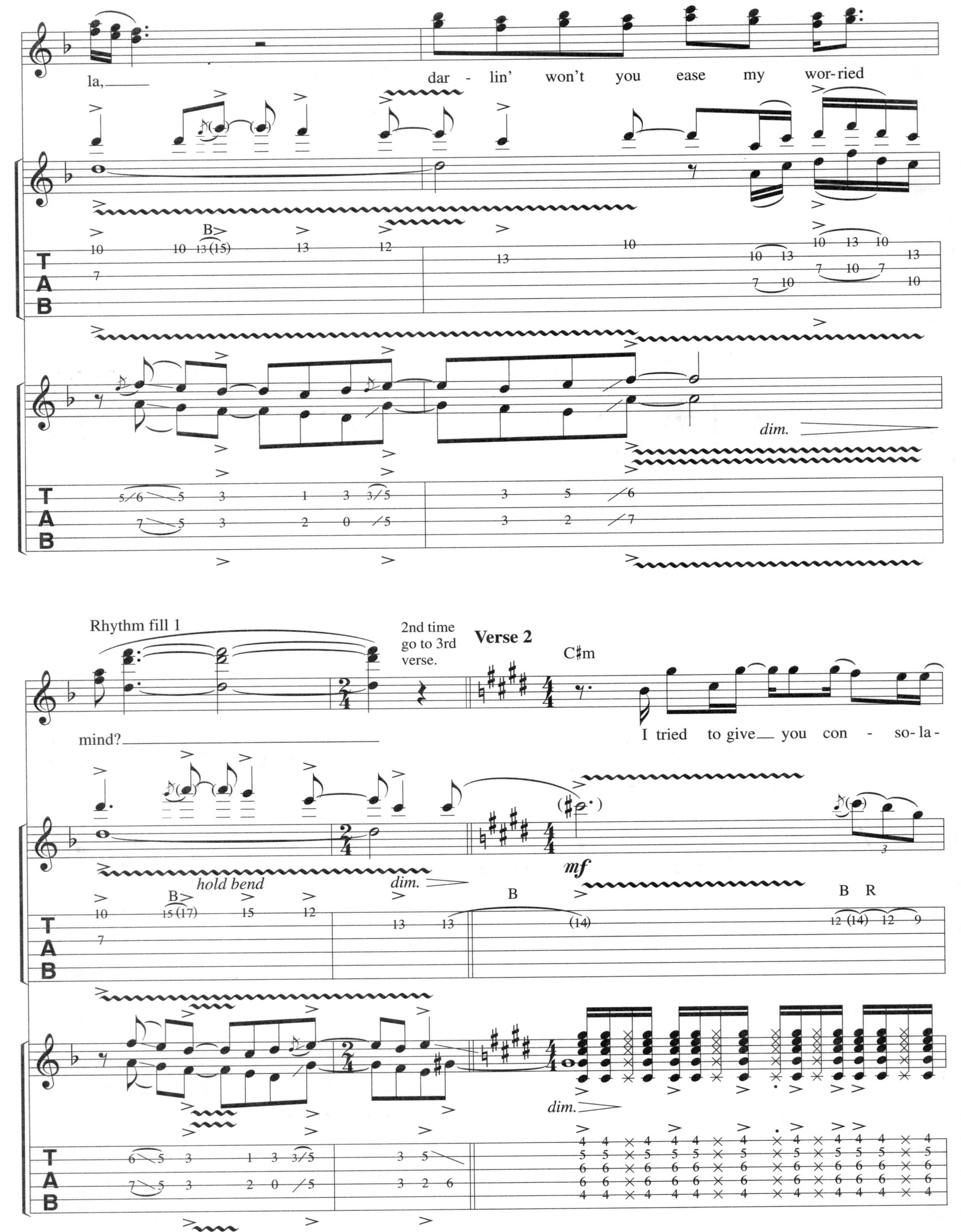
la,
dar - lin' won't you ease my wor-ried
B
mind?
Rhythm fill 1
2nd time go to 3rd verse.
Verse 2
C♯m
I tried to give you con - so-la-
hold bend
dim.
mf
B
B R
dim.

G♯m7 C♯m7 C7 D7

tion when your old man, he let you

hold bend

E F♯m B

down. Like a fool, I

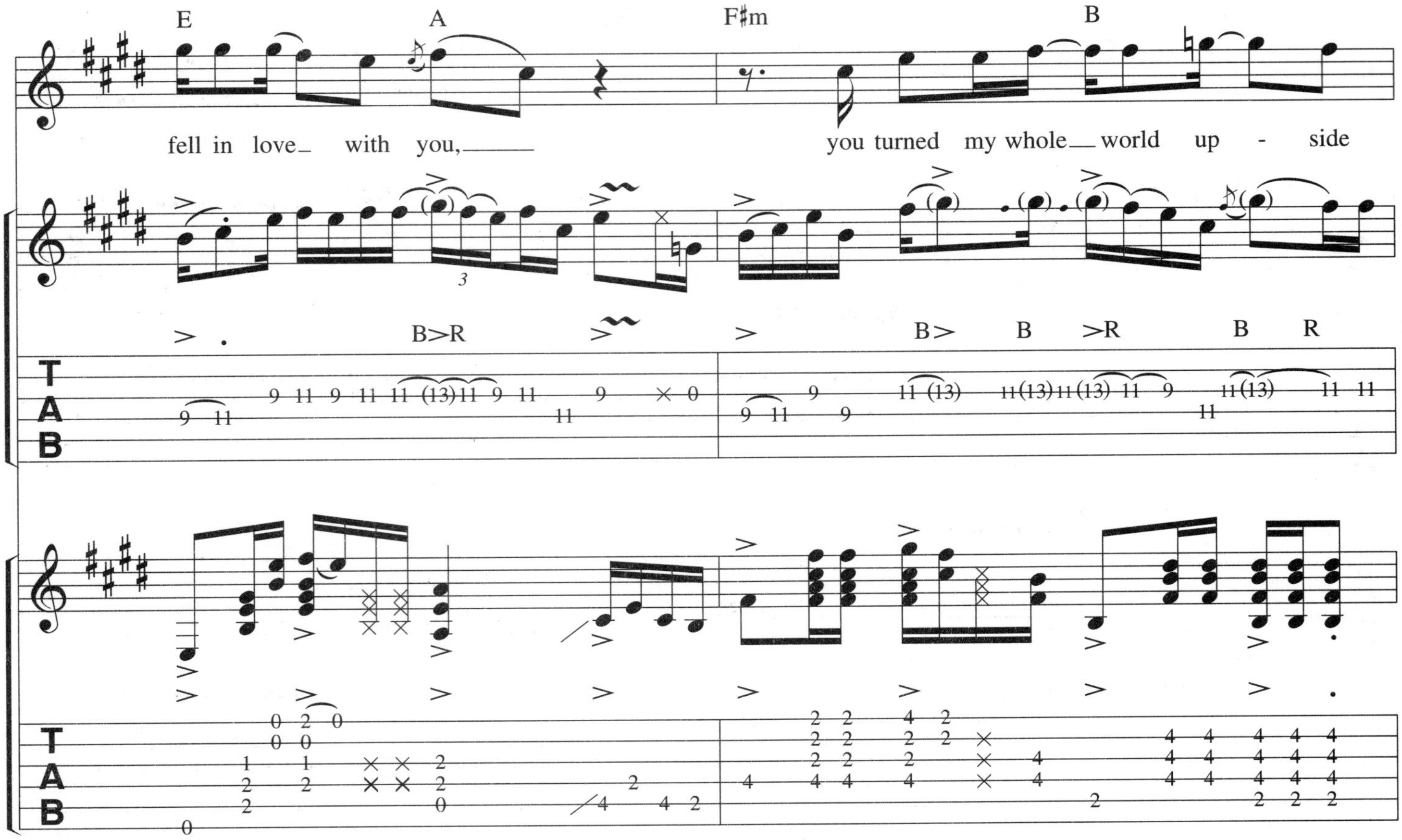

E A F♯m B

fell in love_ with you,___ you turned my whole_ world up - side

B>R B> B >R B R

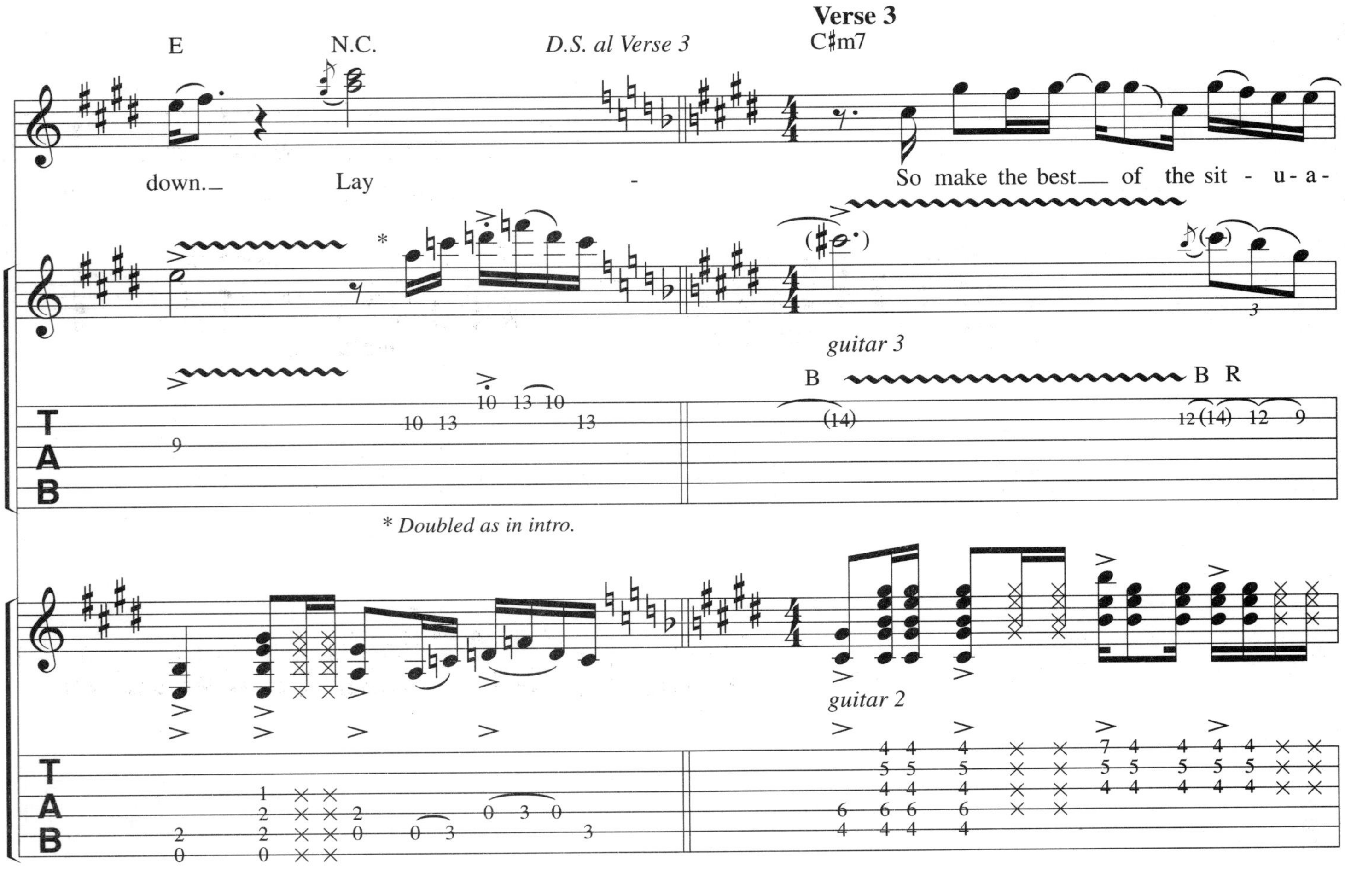

E N.C. *D.S. al Verse 3*

Verse 3

C♯m7

down._ Lay - So make the best_ of the sit - u - a -

guitar 3

B B R

** Doubled as in intro.*

guitar 2

G♯m C♯m7 C7 D7

tion, before I fin - 'ly go in -

guitar 2

guitar 3

B B R B B R

E7 F♯m

sane. Please don't say we'll

hold bend

B B B R

E
A
F♯m
B
nev - er find a way,
or tell me all my love's in
hold bend
accel.
B> B
B>R
Chorus
guitar 3 Rhythm figure 1 (eight times) simile
E
N.C.
N.C. (Dm)
vain. Lay - la,
you
guitar 1
guitar 2
divisi
* Doubled as in intro.
guitar 4 *
guitar 5 *
divisi
* with slide

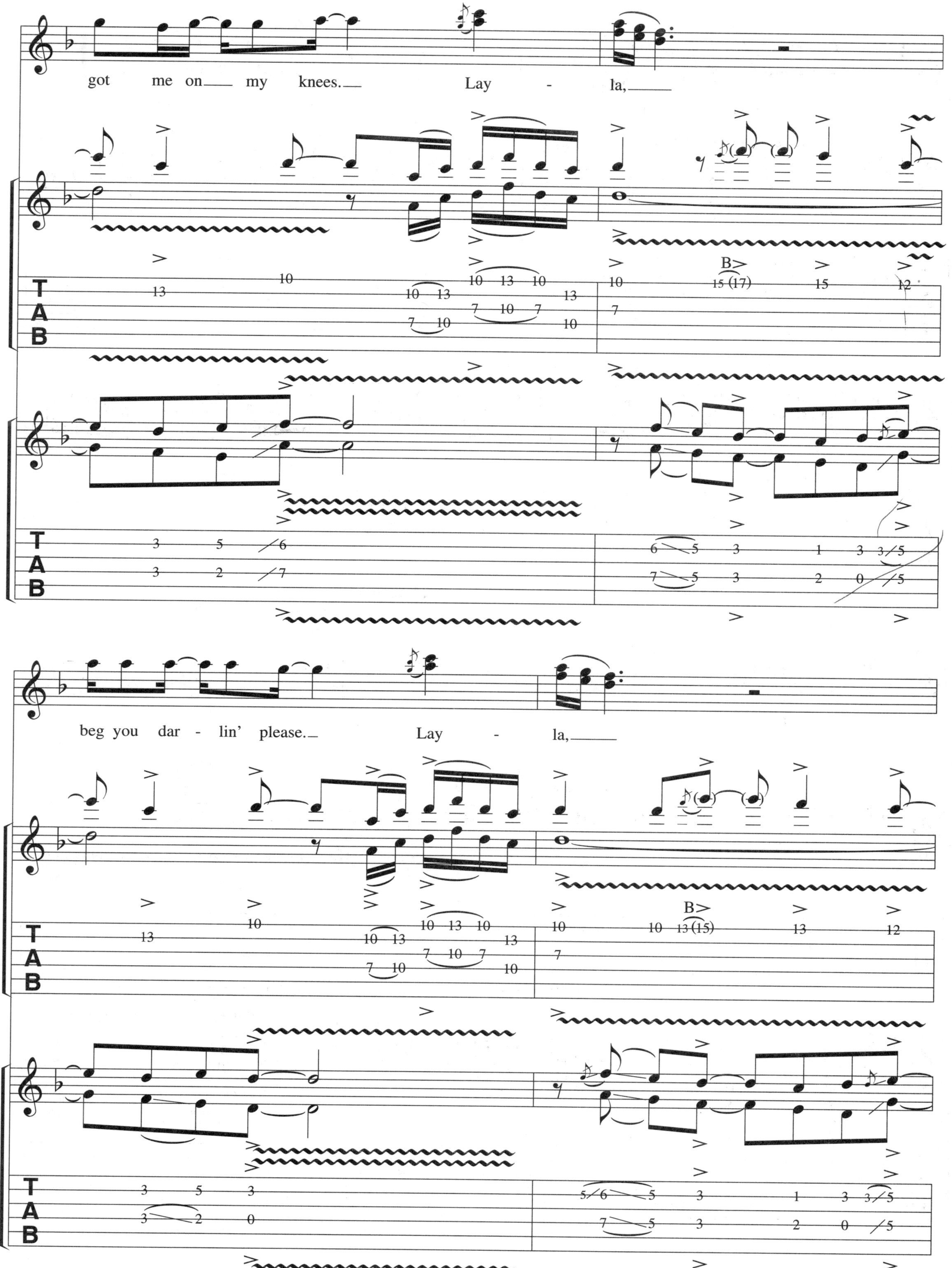
got me on my knees. Lay - la,
T
A
B
13
10
10 13
7 10
10 13 10
7 10 7
13
10
10
7
B
15 (17)
15
12
3 5 6
3 2 7
6 5 3 1 3 3 5
7 5 3 2 0 5
beg you dar - lin' please. Lay - la,
13
10
10 13
7 10
10 13 10
7 10 7
13
10
10
7
10 13 (15)
13
12
3 5 3
3 2 0
5 6 5 3 1 3 3 5
7 5 3 2 0 5

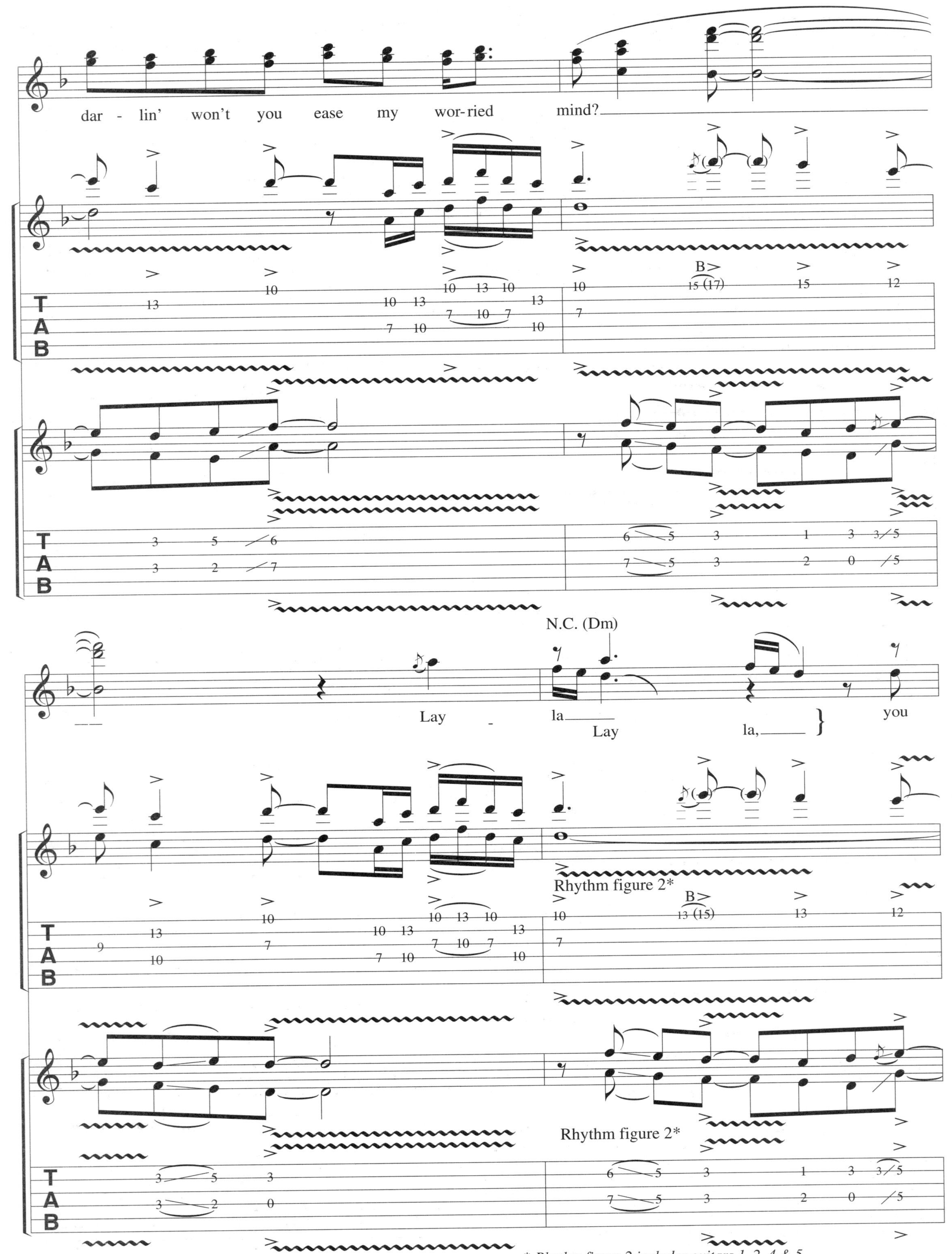

* *Rhythm figure 2 includes guitars 1, 2, 4 & 5*

got me on my knees. Lay - la,
I
T
A
B
beg you dar - lin' please. Lay - la,
Whoa.

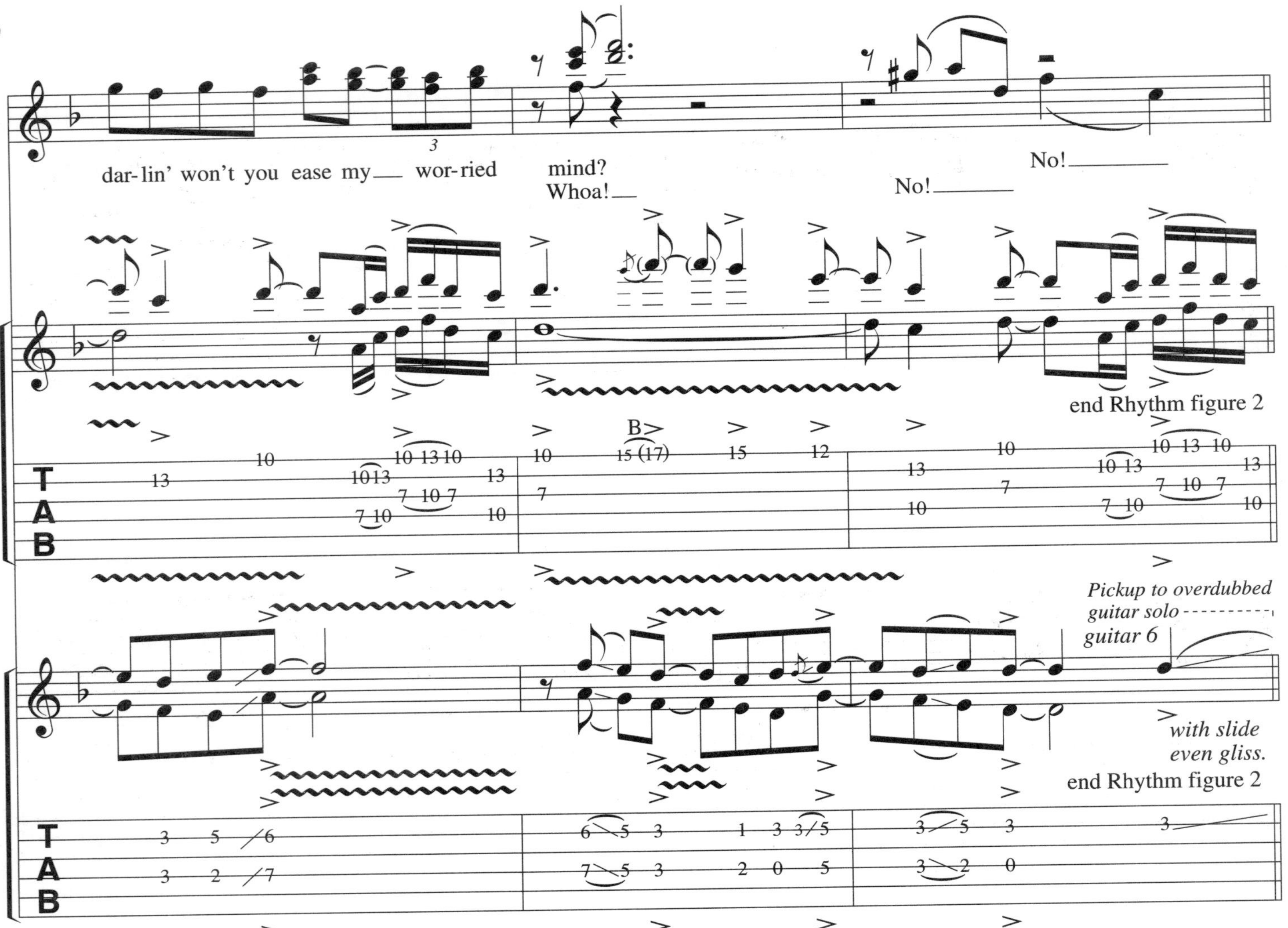

dar-lin' won't you ease my___ wor-ried mind?
Whoa!___

No!___ No!___

end Rhythm figure 2

Pickup to overdubbed guitar solo
guitar 6

with slide
even gliss.
end Rhythm figure 2

Guitar solo
guitar 3 Rhythm figure 1 (eight times) *simile*
guitars 1, 2, 3, 4, & 5 Rhythm figure 2 (two times) *simile*

* *TAB numbers based on location of notes beyond fretboard*

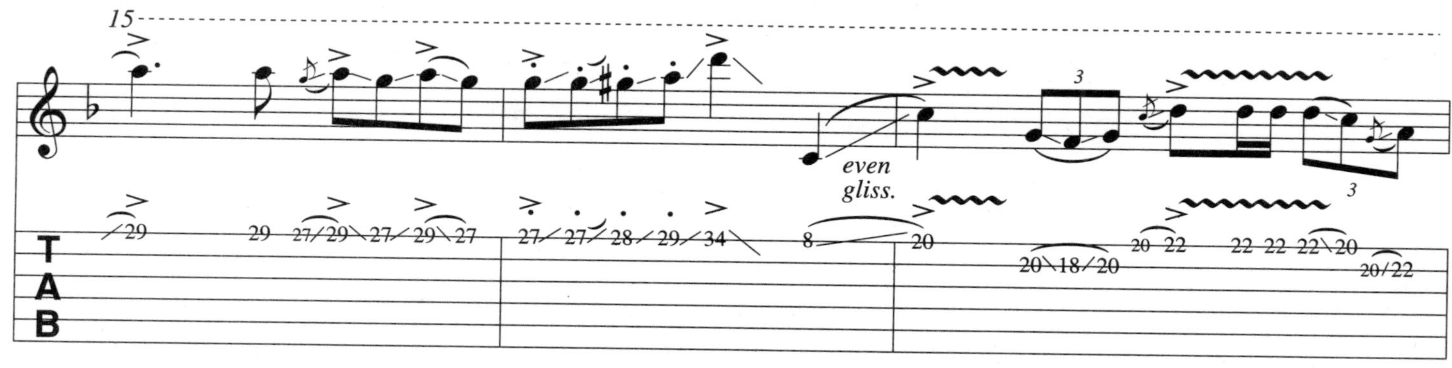
even
gliss.

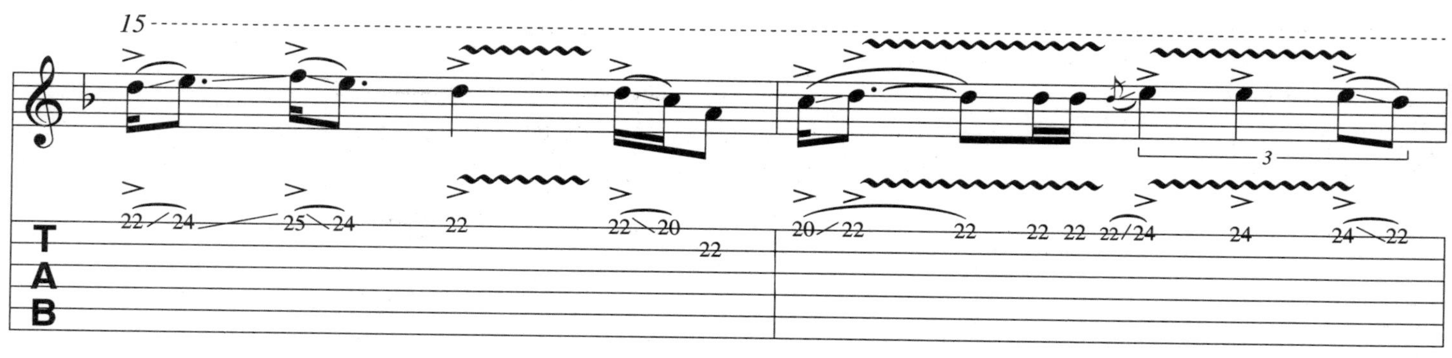

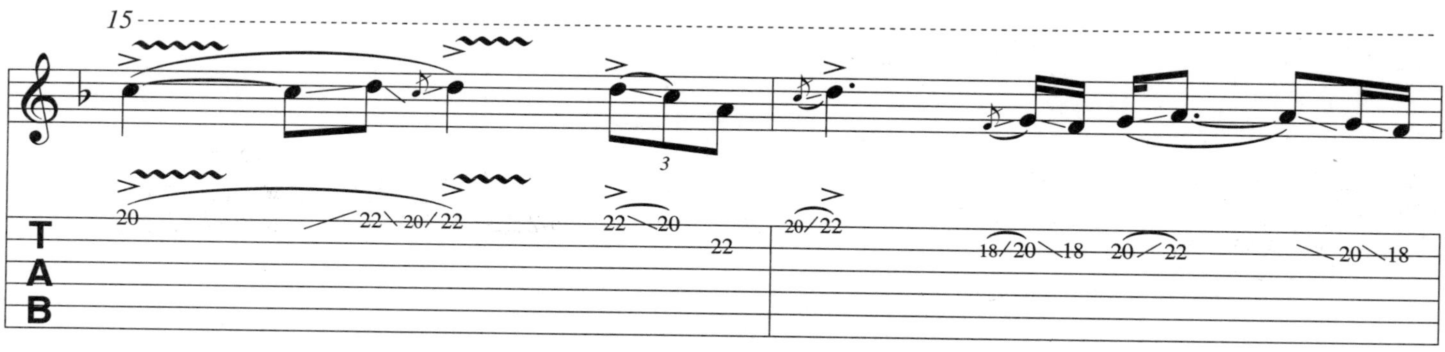

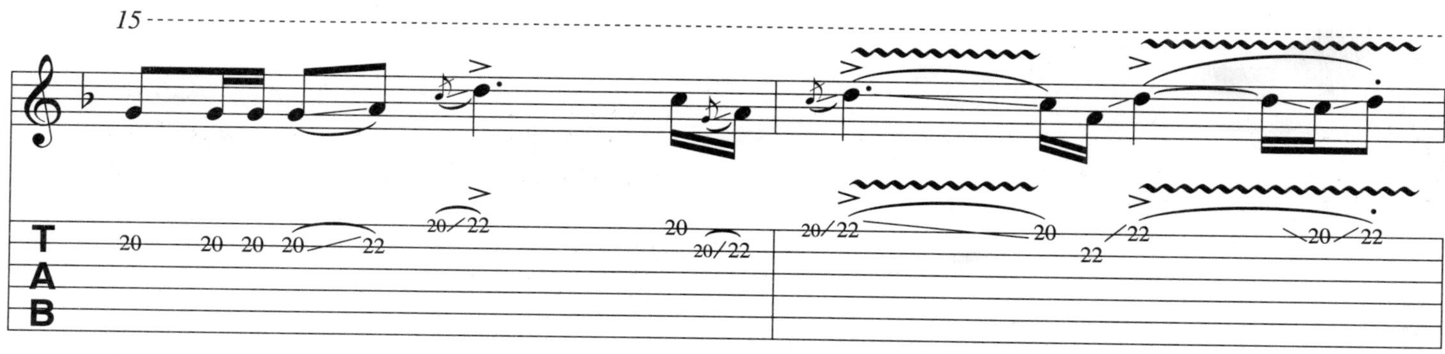

guitar 3 Rhythm figure 1 (three times) *simile*
guitar 4 & 5 Rhythm figure 2 *simile*
guitar 1
guitar 2
B
10 7 13 (15) 13 12
15
guitar 6
accel.
20/22 22 24 22 22 20 22
22 24 24/25 24 22 20 20 20
B
13 10 10 13 7 10 10 13 10 7 10 7 13 10
10 7 15 (17) 15 12
15
let ring
even gliss.
20 24 20 22 22 20 22 20
22 22 22 22 22 22 22 22 22 22 22 22 22 22 22 25

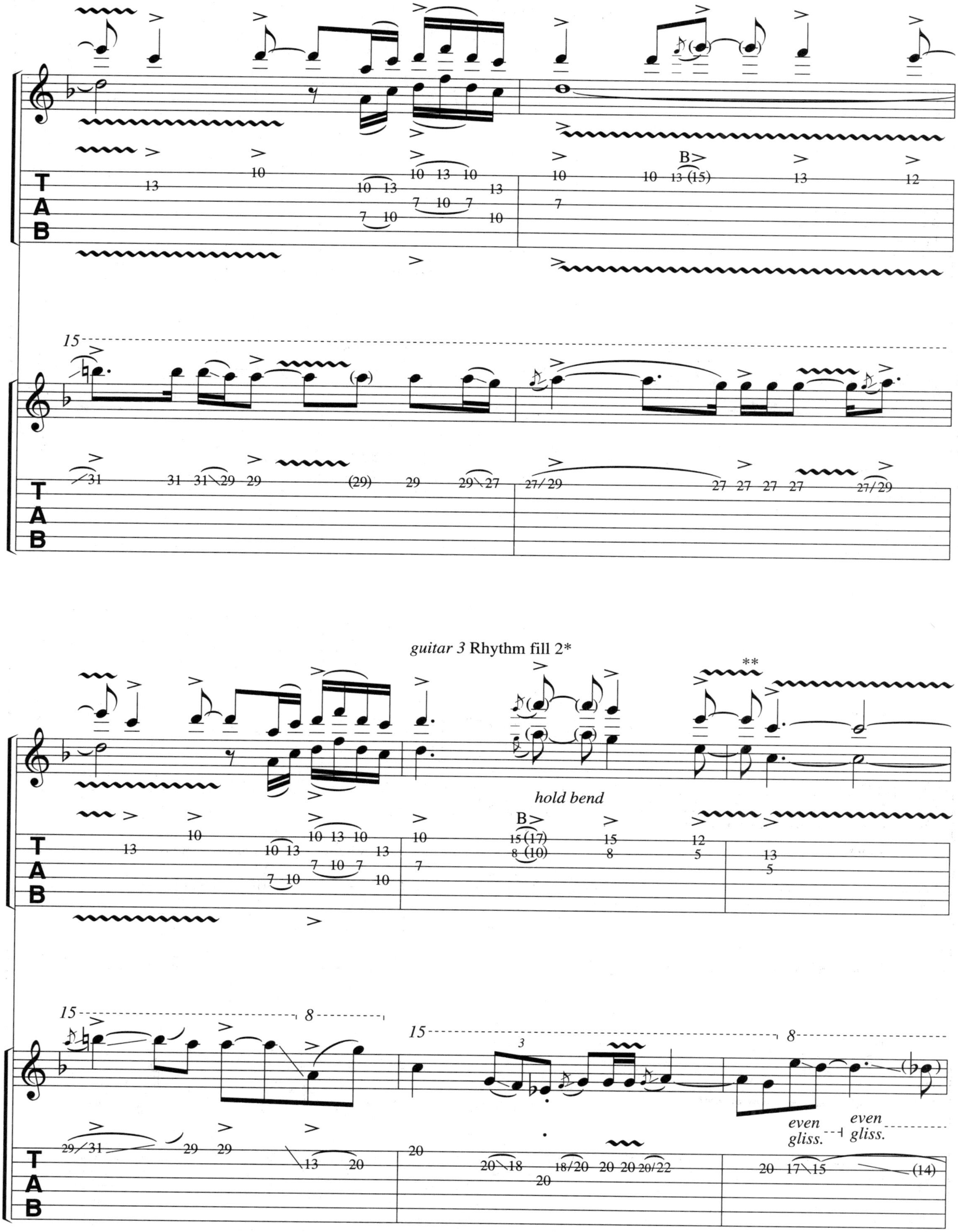

guitar 3 Rhythm fill 2*

hold bend

even gliss. *even gliss.*

* *Rhythm fill 2 -- Play 1st measure of Rhythm figure 1 and sustain last eighth note diad.*
** *guitars 4 & 5 hold last note of previous measure.*

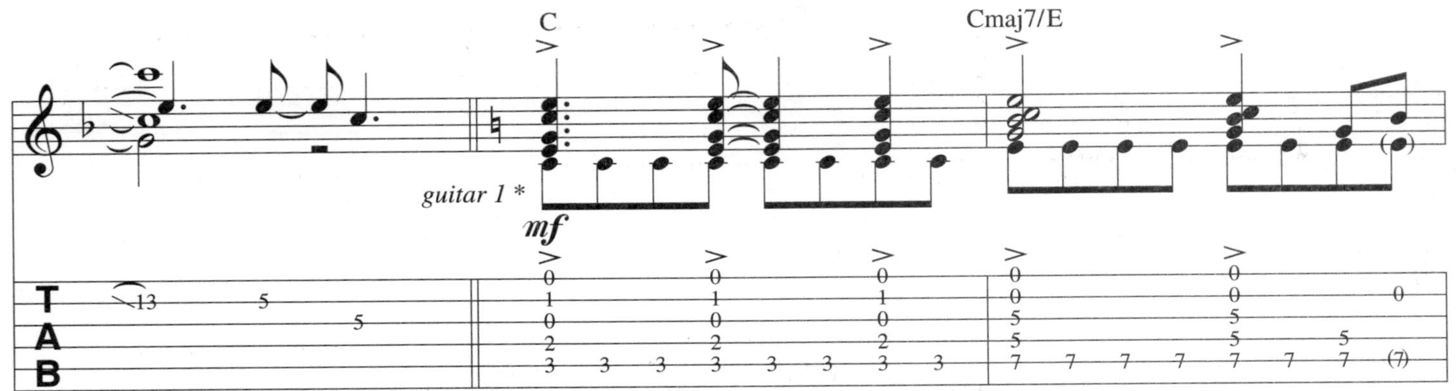

* Piano part arranged for guitar.
All guitars are re-numbered for the remainder of the song.

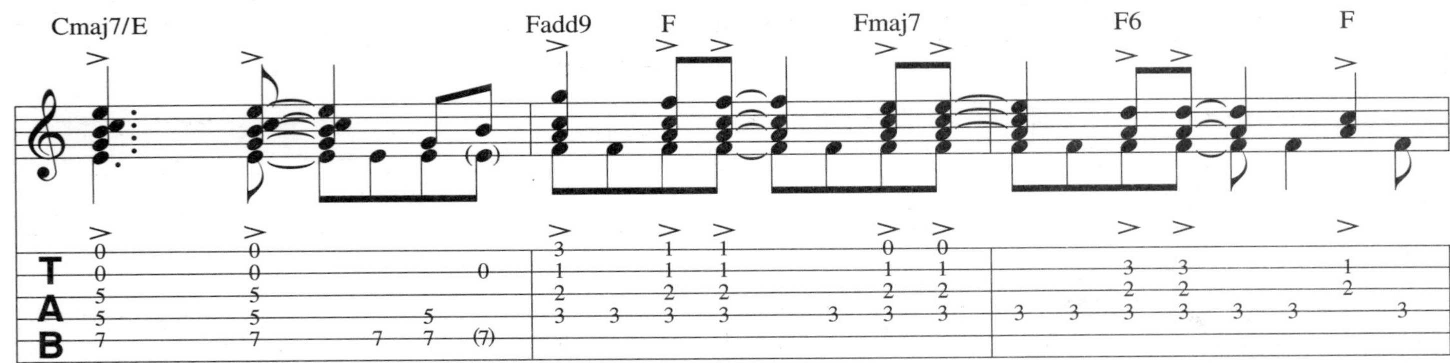

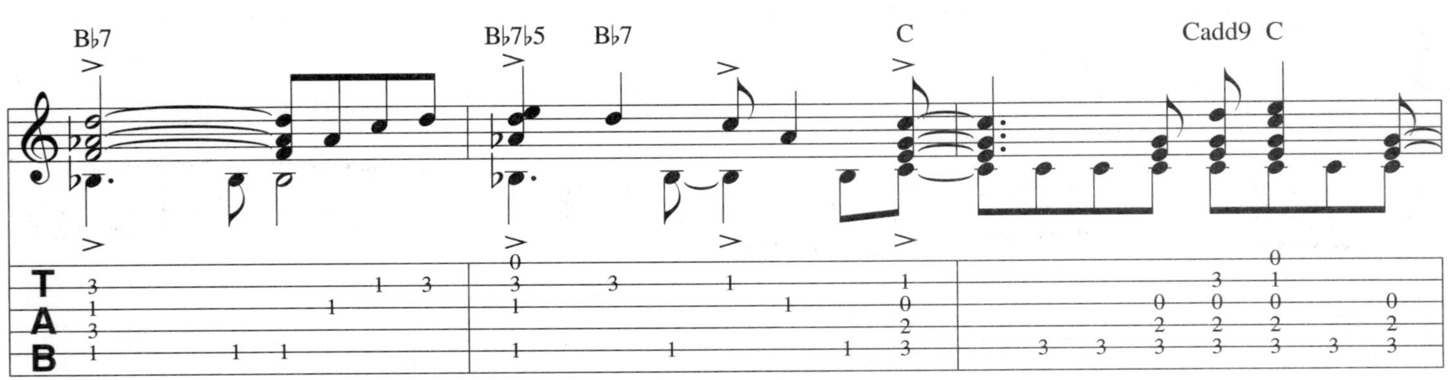

guitar 1 Rhythm figure 3 simile
C
Cmaj7/E
end Rhythm figure 3
mf guitar 2 with slide
f guitar 3 with slide
guitar 4
mf let ring
Rhythm figure 4
Fadd9
F
Fmaj7
F6
F
B♭7
end Rhythm figure 4

B♭7♭5
B♭7
C
8
loco
let ring
guitar 1 Rhythm figure 3 (first seven measures only)
C
Cmaj7/E
Fadd9
F
Fmaj7
Rhythm figure 5

* Piano part arranged for guitar.

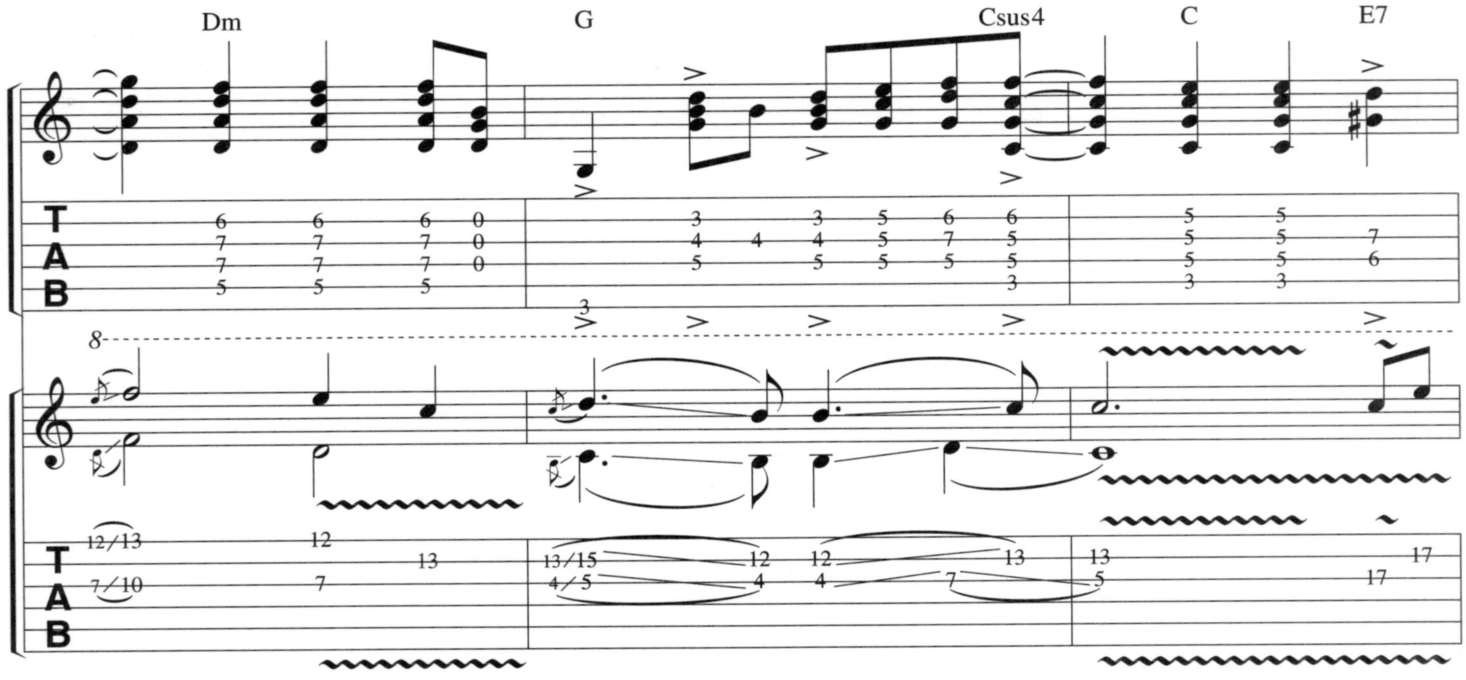

Dm G Csus4 C E7

8

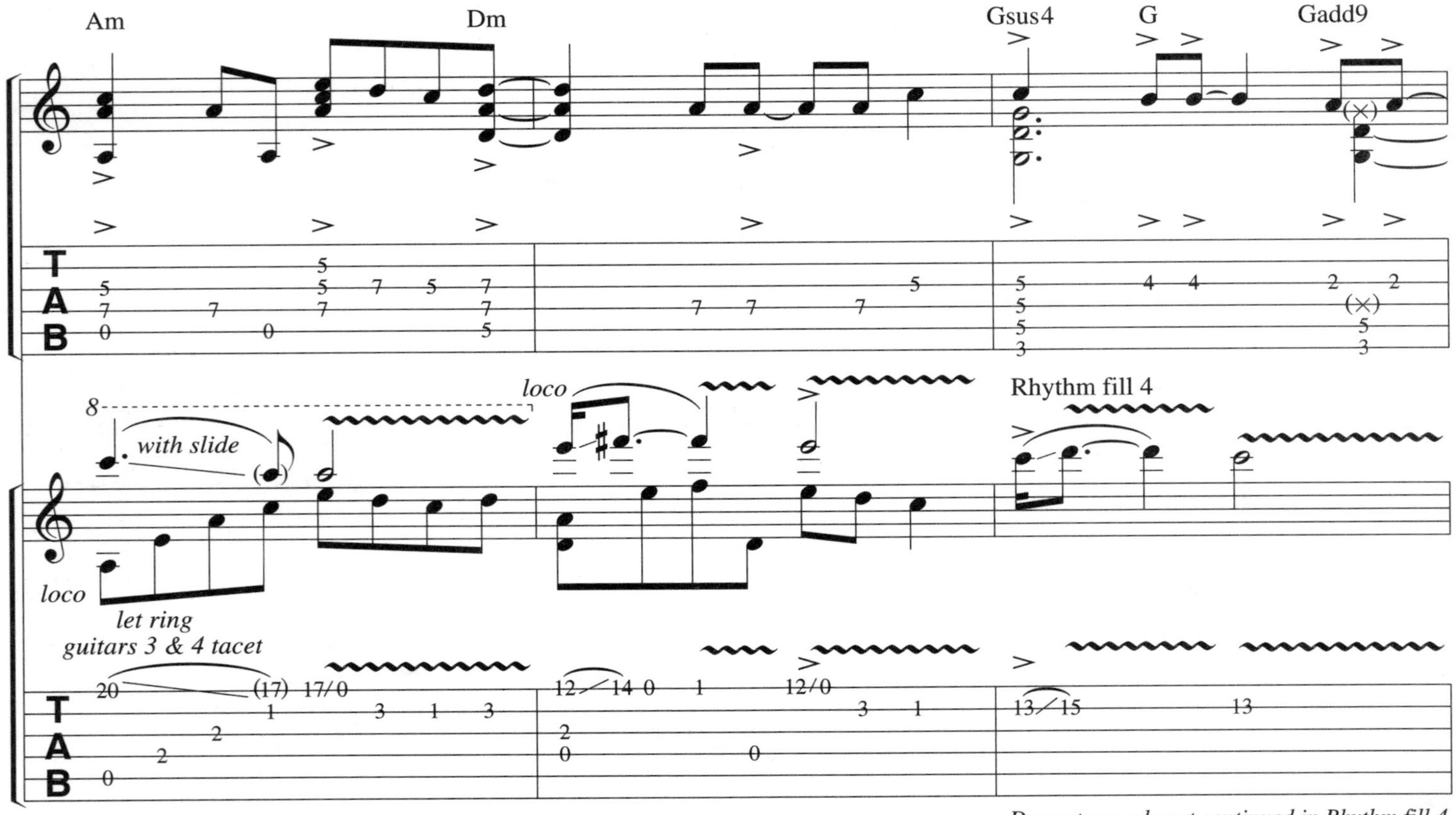

Am Dm Gsus4 G Gadd9

8 *with slide* *loco*

loco

let ring

guitars 3 & 4 tacet

Rhythm fill 4

Downstemmed part notated to right of / in TAB.

Downstemmed part continued in Rhythm fill 4.

G5
end Rhythm figure 6
C
Rhythm figure 7
C/E
guitar 1 *
* Piano arranged for guitar.
guitar 4 Rhythm figure 4 simile
guitar 2
guitar 3 with slide
Fadd9
F
Fmaj7
F6
F
C

C/E
Fadd9
F
Fmaj7
F6
F
8
8
B♭7
B♭7♭5
B♭7
C
8
even gliss.
8
loco

end Rhythm figure 7
guitar 1 Rhythm figure 3 & 5 simile
Cmaj7/E
Rhythm figure 8 *
* Acoustic guitar overdub
Fadd9
F
Fmaj7
F6
F
B♭7

B♭7♭5
B♭7
C
end Rhythm figure 8
Rhythm figures 3, 5, & 8 *simile*
C
Cmaj7/E
Fadd9
F
Fmaj7

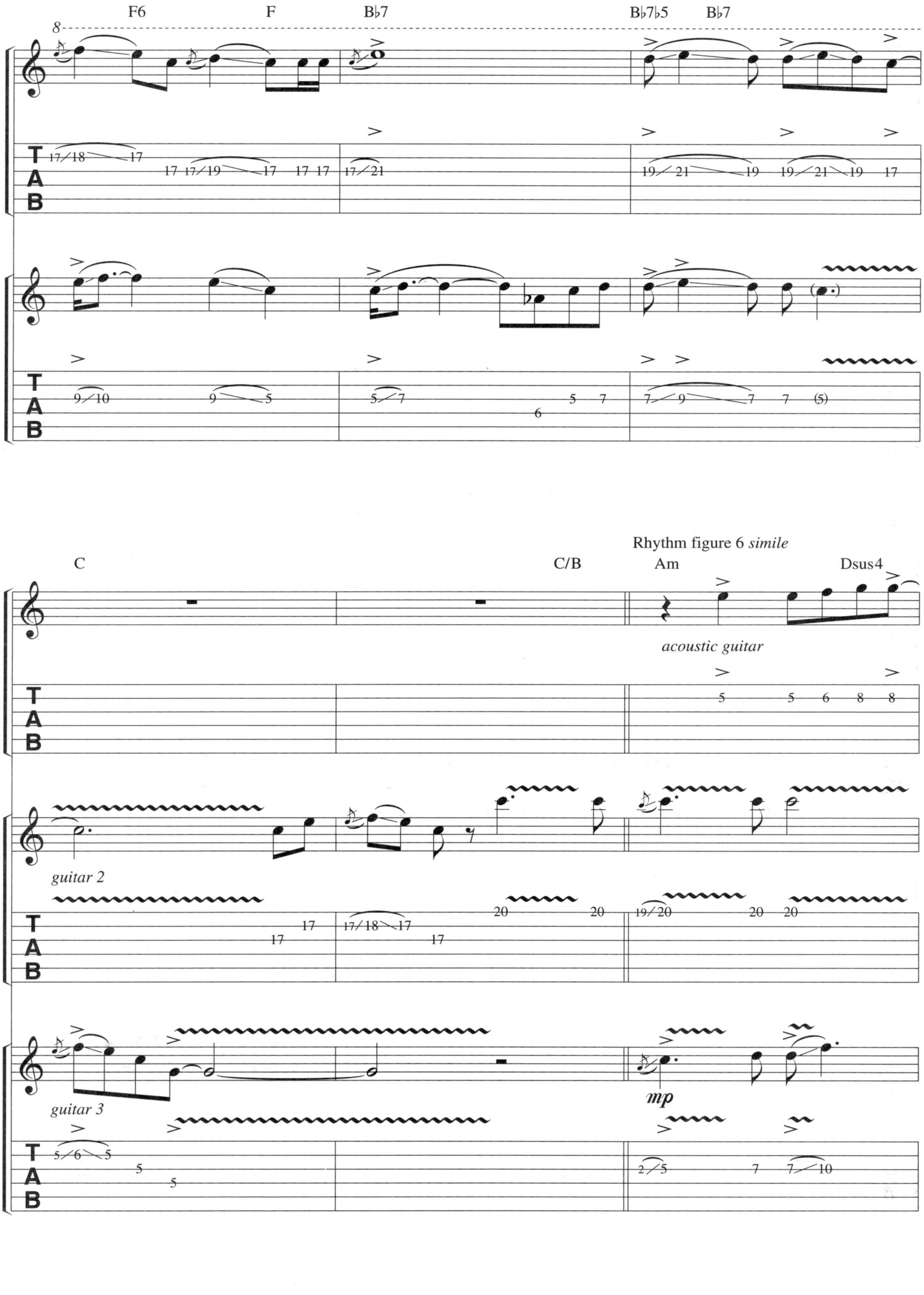

Rhythm figure 6 *simile*

C | C/B | Am | Dsus4

acoustic guitar

guitar 2

guitar 3

mp

Dm
G
Csus4
C
E7/B
Am
D

C
C/E
Rhythm figure 9
even gliss.
Fadd9
F
Fmaj7
F6
F
C
end Rhythm figure 9

C/E
Fadd9
F
Fmaj7
F6
F
loco
B♭7
B♭7♭5
B♭7
C

Rhythm figure 7 (first eight bars only)
Rhythm figures 4 & 9 (five times) simile
C
C/E
Fadd9
F
Fmaj7
even gliss.
mf
dim.
F6
F
C
C/E
Fadd9
F
Fmaj7
F6
F
Rhythm figure 7
(first eight bars only)
C

C/E
Fadd9
F
Fmaj7
F6
F
C
C/E
Fadd9
F
Fmaj7
even gliss.
F6
F
C
C/E

Piano arranged for guitar ritards simile.

from Unplugged

Malted Milk

by Robert Johnson

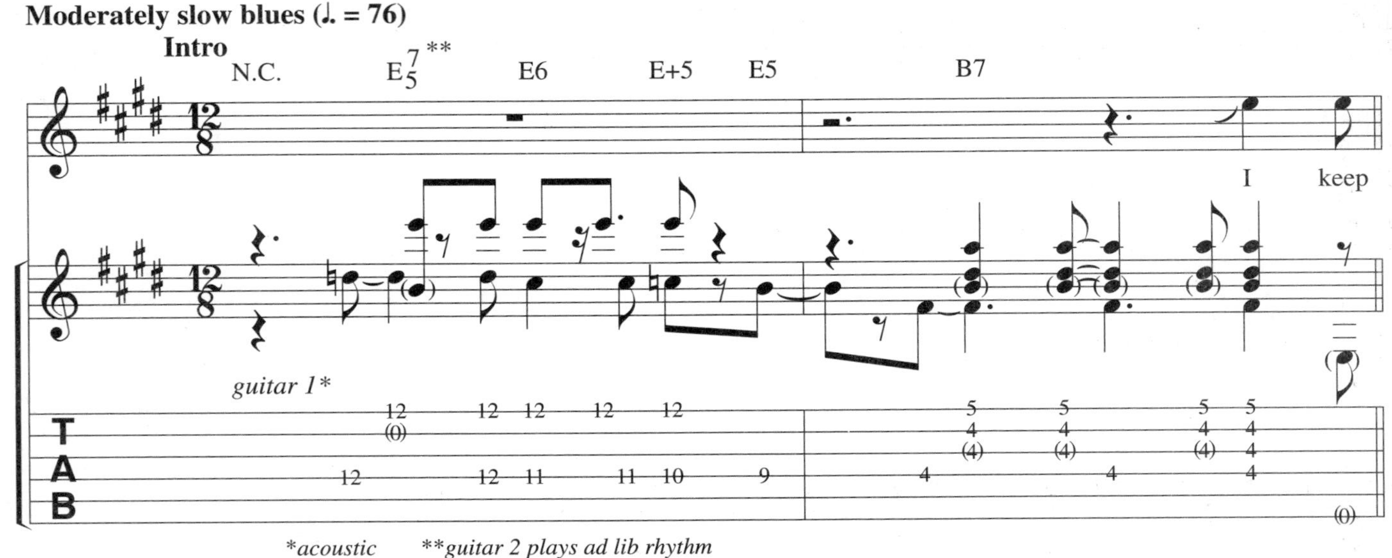

A7
2:3
drink - in' malt - ed milk
try - in to drive my blues a - way.
E7
Ba - by, you're just as
B7
A7
wel - come to my lov - in' as the flow - ers is in May.
E5
C♯7/G♯
C7/G
B7
Malt - ed
T
A
B

Verse 2
E7
A7
2:3
2:3
milk, malt - ed milk,
keep rush - in' to my head.
E7
Malt - ed
A7
milk, malt - ed milk,
keep rush - in' to my head.
E7
And I have a

B7
A7
fun - ny, fun - ny feel - ing and I'm talk - in' all out my head.
E5 N.C. C♯7/G♯ C7/G
B7
Ba - by,
Verse 3
E7
A7
2:3
fix me one more drink 'n' hug your dad - dy one more time.
E7
Ba - by,
TAB

A7
fix me one more drink 'n' hug your dad - dy one more time.
E7
Keep on stir-rin'
B7
2:3
my malt-ed milk, ma-ma,
A7
un - til I change my mind.
E5
N.C. C♯7/G♯
C7/G
B7/F♯

Guitar solo

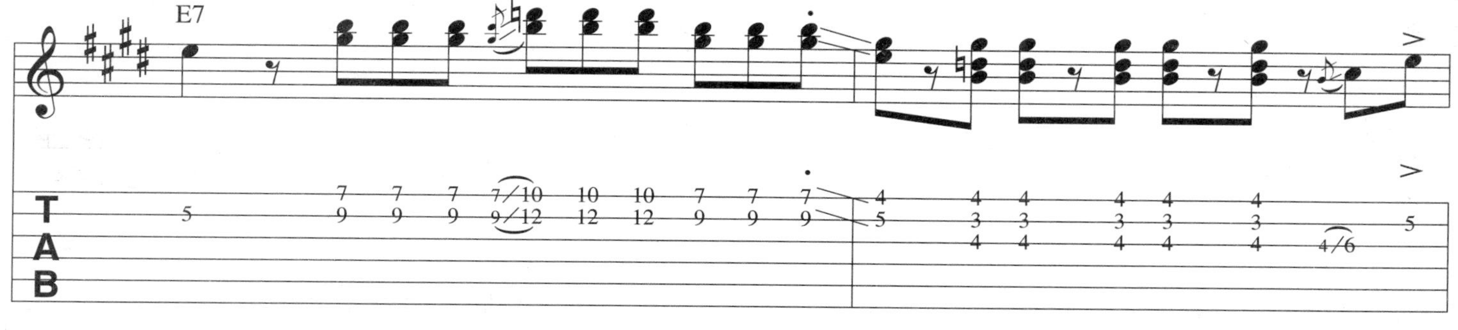

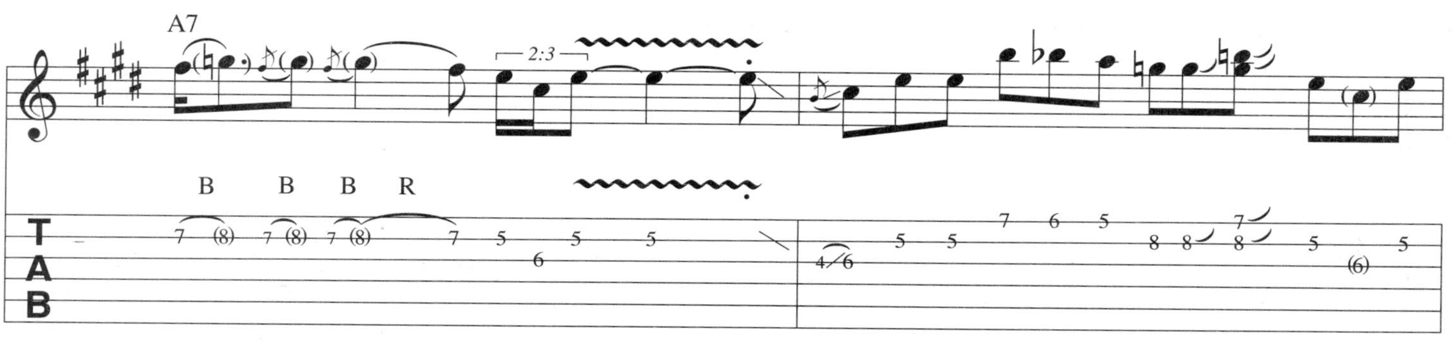

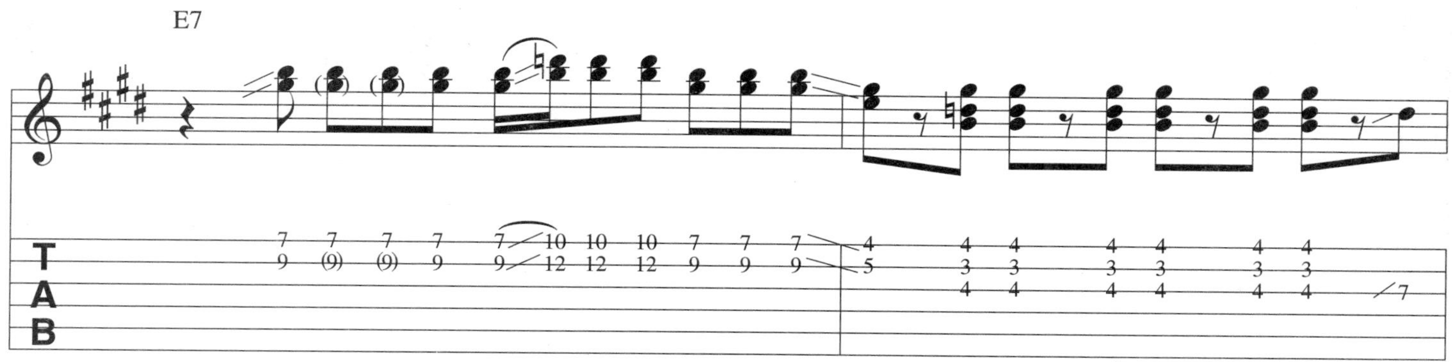

N.C.
C♯7/G♯
C7/G
B7
My door
Verse 4
E7
A7
knobs keeps on turn-in', there must be spooks a-round my bed.
E7 N.C.
E7
A7
My door knobs keeps on turn-in', there

(E)
N.C.
must be spooks around my bed.
E7
An' I have a
2:3
B7
fun-ny, fun-ny feel-in',
and the
A7
hair ris-in' on my head.
(E)
N.C.
Free time
⑥ open
E
E
B
B
R
rit.
let ring

from John Mayall's Bluesbreakers with Eric Clapton

Ramblin' On My Mind

by Robert Johnson

A5
A6
A7
A6
A5
A6
A7
A6
A5
ram - blin',
down to the sta-tion,
girl, lit-tle girl,
I've got ram - blin' all on my mind.
catch that old fast milk - train, you'll see.
I've got mean things all on my mind.
E
with Rhythm fill 1
end Rhythm fill 1
Is to leave
I've got the
Is to leave
1., 3.
B7
A7
to Coda
my ba - by,
'cause she treat me so un - kind.
E7
B7
I'm go - in'
2.
B7
A7
blues 'bout Miss So and So.
and the sun got the blues 'bout me.

E
B7
tr
T
A
B

Guitar solo

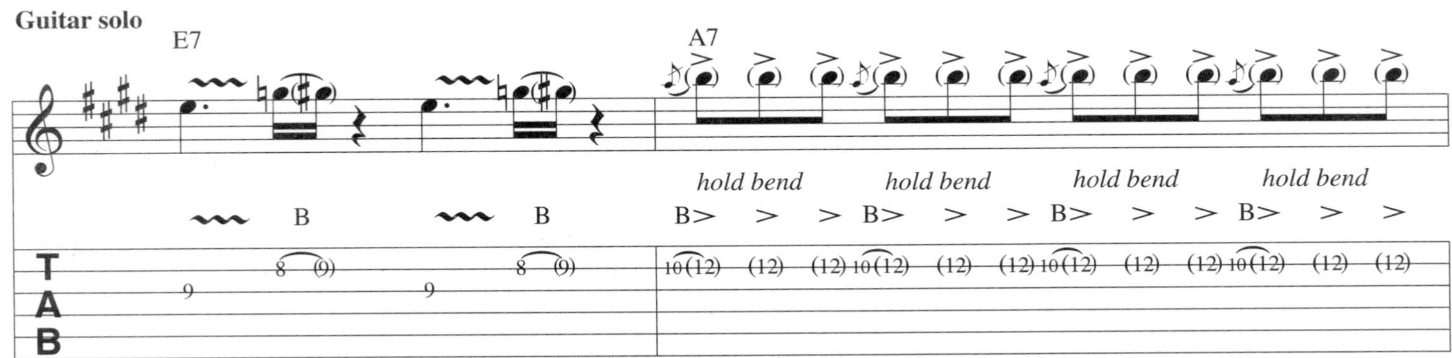
E7
A7
hold bend
hold bend
hold bend
hold bend
T
A
B

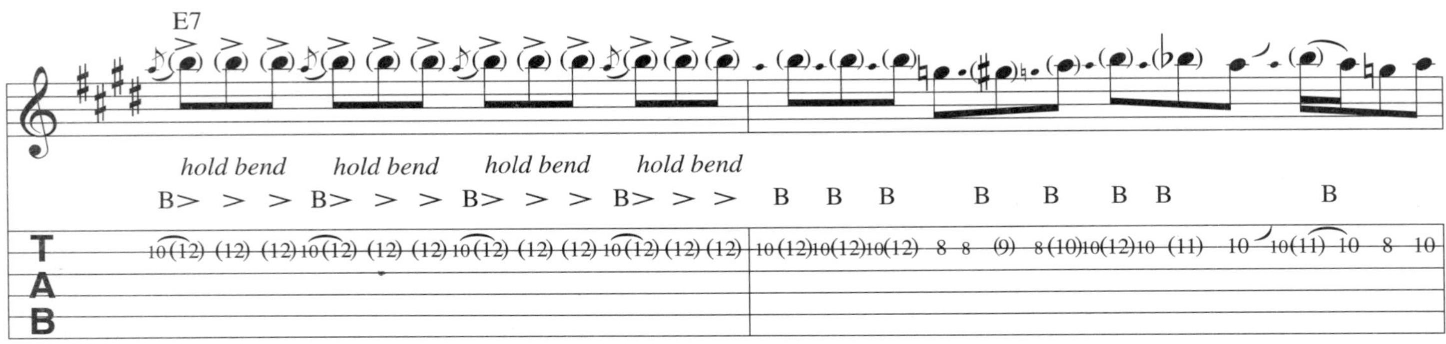
E7
hold bend
hold bend
hold bend
hold bend
T
A
B

A7
T
A
B

E7
T
A
B

B7
A7
tr
B B
B
T
A
B

E
D.S. (third verse) al Coda
3. I got
T
A
B

Coda
E
D♯7 E7
tr
T
A
B

from From The Cradle

Reconsider Baby

by Lowell Fulson

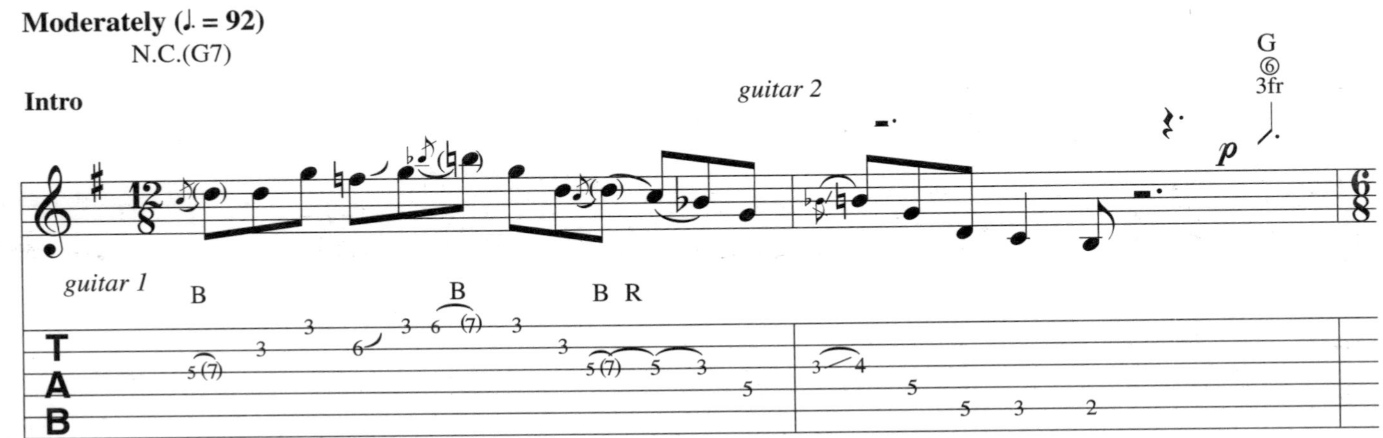

C9
B R
B
B R
B
B R
G9
4
B
B R
B
D9
B
C9
G9
end Rhythm figure 1
1. So
B

Verse 1
guitar 2 Rhythm figure 1
G9
C9
long,
oh, how I hate to see you go.
G9
C9
So long,
B
B
oh, how I hate to see you go
G9
B
B
B
D9
and the way that I will miss you.
B
B R

C9
G9
I guess you would never know.
B
B R
Verse 2
guitar 2 Rhythm figure 1
G9
2. We've been to-geth - er so long
B
C9
G9
to have to sep- a- rate this way.
B
R
B R
C9
We've been to- geth - er so long
B

G9
to have to sep- a- rate this way.
B
B R
D9
I'm gon- na let you go head on now, ba - by,
B R
C9
G9
pray that you come back home some day.
B hold bend B
Guitar solo
G9
guitar 2 Rhythm figure 1 (two times)
B
B

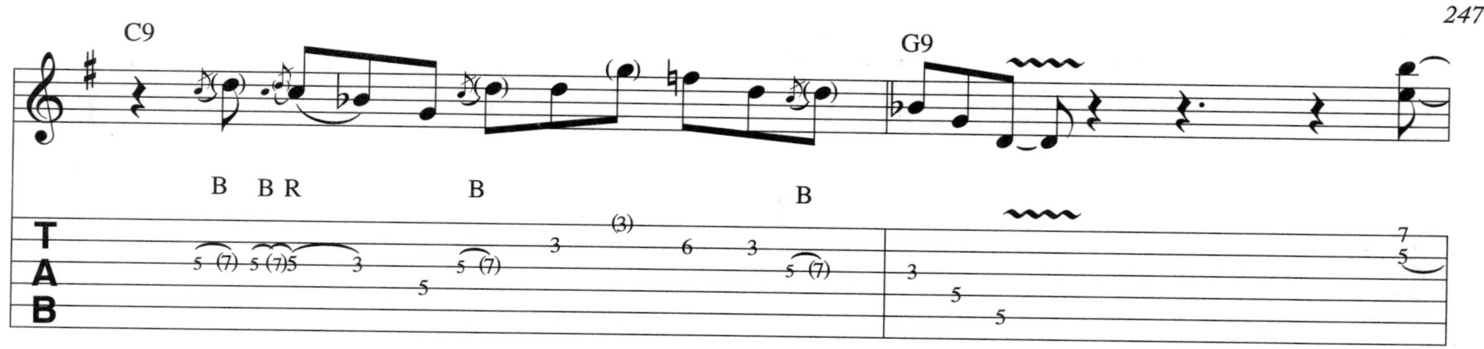
C9
G9
B
B R
B
B
T
A
B

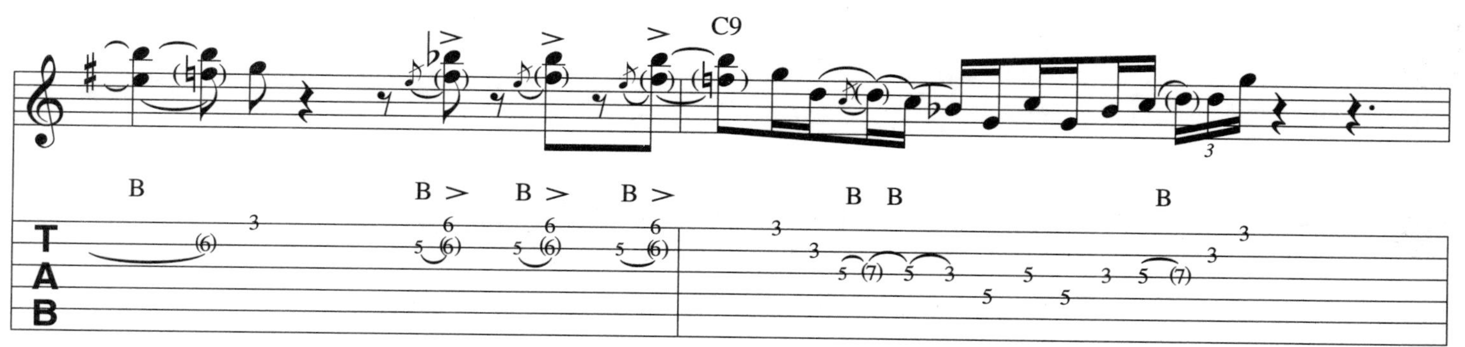
C9
B
B
B
B
B B
B
T
A
B

G9
B
B R
B
B R
T
A
B

D9
B
B
B
B R
T
A
B

C9
G9
B
T
A
B

C9

G9

C9

G9

D9
G9

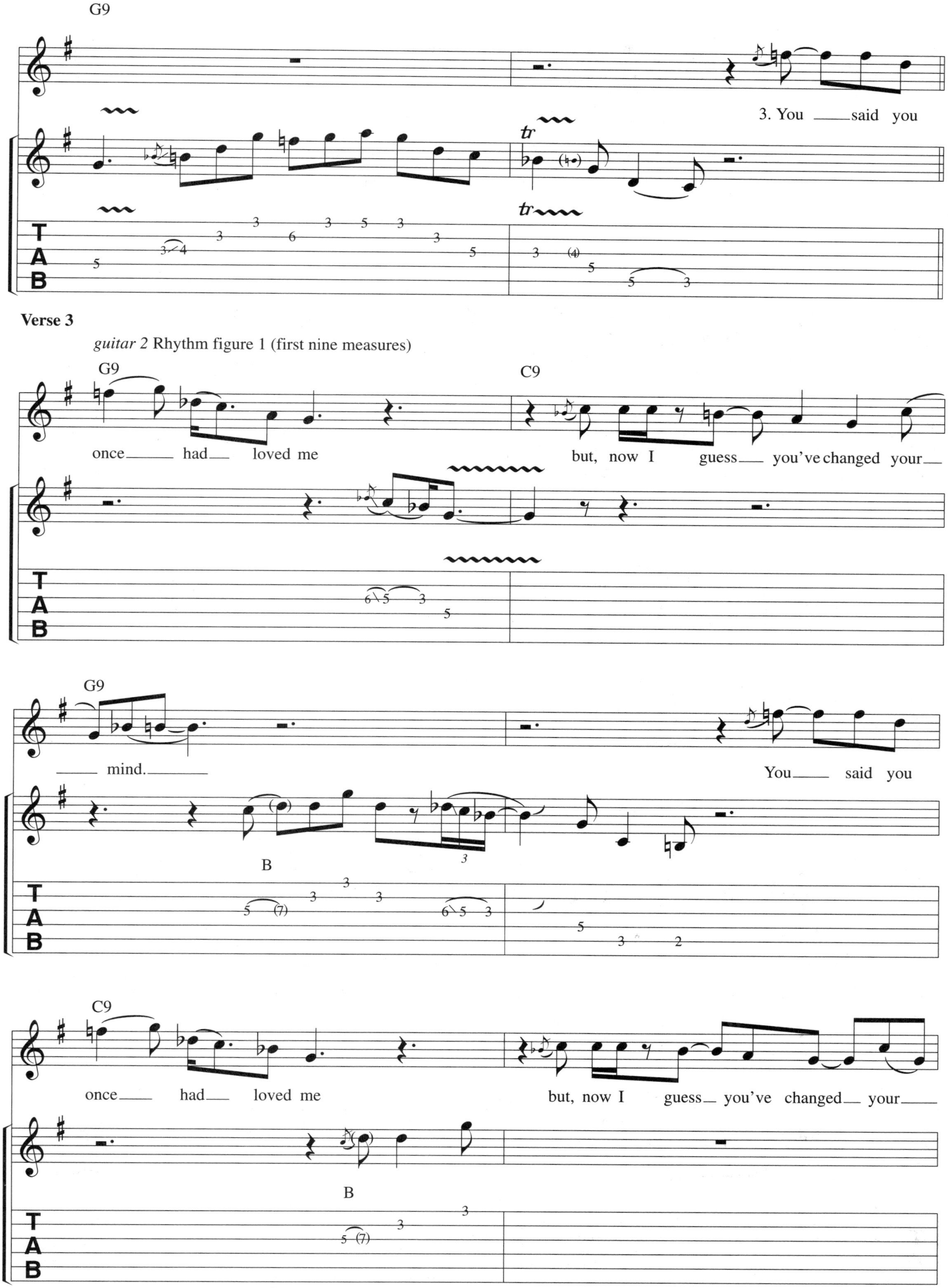

G9

3. You said you

Verse 3

guitar 2 Rhythm figure 1 (first nine measures)

G9 C9

once had loved me but, now I guess you've changed your

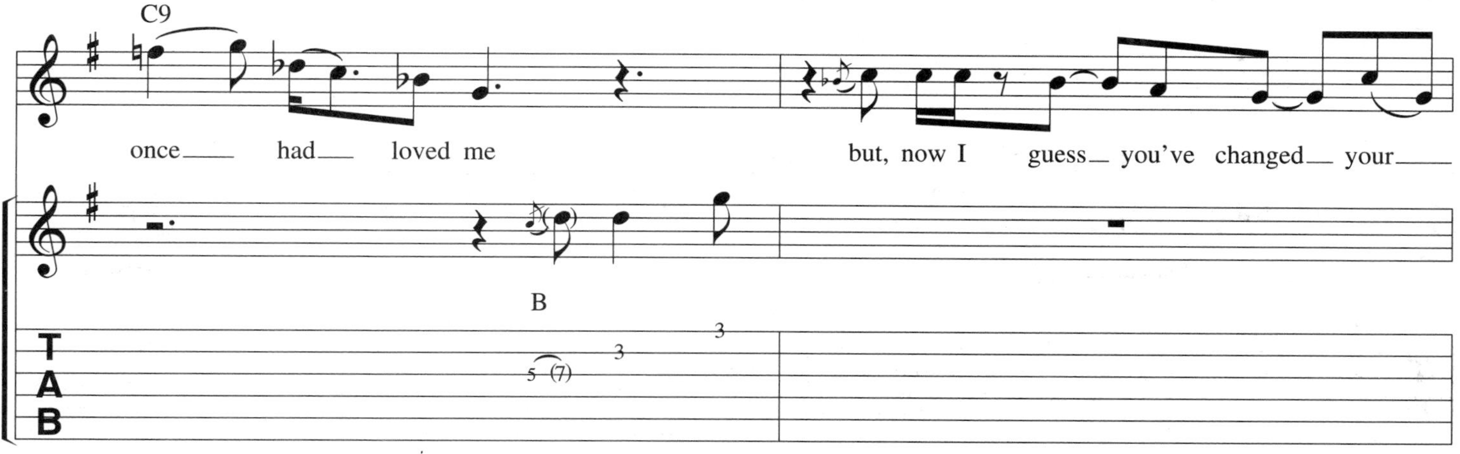

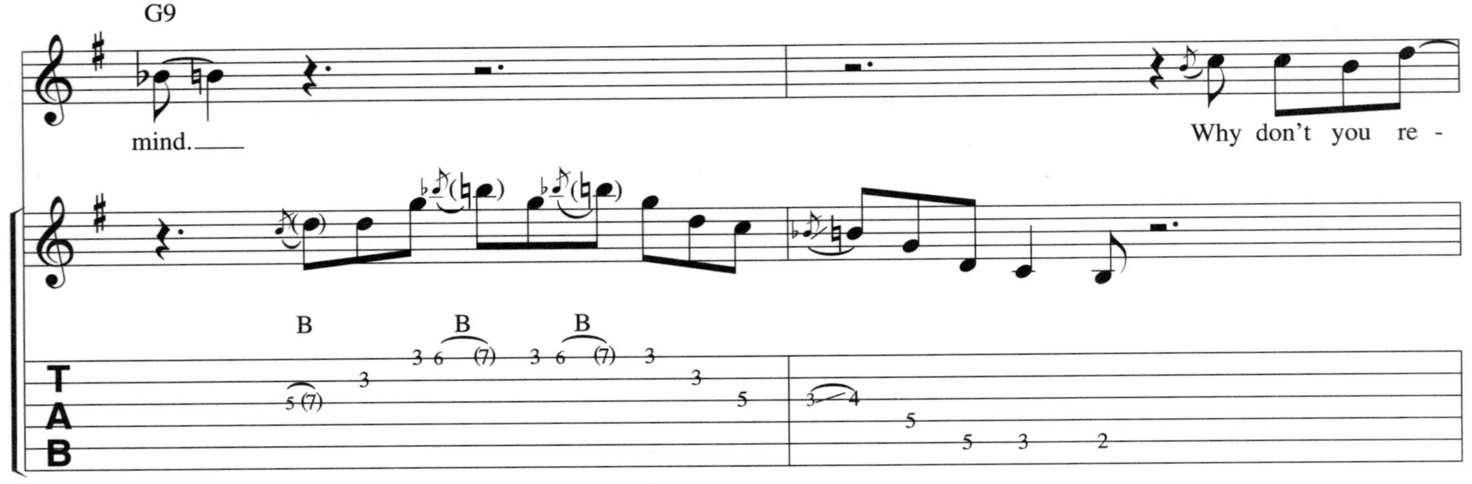
G9
mind.
Why don't you re -
B
B
B
T
A
B

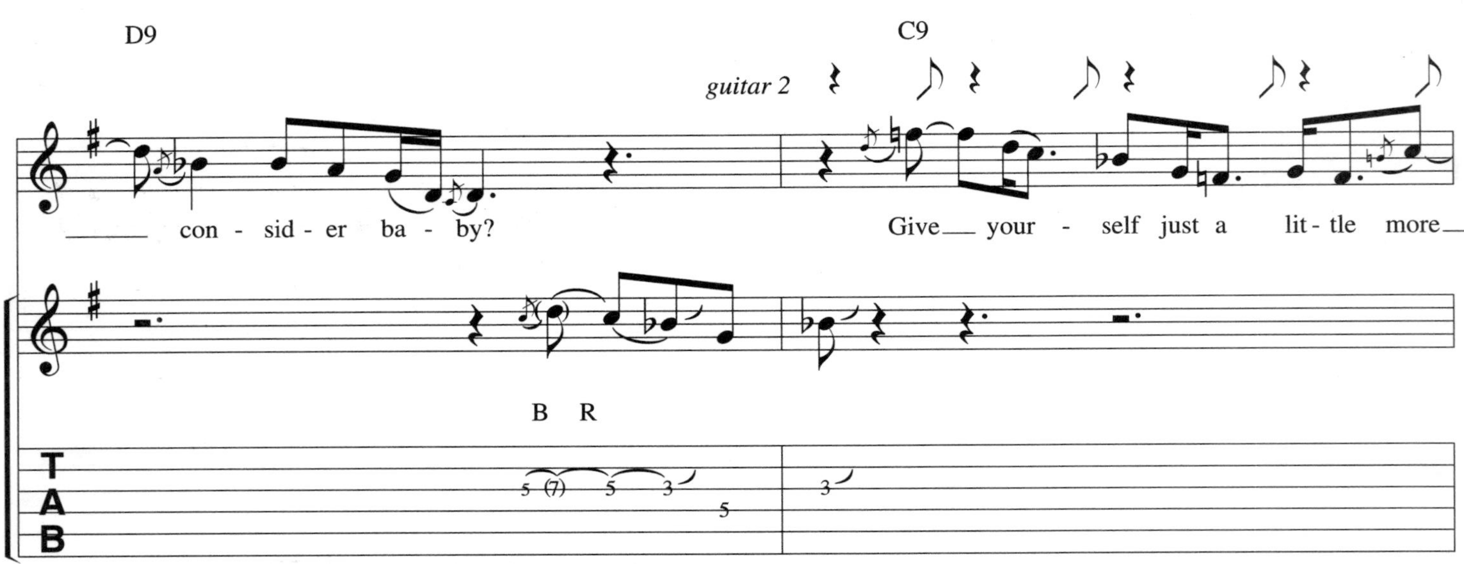
D9
C9
guitar 2
con - sid - er ba - by?
Give your - self just a lit - tle more
B R
T
A
B

A♭9
G9
time.
B
T
A
B

from Crossroads

Roll It Over

Words and Music by Eric Clapton and Bobby Whitlock

Verse
E
Go down eas - y
Roll it o - ver
guitar 3 (slide fills only on repeat)
guitar 1
let ring
guitar 2
and let me take my time.
let's take it from be - hind.
let ring

A7

Go down eas - y
Roll it o - ver,

let ring

E

and let me take my time.
let's take it from be - hind.

D7

Rock me slow
S'on - ly love,

F♯7 F7 E7

'til I lose my mind.
God knows it ain't no crime.

let ring

1.
guitar 3 tacet
let ring
Bridge
2.
F♯7
G♯7
C♯m
You don't know how much it's means to be
guitar 1 tacet
let ring
guitar 2
F♯7
G♯7
C♯m
C♯m/B
A7
N.C.
here in your arms. Roll it o -

E
ver.
Roll it o - ver.
guitar 1 with slide
let ring
guitar 2
let ring
Verse
E
Go down eas - y
and let me take my time.
Roll it o - ver
let's take it from be - hind.
guitar 3
guitar 1
guitar 2

A7
Go down eas - y
Roll it o - ver,
guitar 1
guitar 3
guitar 1 tacet
E7
and let me take my time.
let's take it from be - hind.
guitar 3
guitar 1
let ring
T
A
B

D7
Rock me slow
S'on - ly love,
F♯7
F
E7
'til I lose my mind.
God knows it ain't no crime.
guitar 1
guitars 1 & 3
guitar 3
let ring

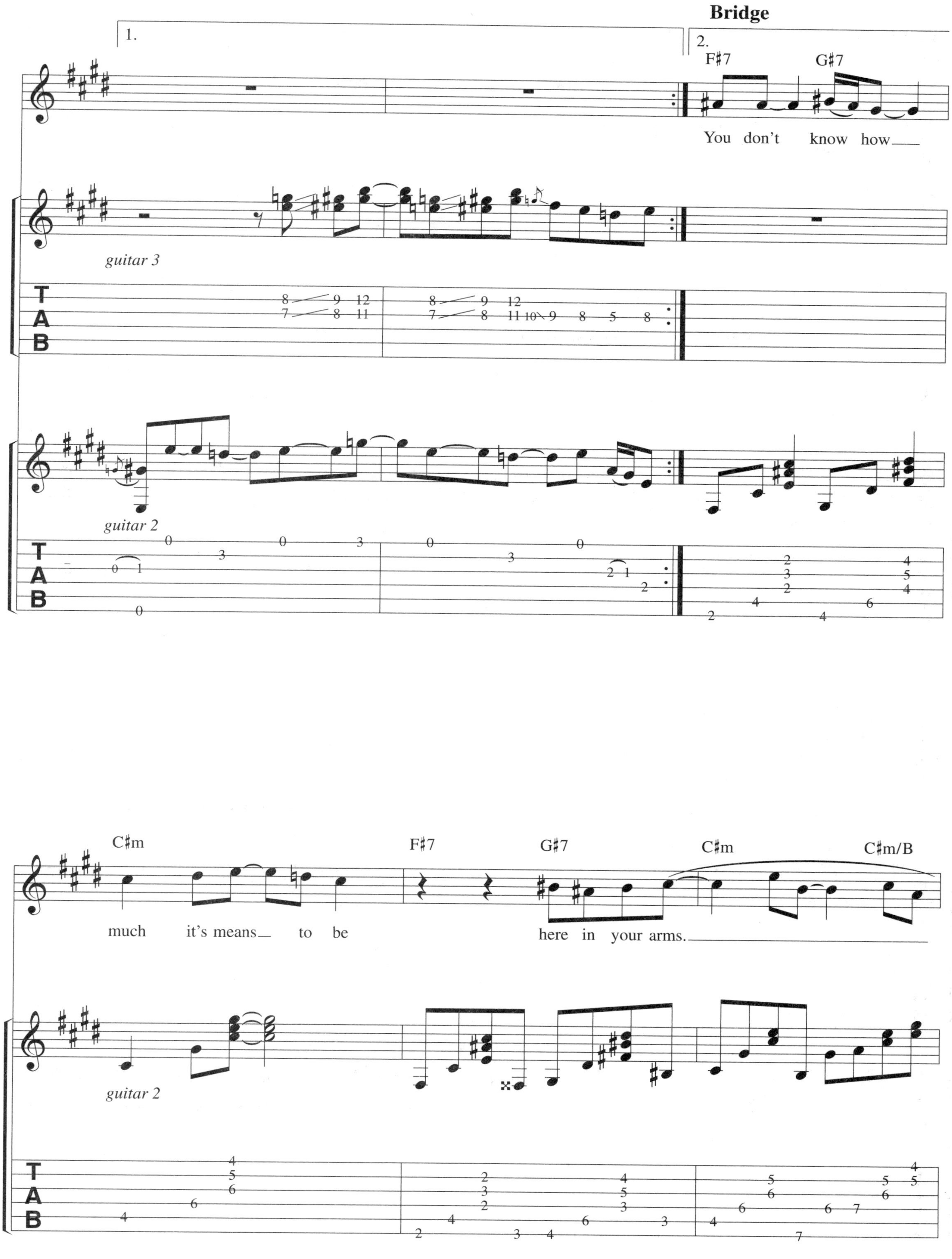

1.

Bridge

2.

F♯7 G♯7

You don't know how

guitar 3

guitar 2

A7
E7
Roll it o - ver.
Roll it o -
guitar 1
guitar 2
ver.
Guitar solo
E7
let ring
guitar 1 ** with Wah pedal
U.B.
R
** Standard tuning
①E ②B ③G
④D ⑤A ⑥E

A7
U.B. R
B R
U.B.
U.B.
U.B.
B U.B. B
TAB
E7
B B B B R
U.B. U.B.
TAB
D7
F#7
F7
E7
B
U.B.
TAB
let ring
U.B.
U.B.
U.B.
U.B.
B
B R
TAB
B R
TAB

A7
B R
B
B
B
E7
D7
F♯7
F7
E7
very light
B R
B
B R
U.B.
U.B.
U.B.
U.B.
U.B.
U.B.
U.B.
U.B.
U.B.
U.B.

U.B.
B
R
A7
E7
D7
F♯7
F7
hold bend
rit.

from No Reason To Cry

Sign Language

Words and Music by Bob Dylan

Em
D
lan - guage
er - y,
as I'm eat - ing a sand - wich
this is my sto - ry

Em
E5
in a small ca - fé
and still I'm still there.

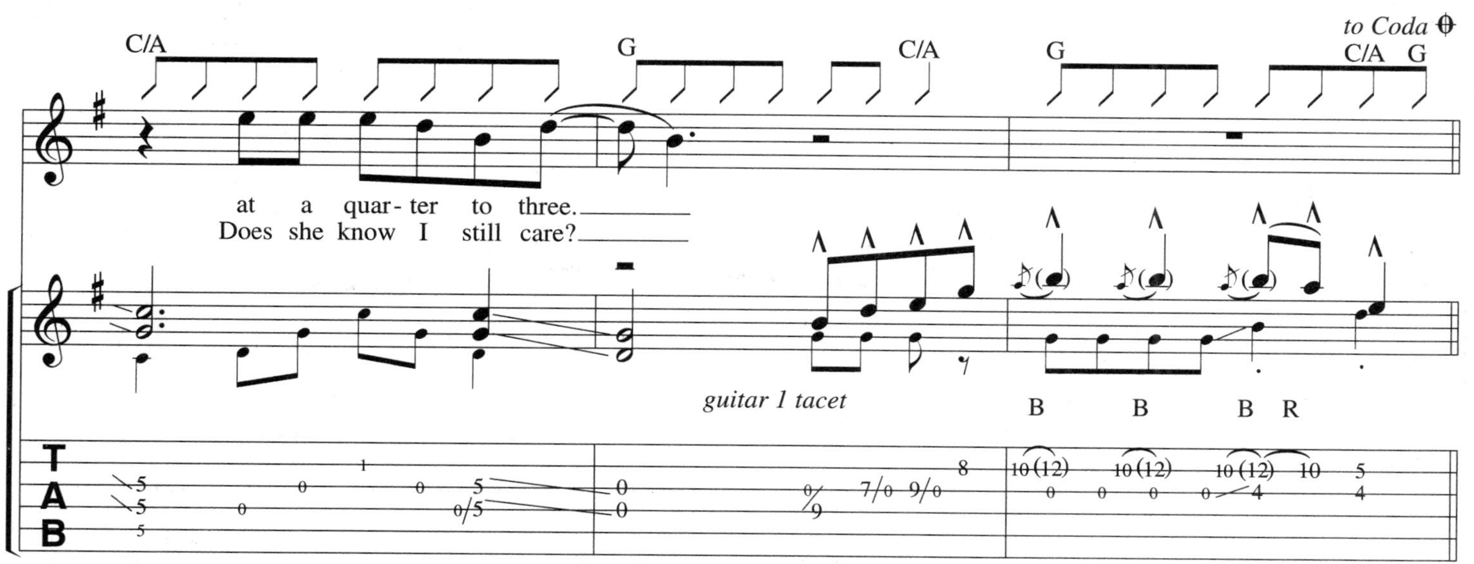
C/A
G
C/A
G
to Coda
C/A G
at a quar - ter to three.
Does she know I still care?
guitar 1 tacet
B B B R

Bridge
guitars 3 & 4
D
C/G
Well, I can't re - spond
Link Wray was play - in'
to your sign
on the juke - box I was
guitar 2
guitar 1
guitar 2 tacet
P.M.

Em
D
lan - guage;
pay - in'
you're tak - ing ad - van - tage,
for the words I was say - in',

Em
bring - ing me down.
so mis - un - der stood.
guitar 1

D.S. al Coda
to Coda
G
C/G G
C/G G
Can't you make an - y sound?
It did - n't do me no good.
guitar 2
Coda
G
D
guitar 2
C
G
D
Em
guitar 1
guitar 1
guitar 2 tacet
guitar 2

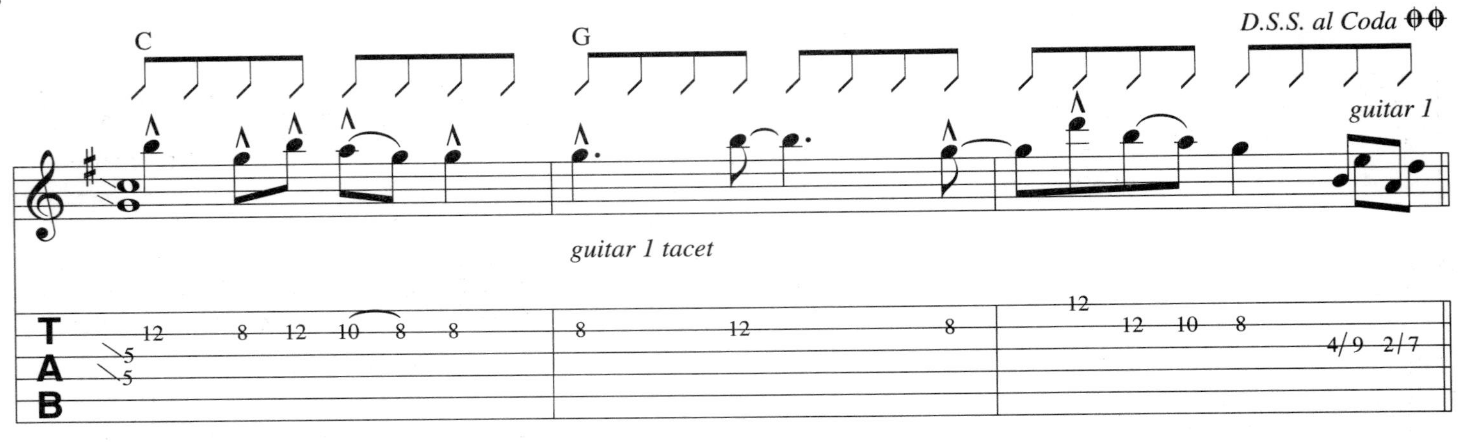

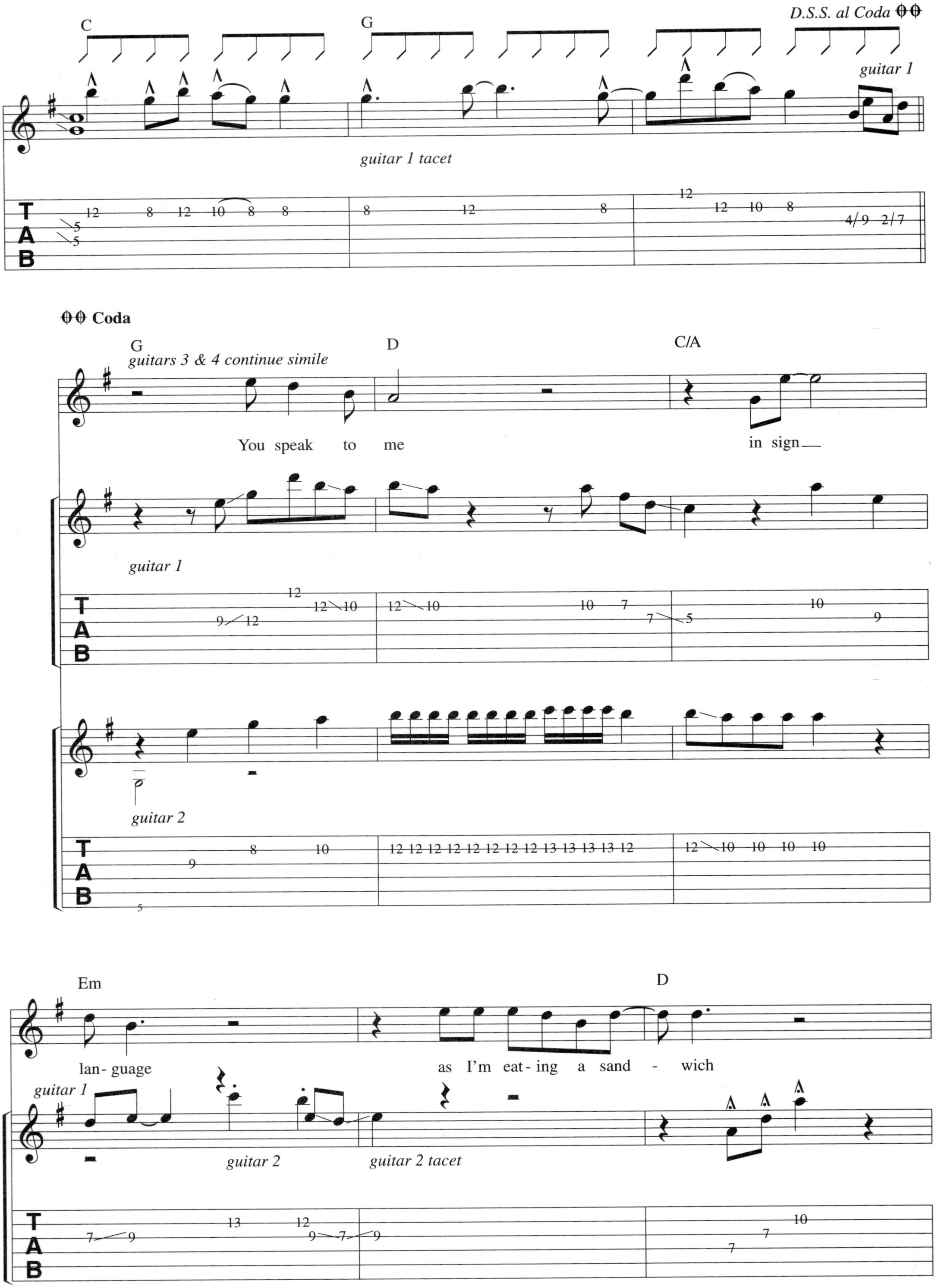

D.S.S. al Coda
C
G
guitar 1
guitar 1 tacet
Coda
G
D
C/A
guitars 3 & 4 continue simile
You speak to me in sign
guitar 1
guitar 2
Em
D
lan- guage as I'm eat- ing a sand - wich
guitar 1
guitar 2
guitar 2 tacet

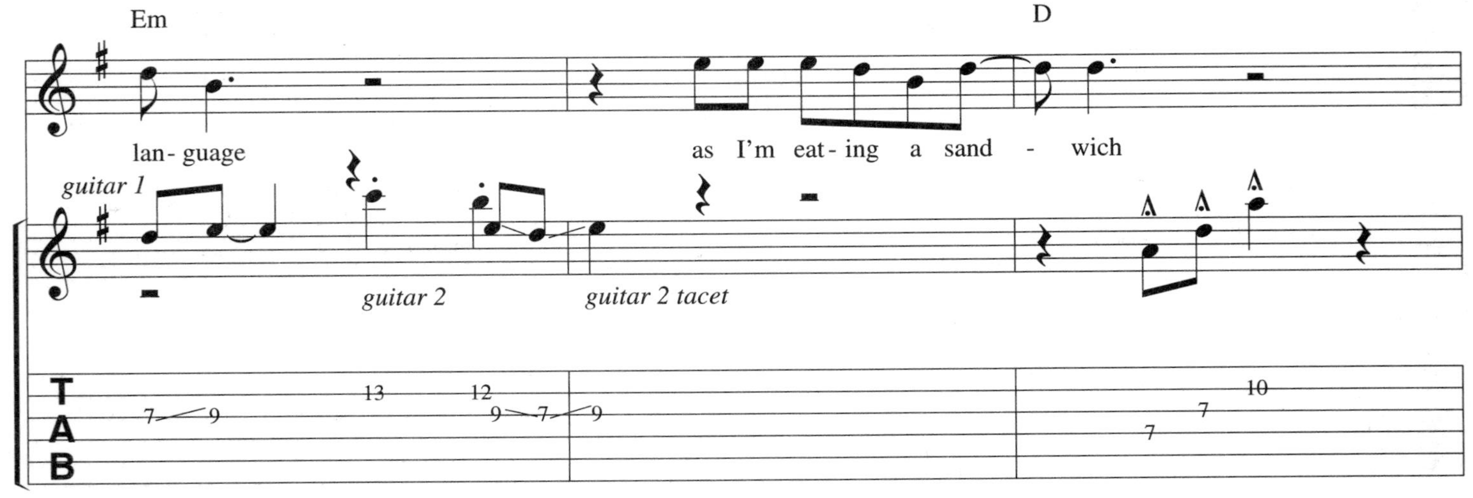

Em
C/A
in a small ca - fé
at a quar- ter to three.
guitar 1
B R
guitar 2 tacet
G
Well, I can't re -
pp
D
C/A
Em
spond
to your sign
lan- guage;
guitar 1
guitar 2
B
B
B

D
you're tak - ing ad - van - tage,
bring - ing me down.
T
A
B

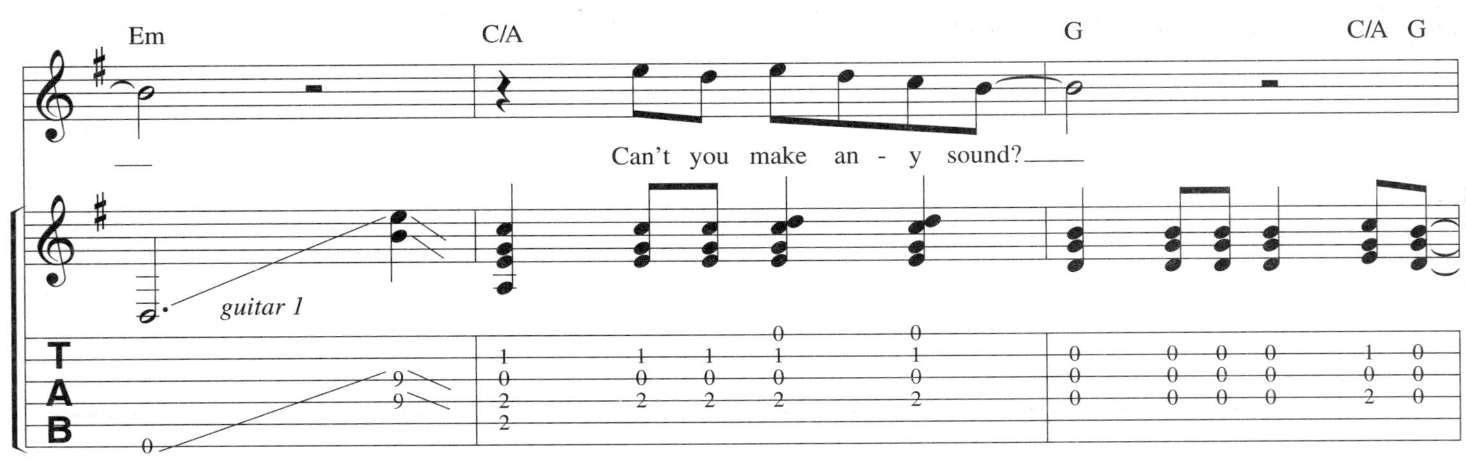
Em
C/A
G
C/A G
Can't you make an - y sound?
guitar 1
T
A
B

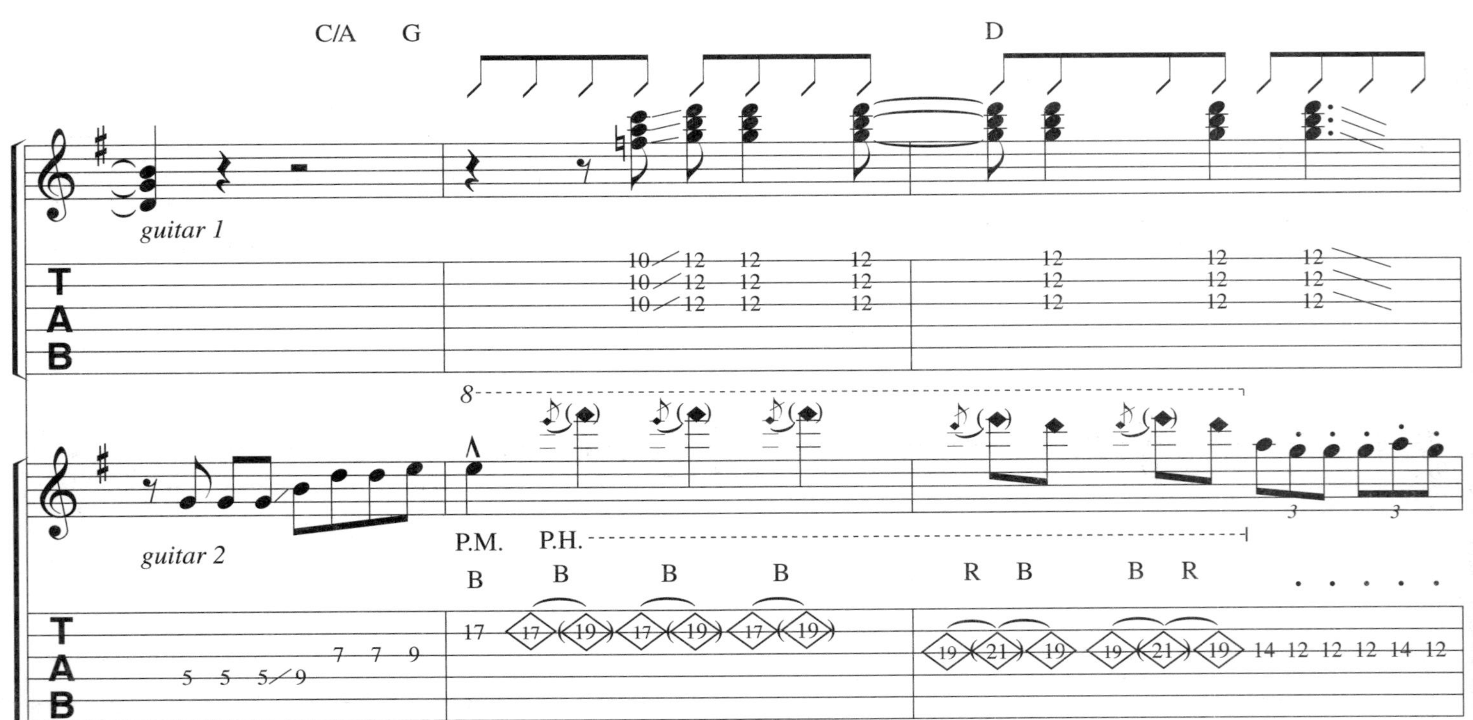
C/A G
D
guitar 1
guitar 2
P.M.
P.H.
T
A
B

C
G
T
A
B
5
5
5
5
5
5
2
4
3
12
14
12
14
12
14
14
14
12
12
12
12
B
B
R
14
(16)
D
3
4
7
19
(20)
15
16
9
8

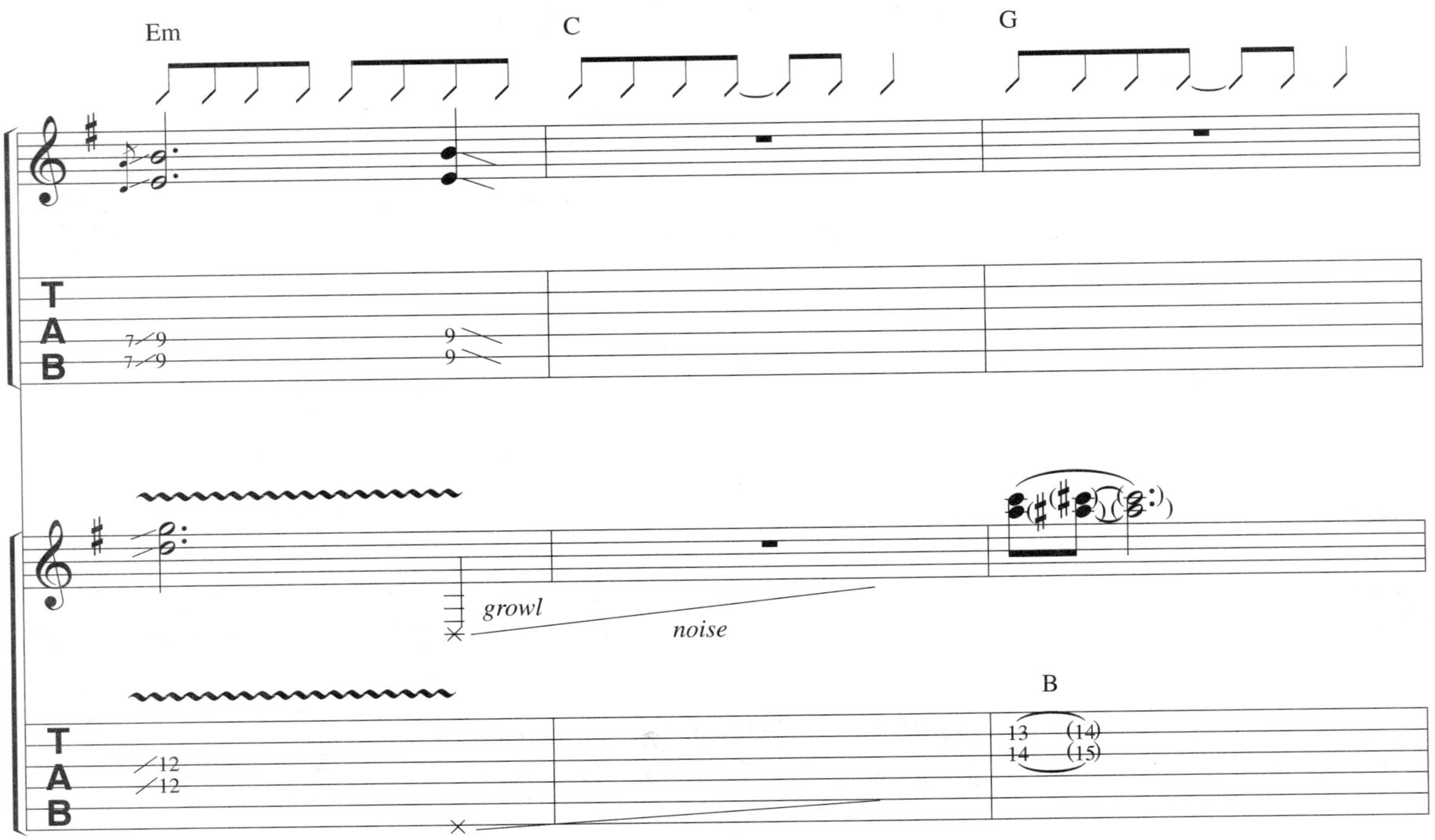

Em C G

growl *noise*

B

from Unplugged

Rollin' And Tumblin'

by Muddy Waters

Verse 2
C
2. Well now, come here ba - by,
3. & 4. See additional lyrics
G
sit down on da - dy's knee.
C
Well now, come here ba -
by,
G
sit down on dad - dy's knee.
even gliss.

I wan - na
with fingers
with slide
D
C
tell you a - bout the way they treat - ed me.
G
to Coda
D.S. (fourth verse) al Coda
Guitar solo 1
C
TAB

G
C
G
D
C
G

Coda
3. Well, I
Guitar solo 2

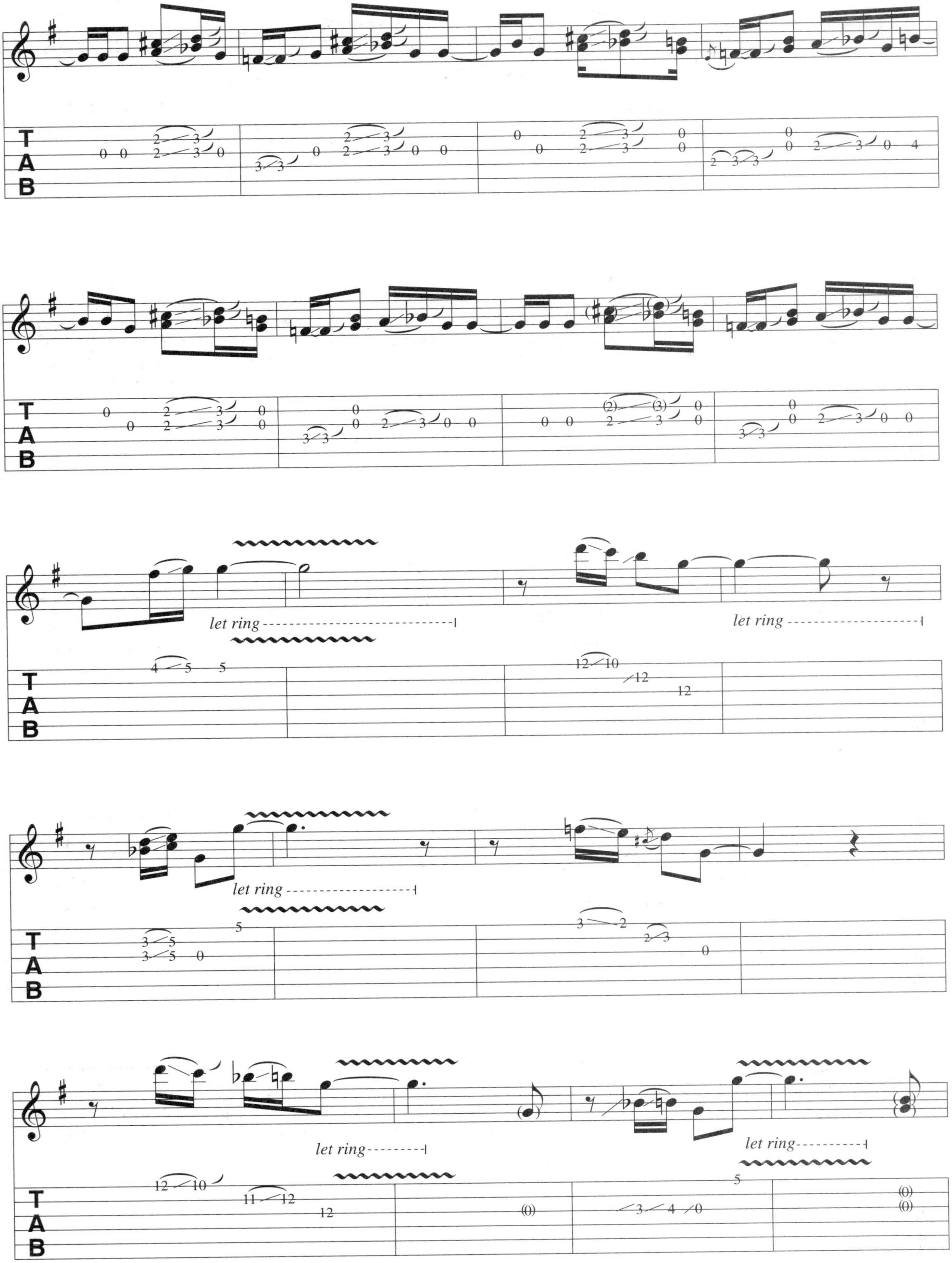

let ring

let ring

let ring

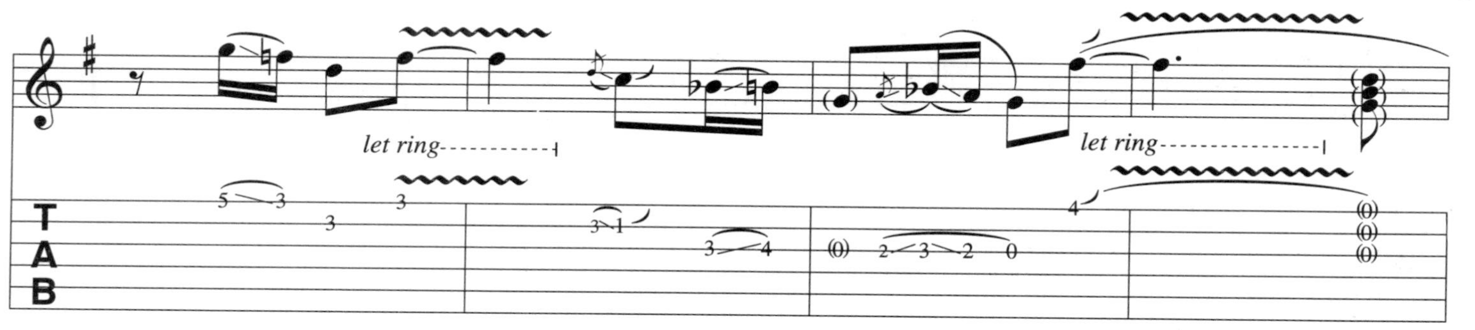
let ring
let ring

let ring
let ring

let ring
let ring

let ring

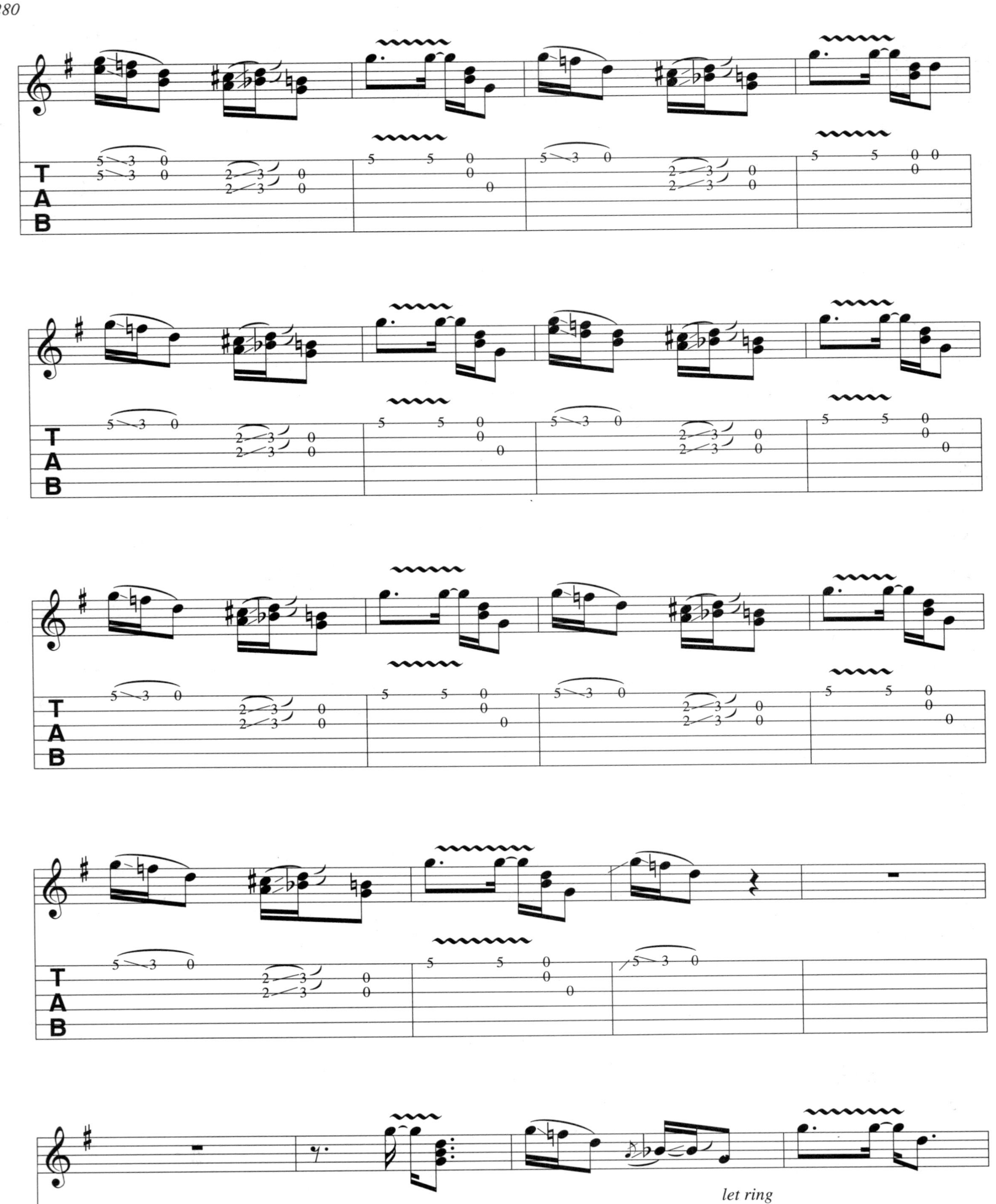
let ring

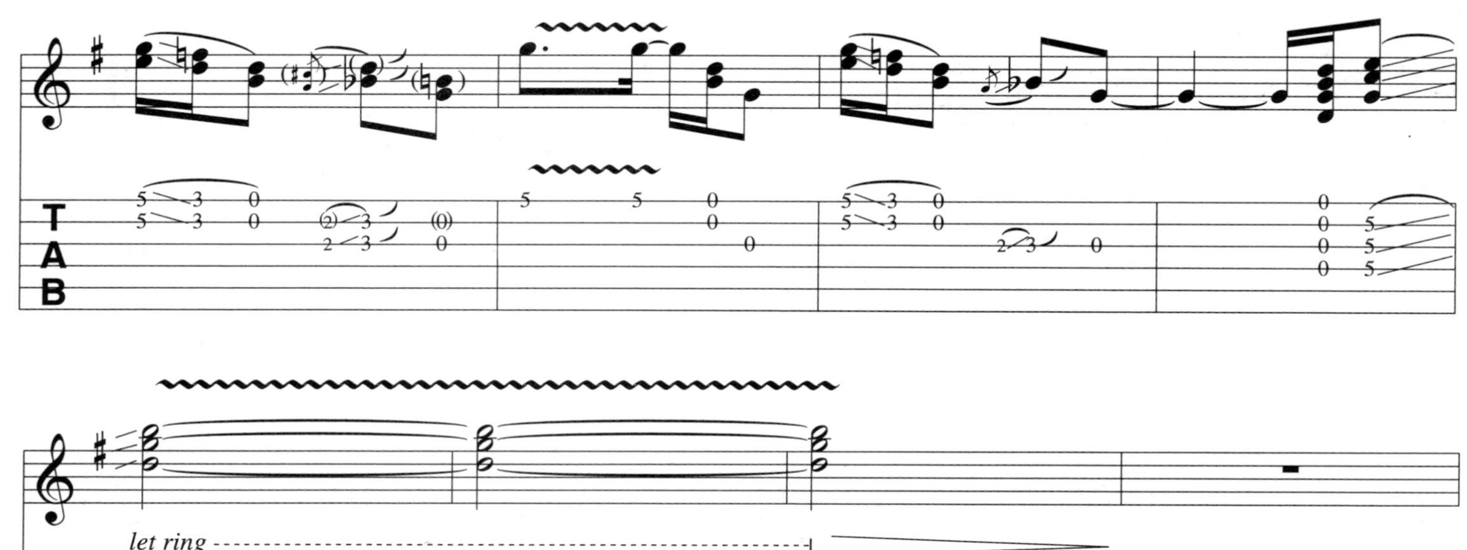

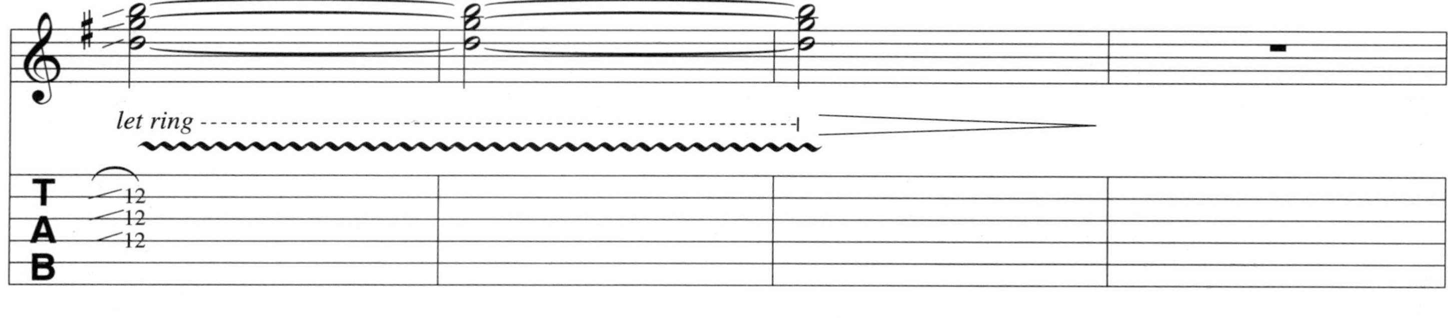

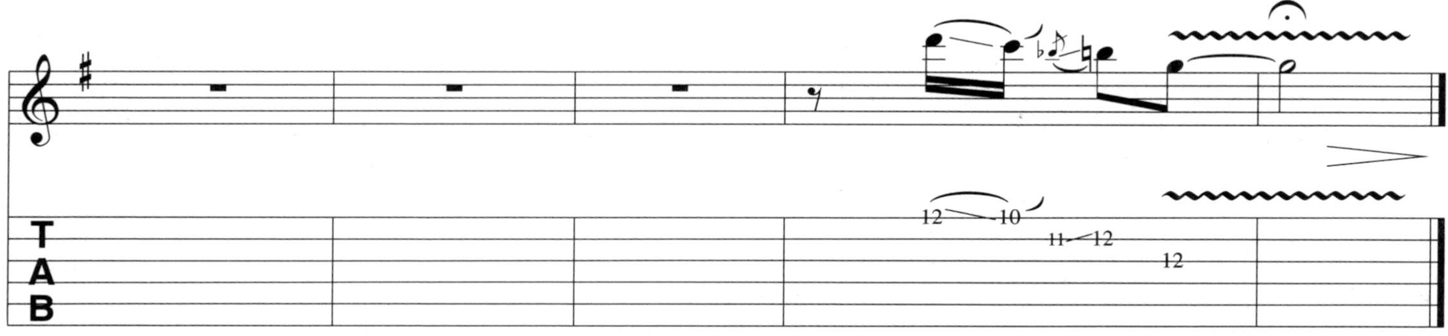

Additional Lyrics

3. Well, I rolled an' I tumbled,
   Cried the whole night long.
   Well, I rolled an' I tumbled,
   Cried the whole night long.
   When I woke up this mornin'
   All I had was gone.

4. Well, I hmm, mmm, ah.
   Well, I hmm, mmm,
   Mmm, mmm, mmm.
   Ah, ah, ah, mmm, whoa.

from From The Cradle

Standin' Around Cryin'

by Muddy Waters

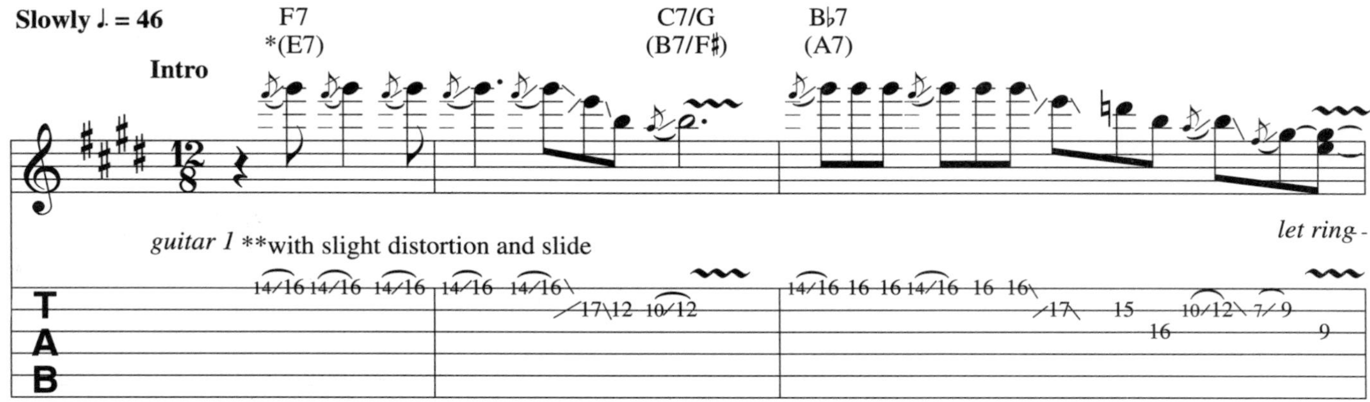

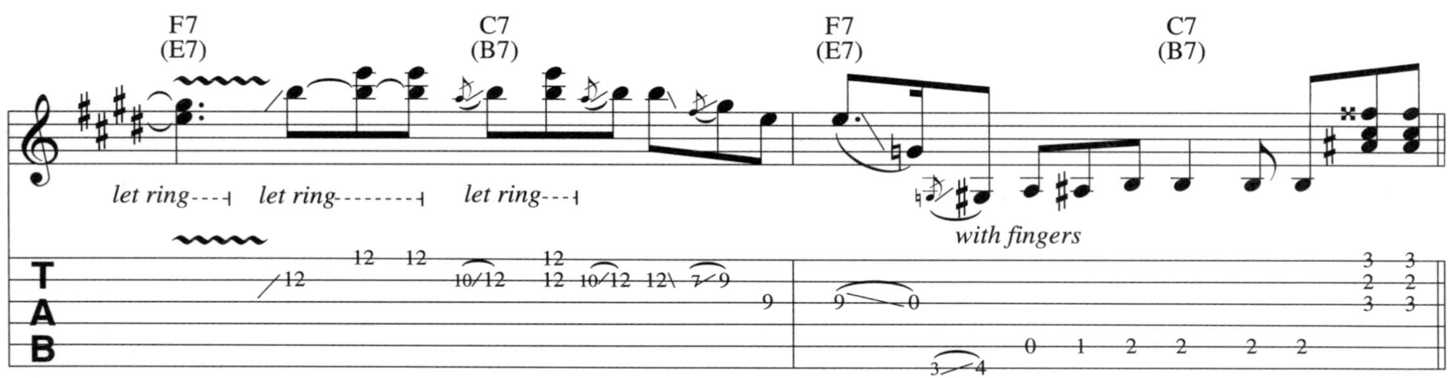

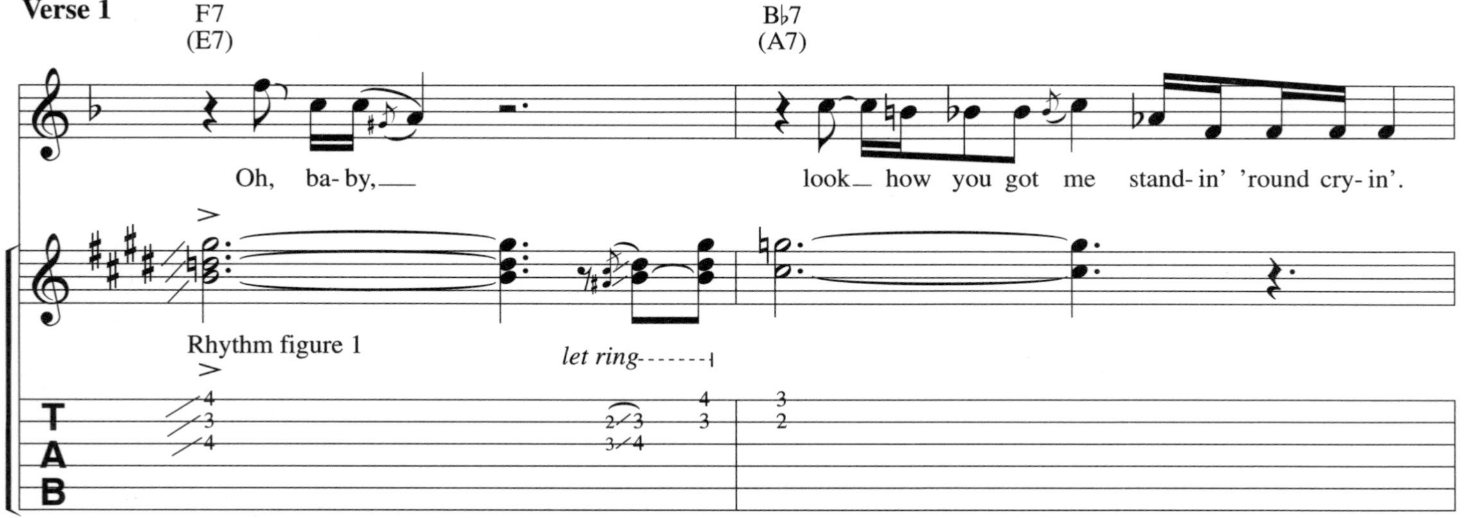

F7
(E7)
let ring

B♭7
(A7)
Oh, ba-by,
look how you got me stand - in' 'round cry - in'.

F7
(E7)
with slide

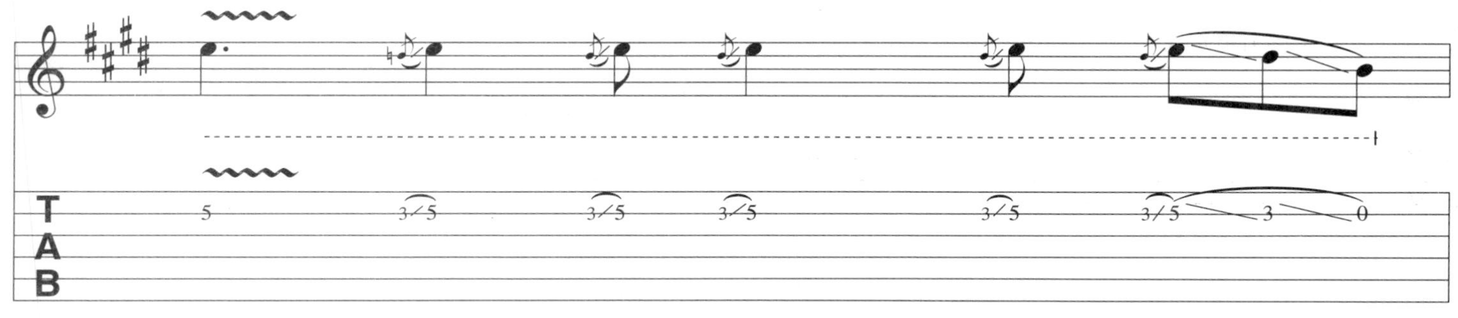

C7
(B7)
B♭7
(A7)
No, I don't love you lit- tle girl,
but you're al-ways rest-in' on my mind.
let ring
end Rhythm figure 1
F7
(E7)
C7
(B7)
Verse 2
guitars 1 Rhythm figures 1 simile
guitar 2 continues ad lib rhythm
F7
(E7)
B♭7
(A7)
Oh, ba-by,
I ain't gon-na be rid- in' you 'round in my au- to- mo- bile.
F7
(E7)
B♭7
(A7)
Oh, ba- by,
I ain't gon- na be rid- in' you'round in my au- to- mo- bile.
F7
(E7)
C7
(B7)
F7
(E7)
C7
(B7)
B♭7
(A7)
You got so man - y men,
that I'm a - fraid you may get me killed.

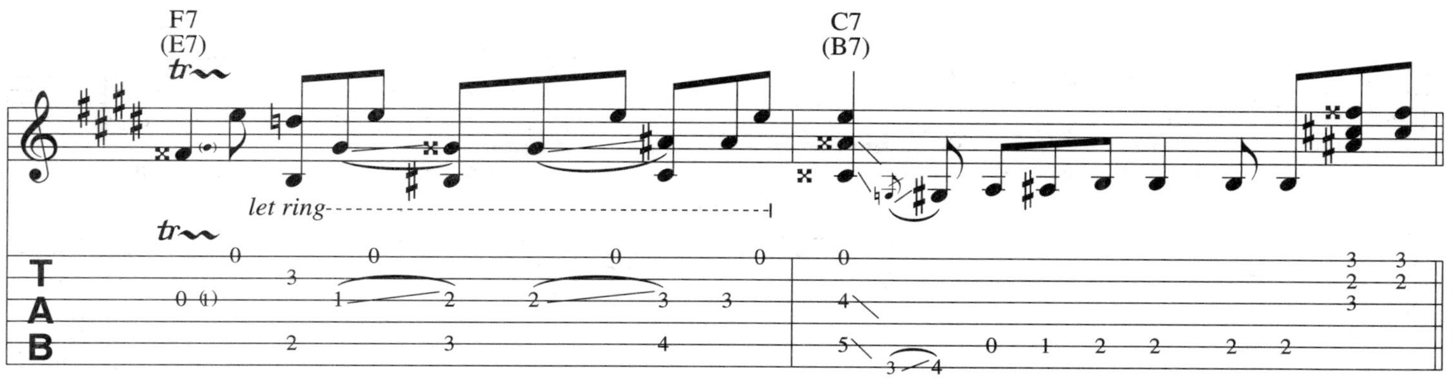
F7
(E7)
C7
(B7)
let ring
T
A
B

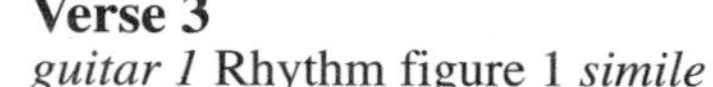
Verse 3
guitar 1 Rhythm figure 1 simile

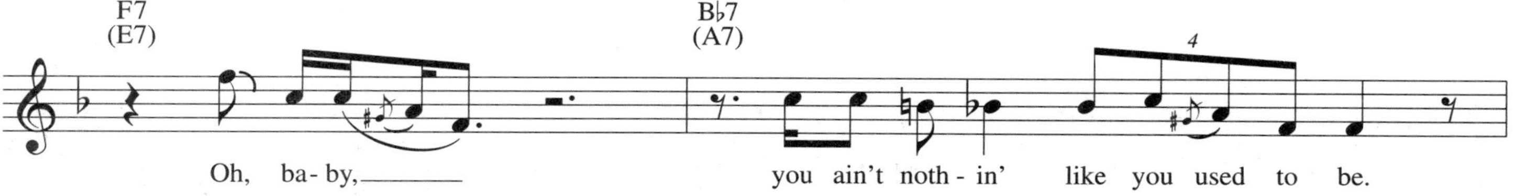
F7
(E7)
B♭7
(A7)
Oh, ba- by,
you ain't noth - in' like you used to be.

F7
(E7)
(spoken): No, don't get me killed, hon - ey.

B♭7
(A7)
Oh, baby,
you ain't noth - in' like you used to be. (spoken): Oh, man leave

F7
(E7)
that wom- an a - lone.
guitar 2
U.B.
T
A
B

C7
(B7)
When I was deep in love with you, lit - tle girl,
let ring
B♭7
(A7)
you were just sweet as an ap – ple on a tree.
F7
(E7)
F7/A
(E7/G♯)
B♭7
(A7)
B°7
(A♯°7)
let ring
C7
(B7)
F♯9
(F9)
F9
(E9)
poco rit.

from Unplugged

San Francisco Bay Blues

Words and Music by Jesse Fuller

Moderately fast with swing feel ♩=162

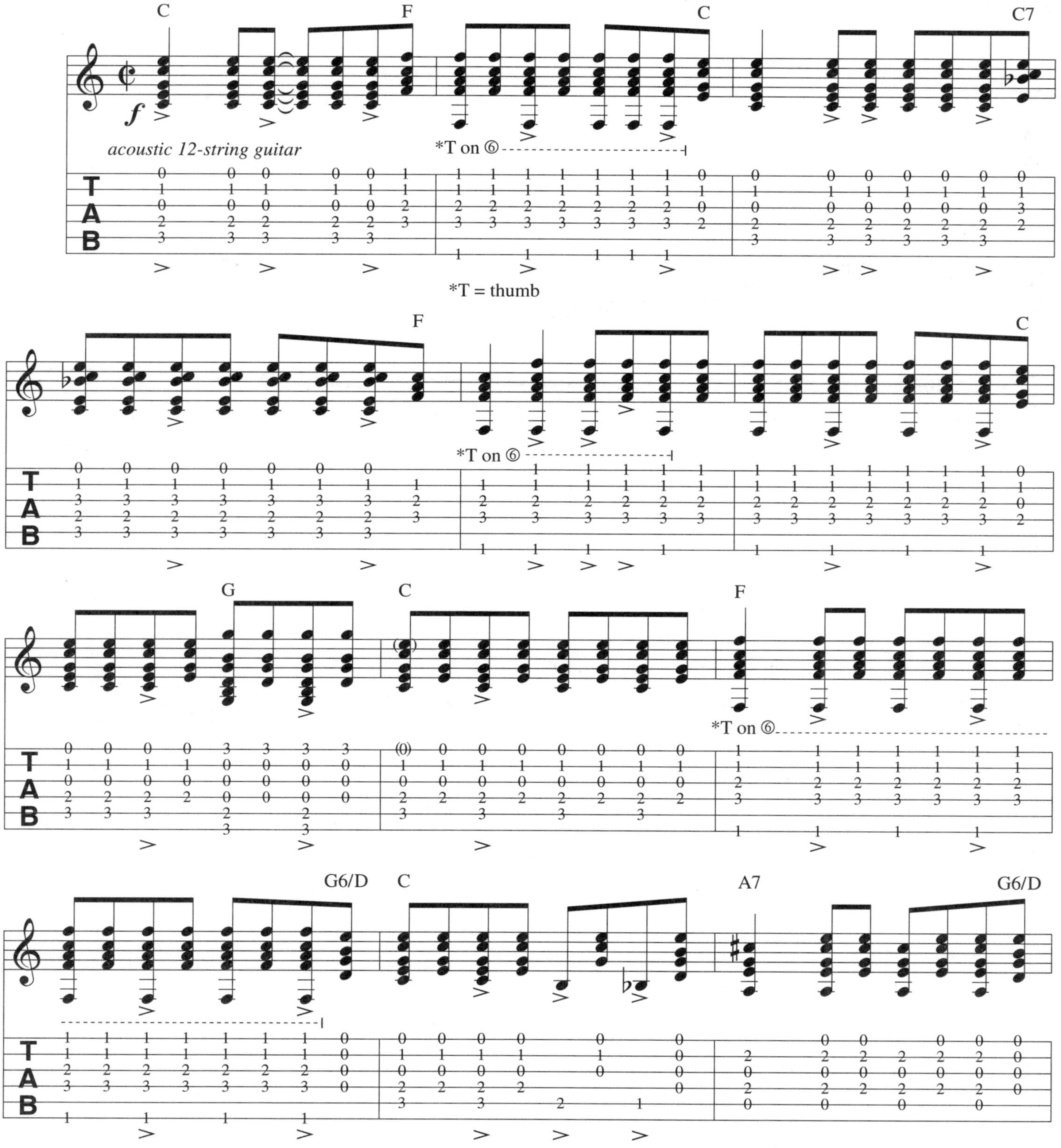

C F C C7

f

acoustic 12-string guitar

*T on ⑥

*T = thumb

F C

*T on ⑥

G C F

*T on ⑥

G6/D C A7 G6/D

D7/F♯
G6/D
G7
*T on ⑥
Verse 1
C
F
1. I got the blues from my ba - by liv - in' by the San Fran - cis - co bay.
C7
The o - cean lin - er's not so far a - way.
G6
(I)
C/B
⑤1fr
B♭ A7
did - n't mean to treat her so bad. She was the best girl I ev - er have
⑤open
A A7 Am7
D7
had. (I) said good - bye, I can take a cry.

Verse 2
G7 C F G6/D C7 F6 E5 E Em E E7 C/B ⑤1fr B♭ A7 D7 D7/F♯ 1. G 2. G
Verse 3
I wan-na lay down 'n' die.
I ain't got a nick-el an' I ain't got a lou - sy dime.
(with kazoo solo on repeat)
She don't come back, ain't gon-na lose my mind.
(Ya) ev-er get back to stay, it's gon-na be an-oth-er brand new day,
walk in' with (my) ba - by down by the San Fran-cis-co bay.
(Sit-tin') down, look-in' from a back door,

F
C
F
won-d'rin which way to go.
(The) wom-an, I'm so
C
F
cra - zy 'bout,
she don't love me no more.
G6/D
C
C/B
⑤2fr
B
G6
Think I'll catch me the freight train
be-cause I'm feel - in'
A7
D7/F♯
G7
blue
ride all way to the end of the line,
Verse 4
G6/D
C
F
C
Think-in' on-ly you.
Mean - while, liv - in' in the
F
C
F
cit - y,
just a-bout to go in-sane.
G6/D
E7
All I heard my ba - by, Lord,
wish-in' you could call my name

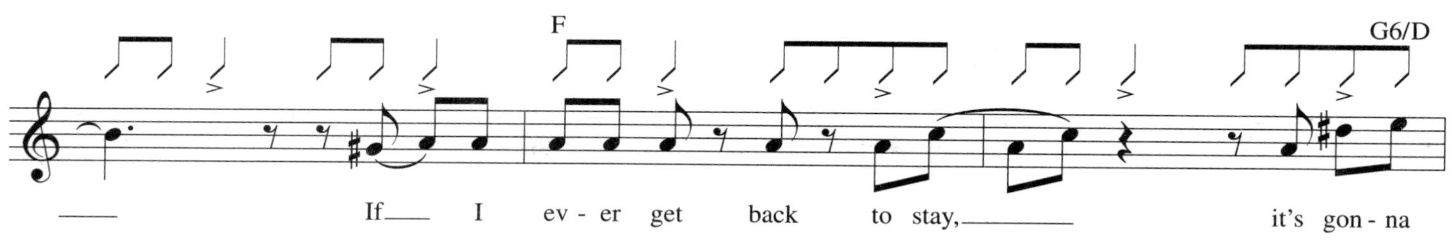
F
G6/D
If I ev - er get back to stay, it's gon - na

C
C/B
⑤1fr
B♭ A7
A7
D7/F♯
G7
be an - oth - er brand new day,
walk - in' with my ba - by down

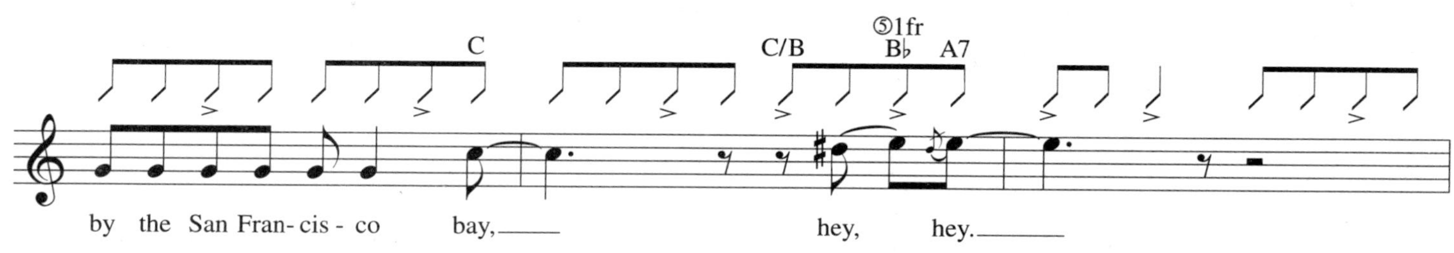
C
C/B
⑤1fr
B♭ A7
by the San Fran - cis - co bay,
hey, hey.

D7/F♯
G7
C
C/B
⑤1fr
B♭ A7
Walk - in' with my ba - by down by the San Fran - cis - co bay.

D7/F♯
G7
Yeah, I'm walk - in' with my ba - by down by the San Fran - cis - co bay.

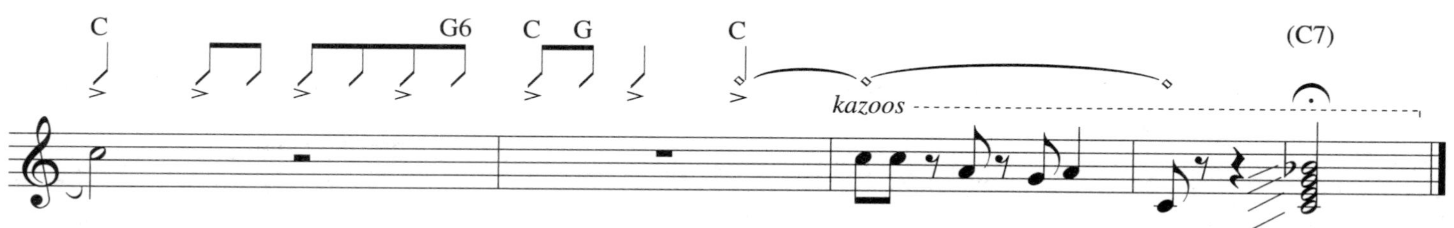
C
G6
C G
C
(C7)
kazoos

from From The Cradle

Someday After A While
(You'll Be Sorry)

by Freddie King and Sonny Thompson

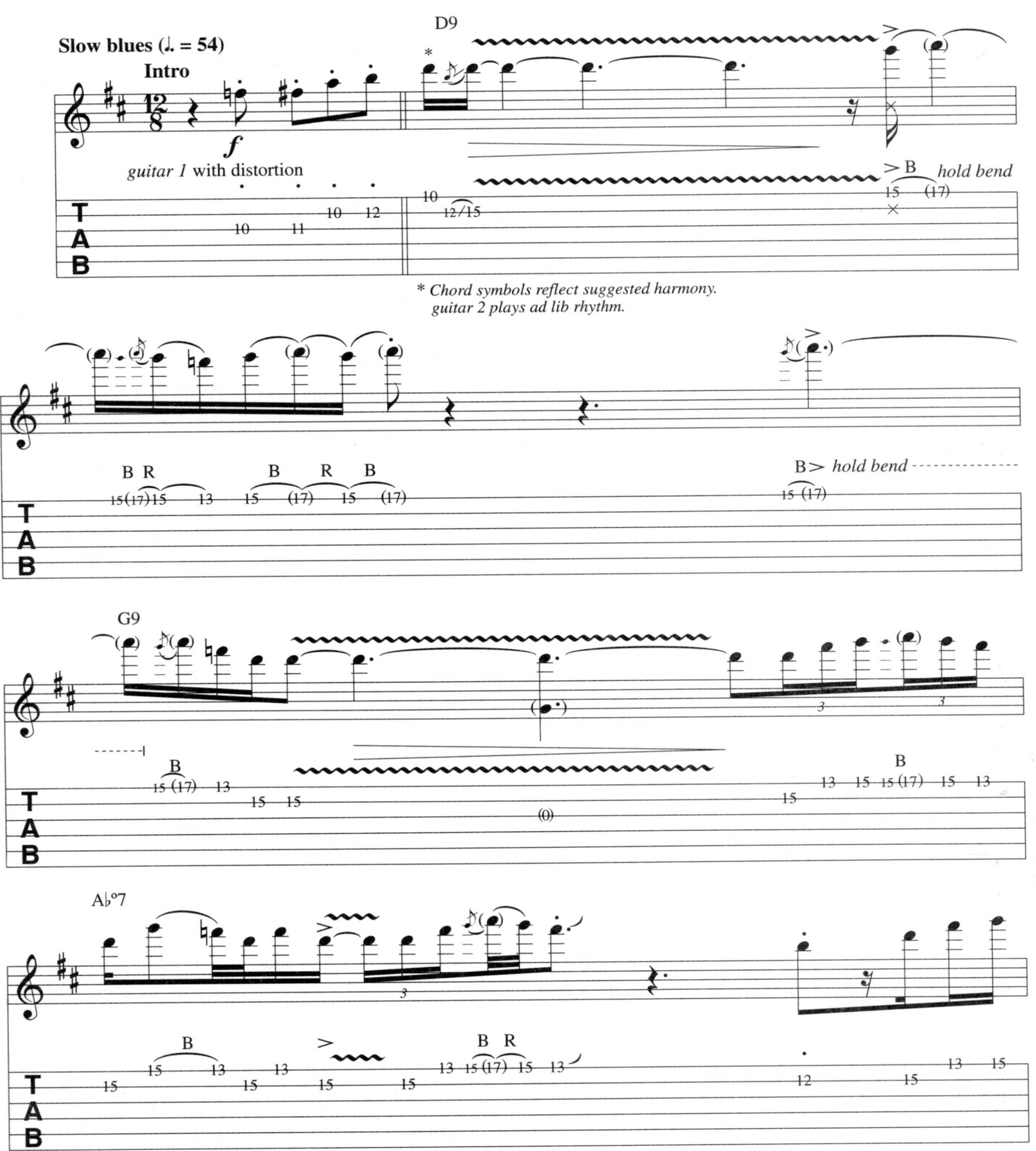

* Chord symbols reflect suggested harmony. guitar 2 plays ad lib rhythm.

D9
Bm7
let ring
Em7
A7
D
D/F♯
G
A♭°7
D
A7
I got
Verse 1
D9
to ride
that lone - some train.
My - heart
let ring

G7
A♭°7
is heav-y with aches and in pain. I said
B R
D
Bm7
Em7
A7
but some-day, some-day, ba-by, af-ter a-while you will be
guitar 2
D
D/F♯
G
A♭°7
sor - ry.
B
B
Verse 2
D
A7
D9
Ev - 'ry day my clouds

G9
— are grey, —
takes you to roll —
all
B
B
10 12
10 12 12 (13) 12 10 12 (13)
A♭°7
those clouds a - way. —
I said, —
B
B R
12 (14) 12 10 12 12 12 10 12 (14) 12 10
D9
Bm7
Em7
A7
— that some-day, some - day, ba-by, af-ter a - while —
you will be —
D
D/F♯
G
A♭°7
— sor - ry. —
B
13 (15) 10 10 10 0 0 0 10 13 10 12 10 12 10 12 12 12
Bridge
D
D7
G7
Trou-ble, trou-ble, —
trou-ble
10 11 10 12 10 11 12 12 10 11 10 10 13 10 13 10

on my mind.
B R
B
D7
Trou - ble, trou - ble,
lay
down the line.
hold bend
hold bend
B
B
B
B
B
let ring
E7
I don't need, I don't need no
sym - pa - thy,
so

A
A11
babe, babe, don't you, don't you pit-y me.
B
B
Verse 3
D9
I may be blue I,
let ring
B
but I don't mind,
B
let ring
G9
A♭°7
be-cause I know way down the line. I said
B
B

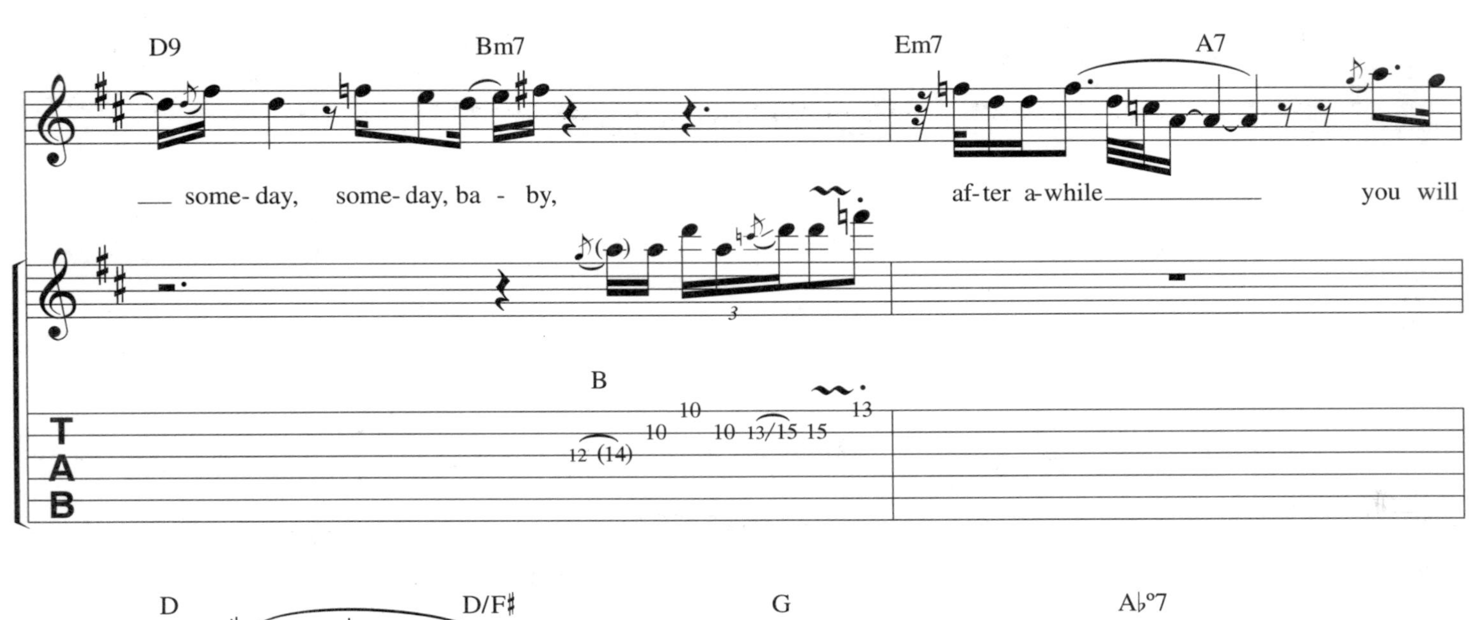
D9
Bm7
Em7
A7
— some- day, some- day, ba - by,
af- ter a-while
you will
B
10
10
10 10 13/15 15
13
12 (14)
T
A
B

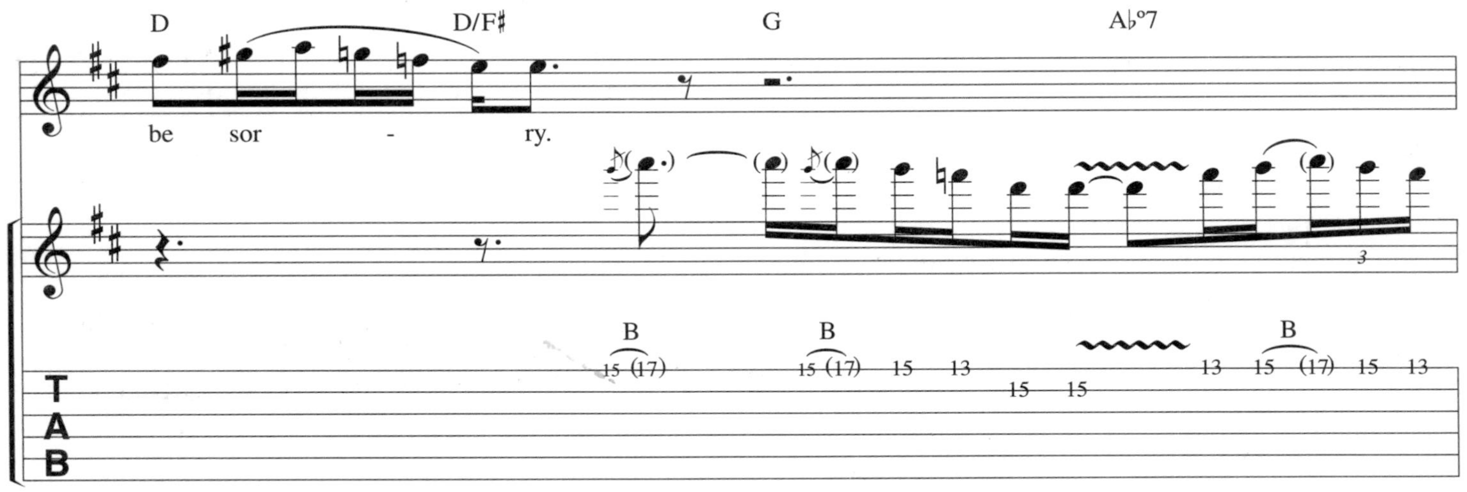
D
D/F♯
G
A♭°7
be sor - ry.
B
B
B
15 (17)
15 (17) 15 13
15 15
13 15 (17) 15 13
T
A
B

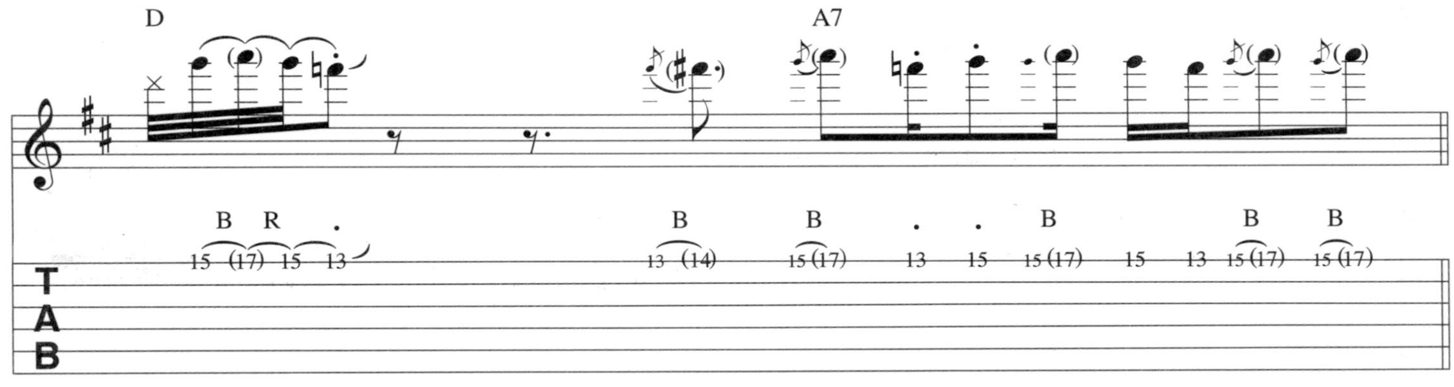
D
A7
B R
B
B
B
B B
15 (17) 15 13
13 (14)
15 (17)
13 15 15 (17)
15 13 15 (17) 15 (17)
T
A
B

Guitar solo

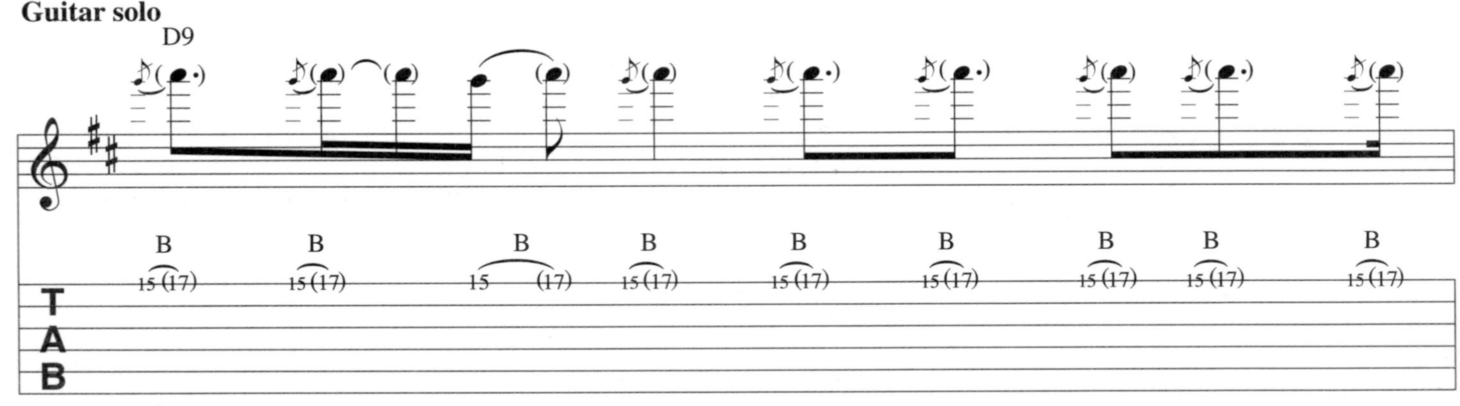
D9
B B B B B B B B B
15 (17) 15 (17) 15 (17) 15 (17) 15 (17) 15 (17) 15 (17) 15 (17) 15 (17)
T
A
B

G9
A♭°7
D9
Bm7
loco
Em7
A7

D
D/F♯
G
A♭°7
D
A7
hold bend
D9
loco
hold bend
G9

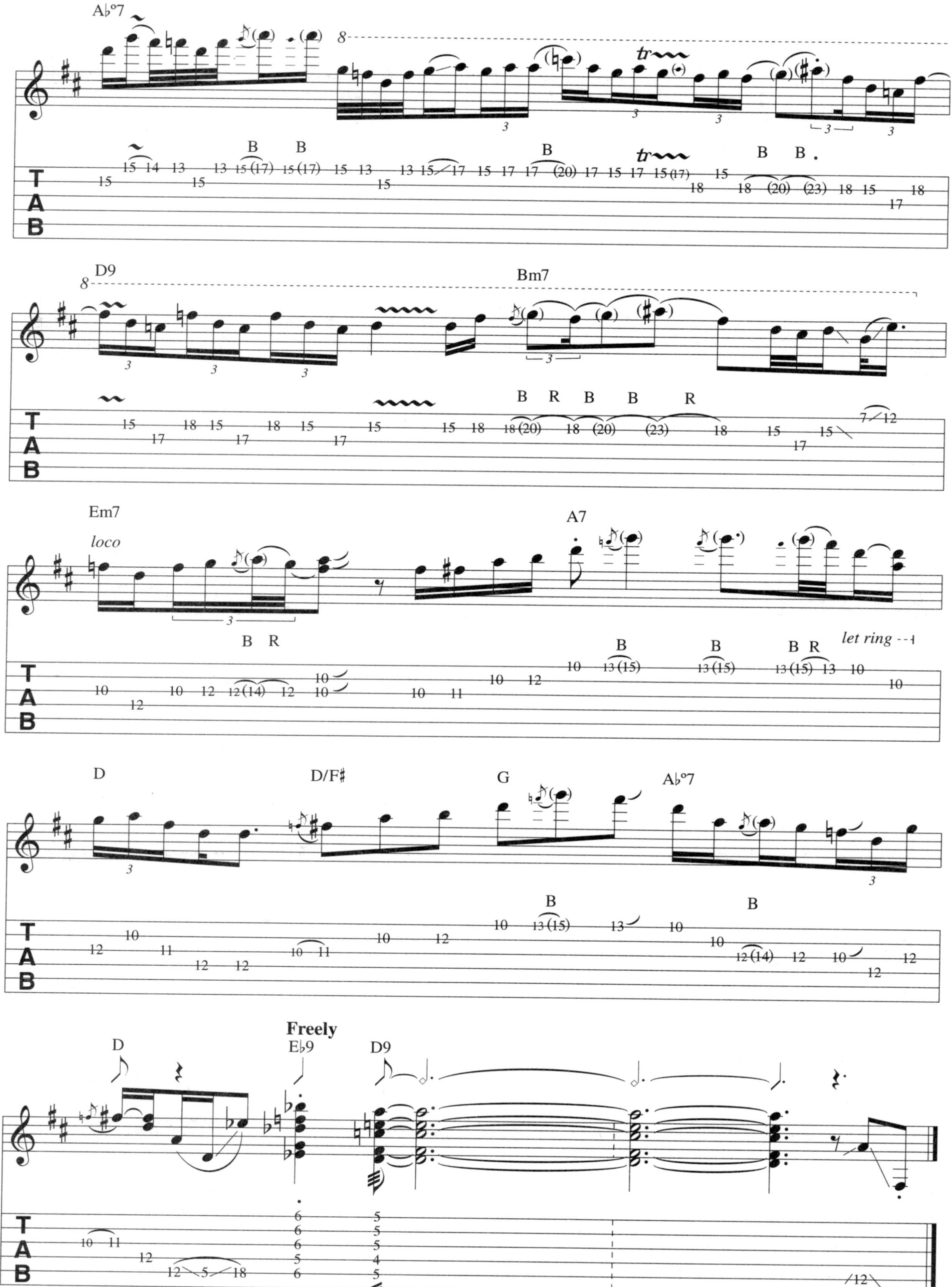

A♭°7
8
tr
B
B
B
B
D9
Bm7
B
R
B
B
R
Em7
loco
A7
B
R
B
B
B
R
let ring
D
D/F♯
G
A♭°7
B
B
Freely
D
E♭9
D9

from Fresh Cream

Spoonful

Written by Willie Dixon

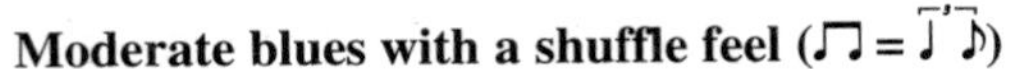

Just a lit-tle spoon of your pre-cious love
B hold bend R
N.C.
sat - is - fy - my soul.
Men lies a - bout it;
some of them cries a - bout it.
Some of them
dies a - bout it.
Ev - 'ry-thing's a fight-in' a - bout the

spoon - ful. That spoon, that spoon, that spoon - ful. That
B B B
spoon, that spoon, that spoon - ful. That spoon, that spoon, that
spoon - ful. That spoon, that spoon, that spoon.
harp solo
TAB

Could fill a spoon's full of cof - fee; could fill a spoon's full of tea.
Just a lit- tle spoon of your precious love, is
that e- nough for me?
Em
Men lies a - bout it;
hold bend
B
B hold bend R
B

some of them cries a - bout it. Some of them
B
dies a - bout it. Ev - 'ry - thing's a fight - in' a - bout the
B
spoon - ful. That spoon, that spoon, that spoon - ful. That
B
spoon, that spoon, that spoon - ful. That spoon, that spoon, that
B

spoon - ful.
That spoon, that spoon, hey.
Guitar solo
B hold bend R B B
B
B
B R B
B

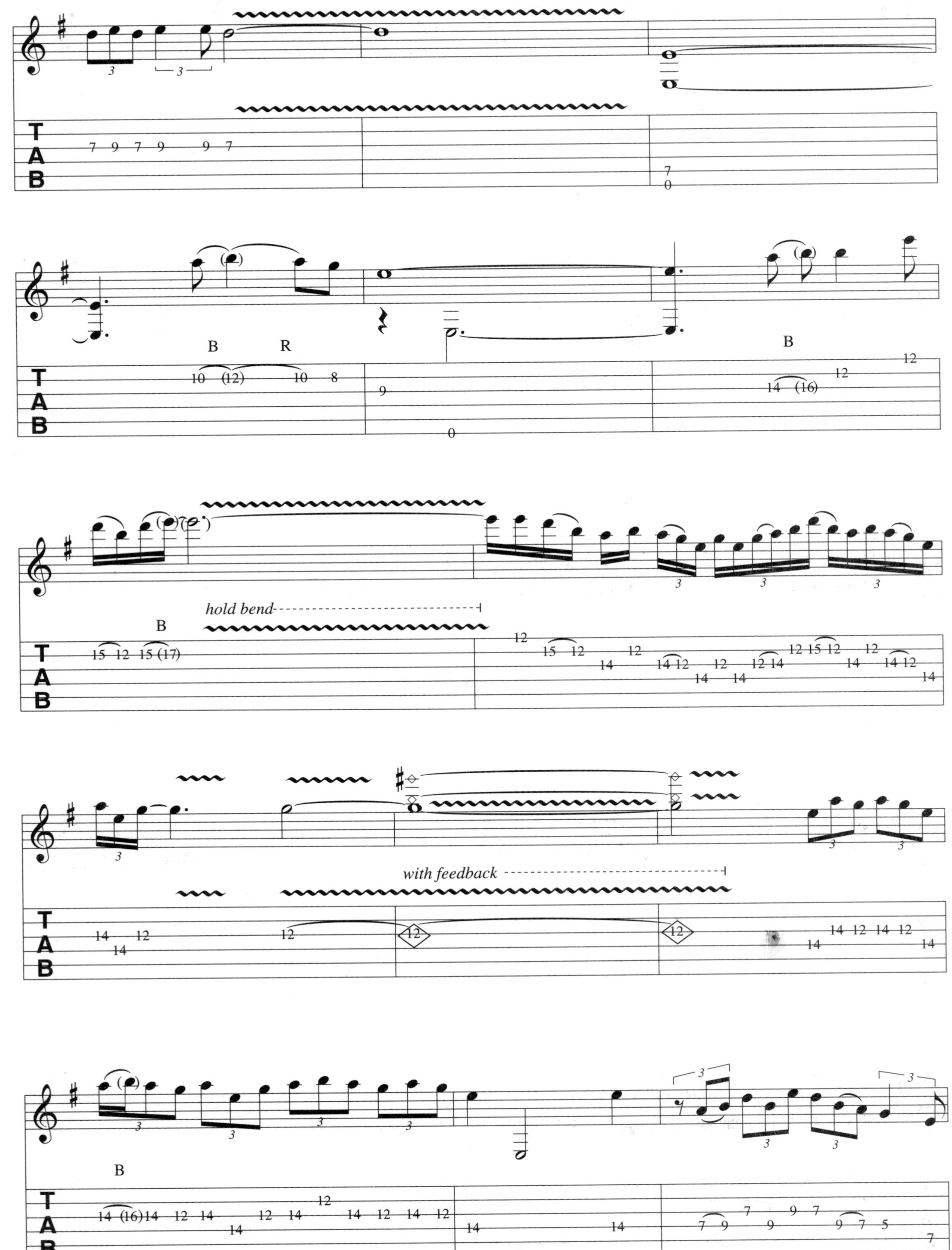
hold bend
with feedback
B
R

B
B R
B
TAB

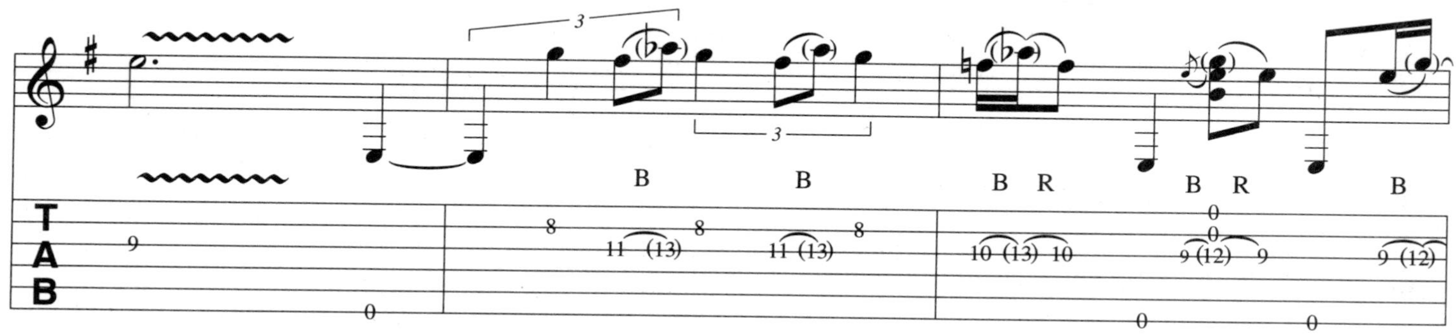
B
B
B R
B R
B
TAB

R
B R
B R
TAB

B R
TAB

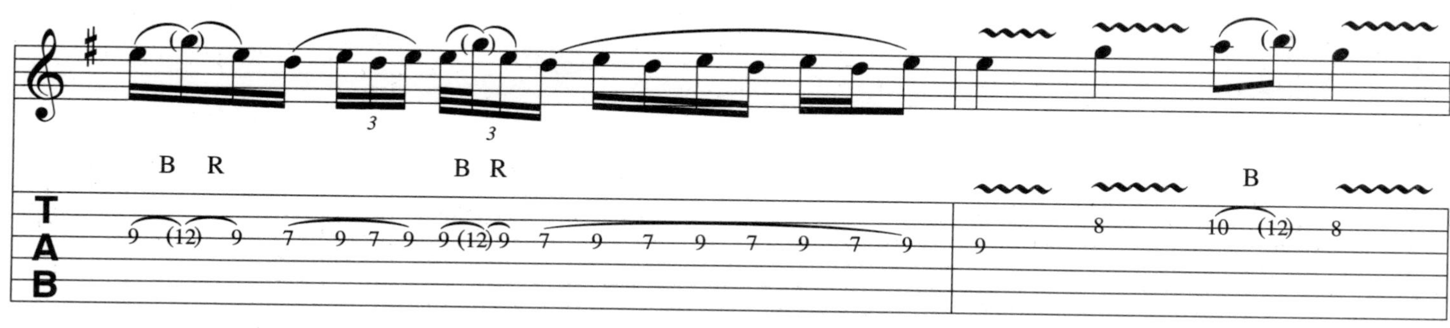
B R
B R
B
TAB

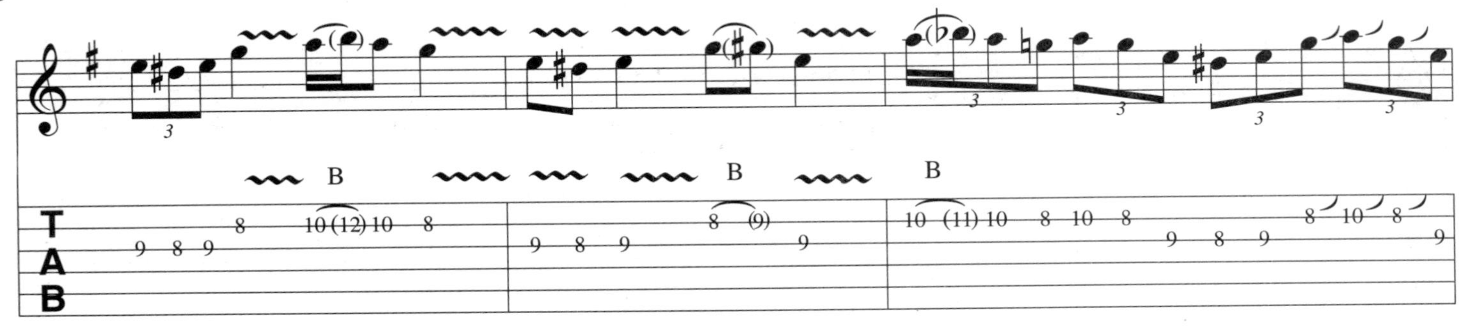
B
B
B
TAB

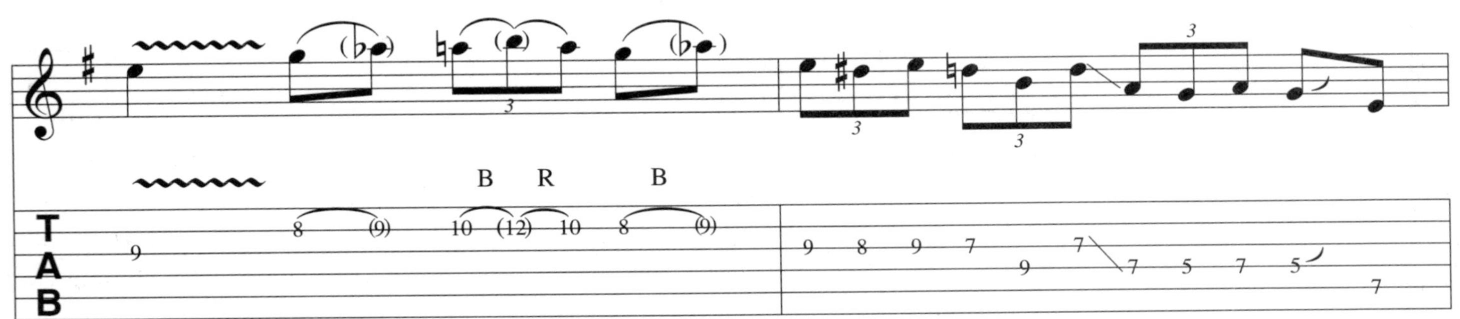
B R B
TAB

TAB

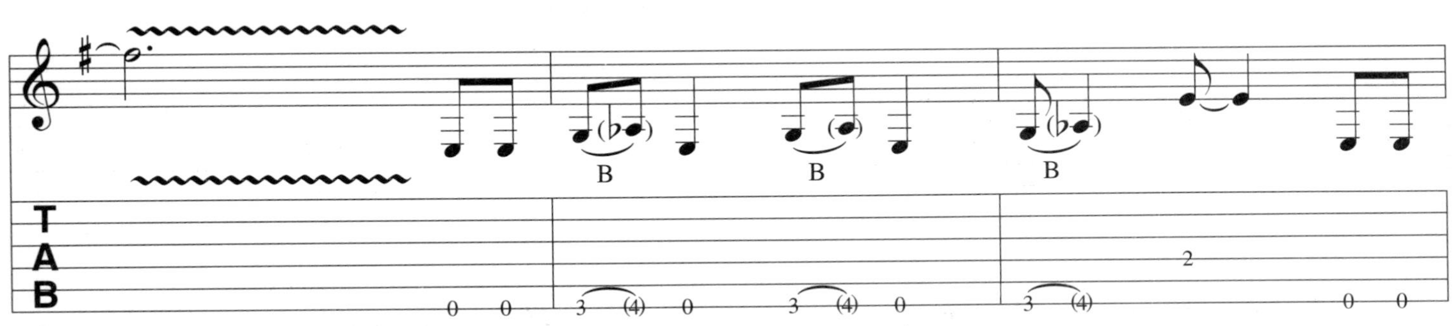
B
B
B
TAB

B
B
B
TAB

B B B
Could fill a spoon's full of wa - ter,
saved them from the des - ert sands.
Was a lit - tle spoon of your love, ba - by,
B hold bend B R
B
saved you from an - oth - er man.
Men lies a
B

some of them cries a - bout it.
Some of them
dies...
Ev - 'ry - thing's a - fight - in' a - bout it, uh!
Ev 'rything's a - cry - in' a - bout it, uh!
Ev 'ry - thing's a, ev - 'ry - thing's a - die - in' a - bout it.
Ev - 'ry - thing's a -
TAB
TAB
TAB
TAB

cry - in' a - bout it. Ev - 'ry - thing's a - ly - in' a - bout it.
Lil'l' old, lil'l' old, spoon - ful,
spoon ful. Hey!
Ev - 'ry - thing's die - in' a - bout it, uh!
B
B
B
B
B
T
A
B

All right, just cry-in' a-bout it.
That
B
B
spoon, that spoon, that...
Lit-tle old spoon,
Lit-tle old spoon,
lit-tle old...
B
Lit-tle old spoon, lit-tle old spoon, lit-tle old spoon - ful.
That
B
B
spoon, that spoon, that spoon - ful.
Spoon, that spoon, that
(3rd string sounds sympathetically)
T
A
B

spoon - ful. Yeah!
(ad lib vocal humming)
(4th string sounds sympathetically)
(2nd string sounds sympathetically)
(harp and drums)
N.C.
Freely
G
E7♯9
Ev - 'ry-thing's a - die-in' a- bout it.
Hey!
8va
with feedback

from Disraeli Gears

The Sunshine Of Your Love

Words and Music by Jack Bruce, Pete Brown and Eric Clapton

D7 C7 D7 N.C.
G F G N.C.
give you my dawn sur - prise.
morn-ing and just we two.
I'll be with you dar - ling, soon.
I'll stay with you dar - ling, now.
G F G N.C.
I'll be with you when the stars start fall - ing.
I'll stay with you 'til my seeds are dried up.
D7 C7 D7 N.C.
D7 C7 D7 N.C.
to Coda
play 2nd time
A5
C5
G5
A5
I've been wait - ing so long to be where
C5
G5
A5
C5
G5
I'm go - ing in the sun - shine of your
1. A5
D7 C7 D7 N.C
with Rhythm figure 1 simile
love.

Guitar solo

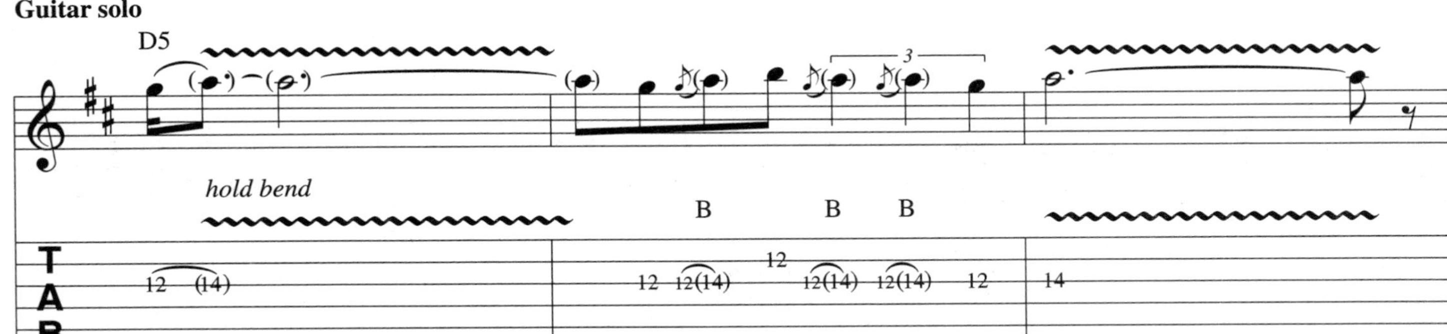

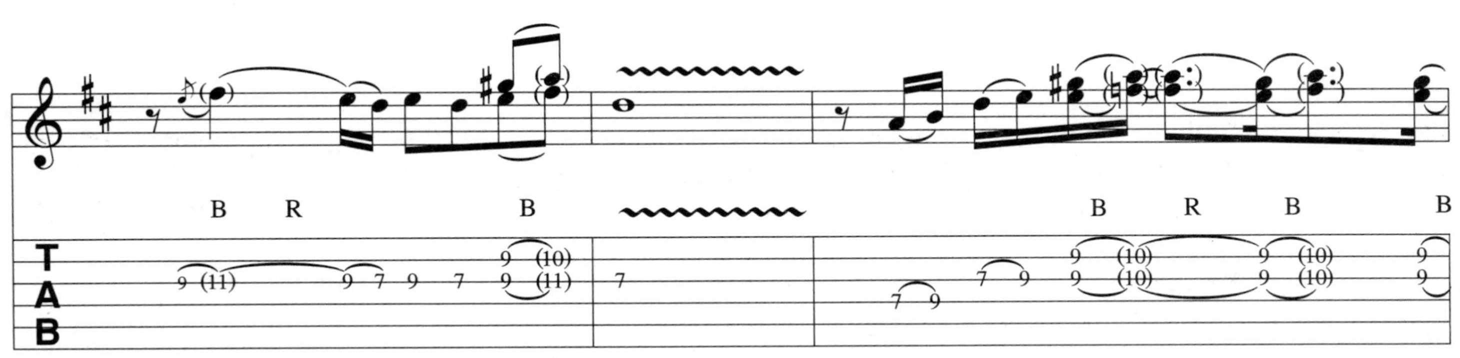

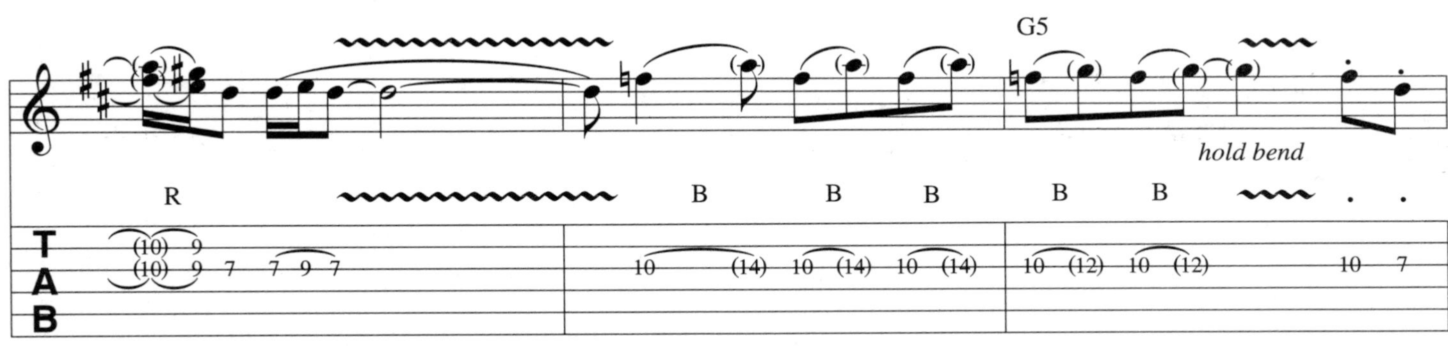

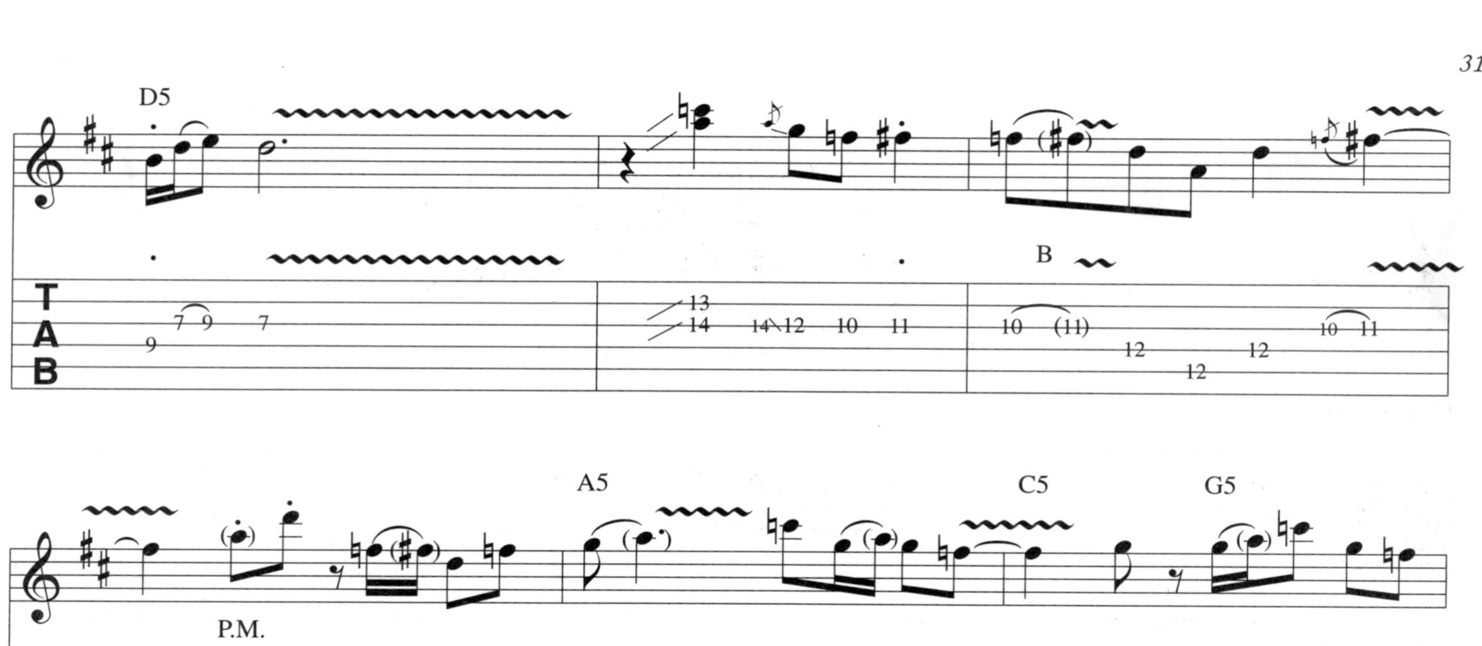
D5
B

A5
C5
G5
P.M.
B

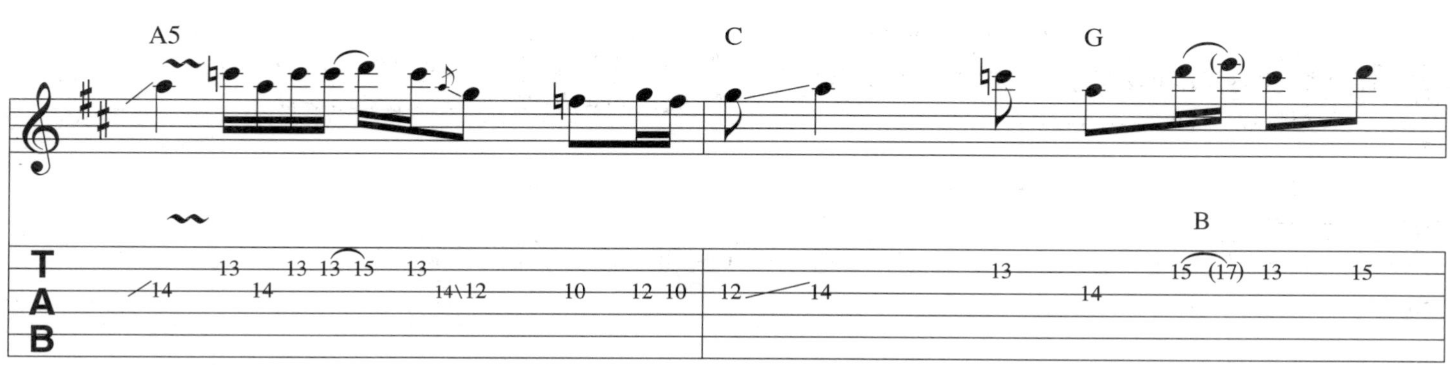
A5
C5
G5
B
B R

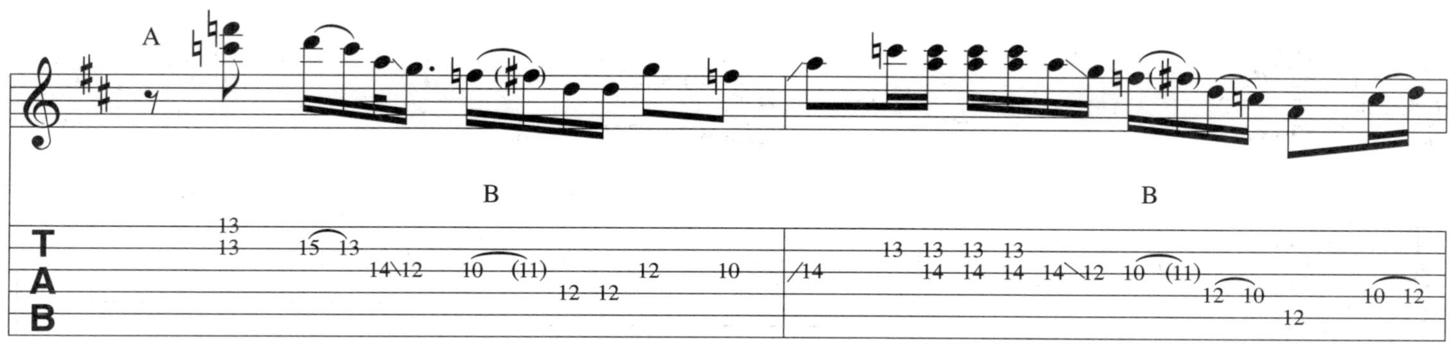
A5
C
G
A
B

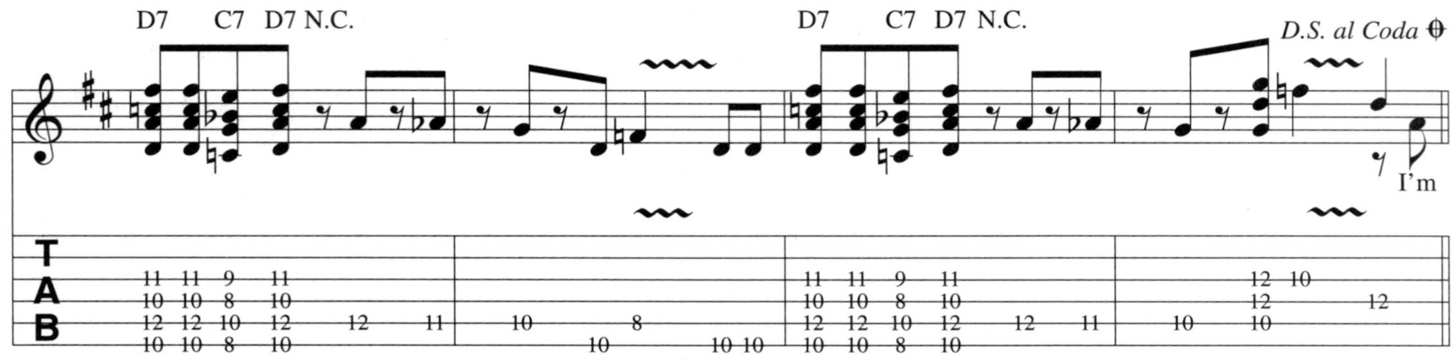
D7 C7 D7 N.C.
D7 C7 D7 N.C.
D.S. al Coda
I'm

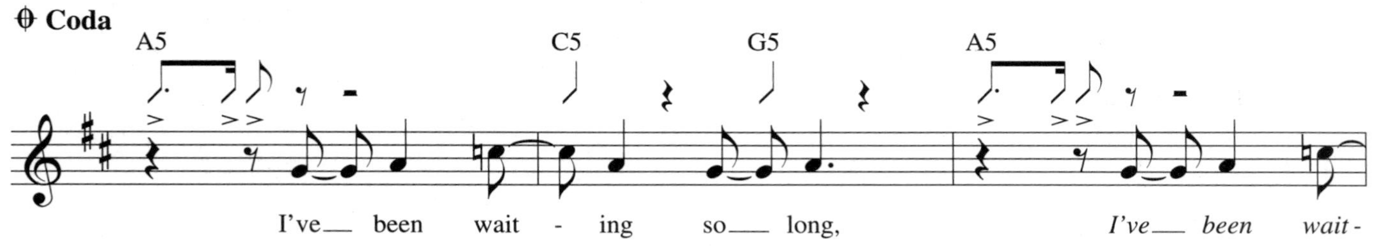
Coda
A5
C5
G5
A5
I've been wait - ing so long,
I've been wait -

C5
G5
A5
C5
G5
ing so long,
I've been wait - ing so long

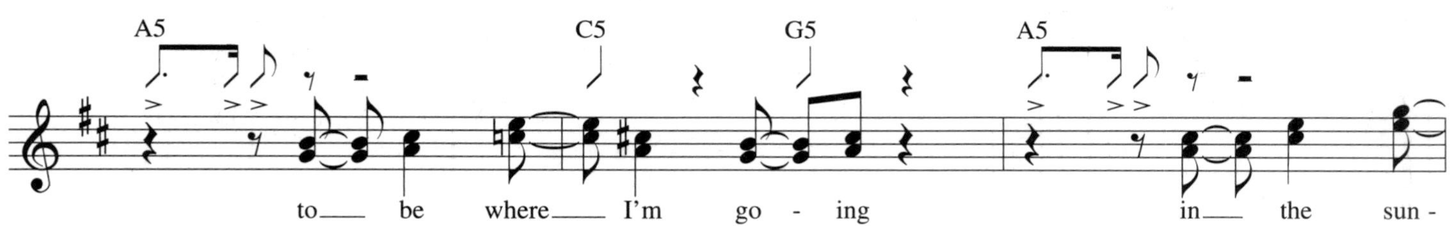
A5
C5
G5
A5
to be where I'm go - ing
in the sun -

C5
G5
A5
Continue simile (seven measures) & fade
shine of your love.

from Layla And Other Assorted Love Songs

Tell The Truth

Words and Music by Eric Clapton and Bobby Whitlock

Moderate blues (♩ = 101)
Intro

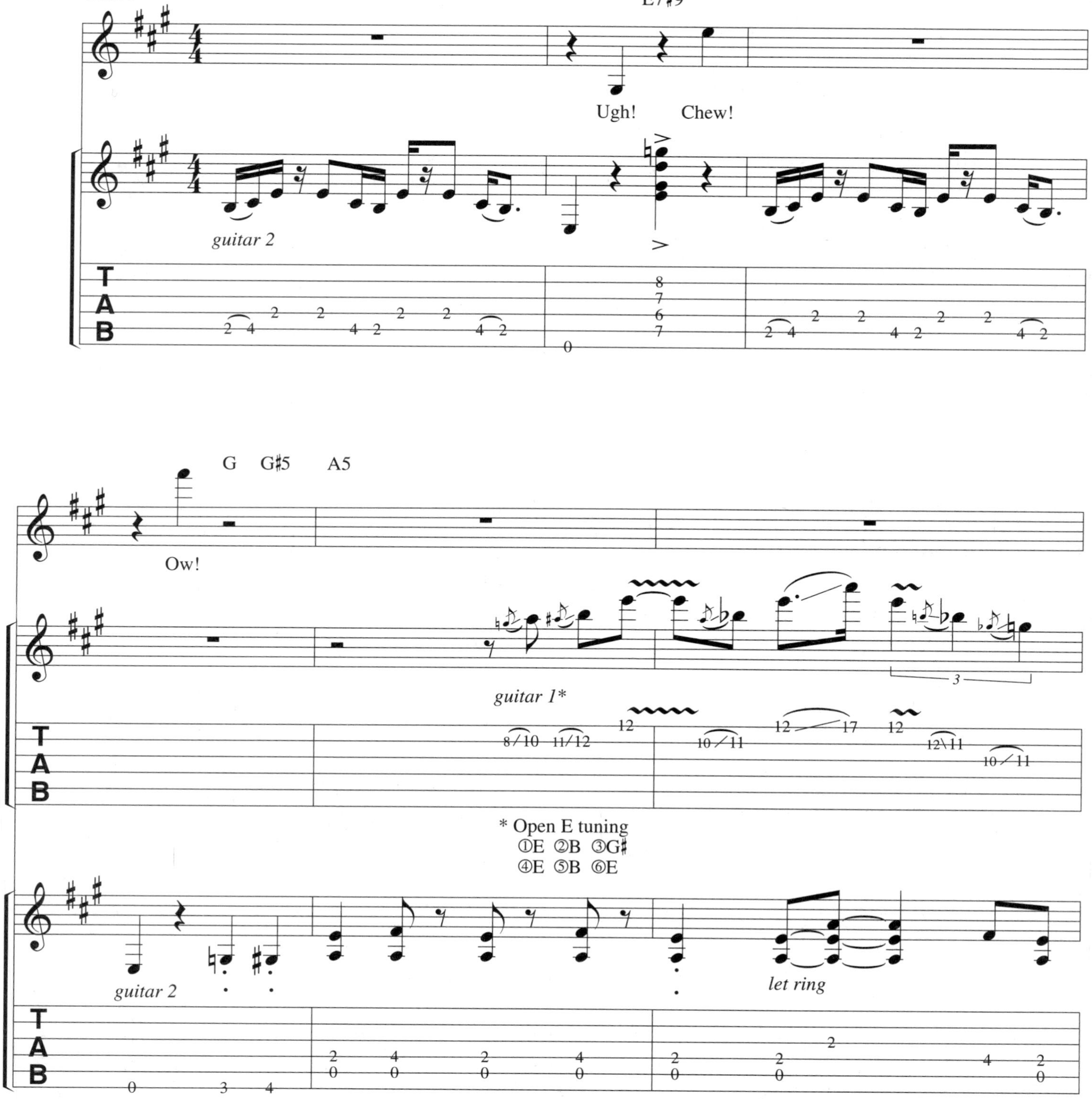

G G♯5 A5

Ow!

guitar 1*

guitar 2

let ring

* Open E tuning
①E ②B ③G♯
④E ⑤B ⑥E

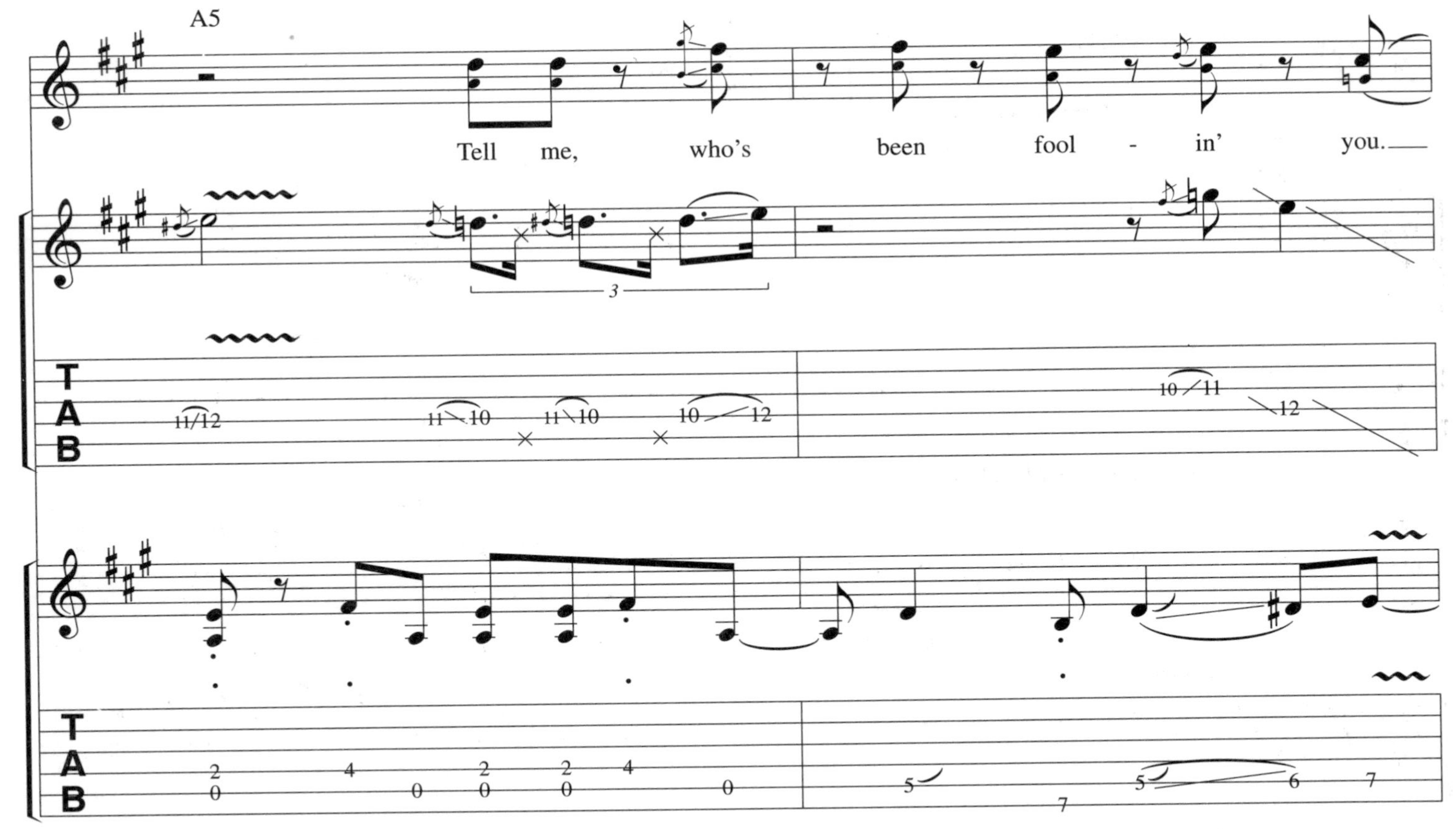

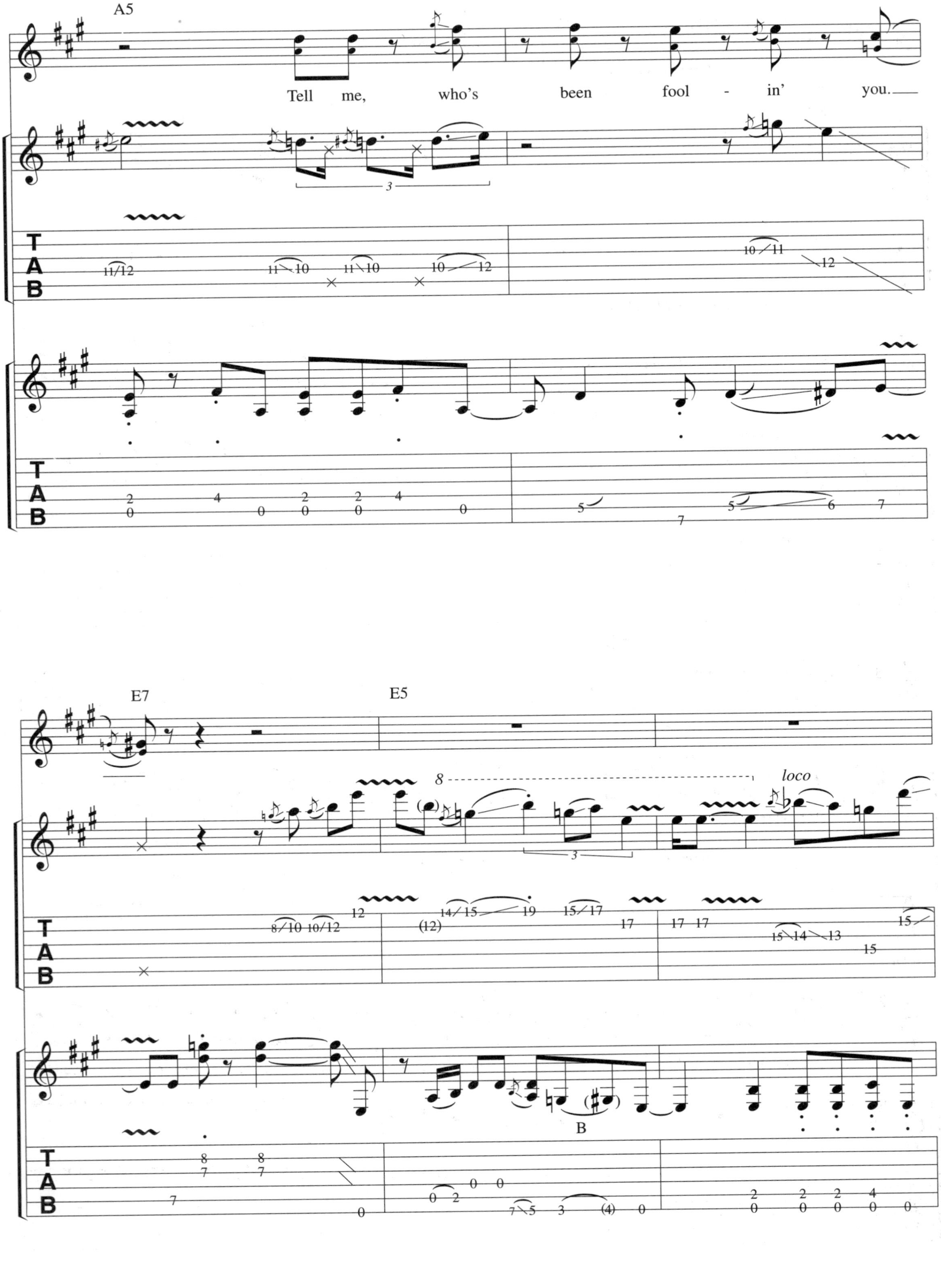
A5
Tell me, who's been fool - in' you.
TAB
E7
E5
8
loco
B

*
A5
Tell the truth.
* guitar 2 continue ad lib rhythm simile
B5
Ah, who's been fool - in' you hoo hoo?
even slide
Verse 1
A5
E5
A5
Yeah, you sit there look - in' so cool while the whole show was pass - in' you by.

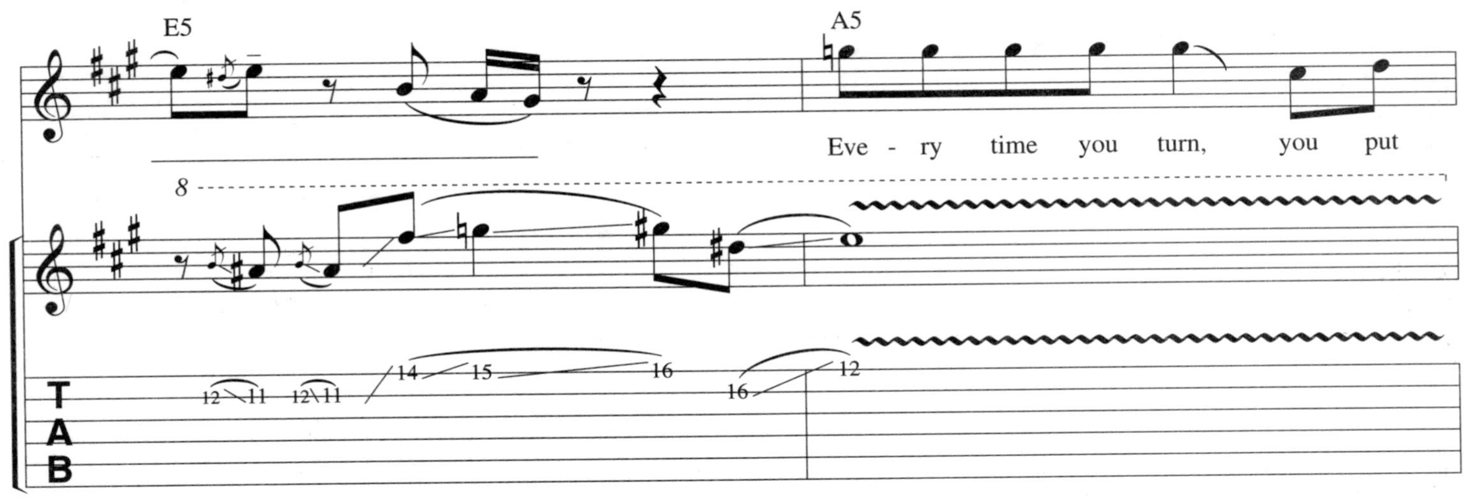
E5
A5
Eve - ry time you turn, you put
8
TAB

Bridge
E5 Eadd6 E5 Eadd6 G G G6 G G6 D5 Dadd6 D5 Dadd6 D5
guitar 1
down a man's faith hon - ey. Whole world is shak - in' now, can't ya feel
guitar 2
TAB
*guitar 3 plays rhythm fills in Open E tuning with slide

E B5 E5 B5 E5 B5 G
it. ooh. You got me think-
TAB

D5 Dadd6 D5
A5
B5
in' now. Can't you see it?
Tell the truth
guitar 1
guitar 2
Chorus
A5 guitar 2 continue ad lib rhythm simile
oh, oh - oh. yeah
Tell me who's been fool - in' you.
E5
Ah.
guitar 1

Tell the truth,
oh, oh
loco
rake
B♭ B B5
oh who's been fool - in' you,
ooh.
Yeah! whoa!
Verse 2
A5 E5 A5
It does-n't mat-ter just a who you are, or where you're goin' to dance,

E5
E5 E6 E5 E6 E5
guitar 1
— yeah. Hey, o - pen your eyes — look at your — poor — boy.
guitar 2
guitar 3*
* Open E tuning
①E ②B ③G♯
④E ⑤B ⑥E
Bridge
G5
D
E
B
Whole world is shak - in' now, — can't ya feel — it? yeah! —
Whoa!
guitar 2 tacet

B E B G D G
Ho yeah! You got me think - in' now. Can't ya see
T
A
B
B5 B6 B5 B6 B5 G D G B5 B6 B5 B6 B5
it? I said see. You got me think - in' now. Can't ya see it? I said see
T
A
B
B5 B6 B5 B6 B5 B6 B5 B6 B5
it yeah. You see it, can't ya see?
B6 B5 B6 B5 B6 B5 B6 B5 B6 B5 C5
it yeah, can't ya see it. I can see it yeah. ooh

Guitar solo
C♯5 C♯6 C♯5 C♯6 C♯5 C♯6 C♯5 C♯6 C♯5 C♯6 C♯5
Woo hoo hoo hoo.
guitar 3
let ring
C♯6 C♯5 C♯6 C♯5 G♯5 G♯6 G♯5 G♯6 G♯5
G♯6 G♯5 G♯6 G♯5 G♯6 G♯5 G♯6 G♯5
let ring
A♯5 B5 B6 B5 B6 B5
slow steady slide
T
A
B

B6 B5
B6 B5
B6 B5
B6 B5
B5
Tell the truth,
8

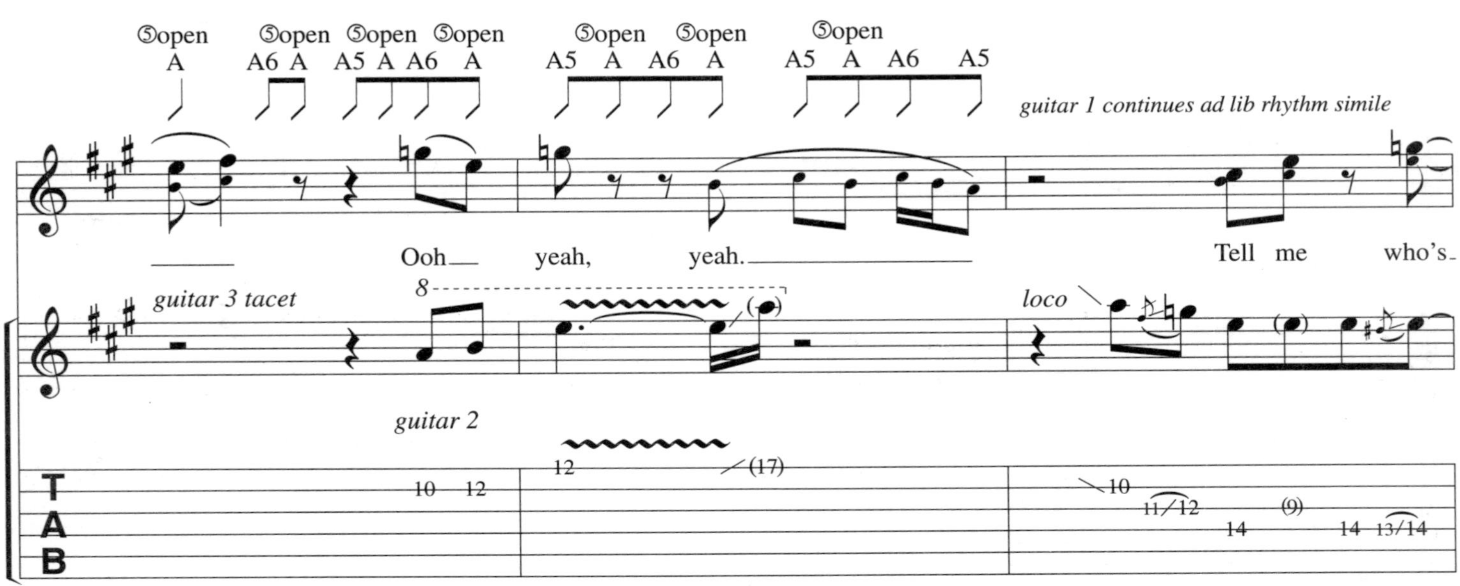
⑤open
A
⑤open
A6 A
⑤open
A5 A
⑤open
A6 A
⑤open
A5 A
⑤open
A6 A
⑤open
A5 A A6 A5
guitar 1 continues ad lib rhythm simile
Ooh yeah, yeah.
Tell me who's
guitar 3 tacet
8
loco
guitar 2

E5
been fool - in' you.

A5
Tell the truth, oo.
8
T
A
B
12 14 14 11 13 14 14
10 12 10 12 10 12 10 12 12
10 12

ah, Who's been fool - in' you?
8
loco
3
T
A
B
10 12 10 17 19 15 16 15 16 17 (0) 10 11 12
10 11

B
Ooh whooo
T
A
B
(10)
7 7 7 9 7 8 9
7 7 9 7 7 8 8

Verse 3
A5
E
Hear what I say! 'Cause ev - 'ry word is true,

A5
E
A
God, I would - n't tell you no lie.
Your time's com - in',

E5
guitar 3 play Bridge simile
guitar 2 tacet
Bridge
G
guitar 1
D5
gon - na be soon boy.
Whole world is shak - in' now.
Can't ya feel

E5
B
E
B
E
B
G
D5
it? Whoa, whoa!
You got me think - in' now.
Can't you see

B5 B6 B5 B6 B5 B6 B5 B6 B5 B6 B5 B6 B5
it? I said see__ it yeah. Ya see__ it. Can't you see_
guitar 2
T
A
B
10 12 10 11 12 7 8 8 9

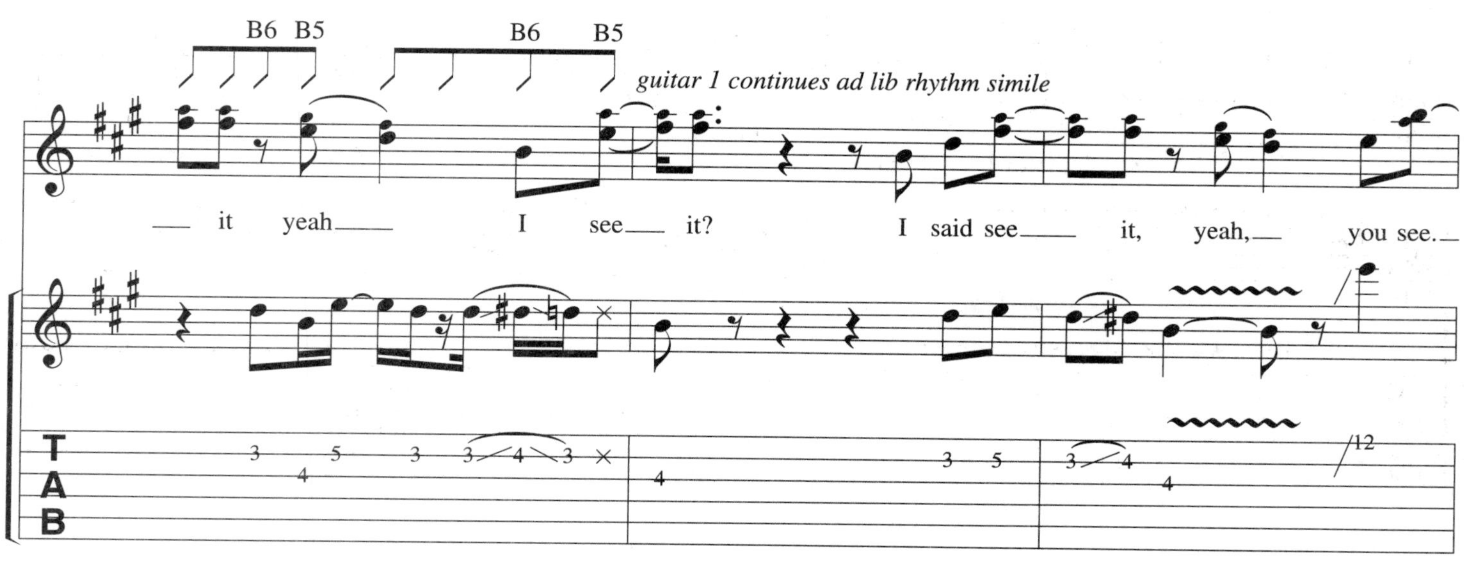
B6 B5 B6 B5
guitar 1 continues ad lib rhythm simile
__ it yeah__ I see__ it? I said see__ it, yeah,__ you see.__
T
A
B
3 4 5 3 3 4 3 4 3 5 3 4 4 12

__ I said see__ it, yeah,__ said see it. I said see__
T
A
B
10 11 12 10 11 12 7 5 7 9 9 9 7 (9) 9 (9) 7 8 9 7 9 7

it, yeah, you see.
I said see.
continue vocal ad lib simile

E5 E6 E5 E6 E5 G D5
guitar 1
Whole world is shak - in' now. Can't ya feel
guitar 3 play Bridge simile
guitar 2
E5 B E B E B G D5
it?
You got me think -
G B5 B6 B5 B6 B5
guitar 1 continue ad lib rhythm simile
guitar 3 tacet
in' now. Can't you see it? I said see it, yeah, you see.
Can't you see it, yeah, 'cha see?

Can't you see it, yeah, can't you see
guitar 2
T
A
B

it. Ooh, can't you see it yeah, 'cha see
T
A
B

it. Ooh, can't you see it yeah, can't you see
T
A
B

it,
ooh,
can't
you
see
oh,
yeah.
⑤open
B
B
B6
B5
B
B6
B5
B
⑤13fr
B♭
⑤14fr
B
⑤13fr
B♭
⑤14fr
B
guitar 1 continue ad lib rhythm simile

E5
E6
E5
E6
E5
8
T
A
B
21 19 21 19 21 18 20 (21) 21 19 (21) 18 20 21 21 19 (21) 18 20
21 19 21 19 21 21 19 21 21 19 21 19

Outro

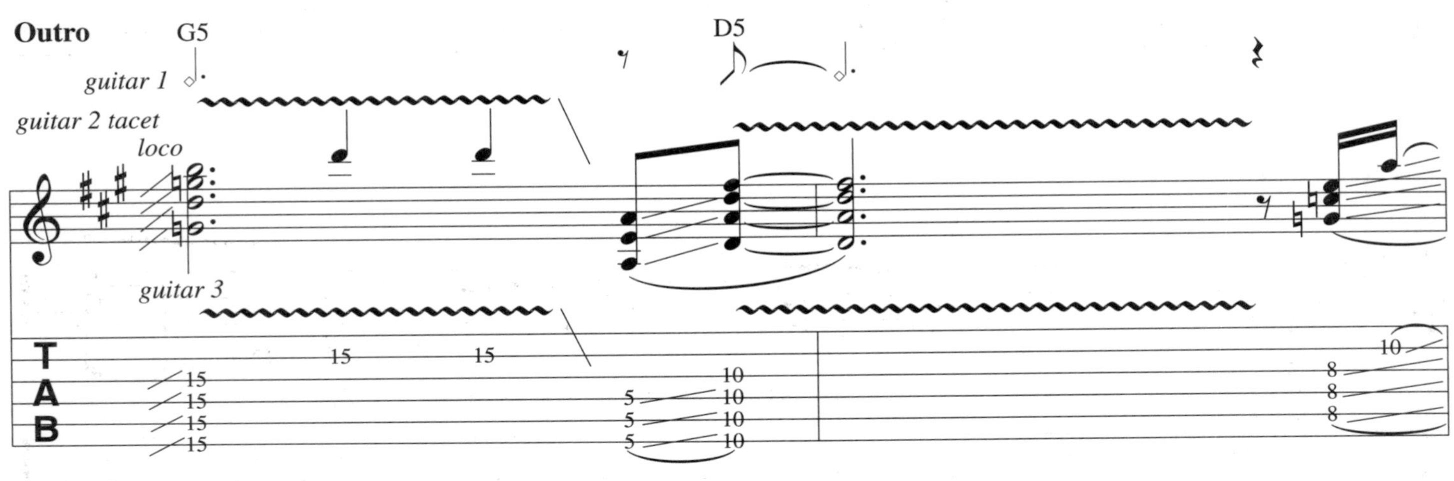
G5
D5
guitar 1
guitar 2 tacet
loco
guitar 3
T
A
B
15 15 15 15 15 15
5 5 5 10 10 10 10
10 8 8 8

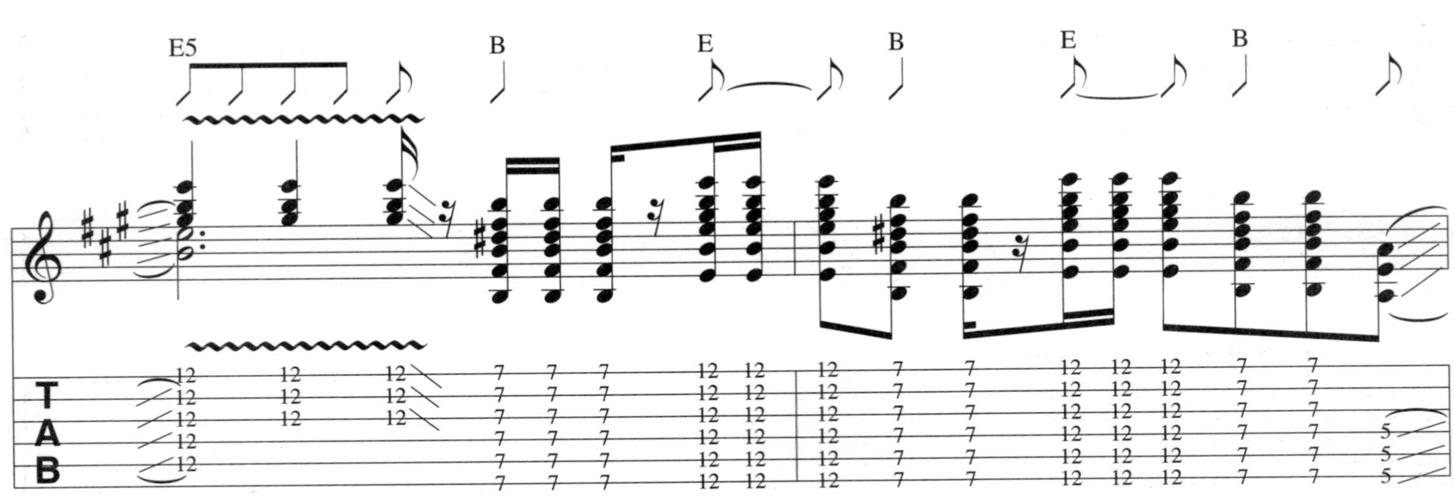
E5
B
E
B
E
B
T
A
B

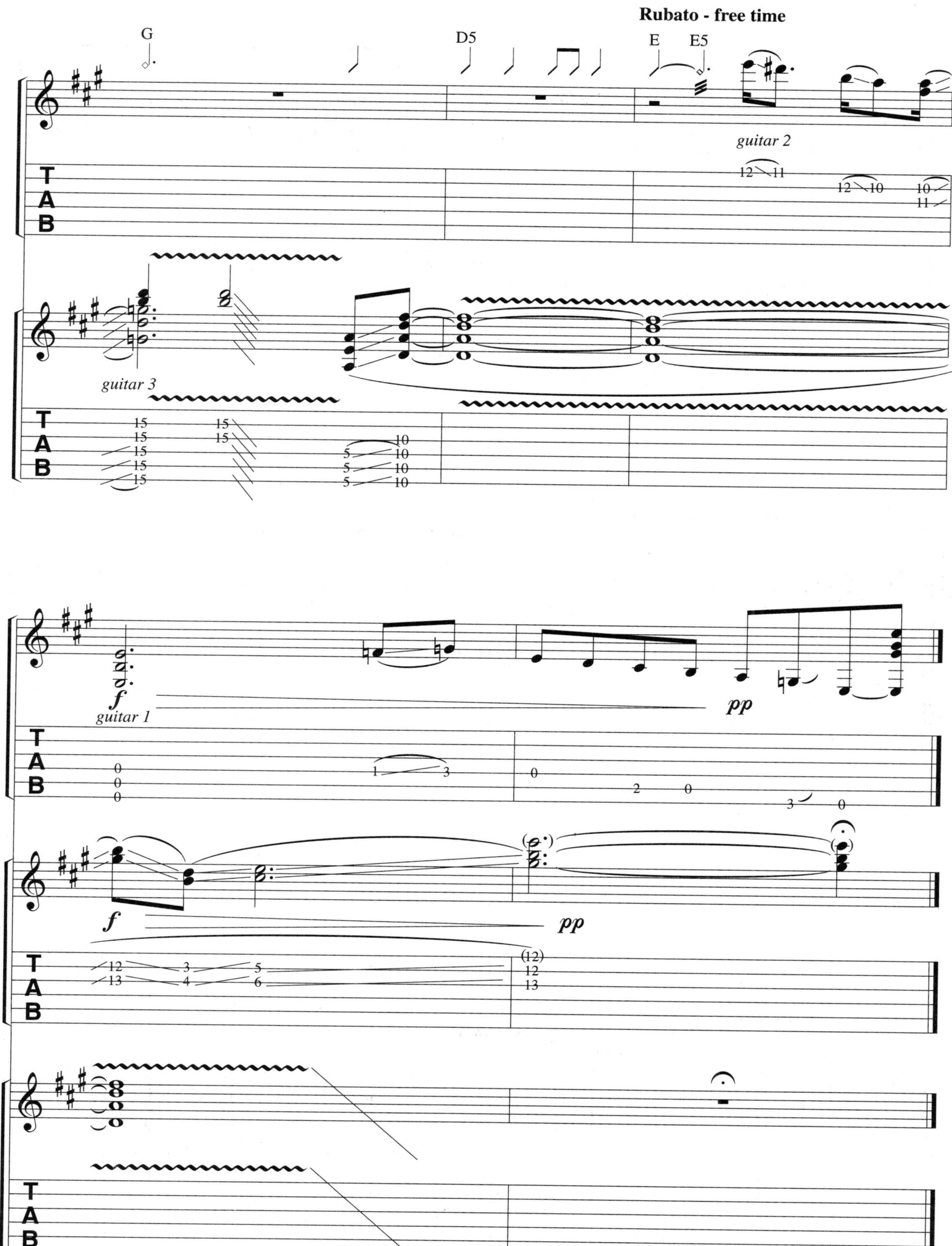
Rubato - free time
G
D5
E
E5
guitar 2
guitar 3
guitar 1
f
pp

from Layla And Other Assorted Love Songs

Thorn Tree In The Garden

Words and Music by Bobby Whitlock

A6/9
Emaj7
A6/9
guitar 1 Riff B (two times) simile
not the way it seems, 'cause I miss her.
T.H.
end Riff B
Emaj7
A6/9
Emaj7
She's the on - ly girl I've cared for, the on -
A6/9
Emaj7
ly one I've known and no one ev - er shared more love
A6/9
Emaj7
end Riff B
E7
than we a-lone and I miss her.
But
T.H.
A
Emaj7
it all seems so strange, ya see, *(Inhale) 'cause she'd nev-er turn her back on me

A
B
E
E7
and leave without a last good-bye.
T.H.
A
Emaj7
And if she winds up walk - in' the streets lov-in' ev-'ry oth-er-man she meets.
A
Emaj7(no 3rd)
B7
Who'll be the one to an-swer why?
Lord, I hope it's not
Emaj7
E7
A
Am6
E
me, oh, it's not me.
T.H.

Emaj7
*
And if I nev - er see her face a - gain or
T
A
B
19 18 14
A6/9
guitar 1 Riff A (repeat to end)
Emaj7
3
nev - er hold her hand, and if she's in some - bod - y's arms I
A6/9
Emaj7
know I'll un - der - sand, but I miss that girl, oh
E7
A
Am
I still miss that girl.
Emaj7
E7
A6
Am6
Emaj7
E7
May - be some
A6
Am6
*
Emaj7
day soon, some way.
E7
*
A6
Am6
continue simile 12
E
Oo

from Unplugged

Walkin' Blues

by Robert Johnson

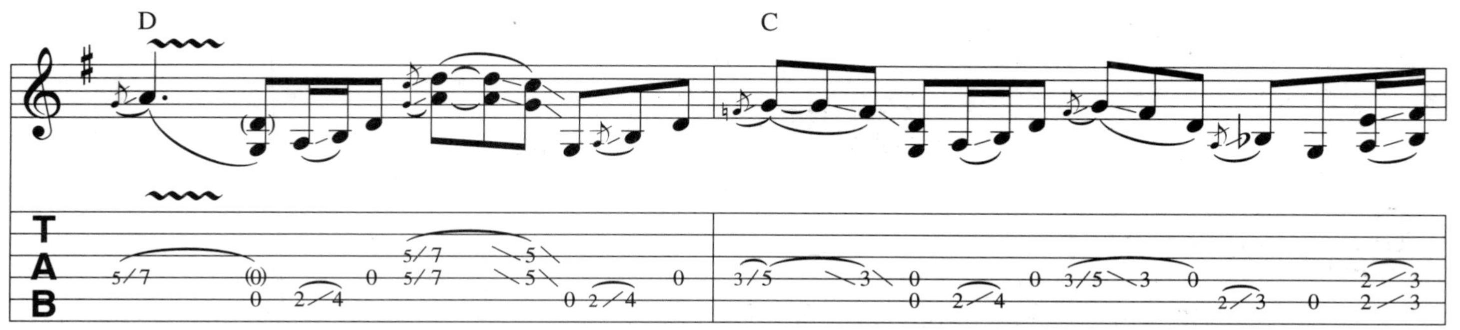
D
C
T
A
B

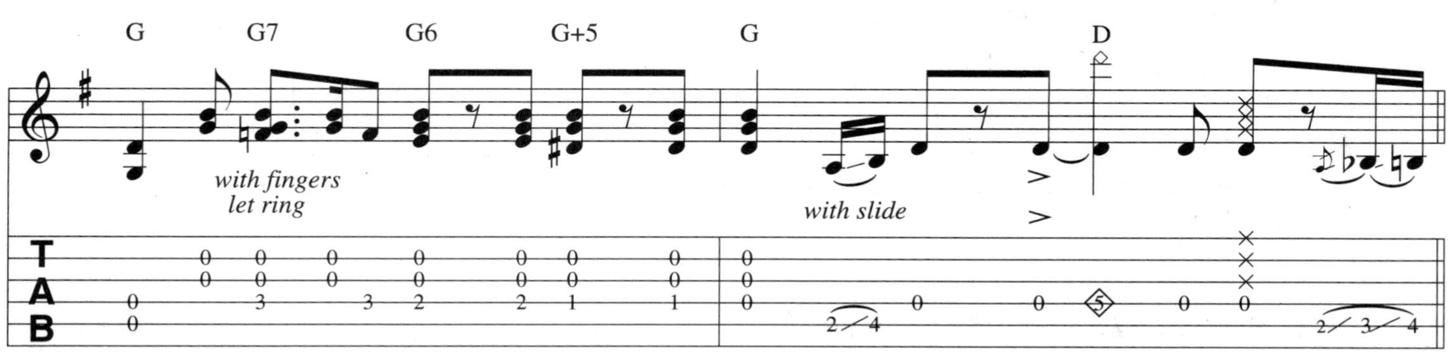
G
G7
G6
G+5
G
D
with fingers
let ring
with slide
T
A
B

Verse 1

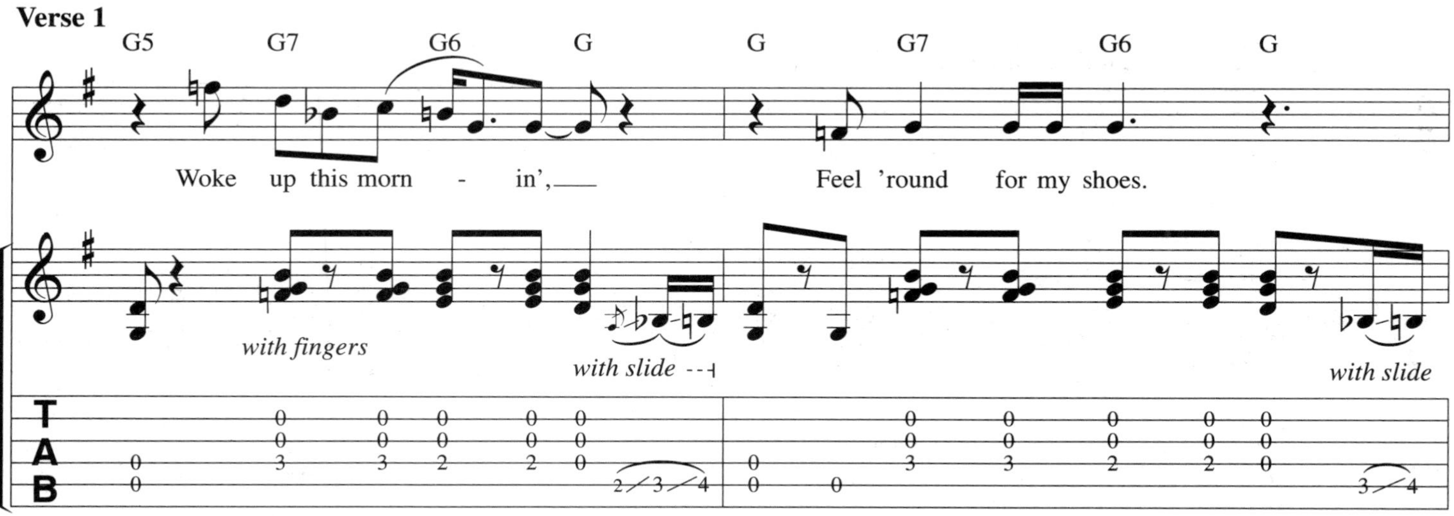
G5
G7
G6
G
G
G7
G6
G
Woke up this morn - in',
Feel 'round for my shoes.
with fingers
with slide
with slide
T
A
B

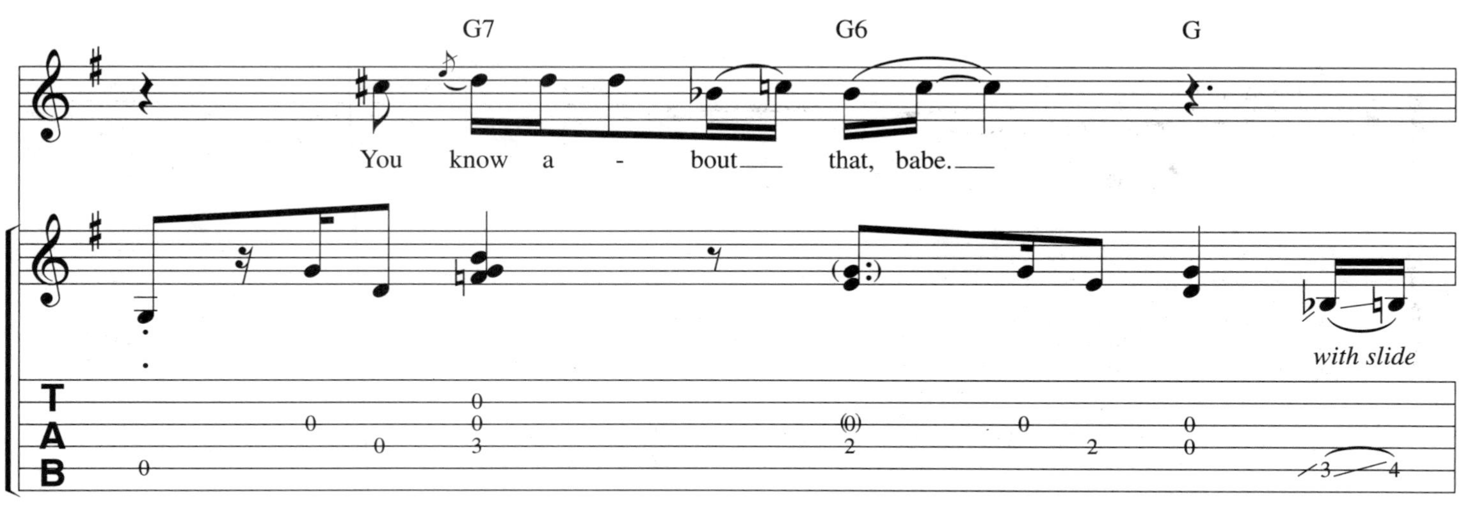
G7
G6
G
You know a - bout that, babe.
with slide
T
A
B

G5 (2:3) G7 G6 G — C

I have them old walk-in' blues. Woke up this morn - in',

with slide
let ring

let ring

G

I feel 'round for my shoe.

let ring

(2:3)

D

You know a-bout that ba - by,

let ring

C (3 2:3 3) — G G7 G6 G+5

woo Lord, I had them old walk - in' blues.

let ring

let ring
with fingers

Verse 2
G5
D
G5
G7
G6
G
I'm leav-in' this morn - in',
with slide
with fingers
with slide
G5
G7
G6
G
G5
G7
G6
G
I have-ta go ride the blinds.
I been mis-treat - ed.
with slide
G5
G7
G6
G
C
I don't mind dyin' this a-morn - in',
with slide
let ring
let ring
let ring
G
if I have-ta go ride the blinds.

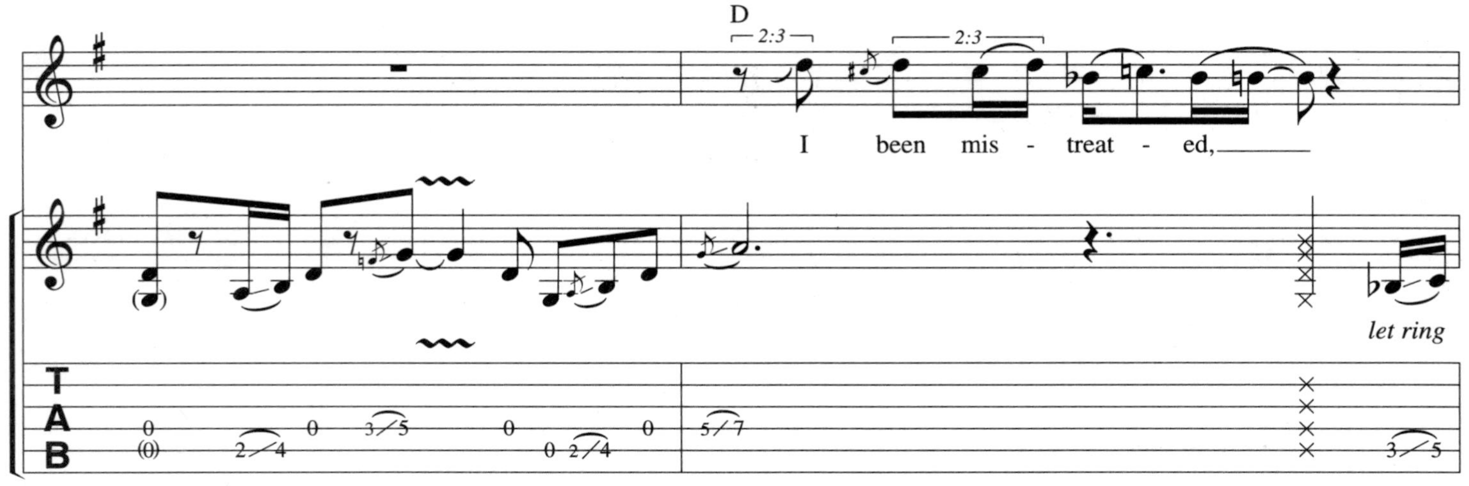
D
2:3
2:3
I been mis - treat - ed,
let ring

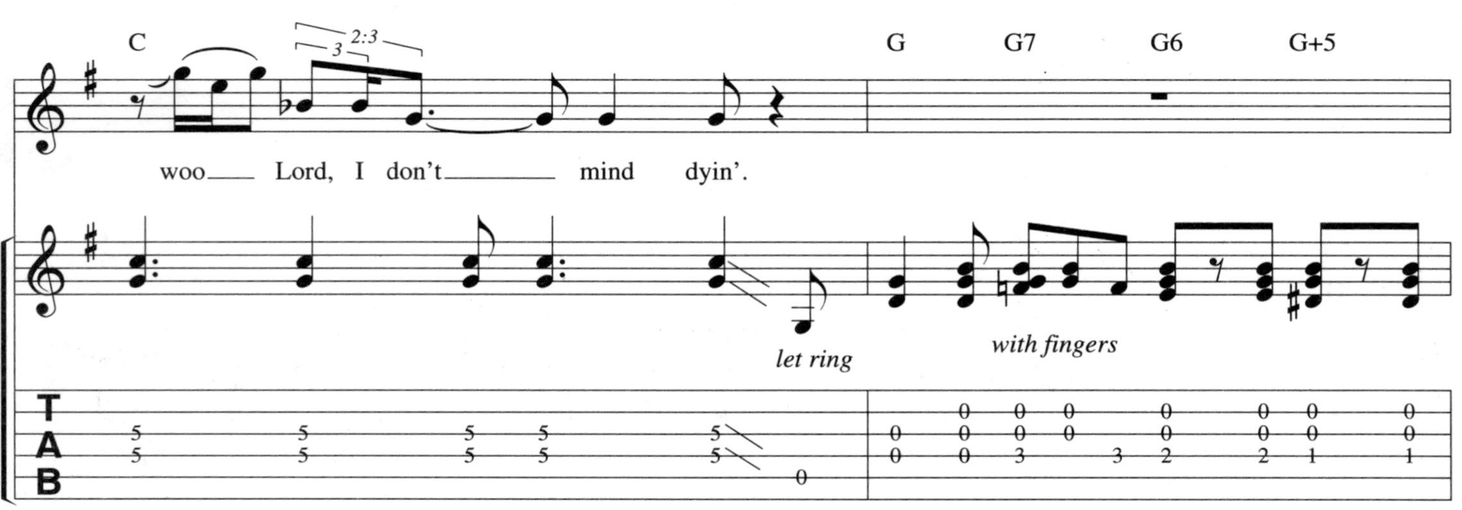
C
3
2:3
G
G7
G6
G+5
woo Lord, I don't mind dyin'.
let ring
with fingers

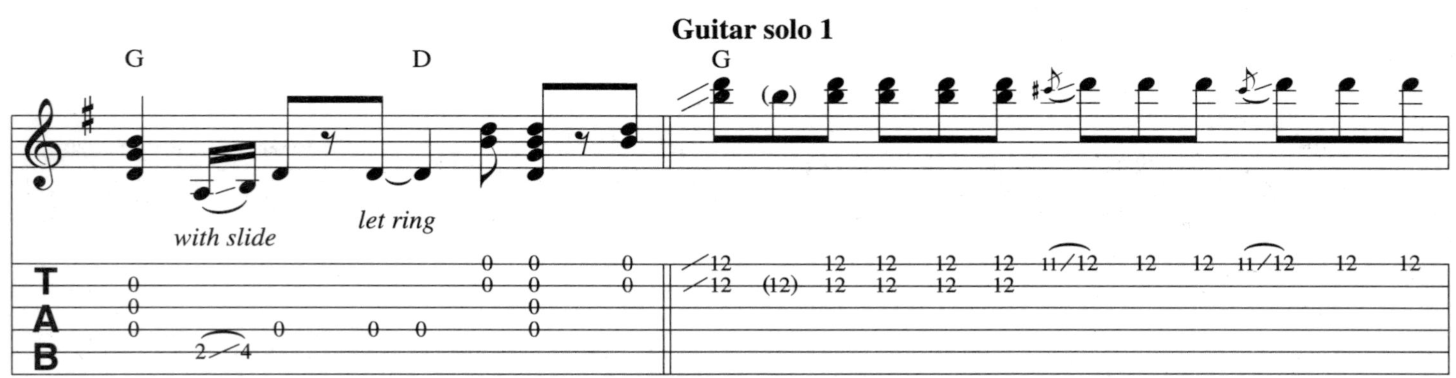
G
D
Guitar solo 1
G
with slide
let ring

let ring

G♭
F(/G)
C
G
p
mp
mf
D
C
G
G7
G6
G+5
G
D
with fingers
with slide

Verse 3

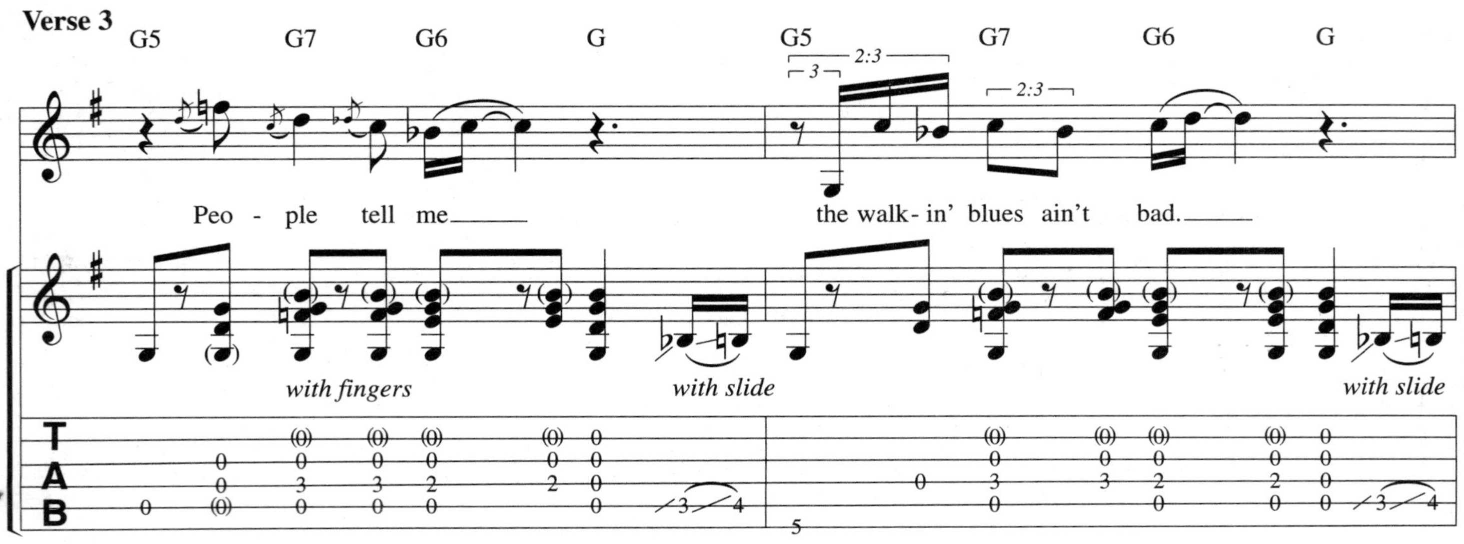
G5
G7
G6
G
People tell me
the walk-in' blues ain't bad.
with fingers
with slide
with slide

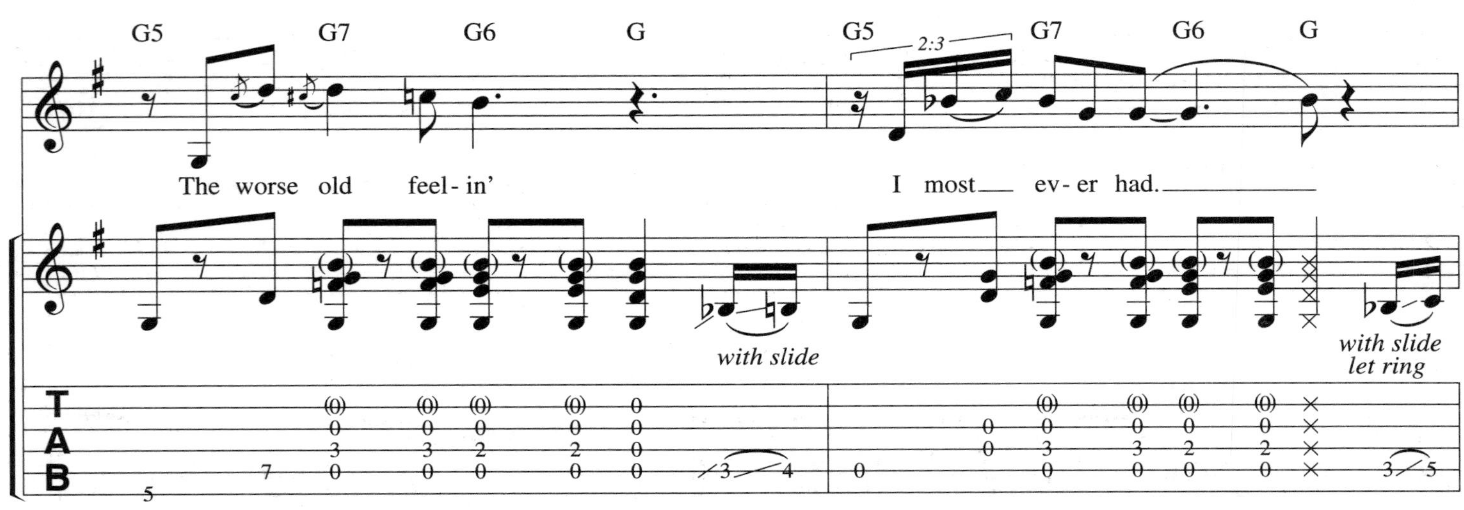
G5
G7
G6
G
The worse old feel-in'
I most ev-er had.
with slide
with slide
let ring

C
People tell me
the old walk-in' blues ain't bad.

G

Well, it's the

D C

worse old feel - in', woo Lord the most I ev - er had.

G G7 G6 G+5 G 2:3 D

with fingers

let ring

Guitar solo 2

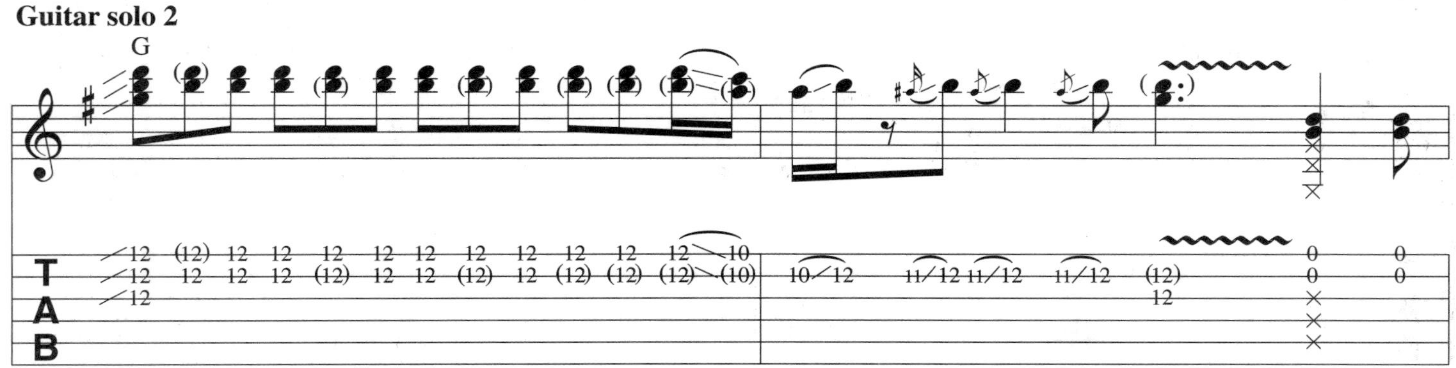

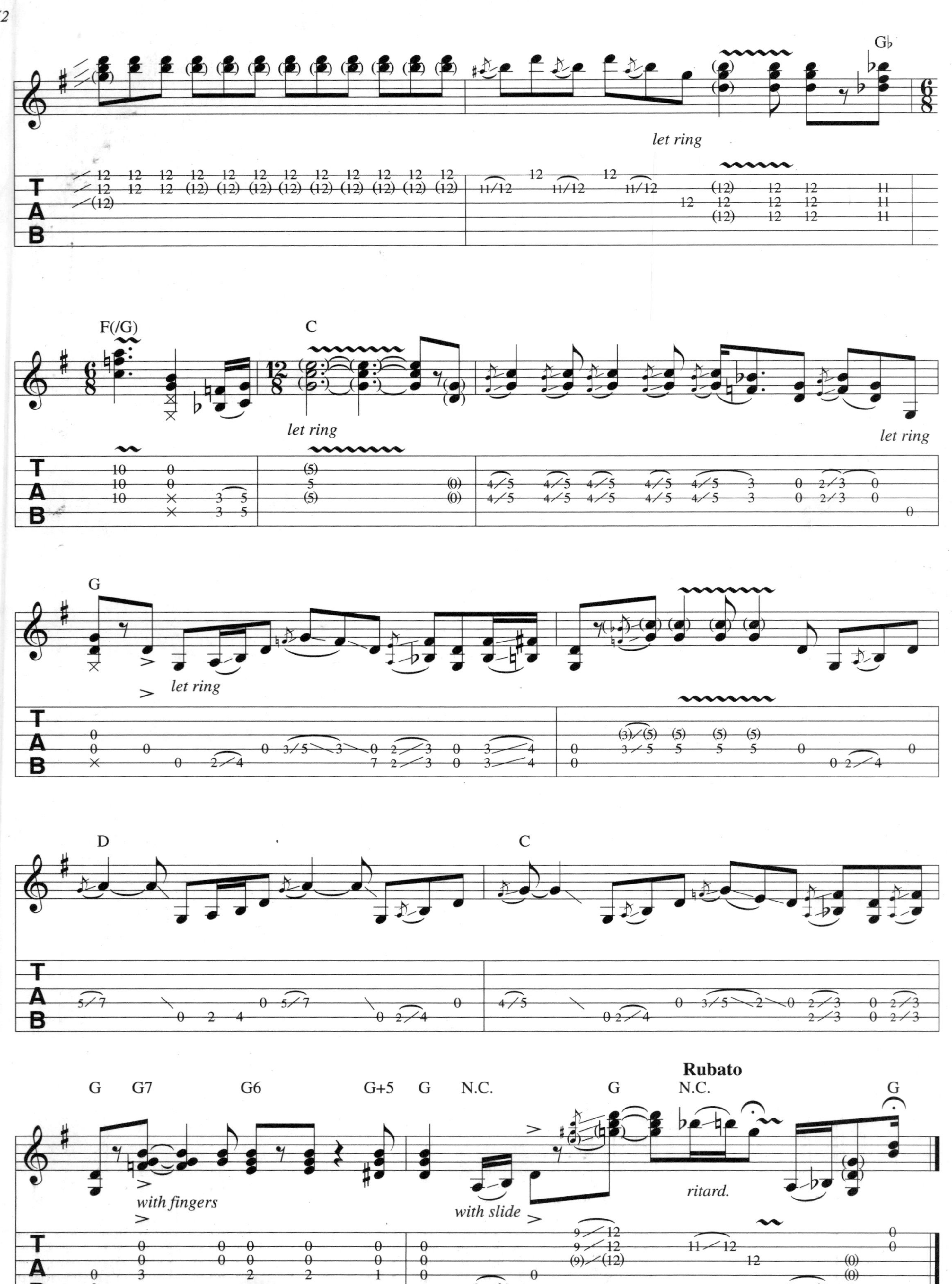
G♭
let ring
F(/G)
C
let ring
let ring
G
let ring
D
C
G
G7
G6
G+5
G
N.C.
G
N.C.
G
Rubato
with fingers
with slide
ritard.